LATER MEDIEVAL EUROPE

From Saint Louis to Luther

by

DANIEL WALEY

LONGMAN
London and New York

LONGMAN GROUP LIMITED
London
Associated companies, branches and representatives
throughout the world
Distributed in the United States by Longman Inc., New York

© *Daniel Waley 1964*
This edition © *Longman Group Ltd 1975*

First published 1964
Revised edition and first appearance in paperback 1975
Second impression in paperback 1976

ISBN 0 582 48407 3
Library of Congress Catalog Card Number: 74—82568

Set in Monotype Garamond
Printed in Hong Kong by
Sheck Wah Tong Printing Press

TO

PHILIP, CATHARINE and HARRIET

CONTENTS

		PAGE
PREFACE		xi
PREFACE TO THE REVISED EDITION		xii
I. GOVERNMENT IN THE LATER THIRTEENTH CENTURY.	.	1
II. ITALY AND THE MEDITERRANEAN IN THE SECOND HALF OF THE THIRTEENTH CENTURY: THE RIVALRY OF FRENCH, GREEKS AND ARAGONESE, AND THE INVOLVEMENT OF THE PAPACY		33
III. THE AGGRANDIZEMENT OF THE FRENCH MONARCHY .		56
IV. DISINTEGRATION IN GERMANY		73
V. ECONOMIC SETBACKS AND DEVELOPMENTS IN THE LATER MIDDLE AGES		95
VI. THE TROUBLES OF THE ROMAN CHURCH . .	.	116
VII. FRENCH DEFEATS AND CHIVALROUS IDEALS: THE HUNDRED YEARS WAR		140
VIII. THE EARLY RENAISSANCE		161
IX. BURGUNDY, THE GREAT DUCHY OF THE WEST .		178
X. THE TURKISH CONQUEST OF SOUTH-EASTERN EUROPE		198
XI. THE TYRANNIES IN ITALY		213
XII. THE FRENCH RECOVERY		232
XIII. THE UNIFICATION OF SPAIN		246
XIV. GERMAN DISUNITY AND THE ORIGINS OF THE REFORMATION		260
XV. POLITICAL WRITERS AND THE STRONGER STATE .		277
INDEX		291

MAPS

		PAGE
I.	Europe in the middle of the thirteenth century	2
II.	The Duchy of Burgundy in the fifteenth century	182
III.	The eastern Mediterranean, c. 1340	201
IV.	South-eastern Europe, 1481	211
V.	The Italian States in 1494	279

PLATES

FACING
PAGE

Drapers selling their wares at stalls in Bologna. See Chapter V

   Alinari photograph 84

Hawking: scene from a fresco in the Papal Palace at Avignon by
Matteo Giovanetti. See Chapter VI

   Giraudon photograph 85

Excavation on the site of the battlefield of Aljubarrota (1385) in
Portugal, showing pits probably dug by English archers. See
Chapter VII

   From *Antiquity*, December 1963, by permission of the Editor
   and Colonel Afonso do Paço 100

A Tournament, from an illustration to Froissart's *Chronicle*. See
Chapter VII

   British Library, Department of MSS. 101

A Renaissance ruler and his son: Federigo and Guidobaldo da
Montefeltro. See Chapters VIII and XI

   Anderson photograph 164

Chancelier Rolin, adviser to Philip the Good of Burgundy (by
Van Eyck). See Chapter IX

   Bulloz photograph 165

The Entry of Ferdinand and Isabella into Granada. See Chapter
XIII

   Foto Mas, Barcelona 180

The Pope as the Whore of Babylon in Luther's Bible. See Chapter
XIV

   British Library, Department of Printed Books 181

ACKNOWLEDGEMENTS

We are grateful to the following for permission to quote copyright material:

Cambridge University Press for material from the Ingolstadt Address in *Selections* from the works of C. Celtes edited by L. W. Forster; Chapman and Hall Ltd. for material adapted from *The Chronicle of James I, King of Aragon*, Volume II, translated by J. Forster; Orbis for material adapted from the 'Articles' of Tabor in *The Hussite Movement in Bohemia* by Josef Macek, 2nd edition, 1958; Oxford University Press for material from *Selections from the Notebooks of Leonardo da Vinci*, edited by I. A. Richter (World's Classics 530), and G. P. Putnam's Sons for material from Petrarch's *Familiarium Rerum*, translated in *Petrarch: the First Modern Scholar and Man of Letters* by J. H. Robinson.

PREFACE

THE aim of this book is to serve as an introduction to the history of Europe between the middle of the thirteenth century and the early part of the sixteenth. I hope to persuade my readers that this is an interesting period, and I have quoted a good deal from contemporary writings, because men's *ipsissima verba* are surely bound to be more striking and more convincing than the 'secondary' conclusions drawn from them. I have also assumed in my readers diverse intellectual temperaments. Those who are not attracted by past politics may find more interest in past economics, or in religion or art or the history of ideas, and quite substantial sections of the book are devoted to each of these topics. Yet politics remain the staple diet of the historian, and I have taken as my principal subject the growth of the power of the State and the manner in which this is reflected in ideas concerning politics. In treating a series of diverse themes I have tried to keep this main thesis in view. Thus, while the book begins and ends with contrasting chapters on the State and men's notions about it in the thirteenth century and the early sixteenth century, the chapter on the early Renaissance touches on the intensification of civic spirit, while, of the two chapters primarily concerned with religion, the former emphasizes the patriotic element in the Hussite movement and the latter the decisive religious consequences of Germany's uncharacteristic political disintegration.

My thanks are due above all to my wife and to my friend Dr E. B. Fryde, who read the work in typescript: both of them have helped me with many suggestions. I have also benefited gratefully from the advice of Dr A. R. Bridbury (on Chapter V) and of Dr Nicolai Rubinstein and Dr A. T. Hankey (on Chapter VIII).

D. P. W.

PREFACE TO THE REVISED EDITION

The issue of a paperback edition of *Later Medieval Europe* has provided me with the opportunity to make some changes. These have had to be confined to minor verbal alterations in the text and to changes in the suggestions for further reading. Ten years having passed since the book appeared, a number of works have been published which I wished to add to these reading lists. The passing of a decade has also led to further thoughts about some of the subjects discussed in the book. Only in very few instances have these been translatable into verbal changes of the sort which could be made in a reprint; they have tended rather to reflect differences in approach and outlook.

A friendly critic has suggested that the title of Chapter IV, 'Disintegration in Germany', is misleading. The very size of Germany and the other imperial territories was the most important of all the reasons for the emperor's lack of authority and the word 'disintegration' implies a higher degree of imperial control before the thirteenth century than existed in fact. Also the emphasis on the disadvantages of elective kingship (p. 74) should have been accompanied by a reminder that this institution also had its advantages: it obviated tension between the ruler and his heir and ensured that the crown did not pass to a minor or an imbecile.

Chapter IX was written when only the first of Professor Richard Vaughan's four volumes on the Valois dukes of Burgundy had appeared. Now I would emphasize that John the Fearless, like his father, envisaged Burgundy as a potentially separate entity, but that Philip the Good did 'little to consolidate his dynasty's precarious power'. Also the role of Louis XI in Charles the Bold's defeat is perhaps exaggerated, that of the towns understated. It should be explained too that the figures quoted on p. 191 refer only to the Burgundian receipt-general of finances and exclude surpluses from individual territories and some revenue from *aides*. Probably I have exaggerated (on pp. 186, 238 and 285) the degree of Louis XI's danger at Péronne in 1468: and in other respects I have been over-indulgent towards what Professor Vaughan calls Commynes's 'unparalleled mendacity'.

There are, inevitably, other points of fact on which doubt has been cast by recent historical writing. This is true, for example, of two passages in Chapter V. Villani's figures of Florentine cloth production (p. 106), sometimes attacked and sometimes defended by historians, have recently been in disfavour. And the Ciompi troubles (p. 107) are now seen by Professor Gene Brucker as the effect of the discontent of 'petty entrepreneurs', not of the clothmaking proletariat.

If the book were to be written now it would certainly differ less because 'facts' have been challenged or new interpretations offered than because books have been written which deal with history in new ways. Above all the approach of French writers to regional social and economic history has made the subject—not merely later medieval Europe—look different. Guy Fourquin's *Les Campagnes de la Région Parisienne à la fin du Moyen Age* (1964) and Robert Fossier's *La Terre et les Hommes en Picardie jusqu'à la fin de 13e siècle* (1968) are two outstanding examples of books dealing with this period which have had a subversive effect. One respect in which the approach of such works has been revolutionary is that it casts increasing doubt on the assertion, made above, that 'politics remain the staple of the historian'.

March 1974.   D. P. W

FURTHER READING

There is a short list of suggestions for further reading at the ends of chapters. I have limited these to books in English and French that are likely to be available in school and college libraries. I have indicated which works are available in paperback editions by citing the series in which these are published.

The following series are of general utility. They are not normally cited in the lists at the ends of chapters:

The Cambridge Medieval History, ed. J. R. Tanner, C. W. Previté-Orton and Z. N. Brooke, Vols. V–VIII (1926–36)

The New Cambridge Modern History
  Vol. I (The Renaissance, 1493–1520), ed. G. R. Potter (1957)
  Vol. II (The Reformation, 1520–1559), ed. G. R. Elton (1958)

Histoire Générale: Histoire du Moyen Age, ed. G. Glotz (Paris):
  Vol. IV, Pt. I. E. Jordan, *L'Allemagne et l'Italie aux 12e et 13e siècles* (1939)
    Pt. II. C. Petit-Dutaillis and P. Guinard, *L'Essor des États d'Occident* (1937)
  Vol. VI. *L'Europe Occidentale de 1270 à 1380*
    Pt. I (1270–1328) by R. Fawtier (1940)
    Pt. II (1328–80) by A. Coville (1941)
  Vol. VII. J. Calmette and E. Déprez, *L'Europe Occidentale de la Fin du 14e siècle aux Guerres d'Italie*
    Pt. I. *La France et l'Angleterre en Conflit* (1937)
    Pt. II. *Les Premières Grandes Puissances* (1939)

I

GOVERNMENT IN THE LATER THIRTEENTH CENTURY

THE main theme of this book is the development of government during two centuries and a half, culminating in the 'modern' nation-state of the age of the Reformation; so we may begin by describing some of the ways in which political power was exercised at the start of our period.

In France, where St Louis IX (1226–70) had added his imponderable offering of prestige to the territorial and administrative gains of Philip (II) Augustus (1180–1223), as well as in Christian Spain and in England, the monarchy already displays the powerful basis of its later achievements.[1]

In their relationship with the great men whose attitude would do most to determine their success as rulers, kings were feudal overlords. The magnates, lay and ecclesiastical, owed the king fealty as vassals and in particular had the obligations of attending his court when summoned to give counsel and of rendering him military service—the amount of which was normally defined in some detail. In that he had been crowned a king and anointed as a sign of his semi-sacred calling—everything possible was done to exploit in his interest the numinous aspects of kingship—the monarch was more than *primus inter pares*, and in thirteenth-century France the doctrine was becoming accepted that in no circumstances could he be himself a vassal of an uncrowned lord.

The western emperors, heirs to Charlemagne, had uncertain claims to suzerainty over these kings, but in practice the lands of Germany and northern Italy had no ruler between the death in 1250 of Frederick II and the election in 1273 of Rudolf of Habsburg, a princeling from south-western Germany who enjoyed

[1] See Map I.

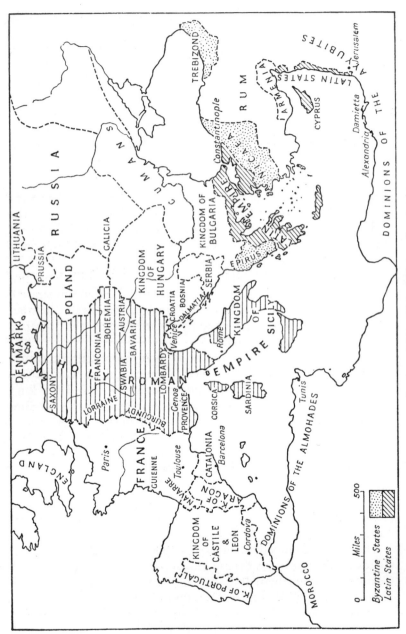

I Europe in the middle of the thirteenth century

papal support but had no resources to compare with those of the kings. Germany was a feudal body without a head. The eastern emperor, restored to Constantinople from the time of Michael Palaeologus (1261), ruled over 'the shade of that which once was great'; most of what had been Byzantine territory was now parcelled out among the Turks, Bulgars, Italian maritime republics and Frankish lords. Poland and Bohemia were Slav kingdoms in part populated by Germans and often unsettled by pressure from the rulers of Germany. Russia was overshadowed by Tartar domination and Hungary by the power of both Tartars and Germans. The Scandinavian kingdoms had not yet achieved even the relatively civilized techniques of government in western Europe and have left little written testimony to their activities.

It is with France and Spain that we shall be principally concerned, then, in describing the characteristic structure of the feudal kingdom, with its *imperia in imperio* or, more accurately, its series of 'Chinese boxes' intervening between the all-inclusive monarchy and the humble individual in his own locality (in 'le dernier pays du monde', as I once heard a French peasant describe his village). 'Every baron is sovereign in his own barony', says Beaumanoir, the French lawyer, and indeed each was entitled to wage his own wars, so long as these were not incompatible with his fealty to the king. Linguistic differences accentuated this social and political localism. In France the great dividing-line ran between the Provençal south, whose tongue (the 'langue d'oc') had received a smaller element of Teutonic influence from the barbarians, and the northerners whose 'yes' was 'oui' (the 'langue d'oïl') and who have shaped the French language of today. Brittany, of course, spoke an entirely different, Celtic, tongue. The great French fiefs were Acquitaine (whose duke was the king of England), the duchy of Burgundy, and the counties of Flanders, Brittany and Champagne. At St Louis' death (1270) the other powerful counties were in the hands of the king or his immediate family; his brother Charles held Anjou and Provence and a nephew Artois.

Each of these lordships was a state in itself, with its own machinery of central and local government, exercising legislative and judicial powers, taxing and coining money, exacting military service and counsel. Even excluding Acquitaine, which was altogether exceptional through its connection with the English crown, these fiefs rivalled and in some cases surpassed the king's own administration in the degree to which they had developed an intricate structure of government. Both Champagne and Flanders had local *baillis* at least as early as the crown—in the late twelfth century—and indeed the Flemish counts, who had a precocious chancery in the eleventh century, tapped the wealth of their industrial cities through a highly-organized office for receipts by the middle of the thirteenth. For the majority of French nobles, their lord was one of these great magnates. Before St Louis set out on crusade he had called his barons to Paris to swear that they would 'keep faith and loyalty to his children if anything happened to him on his journey'. Joinville, the king's future biographer, refused to take this oath, 'for I was not his man'.[1] He was a vassal of the count of Champagne only and his refusal was entirely justified. Nearly two hundred years later the royal official at Vaucouleurs in the county of Bar—between Champagne, which had now come to the Crown, and Lorraine—was Robert de Baudricourt. When a shepherdess came to him with a strange tale of supernatural visions, it was to the duke of Lorraine that she was sent. Only later did Baudricourt reluctantly despatch the persistent Joan to Charles VII at Chinon.

But it would be misleading to give an impression of France as a neat pattern of clearly demarcated territorial lordships. The situation was much more intricate than this. The count of Champagne, for example, held lands of the emperor, the duke of Burgundy, the archbishops of Reims and Sens and of several bishops, as well as of the king of France. The title of count was not an indication of tenancy-in-chief (i.e. of the king) and many counts were numbered among the count of Champagne's own vassals. The powerful subjects of later medieval England were still less regional in the basis of their strength. Edward III's sons, the Black Prince and John of Gaunt, were little less than kings, and the latter (who was, indeed, titular king of Castile) on occasions raised about half the nation's armed forces from his own men. The Black Prince was prince of Wales and Acquitaine, duke of Cornwall and earl of Chester; Gaunt was duke of Lancaster, but geographical titles gave little indication of their power and Gaunt's 'palatinate' was more independent and stronger.

[1] *Life of St Louis*, ch. XXVI.

The Spanish monarchies present a different picture in some respects, for they were themselves composite structures. Alfonso X was king of 'Castile, Toledo, León, Galicia, Seville, Cordova, Murcia, Jaen and Algarve' and the Aragonese ruled not merely Aragon but also Catalonia, Valencia, the Balearics and the county of Barcelona. These titles to some extent corresponded to divisions in the work of government: the component parts of the Aragonese kingdom had their own royal households and councils, their own stewards and chancellors, courts and parliaments. The absence here of a small class of great lay feudatories did not imply that the king exercised greater power, indeed it could not, for all kings faced the same situation and lacked the financial means to secure direct obedience over wide areas. Hence all were compelled to divide the work of government with local powers such as feudal magnates or municipalities. The degree of independence achieved by urban institutions serves as a sort of barometer of the king's strength, for where he is most powerful—in southern Italy and in England—the town receives a strictly limited right to order its own internal affairs, and where he is weakest—in the imperial territory of northern Italy—republics arise paying at the most occasional lip-service to their overlord.

Since the Carolingian period, in circumstances that had been unpropitious to central control, western Europe's most characteristic institution had been the zone of private jurisdiction, the 'liberty' or 'immunity'. The king's efforts had to be directed to seeing that 'self-government at the king's command' was performed satisfactorily and on terms which were clearly defined and as much as possible in accordance with his own interests. His vassals owed him aid in war and peace and he would also attempt to reserve the right to hear judicial appeals. He would normally reserve the right to intervene if his vassal failed to render justice, and might even reserve for his court all major criminal suits. A grant made by Alfonso IX of Castile to the Order of St James (1229) will serve as an illustration.[1] The Order received from the king jurisdictional rights in certain places in return for normal feudal services. 'Moreover I (the king) am to exercise justice in these *villae* should either you or the representative (*vicarius*) deputed by you for this purpose be negligent in doing justice.' Should this

---

[1] *Bullarium Equestris Ordinis Sancti Jacobi*, p. 150.

B

circumstance arise, however, the Order was nevertheless to receive the property of the criminal. The king also reserved to himself the power to hear appeals from the Order's court.[1]

Arrangements of this nature prevailed all over Europe (and others bearing some resemblance to them over a good deal of Asia). The Spanish kingdoms were not exceptional in the ubiquity of ecclesiastical lords. In imperial territory north of the Alps (that is, roughly, modern Germany) the pious donations of lay magnates had combined with the policy of emperors intent on securing a literate and celibate governing class to place a very high proportion of the land in the hands of the Church, a situation which had been fateful for German history in the eleventh century, when the emperors fought the new claims of the papacy to control the whole Church, and was to be so again in Luther's time.[2] In the Slav lands, Germany east of the Elbe and Scandinavia, bishops and monasteries occupied a dominant position in society as the heirs of recently triumphant missionaries. Some churchmen, too, benefited by the general rule that in the 'marches' or border territories the local potentates were entrusted with special powers to strengthen their hand in the military emergencies of frontier existence. Thus the bishop of Durham, the king of England's bulwark against the Scots, ruled a palatinate which was unvisited by the king's sheriffs and normally paid the king no taxes.

The energetic ruler kept himself constantly informed concerning his rights and struggled to increase them or at least preserve them intact. In particular he sought to extend his judicial activity, for this gave him greater control in his kingdom and also, by bringing in money, made possible further gains. Often a vital contest was waged over appellate jurisdiction.[3] The popes of the later thirteenth century fought a long struggle to prevent the communes of the Papal State from hearing appeal suits, but their attempt

[1] The chain of appellate jurisdiction was often a long one. Thus in Castile *c.*1274 appeal from the court of the town *alcalde* was to the local *adelantado* (governor), thence to the king's *alcalde*, thence to the royal court (*adelantados mayores de Castilla*) and finally to the king himself. In León and Andalusia the second court was one of 'three men learned in the law' and the fourth of these five stages was omitted.

[2] It has been calculated that in the late eleventh century fifty-three German counties were in the possession of the episcopate alone.

[3] 'Appeal' as such is not characteristic of Germanic law and did not exist in Flanders, for example, but analogous concepts enabled the party losing a suit to claim denial of justice or false judgment.

to secure a monopoly of these cases was not successful. At the same period (1278) Philip III of France legislated to forbid the setting up of appeal benches by any of his vassals not then in possession of such courts.

The bureaucratic apparatus of the western monarchies will be described later. The king was, in orthodox but somewhat archaic theory, expected to 'live of his own', content with what he received as a lord exploiting his own feudal revenues or domain. To an enormous extent he was dependent on the productiveness of this domain. With some exaggeration, the success of the thirteenth-century French kings may be ascribed to their acquisition of Normandy in 1204, and the failure of the emperors to their inability to acquire the confiscated duchy of Saxony some years earlier. But in the last analysis the king was dependent on the loyalty of his vassals, a virtue doubtless fostered by the knowledge that they in turn needed their own vassals to be loyal.

To these vassals the king was a feudal overlord, but he could be seen in other ways: to legists he was the source of law, to theologians the means through which God worked his purposes on earth. Before going further into the realities of thirteenth-century government it may be well to look at some of the theories expressed concerning rule and rulers and, first of all, to see what kings themselves and popes thought about kingship.

St Louis, handing on to his son Philip III the lessons of a righteous and successful career, explained that a king must love God and strive after justice. He must avoid favouring the rich and powerful and must show complete impartiality in cases in which the Crown's own rights are involved: 'If you should discover that you are in wrongful possession of anything, even if possession of it was acquired by your ancestors, surrender it forthwith'.[1]

A few years before this, St Louis' brother, Charles of Anjou, had been the recipient of similar advice from Clement IV on acquiring the throne of Sicily and Naples.[2] The pope too had emphasized justice. Royal judges should sit daily and should be salaried and incorruptible. Any complaints against officials should

---

[1] Joinville, *Life of St Louis*, ch. CXLV. A number of different versions of these 'Instructions' have survived.

[2] Martène (E.) and Durand (U.), *Novus Thesaurus Anecdotorum*, II, cols. 505–8.

be investigated rapidly and there should be a special post (held by
a monk or some *miles affabilis*, a good-natured knight) concerned
with petitions, to ensure that these were heard expeditiously. The
king should never take innocent parties as hostages or make them
pay for the guilty. When enquiries were held concerning royal
rights the burden of proof should only be placed on his subjects
when circumstances made this reasonable.[1] The pope had also
some advice to offer on administration and the king's relations
with his baronage; he should be careful not to abuse his feudal
right to intervene concerning marriages (of his tenants' daughters)
and above all he should remedy the serious trouble about this
present year's taxes by reaching agreement with his barons, prelates and men of the towns about the circumstances in which he
may impose taxation.

   Both Philip and Charles may well have thought that their duties
were being emphasized at the expense of their rights, but this was
in keeping with medieval views of kingship. The king was, by
general consent, bound by the law—and whatever doubts there
might be as to what constituted 'the law', the essential point was
that the monarch had responsibilities and did not wield absolute
power. In England the king took an oath at his coronation to
keep peace with the Church, exercise justice in his judgments,
preserve good customs and extirpate bad ones,[2] and Magna Carta
—reissued several times in the thirteenth century—was testimony
to circumstances in which a king's powerful subjects might force
him into less imprecise promises. It was not the attitude of
theorists, but the relative strength of king and subjects and their
interdependence in practice which effectively determined the king's
position. Coronation oaths reveal this clearly enough, particularly in Aragon, where the nobles probably swore to the king that
'We who are each worth as much as you, and, united, more than
you, offer you our obedience if you keep our liberties, and if not,
not.'[3] It was orthodox doctrine in thirteenth-century France that

---

[1] The pope refers here to the 'enquiry' allegedly held by Charles's predecessor
Manfred into the possession of horses and sheep. When the owner could not prove
the animals were his they became the king's.

[2] W. Stubbs, *Select Charters* (Ed. 9), p. 244 (oath of Richard I, 1189: cf. the similar
oath of Henry I, 1100, p. 116).

[3] Quoted in R. B. Merriman, *The Rise of the Spanish Empire* ,I, 458-9. The source
is a late sixteenth-century one.

a vassal denied justice might declare war on the king, hence St Louis was doing more for his son than enumerating personal virtues. In the crusading kingdom of Jerusalem, where a monarchy had been installed ready-made rather than growing up by evolutionary processes, the mutual duties of ruler and ruled were yet more clearly defined. The 'Assizes' declared it the duty of the people to prevent their lord from breaking his oath and refusing to administer law and justice, and the court of all the king's vassals, the 'Court of Burgesses of Jerusalem', could declare any vassal absolved from his obligations.

The constitution of the crusading state was the *ne plus ultra* of feudal monarchy, emphasizing the weak position of a king chosen as the ostensible apex of a pyramid whose sturdier blocks were the lords who had carved for themselves slices of formerly Islamic and Byzantine territory in the Levant. In western Europe there were many who claimed for their anointed kings a much less circumscribed and purely utilitarian position. Such men were to be found particularly among the Roman lawyers, for whom law was not a statement of custom (as it was to the men of the early Middle Ages) but a corpus of positive enactments, handed down from the classical period. Inevitably such an outlook implied emphasis on the supreme position of the ruler responsible for enunciating and enforcing the law; indeed a famous Roman maxim had it that 'whatever has pleased the ruler has the force of law'. The study of Justinian's legal code had revived in the west during the eleventh century, and by the thirteenth those who attempted to define the position of the king produced a strangely compounded portrait of two incompatibles, a classical emperor superimposed on a feudal overlord.

We find such a picture in the great legal work of the court of Alfonso X of Castile (1252–84), the *Siete Partidas*, a curious combination of codification with treatises on the law, the constitution, and the duties of different ranks in society. The *Siete Partidas* ('Seven Parts') pronounce that 'no one can make law except the emperor or king or another on their orders', but elsewhere the need to take counsel with subjects is admitted. Statements of custom need 'the counsel of good men . . . the wish of the lord and the consent of those who are to be bound', the king can only rescind laws in a 'great council of all the "good men" of the land, that is the best and most honoured and learned ones', and to amend them he must take counsel with 'the "good men" and those who understand and are learned in law: he must do this with as many good men as he can gather from as many parts as possible, so that they are as much as possible in agreement, *for it is a noble and good thing to make law, and the more it is agreed on and understood the better and firmer it is*'.[1] Even the Romanist lawyers of the Castilian court emphasize that the king has responsibilities, that he must fear God, love justice and truth, and must himself set an example by obeying the law.

Something of the same atmosphere prevails in the political ideas of the best known and most representative of thirteenth-century thinkers, St Thomas Aquinas (*c.* 1226–1274). Aquinas's birth, upbringing and education help to explain his broadly-based outlook, for he was descended from a line of Lombard nobles in southern Italy, and received his earliest schooling at Monte Cassino, the Benedictine mother-house, and at the emperor Frederick II's *studium* at Naples, before embarking on the conventional scholastic training of a Dominican at Paris and Cologne. In his writings is to be found the same characteristically medieval blend of classical influences with those of contemporary society: his views on politics comprise in essence an attempt to apply a Christianized version of Aristotle's thought to the feudal monarchies of his own day. Thus he takes from Aristotle the view that the state is a 'natural' expression of man's nature, thereby departing from St Augustine's pessimistic view of it as a necessary evil, 'the remedy of sinfulness'. From the same source—Aristotle's *Politics* only became widely known in the west in the thirteenth century, through translations into Latin—he adopted the idea of the 'common good' as the touchstone of political action and organization. This was the test of everything, of the justification for levying a tax, for example, and of different types of constitution. A law had to be *ad bonum commune* and 'if rule is ordered not for the common good of the multitude but for the private good of the ruler this is unjust and perverse rule' and 'such a ruler is called a tyrant'. It is typical of Aquinas that he backs up this assertion with a quotation from Ezekiel (34: 2): 'Woe be to the shepherds of Israel that do feed themselves! Should not the

[1] *Siete Partidas*, I, 2, 11.

shepherds feed the flocks?' The concept of the common good—which is as much his key to politics as the 'general will' is Rousseau's—also helps Aquinas to define the role of the individual in the community. 'The good of a single man is not the ultimate end: it should be ordered to the general good' and 'since each man is part of the city [society], no man can be good except in so far as he is well proportioned to the common good'.

When he approaches the question of legislation and the ideal constitution Aquinas reveals more clearly that he is aware of the monarchies of his own day. Custom, he says, is the main source of law, and he gives this statement of Teutonic practice theological and philosophic justification by explaining that men's actions, like their words, are an expression of reason. He does not come down firmly for either prince or people as the source of law, but states that the ruler may change the law if this is expedient. · At this point he again calls in the 'common good'—never long absent from the stage—and explains that it is right to change the law only 'in so far as the common utility is served by such a change'. Moreover there must be 'evident utility'—this concept comes from Ulpian, a Roman lawyer—for custom and law should coincide as far as possible and 'the constrictive force of law is diminished in so far as custom is taken away'. When Aquinas comes to the problem of the best form of government he once again follows Aristotle who, like many writers in antiquity, advocated a 'mixed constitution'. In the *Summa Theologica* (Q. CV, 1) he explains that this means 'a well-combined constitution' (*politia bene commixta*), consisting of elements from monarchy, aristocracy and democracy. Again he is able to clothe his Greek wisdom in Hebrew garments, for he supports his case with the example of Moses and his successors, who ruled with the assistance of chiefs and wise men (Deuteronomy 1: 15, in the Vulgate these are *sapientes et nobiles*) and of 'able men from all the people' (Exodus 18: 21: *de omni plebe viros potentes* in the Vulgate). The conciliar role of the magnates in the feudal kingdoms of his day was doubtless in Aquinas's mind when he advocated an aristocratic element in the government of the ideal state, but it is difficult to see what institutions he had in mind when he spoke of a democratic one. Either its inclusion represents the acceptance of Aristotle without any contemporary reference, or possibly he recalled the burgher representatives of the towns present in the parliamentary assemblies of southern Italy (under Frederick II) and the Papal State and in German *Reichstäge*.[1]

Aquinas's views on the state have been discussed here because they illustrate the supreme exponent of the scholastic outlook face to face with the monarchies of his day. After this preliminary consultation with lawyers and theorists it is time to return to the realities of government, but we cannot leave the quintessential product of thirteenth-century education without a word concerning his general approach and reasoning. St Thomas's political, like his other opinions, are the result of the *deductive* method, that is to say he reasons from the general to the particular. There is no question of considering the workings of particular states, for instance (as Aristotle had done), and of *inducing* from this study general laws applicable to the science of politics as a whole. Instead he begins with universal principles, using his knowledge to illustrate their working. A characteristic passage on the advantages of 'government by one' (kingship) may be cited as an instance:

> That is best which most nearly approaches a natural process, since nature always works in the best way. But in nature, government is always by one. Among members of the body there is one which moves all the rest, namely, the heart: in the soul there is one faculty which is pre-eminent, namely, reason. The bees have one king,[2] and in the whole universe there is one God, Creator and Lord of all. And this is quite according to reason: for all plurality derives from unity. So, since the product of art is but an imitation of the work of nature, and since a work of art is the better for being a faithful representation of its natural pattern, if follows of necessity that the best form of government in human society is that which is exercised by one person.[3]

The right of an overlord to obtain 'counsel', emphasized by the *Siete Partidas* and implicitly mentioned by Aquinas, was no abstract doctrine but a recognition of the obvious fact that orders could only become effective if they had the support of the power-

---

[1] It is less likely that St Thomas knew about burgher representatives in English and Spanish assemblies (for these see below).

[2] This biological fallacy was inherited from the ancient world.

[3] *De Regimine Principum*, ch. 2 (trans. J. G. Dawson).

ful men of the lordship. Moreover their advice would help to decide whether a proposed innovation was practicable. The barbarian kings had held such gatherings of leading warriors and churchmen—witness the Anglo-Saxon *witan*—at which attendance had been less a right than a duty. In the thirteenth century assemblies of great councils—formal meetings of the king and his permanent leading officers reinforced by the presence of powerful men and sometimes by representatives of towns and localities—were becoming characteristic of the monarchies of England, Castile and Aragon. In France, as we shall see, they appear later and their development is stunted. In the south Italian kingdom representatives of the towns had been called by Frederick II to Foggia as early as 1232, and Aragonese influence was later to give Sicily a famous parliament. Pope Innocent III called an assembly of the lands of the Church in 1207 and during the second half of the century several provinces of the Papal State were holding frequent gatherings of this nature. The condition of the Empire was not conducive to the growth of centralized institutions, but Frederick II held spasmodic meetings of town representatives in imperial Italy, and around the middle of the century William of Holland (king of the Romans, 1247–56) gathered several *Reichstäge* or *colloquia generalia* of lords and cities in the Rhineland. In 1274, after the long interregnum, Rudolf of Hapsburg summoned a 'general court' 'for the reformation of the collapsed state of the empire and the common tranquillity of the faithful', but more characteristic of Germany were the *Landstäge* of the princes. Rudolf's summons quoted in support of the king's action the maxim of Justinian's *Codex* that 'what concerns all must be approved by all' ('quod omnes tangit ab omnibus comprobari debet'). In 1295 Edward I of England was to cite the same passage in calling the clergy to parliament, and again one is reminded of how the Roman lawyers could confer classical respectability on rude medieval institutions.

'Institution' is indeed perhaps too exact a term for parliaments in the period of their informal development when they were organs of royal government but occasions rather than institutions. The word *parlamentum* (*parlement* in French and Anglo-Norman) merely meant 'speaking'. Another Latin word, *colloquium* (colloquy = speaking together) was more or less a synonym for *parlamentum* in the thirteenth century and the Spanish equivalents were termed *cortes* (= courts: in Catalan, *corts*). That they were not yet technical terms shows clearly enough in the remark of the English Fleta that 'the king has his court in his council in his parliaments'. At this stage there was no 'parliament' capable of enjoying independent power to check the actions of the king. Yet the gatherings were witnesses to the existence of a *de facto* limitation of the royal power and hence of the possibilities of formal, constitutional, circumscription. In Aragon this situation was exploited by the subjects of Peter II as early as 1283. At the *Cort* of Catalonia held at Barcelona that year a petition made 'in the name of the whole *universitas* [corporation] of Catalonia' was granted, providing that a general *cort* was to be held at least once a year and that representatives of the towns, as well as lay barons and prelates, were always to be present. Statutes were only to be promulgated 'with the approbation and consent of the prelates, barons, knights and citizens of Catalonia, or (providing they have been called) of the greater and wiser part of the same'.[1]

Everything that has already been said on the subject should make it evident that attempts to define and delimit the activities of parliamentary sessions are bound to fail or to end in the vague assertion that they dealt with 'important matters of public concern'. Such a formula at least testifies to a correct reluctance to make anachronistic distinctions. It must include not only consideration of state affairs and all matters requiring publicity,[2] but also the presentation and consideration of petitions, the hearing of judicial suits, the promulgation of laws and consent to taxation. It was natural that consultation on executive action should normally take place only after initial decisions had been made. Thus James I of Aragon was determined on his expedition to the Balearics (1228) and conquest of Valencia (1232) before he summoned his *corts*, though in each case he consulted with them to secure their co-operation. As early as 1188 Alfonso of León had recorded a promise that 'I shall not make war or peace or any judgment [*placitum*: a better translation might be 'treaty'] except with the counsel of the bishops, nobles and "good men", by whose counsel

---

[1] *Cortes de los antiguos Reinos de Aragon y de Valencia y Principado de Cataluña*, I, 145.
[2] It is characteristic that the *Siete Partidas* require public accusations of treason to be made in the king's court and in the presence of at least twelve nobles.

I ought to be ruled.'[1] But in practice the questions 'Shall I wage war?' and so on, were liable to be of the type known to the Romans as 'questions expecting the answer *Yes*'.

We have already quoted the opinion of the Castilian *Siete Partidas* that the king must take counsel when he makes or changes the law and the same view was expressed by the legal writers of other kingdoms. 'Thus it is,' says Beaumanoir, author of a work on the customs of the Beauvaisis, 'the king can make new orders [*établissements*], but he must take great care that he does so for a reasonable cause and for the common good and after taking "great counsel" [*par grant conseil*]'. When a king issued legislation he was careful to precede it with formulae such as 'by common assent and counsel of my court and barons', 'by common deliberation', or 'I, Alfonso, have made this law after much discussion, with the consent of all '

Whatever the king's attitude to his assemblies, there remained the fact that 'counsel' and 'assent' implied the possibility of 'unwelcome advice' and 'refusal'. The most obvious circumstances in which these might arise was a demand for taxation. In England and the Spanish kingdoms it was understood that the ruler could raise 'extraordinary' (i.e. non-feudal) subsidies only with parliamentary consent. The fourteenth century was to see the constitutional exploitation of this notion and in particular the appointment of committees to watch over the administration of grants and other agreed measures. As early as 1301 such committees, to act between parliamentary sessions, were appointed in Catalonia; each represented a locality and its members—a knight, a burgess, a lawyer and a notary—were named by the king.[2] More than a decade before this the pope's rector had met with some outright refusals to grant taxes in the provincial assemblies of Romagna, a region in which papal authority fought in vain against the strength of such tyrants as the Polenta of Ravenna and the Malatesta of Rimini. The denial of scutage (*tallia militum*) by these two cities in 1287 is a reminder that in the last analysis the nature of parliaments depended on the relative strength of ruler and ruled. The presence of representatives of towns—unthinkable in the Teutonic Europe of the early Middle Ages—was testimony to

[1] *Cortes de los antiguos Reinos de León y de Castilla*, I, 39–42.
[2] *Cortes de los antiguos Reinos de Aragon y de Valencia y Principado de Cataluña*, I, 192–3.

an 'urban revolution' and to the need to recognize their weight in the nation. In León the towns were ordered to send men to the *cortes* as early as 1188, and in Catalonia by 1214, but it was only in the second half of the century that they began to play a prominent part in the Castilian assembly; they were then summoned ten times during the reign of Alfonso X (1252–84), four times by Sancho IV (1284–95), and no less than fifteen times by Ferdinand IV (1295–1312). We have already seen that in 1283 the Catalan towns secured a promise from their ruler that they would be consulted annually. The fiction whereby representatives spoke for a community and made promises on its behalf created certain difficulties, for the novel idea that men not present could be bound by the word of others who were present was not easy to grasp— especially the unpleasant financial implications of a blank cheque. Again the Roman lawyers could be of assistance. Justinian's *Code* defined the method whereby a corporation could give its agents full powers (*plena potestas*) to represent its interests and hence to consent to the jurisdiction of judges and to their decisions. By the same means towns could give a mandate to 'proctors' and promise to 'hold firm' whatever these representatives had agreed to in the assembly. Soon kings were insisting that all representatives must have the necessary full powers to bind the corporation or community on whose behalf they were present. Attempts were made by the cautious to confer limited powers or to add powers to defend the town's privileges and liberties, hence Philip IV's instructions that representatives must have full powers 'without the excuse of giving an account'—*plena potestas absque excusatione relationis facienda*—in other words they must not be able to plead the necessity of referring back for further instructions.

The monarchies have been treated hitherto in terms of 'pure' feudalism, but every king had available a certain bureaucratic machinery to assist him in enforcing his will. Inevitably the extent and efficiency of this machine depended largely upon the wealth of the crown, the availability of educated men, and the existence of a tradition of literate and loyal administration. In the later thirteenth century governmental officialdom was probably to be seen at its most powerful in the Sicilian kingdom of Charles of Anjou, though the Palaeologan relic of the Eastern Empire was heir to an even longer and greater tradition. The compact kingdom of England also made an impressive showing, but France on the whole less so—we have already seen that in this respect it as yet barely ranked ahead of some of its own great fiefs. The Iberian kingdoms lacked well-developed systems of administration, while the Empire tended to lag behind all the rest, partly through the tragic adversities of its recent history, but more fundamentally because the elective principle effectively hindered the development of any continuity in personnel, traditions and archives.

The king governed through his 'court' and departmentalization within this court developed very slowly. There was no clear differentiation between the ruler's own finances and the national treasury, and officials did not normally specialize in particular aspects of administration. The seneschal (or steward) and marshal, once the principal men in the king's household, had retained little power, but other officials of the household continued to play a leading part in government, particularly in England. The personnel of central administration consisted of a body of 'familiars' or royal officials, most of whom were normally 'clerks' at least in minor orders, though there was a growing lay element, mainly of men trained in the law. This central civil service was expected to display versatile competence in financial, judicial and military administration. The clerics did not normally receive salaries from the crown but lived mainly on the revenues of their ecclesiastical benefices; naturally they were absentees and pluralists, though this was less serious when they held canonries and prebends without 'cure of souls'. Promotion to the episcopate was the equivalent of promotion today into the higher reaches of the civil service and royal administration was one of the principal routes to ecclesiastical preferment. To govern a diocese conscientiously while remaining in the king's service was beyond the capacity of any normal man, and there were some who expressed dissatisfaction with an arrangement which was taken for granted by most—indeed any other system of paying officials would have placed an intolerably heavy burden on the king's finances and would have led to very heavy taxation or the virtual disappearance of the class of officials.

One occupation of the king's clerks was naturally the drafting of correspondence, a task undertaken by clerics of the royal chapel; as institutions became more formalized the principal of these became known as the chancellor and his office as the chancery. Later these were reinforced by lay notaries, particularly in the Latin countries possessing schools of Roman Law and hence a larger class of literate laymen. Not only did the chancery tend to become something of a separate department within the court, but its head at times assumed an independent status which menaced the king's own supremacy. It was for this reason that the chancellorship was left vacant for long periods in France, England and Castile. The French kings entrusted the headship of the writing-office from 1227 till 1314 to a 'keeper of the seal' who was either a clerk of comparatively low rank (he was never a bishop) or a layman. In Castile the archbishop of Toledo and the archbishop of Santiago became *ex officio* nominal chancellors of Castile and León respectively, while the work was done by a chief notary. We may be justified in applying one general test to these chanceries in an attempt to secure an impression of what degree of bureaucratic efficiency prevailed within them: did they regularly preserve copies of outgoing letters? To do so was a heavy burden on the small staffs of clerks, for dozens of letters, many of them concerning trivial or routine matters, must often have been despatched in a single day—yet how could government be carried on effectively if the king had no record of the orders that he himself had sent? The answer to our question is surprisingly unfavourable to thirteenth century administration. The popes had regularly kept. registers of important out-letters since the eleventh century, and perhaps earlier. The Angevin rulers of southern Italy also made registers of their letters: the full series of 378 volumes survived intact until 30 September 1943, when they were intentionally burnt by the Germans, with the other documents of the Naples State Archive. The English chancery enrolments open on an impressive scale from the reign of John (1199–1216) and the Castilian kingdom had registers (which have disappeared) from the time of Alfonso X. The French court was slow to embark on a policy of regular registration, which was begun only in 1307. In France, as in England, the recipient of a letter had to make a payment to secure its registration.[1]

[1] The chancery of Rudolf of Habsburg seems not to have kept proper registers but many of the king's letters have survived in the 'formularies' compiled by his notaries.

Inevitably the financial aspects of administration, as the essential basis of all the rest, bulked largest, and this is reflected in the emergence of exchequers as separate departments in England and Sicily. Again France was slow to follow suit. At the time of St Louis' death there was no equivalent to the exchequer, the supervision of revenue being entrusted largely to the *chambre aux deniers* in the household and to the occasional sessions of special commissions of the court charged with overseeing the accounts of the officials of the royal domain. The treasury, situated at the Paris house of the Templars' Order, was also much involved with both revenue and expenditure. The consolidation of a separate accounting department (*chambre des comptes*) was again a fourteenth-century development. The Iberian monarchs also lagged behind in financial organization, Castile perhaps inevitably since the king had virtually no domain lands to exploit, while in Aragon finance was the concern of the households of its various parts.

Equally crucial was the field of local administration, and it was here that the French king outstripped the English from whom he had learnt so much. Local government in the Middle Ages could mean anything from the mere recognition of regional magnates (granted office as royal officials and perhaps misleadingly viewed as such from the royal court) to the appointment of men strictly appointed and paid by the crown, responsible and loyal to it, independent of all local ties. Indeed, from the barons of the post-Conquest decades to the royal officials 'raised from the dust', the English sheriffs occupy every position in this spectrum between the eleventh century and the thirteenth. For the king to maintain real control over an official who was truly his servant it was desirable that the man should be imposed from above and without—not recruited locally. He was also more likely to give satisfactory service if he was the recipient of a fixed salary and not a 'farmer' who had secured office in return for a promise of paying a certain sum, and was thus obliged to raise from his zone of activity sufficient money to recoup his farm and achieve a margin of profit for his own pocket. The local representative of French royal power, whose wide functions defy definition, was the bailiff (*bailli* —or, in the south, 'seneschal'). This official met almost all the requirements stated above. He was not a local man and he tended to be moved fairly frequently (on an average every two to three years). Furthermore, if he was a native of the north, he was probably posted to southern France, and vice-versa. He was not permitted to acquire property or even to find a wife or husband for his children within his zone of office, except with the king's permission. He was paid a salary and was required to remain in his bailiwick for forty days after his resignation (or transfer), during which time his finances were subject to a special enquiry. He was also liable to periodical inspection by officials appointed by the king to oversee local administration, the *enquêteurs*. The Aragonese local officers also, unlike the English sheriffs, were salaried, but feudal and municipal powers greatly restricted their activities. The position of the Castilian regional *adelantado* implied recognition of a similar situation and came close to that of the English 'baronial sheriff'; there was virtually no true royal local administration in Castile, for the provinces were ruled by nobles and towns.

/ Hitherto in this chapter municipal government has been mentioned only as detracting from royal control. In a general picture of the exercise of political power this is inadequate, for by the thirteenth century there were two considerable areas in Europe within which the towns were autonomous republics rather than self-governing units within the monarchical structure of rule. These parts were Flanders and northern and central Italy.

Before discussing the institutions of these 'communes' we must consider why more independence was gained in the two areas named and to what extent they may be considered as democracies introducing a broader element of the population to the responsibilities of power. In the first place it is evident that the city-republics were part of an equation in which the other factor was the power of the king or lord; *ceteris paribus*, they were most likely to succeed in asserting their autonomy where external pressure was weakest. In Lombardy, Tuscany and Venetia they benefited by the rarity of effective imperial intervention. In the Low Countries the French king and the emperor made only intermittent appearances on the scene, while the Count of Flanders, by tradition and necessity, was an ally who drew money from the towns rather than sought to rule them. Where the claims of a lord were most effective in limiting municipal independence, as at Liége, Cambrai and Utrecht, the lord was a bishop.

In essence, however, it was the towns' own strength that made of them something more than a 'collective feudatory', and this strength was derived from a sizable population possessing formidable financial and military resources. Such urban nuclei had each some thousands of inhabitants; both Italy and Flanders ran to many towns of around 10,000, but probably only the exceptional places—Bruges and Ghent in the north, Milan, Venice, Florence and perhaps a few others in the south—exceeded 30,000 at the end of the thirteenth century. Their growth was of course connected with the expansion of trade and industry. Many Flemish towns were centres of cloth manufacture, dependent largely on wool shipped from England and exporting their products by North Sea routes (particularly eastwards to northern Germany and the Baltic) and overland to the Mediterranean. Of the larger Italian towns Venice, Genoa and Pisa were most dependent on maritime trade, but these, like the other great towns of Lombardy, Venetia, Tuscany and Emilia, had a mixed economy embracing textile industries and other crafts, long-distance and local trade, banking and finance, shop-keeping and agriculture. The inhabitants of these centres, and still more of the smaller towns, should not be envisaged as a 'new class', urban, mercantile, divorced from and antagonistic to the feudal outlook. In the Mediterranean town-life had a long tradition behind it, and both malaria and the dangers of war and raiding drove men to gather in those hill-top settlements of agriculturalists—often tilling land many miles distant—which still characterize southern Europe. Land-owning knights had been an important element in the formative stage of the Italian commune in the eleventh and twelfth centuries, furnishing its cavalry and often half the consuls (the governing officials). Italy and the Languedoc had also a large and powerful class of lawyers and notaries.[1] Even in Flanders there was no clear-cut division between archaic rustic nobles and slick urban businessmen; money made from the soil was often invested in trade and industry, and in turn the profits of these activities could be converted into nothing safer than land. Such a cycle was still more natural in Italy where the climate encouraged the purchase of a villa for the summer *villeggiatura*. Southern France

[1] Padua, not one of the largest of Italian cities, had over five hundred notaries *c*. 1300.

c

is one obvious exception which disproves the fallacious 'rule' that only communities of merchants could set up independent institutions. Here Toulouse virtually won self-rule in the 1230s as an ally of its Count in the struggle against the military power of northern France, and even smaller places, such as Avignon and Beaucaire, possessed such 'Italian' institutions as consuls and *podestà* and won the vassalage of the surrounding countryside.

Inevitably, self-government was not government 'by the people' or even 'for the people'. 'The rich men possess rule in the towns', says Beaumanoir, and this French generalization holds true elsewhere. The wealthier people had more time at their disposal and more education behind them, to strengthen their speeches and recommend their administrative services. There was much in the government of the town—particularly fiscal policy—that directly and obviously affected their well-being; in such matters to lack interest in politics might be to condemn oneself to poverty. Above all, they possessed the means of bringing pressure to bear upon the rest of the population, dependent on them for employment and patronage and liable to be over-awed, at a pinch, by a show of strength from armed retainers. In a sense the inevitable presence of powerful and interested citizens makes an oligarchy the 'natural' form of government of any autonomous city. In ready recognition of this tendency, contemporaries spoke of *maiores, boni homines, potentiores* and *divites* or *ditiores*—in the Italian vernacular, of *grandi, magnati* and *ottimati*.[1] Rather later the Florentine Francesco Guicciardini thought that a senate of 150 would contain 'all the qualified men of the city'; a larger one would be bound to include the 'ignorant and ill-born'.[2] This oligarchical conformation was typical also of cities enjoying merely municipal status. Beaumanoir explains well the reasons for this and its effects:

> We have seen many disputes in the towns [he says], the poor against the rich, and the rich against each other—when for example, they cannot agree on the nomination of a mayor, or proctors, or lawyers; or when one party accuses another of not dealing properly with the town's revenue and of having spent excessively; or when the administration is in a bad condition on account of the quarrels and hatreds that turn one family against another. . . . There are some

---

[1] Recent writers have tended to prefer the anachronistic 'patricians' and 'patriciate'.
[2] F. Guicciardini, *Dialogo e Discorsi del Reggimento di Firenze*, p. 116.

towns in which the poor burgesses and even those of middle rank take no part in the administration of the town, this being entirely in the hands of the rich because the common people fear them on account of their wealth and connections. Men become mayor or *jurés* or *receveurs* and then the next year they pass on the office to their brothers or nephews or close relatives—so that in ten or twelve years the rich hold all the offices in the towns.[1]

In London, where a similar situation prevailed, the courageous John of Northampton (in the late fourteenth century) led an unsuccessful assault by the lesser crafts and minor members of the greater ones against a well-entrenched régime which, characteristically, followed a monopolistic policy injurious to both small traders and consumers. *De jure* might lag behind *de facto*, but sooner or later the town's constitution was likely to reflect the oligarchical trend. At Ghent this had happened as early as 1228, with the introduction of a sort of rota system whereby the thirteen *échevins* for the year shared power with the thirteen holders of the office for the two previous years. Every three years the same men reappeared as the 'new' *échevins* and in practice office for life was held by 'the thirty-nine'. Venice, the best Italian instance of formalized oligarchy, 'closed' its Great Council in 1297. Thereafter only those whose ancestors had sat in this council were eligible for membership.[2]

A rigid, fossilized system of political oligarchy, however, is doomed to defeat through its very rigidity, for it defies the essential mutability of men's fortunes— or, as the sociologists would have it, 'social mobility'. In an age when a single fortunate trading venture or loan might produce a colossal profit and when taxes (by modern European standards) were low, ability and good luck could rapidly make a poor man rich—the reverse, of course, also held. At times a general increase in wealth might apply to considerable areas—we are perhaps in the realm here of the 'take-off' dear to writers on the economy of under-developed countries— and often many men in a single town were making fortunes contemporaneously. We may see this occurring in Florence in the

[1] Beaumanoir, *Coutumes de Beauvaisis* (ed. A. Salmon), II, 267–9.
[2] Qualification was decided by membership of the council since 1172. Though the *serrata* applied in practice from 1297, the list of eligible families was only drawn up in 1315 and the 'closure' became formal in 1322.

two or three decades after the city's bankers had financed Charles of Anjou's conquest of southern Italy—which became something of an economic colony—in 1265–6. Florence's walls, which had been expanded in 1172–6, had to be extended again after 1284 to take in a vastly increased population. Assisted by the fact that 'conspicuous consumption' is most conspicuous in climates which encourage people to live in the open air, the population was itself aware of such changes. Dante thought that his city's period of true greatness was to be found in the past, before it had become corrupted by wealth. 'New people and rapid wealth', he said, had led to pride and *dismisura* (a lack of proportion), and Florence was already suffering from the effects of this. In a moving passage in the *Paradiso* (written *c.* 1315) he puts into the mouth of his great-grandfather a description of this Golden Age of the twelfth century. 'Within the old walls Florence was at peace, sober and pure.' Women did not wear necklaces and tiaras, skirts and belts covered with ornaments. Fathers were not then appalled at the birth of a daughter, for they married less early and their dowries were smaller. Family homes were smaller and did not seem half-empty, and they too were not over-decorated. Women did not use cosmetics and were not left lonely by husbands going to France on business. They tended their babies in the cradle, chanting the traditional lullabies, or worked at their spinning and told the old tales of Troy, Fiesole and Rome.[1]

Dante's contemporary Giovanni Villani, though writing of a less archaic period, recounted the same contrast, with the same underlying 'primitivist' belief—strengthened perhaps by the Franciscan ideal—in the moral superiority of the simple life:

> And note, that at the time of the said Popolo [1250–60] and before and afterwards for a long time, the citizens of Florence lived soberly, and on coarse food, and with little spending, and in manners and graces were in many respects coarse and rude; . . . but they were true and trustworthy to one another and to their commune and with their simple life and poverty they did greater and more virtuous things than are done in our times with more luxury and more riches.[2]

This knowledge of and admiration for the austerity of the past was not confined to Florence, and the same feeling is to be found

---

[1] *Inferno*, XVI, 73–5; *Paradiso*, XV, 97–126.
[2] G. Villani, *Cronica*, Bk. VI, ch. 70 (translation based on that of Rose E. Selfe).

in Riccobaldo of Ferrara's *Universal History*, written at the end of the thirteenth century:

Manners and ways of living were rough in Italy in the times of this emperor [Frederick II, 1220–50]. The men wore a head-dress of iron mail. Man and wife would eat from one dish and the use of wooden trenchers at table was not yet known. A family would have only one or perhaps two goblets. When people ate at night they lit their tables by oil-lamps or by faggots held by a boy or servant, for tallow and wax candles were not then in use. Men wore leather or cloth cloaks, without a lining, and a light cloth hood. The women wore tunics of the same cloth, both at their marriage and after. For both sexes it was a plain way of life, little if any gold or silver was displayed on their clothing and they were frugal in their meals. The common people ate fresh meat three times a week. They would eat vegetables cooked with meat and keep some of the meat to eat cold in the evening. Not everyone drank wine in the summer, and people thought themselves rich if they had just a little money. Wine-cellars were small then and granaries were not large, for people were satisfied with what was distributed. Girls married with a small dowry because they were frugal in their ways, and before marriage they were content to wear a light cloth tunic and over this a flaxen cloak. Neither maidens nor married women decorated their heads with expensive ornaments. The wives wore a band round their temples and cheeks which tied under the chin. Among men it was thought glorious to be proficient in arms and on horseback, and among the wealthy nobles to possess towers; some of the Italian cities were renowned for the towers which abounded in their midst.[1]

In so far as oligarchy was a formal political structure it had to possess the means of assimilating 'new men', and at times this needed to be a rapid process for many were pressing for admission. There were certainly diehards who objected to the *nouveaux riches*, but their exclusion was a danger and might prevent a town from exerting its full potential strength, as well as weaken it through internal divisions. In the armies of the Italian republics the 'nobles' fought as cavalrymen and it was wasteful not to use in this role a man capable of maintaining a horse and fighting on it. The towns themselves ennobled their own citizens—the ceremony of dubbing had to be performed by one who was himself a noble—

[1] Riccobaldo of Ferrara, 'Historia Universalis', *Rerum Italicarum Scriptores*, IX, col. 128 (also in the same author's 'Compilatio Chronologica', *ibid.*, cols. 247–8).

but some republics compromised by compelling wealthy non-nobles to serve on horseback as *milites pro communi*. The dangers of failing to assimilate at a sufficient rate are illustrated by the 'popular' anti-magnate movements which flourished in many Italian towns in the later thirteenth century.[1] Such movements were essentially an attempt by the leading 'outsiders' to weaken the hold of the 'top people' and in particular to neutralize by legislation their formidable social strength. The nature both of this strength and of the measures used to oppose it are well illustrated by some laws for its members promulgated in 1260 by Perugia's 'Popolo':

> 1. No man is to become the vassal of any other, or swear fealty to him; any one doing so is to be decapitated, as is the man receiving such an oath and the notary recording such a transaction.
>
> 2. No member of the *popolo* may have recourse to any 'magnate' concerning any business he had in the commune's court before the *podestà* or captain or any other official. . . .
>
> 3. No member of the *popolo* is to dare to hold conversation with any magnate or to be in his company when going to or returning from the court or palace of the commune, or in any other part of the city at a time when this magnate is involved in a fight or quarrel. . . .[2]

In Florence similar moves against the 'magnates' began in 1281 with the decision to draw up a list of these, each of whom should be compelled to make a payment of 2,000 *l.* as security for his future good conduct. Twelve years later a more powerful popular movement formulated the 'Ordinances of Justice', whereby an official, the *Gonfaloniere di Giustizia* (Standard-bearer of Justice), was added to the six priors, with the special responsibility of punishing magnates; any magnate killing a member of the *popolo* was to be automatically sentenced to death, his property confiscated, and his house promptly destroyed by the popular militia under the command of the *Gonfaloniere*. If the guilty man could not be traced, his next of kin was liable to punishment; in this way the magnates' family solidarity was exploited and used against them. Magnates were excluded from membership of the gilds and

---

[1] These movements also show the inadequacy of the approach which would describe these towns as 'controlled by a patriciate'.

[2] *Regestum Reformationum Comunis Perusii (1256–60)*, ed. V. Ansidei, pp. 162–6.

hence from the priorate. Any family of which a member during the last twenty years had been a knight was to rank in the black list with 'those whom the general opinion calls *potentes, nòbiles* or *magnates*'. This list included about a hundred and fifty families, seventy-two of which resided mainly in the city.

Opposition to an oligarchy inevitably looked for external allies, and the sort of situation that might arise from this is well illustrated by events in Flanders during the reign of Philip IV of France (1285–1314). At this period the Count, Guy of Dampierre, was co-operating with anti-oligarchic elements in the towns in an attempt to weaken the hold of such cliques as the Thirty-nine of Ghent; the Count's main purpose was of course to gain control himself. The result was the formation in 1287 of a rival coalition between the patriciate (henceforth the *Leliaerts* or 'men of the lilies') and the French king. The long and inconclusive struggle that ensued combined the bitterness of class hatred with the patriotic hatred of Fleming and Frenchman.

We can now turn from this necessarily rather long description of the setting to the institutions of urban government. In origin the communes had taken shape as corporations of individuals undertaking joint political action. Normally the citizens had been united by an oath of mutual co-operation and there is much truth in the view that contrasts this 'horizontal' 'oath between equals' with the 'vertical' feudal oath linking vassal and lord: the double origin of many Italian communes, however, comprising distinct noble and non-noble organizations, is a reminder that even here the democratic element in the towns may easily be exaggerated. In Italy the characteristic institutions of the early communes had been the *arenga* (the parliament of all the citizens) and the consuls, who were administrative officials. By the early years of the thirteenth century divisions within the consular class had led to the replacement of the consuls by a single official called in from another town, a sort of 'town manager'. This man, the *podestà*, was normally in turn dispossessed of the *de facto* headship of the commune by the gild organization, the *popolo*. We have already seen how pressure was constantly exerted on the powers that be by a class of 'new men' and the *popolo* was essentially an organization headed by such men, expressing their interests through the gilds and often forming a military force sub-divided according to the different 'regions' of the town. The *popolo* was usually at first headed by an external 'captain' –in this respect its organization was based on that of the commune itself—but the reverse now occurred to what had happened in the change from consuls to *podestà*, for the captain of the *popolo* often lost his importance to local officials. In Florence the captain, who had come to power in 1250, was virtually superseded in 1282 by gild representatives, the six priors.[1] But there was no secure resting place for the institutions of these towns. No individual was permitted to retain an important office for a long period lest he attempted to set up a tyranny: Florence's priors, for example, held office for two months at a time, after which they were ineligible for the next two years. In this paralysed condition the city-states sought not merely to organize their domestic affairs and to conduct diplomacy and (almost ceaseless) warfare; they also ruled most of the countryside. The *contado*, or zone of subjection, had been acquired in opposition to neighbouring towns for its strategic value, as a source of taxes and soldiers, above all as an insurance against starvation:[2] it was made to provide the town with food. The internal history of most of the towns is a hectic tale of internal class disputes, complicated by feuds inside the nobility, with 'new men' putting forward claims, while the strongest among the 'old' are never dispossessed of power. This explains the numberless constitutional changes, the incurable tendency to experiment with new types of council, new ways of voting, new combinations of the contrasting principles of voting and choice by lot. The constitutional solution to the town's problems was always felt to be just round the corner, and Dante's criticism of Florence was entirely justified:

> Athens and Lacedemon, that did frame
> The ancient laws and were so civilized,
> Made but a feeble feint of living well
> Compared with thee, who dost so subtilly
> Provision make, not to November's midst
> Will reach what in October thou dost spin.
> How often in the time thy memory holds,

[1] A similar change occurred in many towns at this time, the Five taking over power at Perugia in 1270, the Nine at Siena in 1277 and the Seven at Orvieto in 1292.

[2] The view that the *contado* was won primarily to open for trade the roads that had hitherto been dominated by marauding barons is a myth connected with the legend that the communes were essentially congregations of merchants.

Laws, coinage, offices and customs thou
Hast changed and all thy members hast renewed!
If well thou call to mind, with vision clear,
Like a sick woman thou wilt see thyself,
Who on her bed of down can find no rest,
But by her tossing tries to ease her pain.[1]

The conclusion of this tale was almost invariably the same: the *signoria*, government by a single tyrant.

In Flanders and north-western France the characteristic feature of republican institutions was the *échevinage*. The *échevins* (in Latin, *scabini*) were in origin the men chosen by the lord to perform judicial offices in the town, and were appointed to this position for life. As the towns achieved independence the *échevins* were gradually transformed; they ceased to be the lord's men and became the city's governing body or council, no longer holding office for life but now normally for one year only at a time. This at least was the theory, and at first the practice: but at Ghent the annual rotation of thirteen *échevins* was so manipulated that the city was ruled by a closed council of thirty-nine (above, p. 23). In all the city-states the lesson is evident that any constitutional structure was vulnerable to pressure and would be modified and reshaped by the powerful, whether these were Flemish oligarchs crystallizing their control through the Thirty-nine or Italian anti-oligarchs installing their 'popular' institutions to check or supersede those of the magnates. In the towns where a powerful overlord, the bishop of Liége, was able to retain control of the *échevinage* and prevent its development as a town's own council, an analogous process took place: there also two rival governmental structures existed side by side, for the townsmen set up against the bishop's *échevins* their own 'sworn men' or *jurés*.

Monarchical and municipal governments as they existed in the thirteenth century both illustrate that weakness of central control which is the most striking contrast with the modern state. 'Feudalism', even where its institutions are imposed by the monarchy (as in England and southern Italy), is essentially the formalization of this situation. In their lack of salaried officials and full-time soldiers, above all in their implicit compromise with the powerful subject, these monarchies are feeble creatures beside the

[1] *Purgatorio*, VI, 139–51 (trans. A. L. Money).

Leviathans of the sixteenth and seventeenth centuries. Within their limitations, however, great gains could be made. Much depended on the fortunes of family descent, on avoiding minorities and disputed successions. The Capetians of France produced an undisputed male heir in eleven successive generations, from the tenth century to the fourteenth, and it was in part due to this genetic triumph[1] that when they gained new territories—Normandy, Poitou and Toulouse in the thirteenth century, Champagne and part of Flanders early in the fourteenth—they were sufficiently strong for these to prove a source of strength and not an impossible burden. With them one may contrast the unfortunate house of Castile, hopelessly debilitated in the fourteenth century by disputed successions and resultant civil warfare. The collapse of imperial power in Germany must be imputed largely to the failure of earlier rulers to install hereditary succession in place of the archaic elective principle—but that failure is in turn evidence of the feeble resources of these kings and of the dispersion of political power within the Empire.

Further Reading

JOINVILLE, *Life of St Louis* (many editions: trans. by M. R. B. Shaw in *Chronicles of the Crusades*, Penguin Classics, 1963)

ST THOMAS AQUINAS, *Selected Political Writings*, ed. A. P. D'Entrèves (Oxford, 1948)

H. PIRENNE, *Belgian Democracy* (Manchester, 1915): paperback edn. as *Early Democracies in the Low Countries* (Harper Torchbooks, 1963)

D. WALEY, *The Italian City-Republics* (World University Library, 1969).

J. K. HYDE, *Society and Politics in Medieval Italy* (Macmillan paperbacks, 1973)

---

[1] It is of course impossible to calculate the odds against the survival of the father by a legitimate male heir in eleven successive generations over this period, but they must have been enormous.

Appendix

King James I of Aragon negotiates with the Catalan Estates, 1264.
(From *The Chronicle of James I King of Aragon*, chapters ccclxxxiii–
ccclxxxvii. Adapted from the translation by J. Forster, II,
503–7).

I accordingly departed thence, went to Catalonia, and called together
the Estates at Barcelona. When they were assembled, barons, citizens,
and clergy, I asked them, since they and theirs had always helped me in
such undertakings as that of Majorca and others, that they would now
help me in this one, as was much needed. Their answer was that they
would deliberate thereupon, and as the lord Ramon de Cardona and
some of his house claimed redress for some wrongs they had suffered
of me, they would first speak with me thereupon, and then make such
answer as should satisfy me. I replied that anyone in my land who had
any complaint to make, should come forward at once, and right would
be done to him; that ought not to be a reason for refusing me the aid I
asked for. It was not good sense, I said, that whilst I asked them for
one thing, they should reply by talking of another quite unconnected
with it. Wherefore I prayed and commanded them to think better of it,
for certainly the answer they gave did not become such good men as
they were. They deliberated again, and then gave me answer as bad as,
or worse than, the first.

When I saw how badly they behaved to me, I told them that they had
not sufficiently considered what might happen thereafter. If the King
of Castile ultimately lost what was his own, I and they would find it
harder to keep our property than we had done until then. I then
addressed the clergy in these words: 'What will you gain by the churches
where our Lord and His Mother are now worshipped being lost, and
the name of Mahomet proclaimed therein? And if what belongs to me
and to the King of Castile as Christian kings, be lost, how can you
expect to keep what you yourselves own? Why answer me so ill and so
basely! I never thought that I should assemble the Estates in Catalonia
without obtaining from them what was reasonable; for surely had I
asked from you urgently what was unreasonable, I really think I should
have prevailed with you to grant it to me. But since such is your
answer, I will depart from you, as much displeased as any lord ever was
with his people.'

Saying which I arose, and would hear nothing more from them and
went to my house; they prayed me earnestly not to be angry, for they
would again deliberate and give me an answer. But for all that I would
not wait; part of the members followed me to my own house, others

remained behind; but ultimately those who had come with me went back to the others.

And we were in this state, and would not eat, when the Assembly sent us a deputation of four of its members, the lord Berenguer Arnau, the lord Pedro de Berga, and two other barons, whose names I do not recollect, who begged to speak to me. I took them aside and heard what they had to say. They told me on behalf of their colleagues that it had never been, and never should be, the mind of the Estates on any account that I should ask counsel or aid of the prelates and barons of Catalonia without finding it at once. And that as I intended to leave the town, and had said so to some of their colleagues, they begged me to remain, promising, if I did, to behave in such wise that I should be satisfied with them. And this they prayed so much and so earnestly of me, that I had to grant it.

At vespers they came to me again, saying that on no account would they (that I ought to believe) let me leave in anger with them. I ought to hear what they had to say, for their words in the first instance were not intended in bad sense. They therefore begged me, before they granted what I asked of them, to settle Ramon de Cardona's claims. It was, they said, their intention to grant me after that the service known by the name of *bovatge*, although they maintained I had no right to it, having already had it twice since the beginning of my reign; once when I came to the throne, and again when I went to Majorca. They would, however, grant it again, since I wished it, and would serve me in that business so that I should have reason to thank them. I was content with their answer, and called together the Estates in Aragon, to be present at Zaragoza within three weeks.

II

ITALY AND THE MEDITERRANEAN IN THE SECOND HALF OF THE THIRTEENTH CENTURY: THE RIVALRY OF FRENCH, GREEKS AND ARAGONESE, AND THE INVOLVEMENT OF THE PAPACY

THE death of the emperor Frederick II (December 1250) provides a convenient beginning-point for viewing the framework of government in action. Although Frederick had for the most part abandoned the imperial lands north of the Alps to their lay lords and to the towns, his energetic attempt to dominate the Italian peninsula had achieved a sort of crystallization, the dissolution of which marked a decisive change in the course of European history. There is also some convenience in starting in southern Europe because the Mediterranean zone, from the Pillars of Hercules to the Bosphorus, possessed a certain unity; it is conspicuously true of an age of difficult land transport that the sea served to join rather than to divide. In this period the political fates of Aragon, southern Italy and Byzantium were so interdependent that a recent book on the 'Sicilian Vespers' of 1282 has justly borne the subtitle 'A history of the Mediterranean world in the later thirteenth century'.

Throughout Frederick's struggle to dominate Italy, the emperor had employed as a tolerably secure base his Sicilian kingdom, consisting of the island of Sicily and the southern mainland: this was organized along lines not dissimilar to the two great monarchies of northern Europe, France and England. Italy north of Rome, however, contrasted radically with this centralized kingdom, for it was a land of city-states: one might almost say that it was ancient Greece to Frederick's Persia. The central Italian zone claimed by the papacy provided no exception, since the pontiffs could not rule the communes who were their theoretical subjects.

Further north still, in Tuscany, Emilia, Lombardy and Venetia, the towns were yet more pre-eminent. In this alien world Frederick's achievement had been to polarize the rivalries between the cities, one system of alliances relying on his aid while the other defied his pretensions. Even to the former he was no more than an ally; he never came very close to being the ruler of northern Italy. To interpret the history of twelfth- and thirteenth-century Europe as 'the struggle of pope and emperor' is to impart a fictitious unity to a complicated theme and, above all, to neglect the feeble temporal resources of these two contestants. The un-aided power of each was rarely greater than that of one of the more powerful communes, and in writing of Italy the numerous cities deserve much more attention than either pope or emperor. That eyes have often been diverted from the direct evidence of their actions has been in part the effect of the articulateness of these two shadow-boxers; the ingenious pronouncements of their pub-licists have been listened to with unmerited attention, and it has become conventional to discuss this phase of history in terms of allegorical swords at the expense of material ones.[1] It is in keep-ing with this lack of realism in official and semi-official pro-nouncements that Innocent IV should have declared Frederick deposed (Lyons, 1245) and that this deposition should in itself have been virtually without influence on the course of events in Italy. The titular successors found for the emperor achieved no hold south of the Alps.

After Frederick's death the Italian political scene lacked a pattern; the cities were like filings meaninglessly dispersed after the removal of a magnetic force. The situation resembled that of half a century before, when Henry VI had died prematurely, leav-ing Frederick as an infant heir; now Frederick in his turn had no adult legitimate heir in the peninsula. Events at once revealed the readiness of individuals and city-republics to take up the

[1] A modern analogy may illustrate the dangers of relying on propagandists for the reconstruction of history. Ribbentrop's Introduction to the German White Book (1940) refers to 'the magnanimous and infinitely patient statesmanlike endeavours of the Führer to place German-Polish relations on a basis which does justice to the interests of both sides'. This passage is not normally quoted by historians as evidence concerning Hitler's policy during the years before the 1939–45 war. A closer parallel, perhaps, is to be found between the pamphlets of papalist and imperialist writers and the speeches made in the United Nations assembly on behalf of 'western' and com-munist powers, both being intended to influence 'neutral' opinion.

heritage of power in a thoroughly fragmented Italy. In Lombardy and Venetia Ezzelin da Romano and Hubert Pallavicino, hitherto allies of Frederick, were able to construct precocious tyrannies, the former controlling for a time Verona and Padua, the latter Cremona and Pavia. Although neither could hold together a lasting *signoria*, it was already clear that in the north republican institutions were losing ground and would soon normally be replaced by the rule of a single lord. The Estensi dominated Ferrara and the Della Torre and Visconti alternated as rulers of Milan. In Tuscany the time of the dissolution of imperial power was the first great era of Florentine expansion in southern Tuscany and on the Tyrrhenian coast. Further south still, the republic of Rome demonstrated clearly enough by its successful imperialism under a popular leader, the Bolognese Brancaleone degli Andalò (1252–5 and 1257–8), that even in papal territory the towns rather than the pope could benefit by the absence of imperial pressure.

In the Sicilian kingdom, where the towns had long before submitted to the powerful rule of the Normans, the situation evolved in an entirely different manner. Here a struggle for the succession ensued which was decisive for Italy's political geography and for the future of the papacy. The southern kingdom was held, at least in theory, as a papal fief. Thus constitutional right as well as the pressing need to emerge from the century-long nightmare of Hohenstaufen 'encirclement' justified Innocent IV (1243–54) in seeking a new ruler for Sicily. The absence of a legitimate claimant *in situ* (Conrad, Frederick's surviving legitimate son, was in Germany) strengthened Innocent's hopes, but he hesitated between the alternatives of placing the kingdom under direct papal rule and calling in a temporal conqueror to assume the crown. He had not yet made a decision when Conrad (IV) appeared in Italy (January 1252) and began the conquest of his father's kingdom. This setback drove Innocent to negotiate with potential aspirants to the Sicilian monarchy, such as Charles of Anjou (brother of Louis IX of France) and two members of the English royal family, Henry III's brother, Richard of Cornwall, and the king's younger son Edmund.[1] Innocent was still engaged in these

---

[1] The negotiations concerning Edmund, who was a child (b. 1245), were conducted with his father Henry III.

negotiations when he received the news of Conrad's premature death (May 1254).

This renewed incidence, in alternate generations, of early death (Henry VI, like his grandson, had survived his father by less than a decade) was not extraordinary ill-luck by medieval standards. It might have settled the problem of the south decisively in the pope's favour, but there was another contender in the person of Frederick's illegitimate son Manfred, Prince of Taranto. Innocent at first attempted to reach terms with Manfred while himself assuming rule in the Sicilian *Regno*, but this paradoxical alliance was short-lived. Manfred went into revolt and the papal army which entered Apulia was routed. The news of this defeat reached Innocent IV at Naples just before his death in December 1254. His successor Alexander IV encountered a still more decisive defeat in Apulia in the summer of 1255. Manfred was now in a position to assert his succession to his father's standing throughout the peninsula. Beginning with a Genoese alliance (1257) he set about the construction of a system which would serve as a screen against claimants entering Italy from the north. In August 1258 he had himself crowned at Palermo. The same autumn he invaded the March of Ancona, the Adriatic province of the Papal State. He found friends in the north of Italy in Pallavicino and the Estensi and in Tuscany formed links with the Sienese, leaders of the anti-Florentine cause. As well as continuity with the Hohenstaufen tradition—or Ghibellinism, as it was now generally styled—Manfred was able to offer the more tangible asset of a force of German soldiers, well-trained and dependent for their livelihood on successful warfare. These men were the heroes of the great victory of Montaperti (September 1260), a crushing defeat for the Florentines which established Ghibelline authority throughout Tuscany. If any further event was needed to bring home to Alexander IV the revolutionary change in the balance of power to Manfred's advantage, it was the latter's election in 1261 by a pro-Hohenstaufen faction as senator of the city of Rome. Further afield Manfred made a powerful ally and at the same time greatly enhanced the prestige of his line by the marriage of his daughter Constance to Peter, elder surviving son of James I of Aragon (June 1262).

The story of Manfred's overthrow and supersession begins with the death of Alexander IV and the election of a Frenchman, Urban IV (August 1261), as his successor. This was one of the most fateful of all papal conclaves, for Urban's decision that unfavourable terms with a French prince were preferable to a continuance of Hohenstaufen domination inaugurated an era of French predominance in southern and central Italy. Urban promptly relinquished the lengthy and fruitless negotiations carried on by his predecessor with the foolish Henry III of England, whose 'appetite was much better than his teeth'. To renew the approaches already made to Charles of Anjou was not altogether easy, for Charles would require the consent of his brother Louis, and, as a king, Louis was bound to consider more seriously than did the pope the claim to the Sicilian kingdom of Conrad, the young son of Conrad IV. The scruples of the future saint were overcome and in June 1263 Urban was able to announce that he had chosen Charles as king. The terms of the agreement then reached provided that Charles should pay the pope 50,000 marks immediately after the conquest of his kingdom and thereafter an annual feudal rent of 10,000 gold ounces. He was to leave Provence within a year with an army of at least a thousand knights and three hundred crossbowmen.

In contrast with Henry III, Charles of Anjou possessed ability to match his ambition. He had achieved a firm hold in Provence, and Marseilles provided him with a port and a fleet, though the enmity of the Genoese and others deterred him from the attempt to bring the bulk of his forces to Italy by the sea route. An energetic cardinal, Richard Annibaldi, helped to bring about Charles's election in 1263 as senator of Rome, but Urban naturally feared an arrangement whereby the city might have remained permanently under Charles's control and persuaded him to give a secret undertaking to relinquish the senatorship after conquering his kingdom. Alliances in northern Italy were essential for the passage of his army, and with great skill Charles secured a league in Piedmont with the Marquis of Montferrat and in Lombardy with Milan and a number of other cities. The critical year for the papacy was 1264, when Manfred, aware of the approaching invasion, launched a three-pronged attack on Orvieto, Urban's Umbrian retreat; this came so near to success that the pope in haste turned everywhere for local crusaders to repel the threat.

D

The leader of one of Manfred's columns was drowned fording a river and his troops somehow failed to press home their attack. When Urban died in October 1264 Charles's preparations were almost complete.

Urban's death greatly strengthened the position of Charles who was already much the stronger partner in the alliance. As well as interrupting the continuity of papal government, it replaced one Frenchman by another who was both less forceful and more French in his loyalties; Clement IV had served as a counsellor of Louis IX. Charles reached Rome by sea in May 1265 and was crowned as king the following month. To raise his army he had had to make a supreme financial effort. About 200,000 *l.* had been loaned to him by Florentine bankers, Guelfs whom Montaperti had driven into exile. These men had every reason to desire the victory of his cause, and his success was to turn southern Italy, from the economic viewpoint, into something of a Florentine colony. From the Roman bankers Charles was able to borrow about 50,000 *l.*, but this still left him desperately short of money, and Clement IV had to raise more by pawning the plate from his own chapel. In January 1266 the pope learnt with relief of the arrival at Rome of Charles's main forces, which had crossed the Alps late in 1265.

Complete success was not long delayed, for on 26 February Charles shattered Manfred's forces near Benevento. Manfred himself was killed in the battle and after it Charles met little resistance in the Sicilian kingdom. His task of organizing government was simplified by Manfred's thorough control: as heir to a highly efficient machine, Charles was content to preserve the bureaucratic traditions of his German and Norman predecessors. Only one break in continuity was essential, the installation as feudatories of Charles's chief French and Provençal supporters. The confiscated fiefs of Manfred's men provided many of these, but the king also found it necessary to part with a good deal of royal domain; he had to content more than seven hundred land-hungry followers.

As has been mentioned already, Conrad IV had an heir in Germany. 'Conradin', king of the Romans, was now fifteen and his advisers persuaded him that Charles of Anjou's conquest had given him a great opportunity of gaining the kingdom that was rightly his. In 1267 he invaded Italy and won a good deal of support among the imperialist towns of the north. Rome, under the senatorship of a Castilian prince, also welcomed him. Clement IV, who had fled to Viterbo, is said to have expressed his pity for the young man whom he saw leading his army, a lamb going to the slaughter, but this pity was very nearly misplaced, for the battle of Tagliacozzo (August 1268) was a 'near-run thing'. A well-hidden corps in reserve ultimately won the day for Charles, after fortunes had fluctuated. This victory, too, was complete and was followed by the capture of the fugitive king. A few weeks later Conradin was executed at Naples.

One important consequence of Conradin's venture was that a frightened papacy granted new powers to its protector. The untrustworthy citizens of Rome were now placed for ten years under Charles's senatorship; in this matter Clement entirely abandoned the position of his predecessor. At the same time, at the invitation of the Tuscan Guelfs and without consulting the pope, Charles assumed the title of imperial vicar in Tuscany; in the following years his representatives exercised much power in that zone, while a host of allies in Lombardy and Piedmont enabled him to play the role throughout the peninsula which Manfred had sought in the 1260s. This northern screen was a 'pattern of alliances', municipal and feudal, rather than overlordship based on direct local power, but it gave to Charles a standing similar to that enjoyed by the man whom he had come to displace, Frederick II.

Frederick had been matched and fought by Innocent IV, Manfred by Urban and Clement, but in the years of his greatest influence Charles had no counterpoise, since the papal see was vacant for more than three years after Clement's death (November 1268— December 1271). During this time the Papal State became virtually a northern extension of the Sicilian kingdom and Charles's long occupation of the Roman senatorship was the clear sign of his dominance; for ten years after Benevento no pope resided permanently in his own see. The problem for the popes was now the choice between full co-operation as an Angevin ally and the alternative policy of relying on family territorial position as a counterweight and source of independence. The first pope in this situation to choose the latter alternative was Nicholas III (1277–1280), who before his election had served a long apprenticeship as leader of the anti-French element among the cardinals. The

Angevin supremacy and Clement IV's creation of many French cardinals had split the papal court into French and Italian factions.[1] Nicholas, an Orsini, came of a family that had long been associated with the papal see and was well entrenched in the feudal territory to the south of Rome. He exploited his local connections by securing for himself the senatorship of Rome on the expiration of Charles's ten-year period of office, having previously issued a constitution forbidding lay rulers and nobles to hold rule in the city in future. He appointed one of his nephews rector of the papal province north of Rome, the Patrimony in Tuscany, and sent two others (one of them a cardinal) to gain control in Romagna, the fertile but warlike zone in the south-eastern part of the Po valley which had been ceded to the papacy by the recently elected king of the Romans, Rudolf of Habsburg. Ruling in Rome through a series of vicars (the first was his brother), Nicholas took up residence in the city itself, thereby emphasizing his intention of putting an end to the era of Angevin domination. But rule in papal territory through nephews had its disadvantages. The cardinal, alleging ill-health, had an understandable tendency to be at Florence when he was supposed to be at Bologna, and the pope was driven to tell him that it would ill befit the dignity of the family that Bertold, the other nephew, should be forced to serve under a legate who was not an Orsini. Both were reminded by their uncle that the assumption of power in Romagna, a land of powerful barons, was no easy matter: 'in matters of this sort you must make much use of dissimulation, keep many things hushed up, and feel your way cautiously'.[2]

The greatest danger of a family policy of this sort was that it evoked the jealous enmity of the other feudal dynasties of the Roman Campagna. No sooner was Nicholas in his grave than the Annibaldi organized a *coup* in Rome and a rising at Viterbo which dispossessed Orso Orsini of his rectorate and overawed the papal conclave; two Orsini cardinals were seized in an attempt to extort

---

[1] These factions are well illustrated by a poem written in 1270 by a French cleric at the papal Court. This derides the south Italians for their 'rustic, clownish ways' and the barrenness of their soil: the author is confident that both lay and ecclesiastical power (*Regnum* and *Sacerdotium*) have been transferred permanently from Rome to France. See G. de Luca, 'Un formulario della cancelleria francescana e altri formulari tra il XIII e XIV secolo', *Archivio per la Storia della Pietà*, I (1951).

[2] F. Kaltenbrunner, *Actenstücke zur Geschichte des deutschen Reiches*, pp. 218-25.

promises from them concerning their votes in the election. After
six months this situation was ended by the choice of a pope
thoroughly acceptable to Charles of Anjou. Martin IV (1281–5),
a Frenchman, had, like Clement IV, been a counsellor of Louis IX.
Urban IV had raised him to the cardinalate and made him legate
in France during the negotiations which preceded the Angevin
conquest. 'He disturbed the Church of God through his love of
his own people and wanted to rule the whole world in the French
manner', says a German chronicler of the time.[1] As rectors for
the major provinces of the Papal State he took councillors of
Charles of Anjou. A 'crusading' tenth levied in France produced
100,000 *l.* towards the expenses of the burdensome campaign
against his unwilling subjects in Romagna. Having been voted
the Roman senatorship, Martin proceeded to pass on this office to
Charles, in defiance of his predecessor's decree, for the duration of
his pontificate. Reverting to the traditions of Urban and Clement,
Martin settled in Umbria, under the protection of an Angevin
garrison. He could thus leave a free hand in the city to the Angevins, while he himself was closer to Romagna—in which region
his armies were composed largely of Angevin and French troops.
The conqueror of southern Italy had by this time extended his
domination throughout the peninsula.

Jean de Meung, who in the late 1270s added a second part to the
Roman de la Rose, took as an instance of that great medieval commonplace, the mutability of human fortunes, the fate of Manfred.

> who by treachery
> Long time unchallenged kept the land,
> Till Charles of Anjou's mighty hand
> O'ercame him, and there rules to-day,
> Where no man dares dispute his sway.[2]

A few years later any Frenchman would have tactfully avoided
this example, for Manfred's conqueror, whose Italian triumph
has been the theme of the first section of this chapter, was in turn

---

[1] 'Notitia saeculi' in Alexander of Roes, *Schriften*, ed. H. Grundmann and H.
Heimpel (Stuttgart, 1958), pp. 162–3. A dictum of Martin IV current in Vienna was:
'I wish I were a stork and the Germans were frogs in the marshes, so I could devour
them all; or else a pike in a lake and they fish, so I could eat them this way,' ('Con-
tinuatio Vindobonensis', *M.G.H.*, SS., IX, 712–13.)

[2] *Roman de la Rose*, ch. 42 (trans. F. S. Ellis).

to suffer a fall. To account for this turn of Fortune's wheel it is necessary to outline developments in the eastern and western Mediterranean, in Byzantium and Aragon.

Byzantium was the traditional goal of ambitious Sicilian rulers; in the late twelfth century Henry VI had planned an invasion, only to have his fleet wrecked in port by a storm. After this the Eastern Empire, already weakened by territorial losses in Asia and by constant dynastic disputes, underwent the tragic and decisive experience of the Fourth Crusade (1204), which left its shattered frame divided among many masters. The legitimate heir fled to Nicaea in Asia Minor, while the largest share of the dismembered empire went to Count Baldwin of Flanders, who became ruler of an upstart 'Latin Empire', within which one-quarter of the land was retained by the emperor, the rest being shared equally between Venice and the knights who had participated in the Crusade. Many others disputed the body of this prototype 'Sick Man of Europe'. A Greek empire in Trebizond was set up as a rival to Nicaea. Another Byzantine, an Angelus, founded a 'despotate' based on Epirus. The Bulgarians soon greatly extended their hold in Thrace, at the expense of the Latins. Among many westerners to pose their own local solutions to this 'Eastern Question' were Boniface of Montferrat, who became king of Thessalonica, and the Villehardouin princes of Achaia.

Those who gained most of all were the experienced economic imperialists, the Italian maritime cities, and in particular Venice, which had organized the 'Crusade' and played the chief part in it. Already dominant along the eastern littoral of the Adriatic, the Venetians were anxious to extend their empire into the eastern Mediterranean. Their share of the spoils, which consisted almost entirely of harbours and islands, extended from Adriatic into Ionian Greece (including Crete) and to the Hellespont and the Sea of Marmora. The principal commodities imported from and through this area by Venice (and thence distributed over western Europe) were 'spices', a comprehensive term for exotic goods which included sugar, dyes, glue, perfumes, pepper, cloves and nutmeg. Other considerable imports were gold, silver and jewellery, cotton and raw silk, and slaves, particularly from the Black Sea. Italian merchants, never specialists, were also sufficiently versatile to turn their hands to banking. Venetian commerce in the Mediterranean was closely regulated by the republic; by the fourteenth century most of it was conducted through a minutely organized annual convoy of some ten to twenty huge armed galleys. Non-Venetians were excluded from trading through Venice and the balance of trade was safeguarded by forbidding the export of currency and limiting that of goods.

Venice, which thus became the insular centre of a great oriental mercantile empire, is in many ways reminiscent of eighteenth-century England. The *chiarissimi*—the equivalent of the 'nabobs' —returned in middle age to take up the political burden of their closely-guarded oligarchy, after having spent much of their lives abroad as holders of territorial fiefs or as merchants. The wealthier firms had permanent representatives in Greece and the Levant, though much commerce was also conducted by agents who sailed as representatives of the owners of shares ('carats') in the cargo. Altogether Venetian wealth was securely based, for the richer Venetians spread their risks not only by thus dividing the cargo, but by having interests in the local coasting trade, in the republic's funds, and in town property, as well as in the rural properties which provided food for their households and villas for their summer holidays.

Although Venetians secured the leading position in east Mediterranean trade after 1204, their advantage was diminished by Genoa's gains later in the century. The Treaty of Nymphaeum (1261) with the Byzantine ruler Michael Palaeologus gave the Genoese the right to trade free of duty throughout the eastern Empire. They received absolute possession of Smyrna and very full extra-territorial rights in Constantinople itself and nine other commercial centres. Finally the Greeks promised to close the Black Sea to other traders, excepting the Pisans, who, however, were no longer serious competitors in this area, their interests being limited mainly to the western Mediterranean. In return for all this the Genoese had only to offer the emperor the aid of fifty vessels whenever he requested it—and the crews were to be paid by the Greeks. Thus the Genoese were able to build up a rival empire in the Levant, which was the scene of the exploits of such men as Benedetto Zaccaria (*c.* 1240–1307) who held the island of Chios, yielding a crop of mastic worth 16,000 *l.* (Genoese) a year, and Phocaea, with its yet more valuable alum. At one time

Zaccaria was chartered by the French to serve as an admiral against England, but here his Midas touch failed him, for Philip IV's projected invasion never materialized. A reminder of the nature of these settlements of home-sick Italians is a Genoese dialect poem which runs:

> So many are the Genoese,
> And so spread over the earth,
> That where they go and settle
> They make another Genoa.[1]

Michael Palaeologus, the emperor who restored Greek rule to Constantinople in these circumstances of economic dependence, was a usurper. Though descended from three imperial dynasties, Michael came to power only through 'by-paths and indirect crook'd ways'. He dispossessed John IV Lascaris in 1258 and later imprisoned him and, on Christmas Day 1261, had him blinded. Michael's victory against the weak Latin Empire was the tardy result of a series of wars which involved the Bulgars and the other successor states. His decisive defeat in 1259 of the allied forces of Michael of Epirus, William of Achaia, and Manfred, opened the way to Constantinople. In 1261 the Latins were finally driven from the city.

Michael, however, as the terms of Nymphaeum suggest, had come into a shrunken and enfeebled heritage.[2] Of what is now Greece, he regained only part of Thessalonica and the Morea; the Franks retained Achaia and the duchy of Athens. His military strength was inadequate—in part, perhaps, because he was afraid to maintain a really powerful army, which might have restored the rightful Lascarid line. Yet the dominant element in his policy was the threat of Charles of Anjou, the heir not only to Manfred's Sicilian kingdom but to his (and Henry VI's) visions of *Drang nach Osten*. Well-placed for an assault in the Balkans (for Albania lies within sight of the heel of Italy), Charles set about uniting the anti-Palaeologan forces. His aim was nothing less than the imperial crown. Since Charles would be able to present his campaign

---

[1] E tanti son li zenoesi
e per lo mundo si distesi
che unde li van e stan
una atra Zena ge fan.

[2] See Map I.

as a crusade on behalf of Roman Christianity against the heterodox and schismatic Greeks, it was important for Michael to detach the popes from schemes for religious conquest in the east. This he was able to accomplish in 1274 by the titular submission of the Greek Church to papal obedience. Such a policy had immense dangers, and this desperate step testifies to the emperor's over-powering fear of Charles: it caused great discontent and unrest in Michael's territories, arousing so much opposition that its application was found impracticable. This policy of religious appease-ment became yet more difficult to justify after 1281, when the new pope, Martin IV, placed his alliance with Charles[1] before any hopes of peaceful religious reunification with Byzantium.

Charles of Anjou was faced, however, with the prospect of a war on two fronts. As well as the not very formidable enemy in the east, whose emergence has been described in the preceding pages, he had to reckon with a more intimidating power in the west, the Aragonese monarchy. There was no danger that the claims of Constance, Manfred's daughter, to the Sicilian throne might be forgotten at the Aragonese court: she had assumed the title of 'Queen of Sicily' immediately after receiving the news of her father's death, and three years later (1269) her husband, the future Peter the Great, made a treaty with a number of Gascon and Aragonese nobles and knights which bound these men to uphold her rights in the kingdom. The Sicilian exiles at James I's court included Constance's relative Conrad Lancia. Moreover Peter himself had old grievances against Charles concerning Provence and Sardinia and Charles's support of Aragonese rebels. In 1276 this very able man succeeded to the throne on the death of his father.

Aragon's emergence as a great sea-power in the Mediterranean, heralded by the conquest of the Balearics in 1229–35, can have been no surprise to Charles. It was made possible by the growth of the naval and mercantile strength of Barcelona, carefully nur-tured by the monarchy. In 1227 James I gave the Barcelonese traders, then already sailing to Ceuta, Alexandria and Syria, a mon-opoly of the commerce of their home port. These merchants and sailors urged the conquest of the Balearics, which would shorten

[1] See above, p. 41.

their routes and make them safer. The planning of the ensuing
expedition—which was of little benefit or interest to the other
citizens of Aragon, who would have preferred an assault on
Valencia—was entrusted to a Barcelonese, Raymond de Plegamans. One hundred and fifty ships took part and the men of
Barcelona benefited greatly by its success, securing rights of free
trade throughout the Balearics. Thereafter James continued to
smile on his fruitful *protégé*. In 1267 he again denied foreign
merchants the right to freight any ships at Barcelona except their
own. The following year he accorded the city the privilege—
which it already enjoyed *de facto*—of appointing consular representatives in foreign ports. Finally, in 1274, a royal grant gave
Barcelona something of the independence of an Italian republic.
The city's five counsellors were to be its real rulers, the royal
vicar and bailiff having to swear to follow their counsel. The king
renounced his criminal jurisdiction within the city and excused it
payment of the heavy bovage tax. Besides all this, Barcelona
gained very considerable weight in the parliamentary assemblies
of Catalonia.[1]

The rapid expansion of Barcelona's trade can be traced in the
city's consular representation and in the diplomatic negotiations
which marked her peaceful economic penetration of North Africa.
She had a consul at Tunis before 1258, one at Alexandria a few
years later, one at Pisa by 1275. Pisan predominance in western
Mediterranean commerce was seriously shaken by Barcelona
around this time and more so still after the disastrous defeat by
Genoa at Meloria (1284). Though her trade with Syria continued,
the great area of Barcelona's activity was the Maghreb, the western
part of the Mediterranean littoral of Moslem Africa. Envoys from
the king of Tlemcen came to the city in 1250 to reach a trading
agreement, and in 1263 it was found necessary to mint a special
currency imitating Moslem coinage. Barcelona's friendly relations
with the North African powers naturally led her to oppose St
Louis' Crusade against Tunis in 1270. The following year a new
commercial treaty was made with the Tunisian ruler Al-Mustansir
and a later agreement with this Sultan also provided for his payment of a tribute and regulated the status of Christian mercenaries
in his service. Meanwhile, in 1274, James I promised the king of

[1] See above, pp. 14–16.

Morocco the assistance of fifty ships for a proposed attack on Ceuta.

The main justification for Barcelona's privileged status within the Aragonese kingdom was, of course, the city's provision of a fleet, there being then no distinction between trading and naval vessels. The activity of the shipyards is constantly mentioned in James I's time (1213–76), when the harbour had frequently to be enlarged. By the 1280s ten galleys could be built at one time. In 1282 the Aragonese put one hundred and forty ships to sea, of which sixty-four were large vessels (galleys, tarids and 'arrows'). Valencia, by then won from the Moslems, and Tortosa helped to provide this great fleet, but the leadership of Barcelona was emphasized by an order to the Valencians that their ships should be 'painted with the arms of Barcelona as well as those of the King'.

There was no danger that the Barcelonese should fail the Aragonese crown, for their interests coincided admirably. The conquest of Sicily by Peter III would assist them to dislodge the Pisans and Genoese from their hold on the island's valuable trade. When this was accomplished, much direct commerce developed between Barcelona and Sicily, which provided food—in particular grain, wine, cheese, oil, fish and vegetables—for the Aragonese. Before the middle of the fourteenth century the Catalans had 'consuls'—and thus trading colonies—in eighteen Sicilian towns. Besides this they naturally took over the Sicilians' own interests in North Africa. The failure of the Aragonese to make gains on the Italian mainland can in part be attributed to the satisfaction of the Barcelonese with their trading bases in the island, which from an economic viewpoint was a much greater attraction. Their hold there had much to do with their triumphant expansion in the fourteenth century, the golden era of Barcelona's commerce.

Though Charles of Anjou looked ambitiously to the east and nervously to the west, the conclusive phase in the story belongs to his own subjects, whose discontent was brought to the boil by the energetic labours of bitter Manfredian exiles. The Sicilian islanders were heavily taxed by the Angevin government, particularly when naval preparations began for the campaign against Byzantium. Charles's officials were perhaps too little supervised by a king who preferred to reside on the mainland. More influential than any precise grievances over methods of rule were Sicily's immemorial opposition to government from the European 'continent' and the natives' xenophobic hatred of the French. There was still a strong Greek element in the Sicilian population, a potential source of disaffection in view of Charles's well-known schemes for a Byzantine conquest. Many, too, must have remembered Manfred's younger children, held by Charles in perpetual imprisonment, and the situation was exacerbated by several years of disastrously poor harvests.

By the spring of 1282 Charles's plans for the conquest of Constantinople were far advanced. He had the Venetians (dissatisfied with their standing in the Palaeologan empire) as powerful allies, and two hundred ships were ready in the harbour at Messina. Michael Palaeologus, who was in deadly danger, had not failed to make diplomatic contact with Peter of Aragon, and was greatly assisted in these moves by the Manfredian exiles. An Aragonese official, Taberner, was probably at Constantinople in 1278 and again in 1279, while Michael's envoy to Catalonia was the Genoese Zaccaria who stood to lose much of his fortune if driven from Phocaea and Chios by the Angevins and Venetians.[1] It is not possible to reconstruct the full story of the conspiracy of these years, over which Sicilian and Italian patriotism has cumulated a great accretion of myth: in these legends the hero's role is allotted to the Salernitan doctor John of Procida, once Manfred's chancellor and subsequently chancellor of Aragon. Undoubtedly Michael sent money contributions to assist Peter III's naval preparations and he probably sent money to Sicily also. He was able to record in his brief autobiography that 'the Sicilians, who had only scorn for the forces remaining to the barbarian king [Charles], dared to take arms and deliver themselves from servitude, and if I dared to claim that I was God's instrument in bringing them liberty, I would be telling only the truth'.[2]

History, like a Shakespearian play, often proceeds on two planes, the lively characters of the sub-plots appearing unaware of the more deliberate proceedings of the dignified actors of the high diplomatic drama. Thus it was in the 'Sicilian Vespers'. On

---

[1] For Zaccaria, see above, p. 43.

[2] Quoted in D. J. Geanakoplos, *Emperor Michael Palaeologus and the West*, p. 367.

Easter Monday of 1282 (30 March) a French sergeant arrogantly pressed his attentions on a young married woman in the *piazza* of the Church of the Holy Ghost at Palermo.[1] He had little time to realize the unwisdom of his behaviour, for the affronted husband stabbed him to death. Soon his companions had been despatched in the same manner. As the church bells rang for Vespers the streets echoed to the cry of 'Death to the French!' and the massacre of the occupying forces became general. The news of the revolt spread rapidly. Within a few days Corleone had followed the example of Palermo and about a month later Charles suffered a supreme blow through the insurrection of Messina, his main naval base. The first action of each of the rebel towns was to declare a commune; undoubtedly their citizens envied the privileged towns of northern Italy and hoped to attain the same independent status. In their innocence they sent emissaries to the papal court to ask for protection, but the reply of Charles's ally Martin IV was excommunication.

In this spring of 1282, though the Latin Christian state in Syria languished unnoticed and near to extinction, the talk was all of crusades. Charles of Anjou's proposed expedition against Constantinople had been duly recognized by Martin IV as a crusade, but the pope was more doubtful about the request of Peter of Aragon that he should be granted a crusading subsidy for the fleet with which he was preparing to go to the assistance of the governor of Constantine, a potential Christian convert, against the king of Tunisia. Peter's real purpose was of course the invasion and conquest of Sicily, though he may have hoped to combine this with a reassertion of his overlordship in Tunis, or even have regarded the African scheme as a second best if the Sicilian venture fell through. Like Charles, he was taken unawares by the Sicilian rising. He appears to have had no contact with the rebels at first. Only in June did his impressive fleet sail for the Algerian coast, where Peter learned of the death of the governor whose protection was the ostensible purpose of his expedition. In August he was still encamped at this site, and it was there that he received

---

[1] The author of this book served in an invading army in Sicily nearly seven hundred years later and official instructions were then issued warning the troops of the dangers of behaviour of this sort. This suggests that the lessons of history can be learnt—at least in a changeless society!

a visit from a delegation despatched by Palermo and Messina to ask him for aid and to offer the throne to his wife Constance, rightful Queen of Sicily. This was the signal for the transference of the Aragonese armada to southern Sicily and on 30 August Peter disembarked at Trapani.

There is no call to recount the endless fluctuations of the ensuing war. Peter was proclaimed king at Palermo on 4 September and soon Charles had to evacuate his forces to the mainland. The naval and military campaigns for the control of mainland Sicily put an end to Charles's oriental ambitions and long outlasted the lifetime of all the principal participants in the opening scenes, for Michael Palaeologus died in 1282 and Charles, Peter and Martin IV in 1285. With the support of the papacy the Angevins continued the struggle, and Peter's son James, his heir in Sicily, was even persuaded to go over to their cause. The war was thus brought back to the island, now defended by James's younger brother, Frederick. The effect of the Peace of Caltabellotta (1302), which put an end to the struggle, was to perpetuate the military situation of twenty years before: the Aragonese Frederick retained the island of Sicily as 'king of Trinacria', while the Angevins were to rule the southern mainland.

The Sicilian war that humbled Charles of Anjou was also a heavy burden to the papacy, which was committed by the policy of the preceding decades to support of the Angevin cause. Boniface VIII, who was pope from 1294 to 1303, expended something like a quarter of a million florins each year: much less than half of this was spent on the papal court and the government of the western Church, and the war ranked very high among the other, political items. With this financial expense should be reckoned the imponderable loss of spiritual impetus entailed by the attention devoted by popes and many of the ablest churchmen to the papacy's temporal business.

Throughout the war the two rival traditions of 'local' popes seeking support from baronial dynasties and 'French' popes dependent on a wholehearted alliance with the Angevins continued to alternate. Martin IV's pontificate revealed so clearly the disadvantages of the second of these that it was natural that a Roman should be chosen as his successor. This was Honorius IV (1285–7) whose family, the Savelli, were prominent baronial landowners and had already provided one pope. Honorius received the senatorship of Rome for life and, like Nicholas III, was able to depute rule there and in the surrounding papal patrimony to relatives; in comparison with the situation in Martin IV's time, this was a considerable territorial gain at the expense of the Angevin ruler of the Sicilian kingdom.

The Savelli stood with the Annibaldi and Caetani in the second rank of the nobility of the Campagna: none of these could attain to the uncontroverted, time-honoured status of the Colonna and Orsini. The originality of Honorius's successor Nicholas IV (1288–92) lay in his decision to base his temporal policy on the support of the Colonna, although he was not himself a member of that family. Nicholas was a friar, the first mendicant to become pope. His own descent was neither Roman nor baronial, but his connection with the Colonna dated back to the period when he had been bishop of Palestrina (this town being the centre of the Colonna estates in Campagna) and Colonna support probably assisted his elevation to the papacy. Like Honorius, he received the Roman senatorship for life and was able to reside in the city ; this office and the provincial rectorships of the Papal State were of course held by members of the Colonna family. Contemporaries were not slow to remark the humiliating element in Nicholas's position, and one cartoonist depicted him as a scarcely visible figure between two substantial columns.

A long vacancy followed Nicholas's death and was only ended by recourse to an eccentric variant of the Angevin tradition. This was the choice of Peter of Morrone (Celestine V), a hermit who had won a great reputation as a saint and reformer. Utterly unskilled in politics and administration, Celestine could be seen by the spiritual as the protagonist of a radical departure from the temporal preoccupations of his predecessors and by the Angevins (for he was a native of Abruzzi and subject of Charles II) as a harmless and convenient tool. The latter proved the better prophets. During the five months of his pontificate Celestine never moved from the kingdom. Eight Frenchmen were raised to the cardinalate and Angevin officials took over the Roman senatorship and most of the papal provinces. The choice of the hermit of Monte Morrone was perhaps too extreme a swing of the pendulum. His office made demands that the pathetic Celestine was quite unable to fulfil and in December 1294 he resigned.

Celestine's eager successor represented the furthest possible swing in the direction of wordly ability and interests and dependence on family territorial support. Benedict Caetani, who now became Pope Boniface VIII, had served a long apprenticeship in the papal court and had been a cardinal since 1281. He was capable and, as a chronicler puts it, 'prudent and wise in the affairs of this world'. This is a euphemism: Boniface was not merely prudent, he was cynical. In recording this it must be remembered that he was no strange sport amid a body of uniformly dedicated men of God. It was normal in the baronial *milieu* for the clever younger sons to receive an education which prepared them for the Church, and those who were able and had a powerful family behind them would reach the top, however little their temperament inclined them to spirituality. It was long indeed before this dilemma disappeared: Stendhal's *Le Rouge et le Noir* is concerned with the perpetuation in the nineteenth century of an analogous situation. The members of the college of cardinals had only to attach a little too much importance to administrative talent or to underestimate a little too charitably a candidate's lack of holiness for them to find themselves saddled with a Nicholas III or a Boniface VIII.

Fearing that his predecessor—whose resignation was unique and controversial—might become the centre of opposition, Boniface arrested Celestine and placed him in confinement, where he died. Within a few years there was certainly no lack of criticism. Dante, exiled from Florence through Boniface's Tuscan policy, proclaims in the *Inferno* that Nicholas III will have to move lower down among the simoniacs to make way for Boniface.[1] Jacopone da Todi, spokesman for a party among the Franciscans, addressed a number of poems to him, one of which begins:

> Pope Boniface, you have led a joyous life in this world,
> But I do not think that you will leave it joyfully.[2]

One of the remarks attributed to Boniface is that 'unless there

---

[1] *Inferno*, XIX, 76–8.
[2] O papa Bonifatio, molt' ai iocato al mondo;
penso che iocondo non te porrai partire.
(*Laude*, ed. F. Ugolini, no. XL.)

is discord between the great families of Rome the pope cannot be a true pope or dominate the city and the lands of the Church'.[1] His own policy was certainly to lead to this type of discord, but this was due less to a calculation that he could divide and rule than to the impossibility of following a policy of family aggrandizement in the Campagna without arousing bitter hostilities. Boniface's great difficulty was that, as has been remarked above, he lacked a really imposing territorial base. To some extent he compensated this by his precocity in embarking on a dynastic policy. During his cardinalate his brother and nephews had strengthened their holdings between Rome and the Neapolitan kingdom (in which they held the county of Caserta), securing a whole chain of strongholds along the Via Appia and Via Latina, the two main routes of this zone, with outliers on a lateral road to the east. There can be no doubt that these moves were based on hopes of the cardinal's promotion, even before becoming pope he made an agreement with a town, promising the cession of some papal land (in the event of his election) in return for a fief which he coveted for a nephew. This deal in due time became effective and enabled Boniface to extend his family's domain to the north of Rome, but his greatest efforts were reserved for the Campagna, the traditional stronghold of the 'local' popes and the region where his rivals were strongest. Linked with and assisting these territorial acquisitions was the control of the Caetani in the papal provinces, which were normally ruled by members of the family. At the same time Boniface strove, with considerable success, to gain the friendship of the numerous towns of his State by granting them, for money, *de jure* enjoyment of rights which they already exercised *de facto*, and by issuing a series of reforming ordinances to check the abuses of his provincial officials and judges.

Boniface took care not to antagonize all the other baronial families, and in particular ingratiated himself with the Orsini. But his megalomania could only be satisfied by the dispossession of those who were already entrenched. The crisis came when his schemes along the Tyrrhenian coast demanded the purchase of Ninfa, which was the property of Cardinal Peter Colonna. Stephen, the man of action among the Colonna, now set an ambush just

---

[1] P. Dupuy, *Histoire du Différand d'entre le pape Boniface VIII et Philippe le Bel* (1655), p. 344.

outside Rome on the Via Appia and was able to capture most of the money intended for the purchase of Sermoneta, a fortress recently bought from the Annibaldi. There followed an extra-ordinary war. This typical feudal dispute was pronounced a crusade, and the Colonna were excommunicated, deprived of their cardinalates and other ecclesiastical offices, and driven into exile. The lands of which they were dispossessed were either retained by the Caetani or used to ensure the neutrality of the Orsini and Annibaldi.

It is possible that Boniface's landed power might have gone on from strength to strength after his defeat of the Colonna had he not also become involved in a desperate quarrel with the French king, Philip the Fair. Philip's younger brother, Charles of Valois, whom Martin IV had ineffectively named king of Aragon at the time of the Vespers, was in 1302 Boniface's chief temporal ally in the Sicilian war. Philip himself, however, was unwilling to accept Boniface's claim to tax and control the clergy of his kingdom. This dispute, which will be discussed in the next chapter, came to a head when, in 1303, Philip despatched his minister Nogaret to Italy with instructions to capture the pope and bring him before a General Council of the Church. Nogaret enlisted the aid of the Colonna and of three other families of the Campagna which had suffered at the hands of the Caetani. Thus was gathered the strangely assorted force which stormed the papal residence of Anagni on 7 September 1303, the day when, in Dante's phrase, 'Christ was made captive in the person of his vicar'.[1]

The sequence of events related in this chapter, which covers half a century, brought about great changes in the situation in southern Europe. The story began with the creation of a power-vacuum in the Italian peninsula after the death of Frederick II, and the most conspicuous of all the changes was the elimination of the emperor as a great power in Italy. Later emperors were to make an occasional reappearance on the Italian stage and in the fourteenth century Dante could believe in an imperial solution to the political problems of the peninsula, but this was the anachro-nistic dream of a poet. The principal beneficiaries of the new state of affairs were the city-republics. The cultural achievements of the town *milieu*, conventionally described as the 'Renaissance',

---

[1] *Purgatorio*, XX, 87.

will be discussed in a later chapter. The commercial hold of the maritime republics in the Levant, mentioned above, contributed greatly to the wealth of these towns and is evidence of their strength. The theme treated here at length, the involvement of the papacy in the political fate of central and southern Italy, was not a new development: Gregory IX and Innocent IV had been as fully involved in the territorial struggle against Frederick II as their successors were in the wars over the Sicilian kingdom. But the support given to Charles of Anjou and the foundation of a new tradition of French pontificates did bring an entirely new element to the Church's political preoccupations. This involvement with the French dynasty and the growth of a strong French party in the Roman court are the essential preliminaries to the fourteenth-century papal developments which are also the subject of a later chapter. Equally striking as a break with the past is the appearance of Aragon as a great Mediterranean power, with Barcelona, virtually an independent ally of the monarchy, now rivalling Pisa in its pre-eminence in western Mediterranean commerce. The great role of maritime trade in all the transformations described in this chapter is noteworthy. Byzantium's weakness shows in its lack of active participation in this no less clearly than in its loss of territory. A Greek Empire was brought back into being, and was enabled by Michael Palaeologus to escape extinction, but this institution, far older in origin than the others discussed here, was now only 'the shade of that which once was great'. Apart from the city-states and the Aragonese (it would perhaps be more accurate to say the Catalans), the power that had improved its position most notably was the French monarchy, with its related Angevin ally. There was more than a little truth in the cleric's arrogant assertion that both *sacerdotium* and *regnum* were now transferred to the French. We must now turn to an investigation of this claim.

Further Reading

E. JORDAN, *Les Origines de la Domination Angevine en Italie* (reprint, New York, 1960): see also the same author's *L'Allemagne et l'Italie aux 12e et 13e siècles* in G. Glotz, *Histoire Générale* (above, p. xii)

S. RUNCIMAN, *The Sicilian Vespers* (Cambridge, 1958: and Penguin Books)

T. S. R. BOASE, *Boniface VIII* (London, 1933)

For works on papal history see also Chapter VI.

III

THE AGGRANDIZEMENT OF THE FRENCH MONARCHY

THE last chapter was largely concerned with a French outlier, the Angevin kingdom in southern Italy. The combination there of a powerful bureaucratic tradition—having successive Byzantine, Arabic, Norman and German strata—and a conquering French baronage made up a formidable state whose ruler not only threatened to control the Mediterranean but also exercised so great an influence over French policy that successive kings of France died invading Tunis and Aragon on his behalf. Yet the kingdom of France itself demonstrates still more clearly what strength monarchy could generate at the turn of the thirteenth and fourteenth centuries whenever the mighty official was not counterbalanced by that rival, feudal, figure stigmatized by generations of loyal historians as the 'over-mighty subject'.

Louis IX of France (1226–70) added to the practical achievements of his grandfather Philip 'Augustus' his own inestimably precious contribution of prestige. The French monarchy was fortunate that these two great representatives should have made their appearance in this order, since Louis' role was essentially a complementary one: France could only afford a king with a burning zeal for justice and the Crusade after she had made territorial gains, particularly at the expense of the kings of England. The reputation of St Louis was reflected in the many requests for his arbitration. He settled the tangled problem of the inheritance of the county of Flanders and a few years later pronounced in favour of Henry III of England in the matter of that king's dispute with his barons (the Mise of Amiens, 1264). His prestige as a crusader and saint (he was canonized in 1297) made men look back on his reign as a golden age: the feudal malcontents of 1314–15 demanded a return to his laws, and Edward III and the later English kings who claimed the throne of France described themselves as 'descendants of St Louis'. Yet Louis had contributed also to his house's tangible assets, in particular by appointing *enquêteurs* to check local officials and protect royal interests, by insisting that the royal currency should be valid throughout the kingdom, and by strengthening his predecessors' alliance with the towns, especially in the frontier zones.

Under St Louis' son and successor, Philip III 'the Bold' (1270–85), there was no strong indication of a move in the direction of bureaucratic centralization. A conventional, pious, mediocre man and an exemplar of the ideals of thirteenth-century chivalry, Philip set himself the aim of imitating his father. As a young man he had been so submissive to parental authority that he had taken an oath to accept his mother's wardship, in the event of his father's death, until he attained the age of thirty: fortunately his father came to hear of this rash promise and persuaded pope Urban IV to free him from it. He nevertheless remained deeply conservative by instinct. What had been good enough for his father was good enough for him, and owing to the brevity of his reign he was not faced with the problem of seeking a new set of servants to replace those of St Louis. Mathieu de Vendôme, abbot of St Denis (who acted as regent during the Tunisian and Aragonese campaigns) was retained as a virtual prime minister by Philip, together with most of his father's other councillors and officials.

Whatever the temperament of the king, deeper and stronger currents were already bearing the French monarchy in the direction of change. The chief of these was an increasingly pressing need for money. Philip III's invasion of Aragon in 1285 cost more than 1,200,000 *l.*, a tremendous sum by the standards of the time. Moreover it was the expensive culmination, inspired by Charles of Anjou and Martin IV, of a series of French interventions beyond the Pyrenees: disputed successions in Navarre and Castile had already involved Philip in a Navarrese war on behalf of an infant heiress who was betrothed to his elder son, and in an abortive invasion of Castile. The Angevin link was a heavy financial burden in other ways, drawing French forces into the war for Sicily (in which Philip's younger brother Peter of Alençon was killed) and the campaigns fought to gain for the papacy the province of Romagna.[1] Philip III had also to pay the remaining expenses of his father's Tunisian campaign and to send much aid to the Latin state in the Holy Land, now *in extremis*. The constant danger of war with Edward I of England over Edward's fief of Acquitaine was another expensive matter, although open hostilities began only in the following reign.

By Philip IV's time (1285–1314) war with Edward had become the main burden, in combination with a series of campaigns in Flanders. The Flemish war was closely connected with the struggle for Acquitaine, since Edward made an alliance with the County of Flanders to threaten the French on two fronts. But in 1297, after four years of warfare, Edward withdrew: it now seemed to Philip that the wealthiest of the great fiefs lay open to royal control. He was soon to learn that industrialization and urbanization made the Flemings formidable and difficult subjects. Following the policy that had succeeded well in the towns of central and northern France, Philip formed an alliance with the dominant oligarchy, only to find that in these textile manufacturing cities the patricians were confronted by powerful popular forces. The first rising against French government and oligarchic control was the 'Matins of Bruges' (18 May 1302), culminating in a decisive victory for the Flemish infantrymen over 10,000 French knights (Courtrai, 11 July 1302). This shattering blow, which drove the French from Flanders, was followed by two years of indecisive campaigning. The battle of Mons-en-Pévèle (18 August 1304) set the seal on French recovery and the following summer peace was made at Athès-sur-Orge. But the terms of Athès were so humiliating to the Flemings that they failed to achieve a settlement. Besides providing a large money indemnity, the Flemings were to send the French king 500 troops, to be at his disposal for a year. Thereafter they were to owe him military service even against their own Count. Ghent, Bruges, Ypres, Lille and Douai were to undergo the razing of their walls, and Bruges was to expiate the revolt of 1302 by sending 3,000 of its men on pilgrimage, 1,000 of them to the Holy Land. The terms also provided that all Flemings aged over fourteen should swear to observe the

---

[1] See above, pp. 41 and 50.

treaty; this oath was to be renewed every five years, besides which officials were always to take it on entering office. If the terms were broken the county was to be placed under interdict. The main consequence of this exigent peace was the prolongation of the period of heavy military expenditure by the French. With victory apparently achieved, the French were still compelled to call out large armies in an attempt to threaten Flanders into obedience, and naturally the expense of these peacetime armies of 1312–15 and 1318–19 was much resented.

The decisive feature in the development of all the western European states in the later Middle Ages is their adaptation to the financial demands of war, but this is particularly true of the French and English monarchies. In their long struggle the sides competed to wage war more continuously and on a larger scale. To fall behind would be to risk defeat, and hence in both countries new demands had to be made on subjects and new ways found of tapping their wealth. Thus the wars were reflected in another, internal, struggle, in which officialdom strove to increase fiscal pressure without yielding constitutional ground. In the early decades of the fourteenth century this situation was making or breaking the power of monarchical governments. The French bureaucracy was gaining as clearly as the English—driven back by baronial discontents and by nascent parliamentary institutions—were losing; there was as yet no sign that Edward III's victories would come to the rescue of the English monarchy. Naturally, heavy taxation could not by itself bring into being a stronger state: that would require also, on the positive side, jurisdictional gains for the crown and the growth of national feeling, on the negative side a weak and divided opposition to the king's expansion. In addition it would require an efficient and devoted corps of royal servants.

A noteworthy development of Philip IV's time was the employment as ministers and officials of a number of men trained in the law. Educated in a discipline which made an ideal preparation for administrative duties, these lawyers were an immense asset to the Crown, and worked hard on its behalf, especially to extract money from the Templars and other clerics, from Lombards and Jews, from ministers who had forfeited the king's favour, and indeed any subject whom it was worth while to harass. Some historians have seen in them a 'new class', raised from the dust by the king to serve his interests, and owing allegiance to no other power. There are, however, various difficulties about this view. In the first place, there was no clearly defined group of 'royal' lawyers, for those who served the Crown normally acted also for members of the nobility and ecclesiastical bodies. Moreover the 'stereotype' of these men has been based too exclusively on the personality of Guillaume Nogaret, keeper of the Seal from 1307 to 1313. Nogaret was a native of the Languedoc who taught law at Montpellier before entering the service of the Crown and being entrusted with the management of Philip's relations with the papacy. He was of non-noble birth and remained a layman— though he was described as *clericus* during the years of his legal studies. Nogaret was not the only royal legist of this type; another was Raoul de Presles, a lawyer of Laon, who had been born a serf and gained great territorial wealth, perhaps in part through his evidence against the Templars. Others of Philip's officials, however, were of noble origin, among them Pierre Flotte, keeper of the Seal from 1298 till his death (in battle at Courtrai) in 1302. Moreover, many were clerics, and some of the most important figures among the lawyer-officials were both nobles by origin and clerics by status. Aicelin was an Auvergnat noble who became archbishop of Narbonne (and later of Rouen), and Pierre de Belleperche, another keeper of the Seal, who died as bishop of Auxerre, also probably came of a noble family. Certainly there was no decision to have recourse to a new breed of godless and unprincipled Machiavellians. Nogaret himself was a man of at least conventionally religious views, perhaps even a pious man: to oppose the pope was not necessarily to be an unbeliever or neo-Albigensian. When on his way to Italy to summon Boniface VIII before a General Council, Nogaret wrote to a bishop, who was a friend:

> May the Lord through His Grace direct your footsteps . . . pray to the Lord that if my way is pleasing to God He may direct me in it and that if it is not He may prevent me from it by death or as He pleases. . . .

and later, after his 'Outrage of Anagni',[1] he sought (and obtained) papal permission to have a portable altar.

[1] See above, p. 54.

We must now return to the Crown's territorial gains, an element of enormous importance in its general advance in authority. The greatest acquisition of this time was the appanage formerly held by St Louis' brother Alphonse of Poitiers, which came to the Crown when Alphonse and his wife died within a few days of each other in August 1271. Philip III thus added to his domain the counties of Poitiers and Toulouse together with much of Auvergne and some rights in the neighbouring lordships of Albigeois, Rouergue and Quercy. Philip acted at once on receiving news of the death of Alphonse and his wife, for the Aragonese and English kings also had claims in these areas: he himself visited Poitou and then entered Toulouse at the head of an army. The *saisimentum comitatus Tolose*, though mainly peaceful, was a long-drawn-out affair of investigating rights, confirming privileges and receiving oaths; the last judicial enquiry concerning baronial rights in the county on the occasion of its being *immediatisé* was not heard until 1285. Even more gradual was the acquisition by Philip IV of the kingdom of Navarre and the counties of Champagne and Brie, through his marriage to the heiress Joan: these areas came under effective royal control in 1285, but the counties were not formally absorbed into the domain until the second half of the following century, by which time the Navarrese kingdom—a source of expenditure rather than profit—had been divided from them.

In total, Philip III's achievement in the territorial extension of royal power almost deserves to rank with that of Philip Augustus. In Acquitaine his officials fought a ceaseless judicial battle on behalf of his rights, and his gains in the south-west coincided with a greatly enhanced degree of overlordship in Flanders, due to a disputed succession and the consequent separation of Hainault from Flanders.

Successes in Acquitaine were double gains, for they were won at the expense of the English king, but they were hardly more important in the long run than the slow, ubiquitous coralline accretion of lands and rights. Philip III bought the county of Guines from its heavily indebted count, the barony of Nemours, the viscounty of Pierrefonds, the town of Harfleur, and many other lordships. Philip the Fair's main purchases were the counties of Chartres, of La Marche and Angoulême, and of Burgundy (Franche-Comté).

The monarchy usually made such purchases by paying the vendor both a lump sum and an annual pension for his lifetime. In two wealthy and important towns the Crown gained control by a process of attrition which eroded the jurisdiction of the previous lords; these towns were Lyons and Montpellier, the evicted lords of which were respectively the archbishop and cathedral chapter and the king of Aragon. The acquisition of Lyons was one of many gains made in the east, often at the expense of imperial rights, but this was certainly not part of a general preconceived plan for a systematic advance eastward; the Capetians took whatever chances came their way and they came from no single direction. The total effect of the additions now made to the royal domain was so overwhelming that by 1328 the domain covered a total area about three times that of the great appanages and fiefs.

At the same time the monarchy was coming to enjoy a thorough control over the internal affairs of the municipalities. This was in part at the wish of the communes themselves, for they frequently had recourse in their disputes to royal arbitration, while indebted towns sought the advice and aid of royal officials concerning fiscal measures and other financial matters. From this it was a small step to unsought royal intervention, since the Crown could demand to inspect a commune's accounts in order to have a check on its taxes and its financial position. The towns' charters were also open to revision by the king. So thorough was this process of monarchical permeation in the government of the towns that municipal officials came to find themselves entrusted with tasks that should more properly have been those of the king's own agents: after 1284, for example, the officers of the gilds took over from the royal serjeants the administration of ordinances concerning currency. Such administrative innovations were the exception. For the most part the king's government was acquiring more work to do and doing it in the old ways. It was the king's business to investigate his rights and to ensure that these were not usurped by other lords, hence innumerable enquiries were held into the exercise of feudal jurisdiction, comparable with Edward I's *Quo Warranto* proceedings in England. The doctrine that all suits touching the king's sovereignty could be called to the king's court lay behind the great development of royal justice at this time, for every 'breaking of the peace' could be interpreted as such a case. The power of hearing appeals was the Crown's other great judicial asset, and from St Louis' reign onwards the appellate business of the royal court grew steadily and rapidly. This was also the principal way in which the French kings were able to assert their overlordship in Acquitaine. All these gains are reflected in Beaumanoir's statement that 'all lay jurisdiction is held as a fief of the king' and in the increasingly accepted doctrine that the king could in no circumstances hold land as a vassal, a principle stated in the time of Philip Augustus, but only formally proclaimed under Philip the Fair, in 1303.

If the French kings were to secure sufficient money for their military enterprises it was vital that they should gain a share in the revenues of the Church. They would have suffered an immense disadvantage—and the laity would have had to bear a far heavier burden—if the possessors of a very large proportion of the nation's wealth had enjoyed exemption from direct taxation. In Philip the Fair's time a levy on the Church of a tenth of its estimated annual income yielded about a quarter of a million pounds, which was one-fifth of the total cost of his father's Aragonese war. Such a tax required, by time-honoured custom, the consent of the pope. In certain circumstances there was no difficulty in gaining this consent. There was no inevitable clash of interests and it was often possible for king and pope to arrange a mutually satisfactory *modus vivendi* whereby each took a slice from the wealth of the French Church. Such a situation prevailed in Martin IV's time, when the pope awarded the French the Aragonese crown, proclaimed their campaign a crusade and aided it with the grant of a clerical tenth for four years, while his royal ally reciprocated by assisting Martin in Sicily and the Papal State.[1] On that occasion papal legates were involved in the supervision of the levy and the atmosphere of co-operation in a joint enterprise was rounded off by an arrangement whereby part of the proceeds—no less than 100,000 *l.* in 1284—was allotted to the pope.

This type of profit-sharing, however, called for good relations between the two sharers and an absence of dogmatic principle and exaggerated rapacity in either party. Philip IV, who had inherited a crown impoverished by the disastrous campaign in

[1] See above, p. 41.

Aragon, was probably anxious to eschew the pro-papal alignment of his father. The election of Boniface VIII (1294) brought about a crisis because the new pope did not relish the diminution of authority implicit in his predecessors' compromises with the French monarchy and he himself coveted the wealth of the French Church for his own Italian policy and the Sicilian war. In 1296 the pope took the initiative by issuing the bull *Clericis laicos* forbidding lay taxation of the clergy except with papal consent, on pain of automatic excommunication: the kings of France and England were warned by Boniface of this measure. Philip IV's retort was to issue a decree forbidding the export of money from his kingdom, thereby depriving the pope also of the possibility of taxing the French Church effectively. His dependence on French support in Italy made Boniface's position a weak one and he soon failed to give the French clergy the backing they required if they were to achieve exemption from royal taxation. Under pressure from Flote and Philip's other administrators the French archbishops and bishops petitioned the pope to be allowed to pay the tenth refused by Boniface. Early in 1297 the pope gave way, a double tenth was granted and the bull *Etsi de statu* proclaimed the king the judge of the expediency of clerical taxation. Thus the French clergy were routed in this first engagement through the defection of their ally. At this juncture Boniface canonized Louis IX, Philip's grandfather: it appeared that the alliance of Martin IV's time had been re-established.

The alliance was a brief one, however, for a second clash occurred, in 1301, this time concerning the general question of jurisdiction over the French clergy. The occasion was Philip's arrest and trial of the bishop of Pamiers, Bernard Saisset. Boniface now revoked Philip's privileges and summoned the leading French prelates to Rome. His letter *Ausculta fili* stated his grievances and claimed for the papacy a position superior to the French crown; Philip's officials had a copy of this bull burnt in Paris and issued a disrespectful parody. The king also summoned clerical representatives to a gathering and secured their support, but almost half the French bishops obeyed Boniface's summons to Rome. Ineffective negotiations both preceded and followed the issue in 1302 of *Unam Sanctam*, the general statement of papal supremacy in which Boniface declared it 'necessary to the salvation of all human creatures' to be subject to the Roman pontiff. By the spring of 1303, despite his defeat in Flanders, Philip made the decision to press his assault on the pope, accusing him of having secured election unjustly, and denouncing him in a conciliar assembly. That summer Nogaret was despatched to Italy to bring Boniface to trial before a general ecclesiastical Council. These were the events which led to the pope's humiliation at Anagni[1] the day before that on which he had intended to declare Philip excommunicated.

The comparative rapidity with which even the bitter dispute of 1301–3 was healed confirms that the logic of the situation— or perhaps one should say the wealth of the French Church— made the pope and king natural allies. When Philip again asked for a tenth (1303), the Church retorted by demanding in return a promise that permanent judicial sessions should be held at Paris and that the currency should be reformed and no monetary changes be made in future except with the consent of the barons and clergy. Rather than make these concessions, Philip abandoned negotiations, but the succession in 1305 of the weak and Francophil Clement V reintroduced the situation that had prevailed under Martin IV. Tenths were granted with papal consent in 1307, 1308, 1310, 1312 and 1313–15, with no compensating constitutional concessions.

The circumstances of the Avignonese papacy (1305–78) will be described in a later chapter, but some reference may be appropriately made at this point to the 'Affair of the Templars', since the suppression of this Order admirably illustrates the power of the French monarchy in the early fourteenth century. The Order of the Temple had been founded to assist the defence of the Crusading State and the disappearance of that State in 1291 removed its principal *raison-d'être* and provided the Order's enemies with a convenient *prima facie* case for their actions. Philip IV's motives in the matter are not entirely clear, but it is highly probable that his principal purpose in seeking the downfall of the Templars was financial gain, although the results achieved in this respect were disappointing. To describe money as the main motive is not to deny that Philip was genuinely convinced that the Templars were guilty of the crimes of which they were accused, nor

[1] See above, p. 54.

to impugn the sincerity of his schemes for the fusion of the two military Orders in the interests of the Crusade. One distinguished historian has even called the king's part in this grim story 'an act of faith', but his constant pressure on the pope, who was persistently threatened with a posthumous trial of Boniface VIII, suggests a more secular outlook. Here we are concerned with the king's methods rather than his psychology. In the years 1305–7 Nogaret was employed in collecting evidence against the Templars, and on 13 October 1307 all members of the Order were arrested throughout the French kingdom: this simultaneous action is in itself a reminder of the power of the monarchy. The charges brought against the Templars included idolatry, sacrilege (on admission to the Order, it was claimed, a knight was compelled to spit three times on a crucifix) and compulsory sodomy. The wholesale confessions obtained, normally under torture, have puzzled many western European historians, but they should present no difficulty at all to those who have read confessions made under duress in totalitarian states in the twentieth century. They cannot be taken as evidence of guilt, but the vulnerability of the Templars to such pressure reflects unfavourably on their mutual loyalty and the profundity of their religious convictions. Throughout the Affair Philip exerted influence on the pope to hasten individual trials and the general suppression of the Order. In 1308, having recourse to a technique already employed against Boniface VIII, he called a general assembly of nobles, prelates and towns, which gave its approval to the royal request that a petition should be forwarded to the pope demanding the judgment and condemnation of the Templars. The matter dragged on, much to Philip's indignation, and it was only in 1312, at the Council of Vienne, that his pressure persuaded Clement to take the ultimate step of suppressing the Order. Many of its members had already died under torture or been burnt as relapsed heretics, and in 1314 this fate overcame the Grand Master, Jacques de Molay. Throughout France and in the territories that were under French domination—such as the Kingdom of Naples and the Papal State—the Templars confessed and were found guilty. That they did not confess elsewhere is the surest evidence of the efficacy of Philip IV's intervention, whether we are to attribute this situation to the Templars' innocence or (less plausibly) to the inability of other rulers to persuade their subjects to assist in the Order's destruction. Philip gained for himself the money deposited at the Paris Temple and the possessions of this house, as well as a handsome gift of 200,000 *l.* from the frightened sister Order, the Hospitallers. This was certainly not a negligible contribution to his hard-pressed finances, but it may be a tribute to papal resistance that the principal beneficiary from the downfall of the Templars was the Order of the Hospital.

The triumphant tale of Philip IV's relations with the French clergy—whom he taxed heavily in twenty-four of the thirty years of his reign—was in part made possible by his success in securing the backing of his subjects. His method was to make use of parliamentary institutions to demonstrate the degree of support that he enjoyed, and though popes must have known that it was not easy for Frenchmen to express disapproval of a carefully prepared royal statement, it was difficult for them to express scepticism in the face of these manifestations of public consent. As early as 1277 Philip III employed this technique and called a baronial assembly which asked Nicholas III's approval for special taxation in support of a projected crusade. We have seen how his son used similar gatherings to demonstrate the nation's solidarity in opposing Boniface VIII's claims to jurisdiction over the Church in 1302-3 and in the matter of the Templars in 1308. The 'publicizing' nature of parliament was also useful to Philip V, who summoned an assembly to recognize his title to the throne on the occasion of his controversial succession (1316) to his brother Louis X.

By far the most important role of these gatherings was their function in assisting the taxation of the laity. Up to Philip the Fair's time the main source of revenue had been the royal domain, supplemented by clerical taxation and by the levying of money fines on the laity in lieu of military service. Philip found these arrangements quite inadequate to meet his expenditure, but it would be misleading to dignify his experimental struggles for cash with the title of 'fiscal policy'. His methods were above all pragmatic and improvisatory. It was normally his custom to 'consult' and obtain consent from some sort of gathering before embarking on taxation, but there was no attempt to give formality to the occasion or to the approval gained. In 1295, for example, some nobles from southern France met in various assemblies to approve a tax of 1½ per cent on real estate in that area. The following year a small but rather more general gathering agreed to a 2 per cent property tax. In 1303 some nobles and a few others gave consent to an income tax, and in 1304 a slightly reinforced conciliar meeting approved a demand for military service. In 1308 some prelates and towns sent representatives to the court to agree to taxation. Even the greater gathering of 1314, designed to assist the raising of an army to fight in Flanders, contained representatives of the cathedral cities only, and it was characteristic that their main task was to hear and disseminate the propagandistic speech against the Flemings of the principal minister, Enguerrand de Marigny. The same informality prevailed four years later when Philip V needed an army to threaten the Flemings. Forty-six towns of northern France were ordered to send representatives to Paris and fifty-six of the south to Toulouse; the towns were selected more or less arbitrarily, and all communes were later asked for a contribution whether or not they had been summoned and whether or not they had offered assistance. Normally these assemblies were merely the preliminaries to local bargaining between the king's officials and towns or feudal lords: indeed one of their purposes was probably to enable the central government to become better informed about the resources of the localities. 'Compounding' or paying a fine for exemption was the usual way of settling a tax demand; each town made some sort of offer and after prolonged haggling agreement was commonly reached over the payment of a lump sum. Occasionally these negotiations had to be eased by small concessions and by (ill-kept) promises of reform, of exemption from other taxes, or of the 'once for all' nature of the levy. Noble support had sometimes to be won by permitting feudatories to keep a proportion of the proceeds of their own lands. The concessions granted in 1304 will serve as an instance of this process. On that occasion currency reform was promised, together with payment for military provisions and the right to deduct from the amount due debts outstanding from the Crown; finally, the towns' own estimates of their population were to be accepted instead of being subject to official inspection. The nobles of Auvergne further gained two charters confirming their judicial rights. Throughout this experimental double process of 'consultation' and local bargaining there was no notion that consent *had* to be given: the purpose of the assemblies was merely to find out public opinion, to influence it, and to commit it.

The informal nature of the French parliamentary gatherings of this time is the main explanation of the fact that, in contrast with contemporary developments in England, they did not lead to constitutional concessions by the Crown. Since no cut-and-dried assent was required, there was no need to win it by granting concessions. Owing to the technique of local bargaining by royal officials, the only renunciations made were local ones, and these tended to take the form of temporary contracts or even meaningless formulae. The multiplicity of assemblies also meant that there was no possibility of a demand for money being rejected unanimously. It is clear, nevertheless, that the French barons had some opportunity of making use of the king's financial needs to check his power, and that they failed to take it. This may have been due in part to a failure to realize that direct taxation was to become a permanent feature of government, but its main explanation lies in the strength of provincial separatism and in the baron's predominant concern with his own lordship. The feudatories were content to seek independence of the Crown, rather than trying (as in England) to gain control of the government. The king's strength did not appear a menace and, paradoxically, the disunity of the French kingdom assisted the monarchy. Thus the nobles made no attempt to co-operate with other classes, seeing no community of interests with them. The prelates alone seem to have relished their role in central conciliar gatherings, for the towns were quite content with the less costly local assemblies.

Thus it came about that the French kings had only to modify their policies in comparatively unimportant ways. The most significant changes made were currency reforms, the decisions after 1297 to drop forced loans and the unpopular sales-tax and, at the end of Philip IV's reign, the return to a form of direct taxation based on the military liability. In any case, Philip's financial stringencies were greatly eased after 1305 by the renewed alliance with the papacy. When a movement of discontented barons was organized early in Louis X's reign (1314-15), the major lords played little part, and the provincial charters

F

issued by the king contained no important concessions. For the most part these charters confirmed feudal rights and embodied vague promises of fiscal moderation: they put no effective limitation on the Crown's power to tax and they positively aided the growth of royal jurisdiction. The assemblies of Philip V (1316–22) were entirely local and no attempt was made to use them to check the power of the Crown: this king, too, was exceptionally successful in threatening to turn clerics and townsmen against the nobles and thus deterring any moves for co-operation between the three estates.

Regional and local feeling was still intensely strong, far stronger than the nascent stirrings of national patriotism. It is extremely difficult to know what the 'average' Frenchman thought, yet there are some signs among the more articulate that the monarchy's increasing strength was reflected in a growing awareness of nationality and a new sense of being bound by French loyalties. It has already been suggested, in connection with pro-French and anti-French sentiments in the papal court in the 1260s,[1] that such feelings were essentially negative in origin, the product, especially in circumstances of antagonism, of meeting strangers speaking a different tongue and reared in an alien environment. That the Curia continued to breed these prejudices is shown clearly enough by the alleged dictum of Boniface VIII that 'he would rather be a dog or an ass than a Frenchman'.

The principal basis for the consequent sentiment of solidarity was certainly linguistic. Though Italy was long to remain a 'geographical expression', Dante had no doubts at the beginning of the fourteenth century of who were the Italians; they were those who spoke Italian, the inhabitants of the area between Pola in Istria and the northern border of Genoese Liguria.[2] Edward I of England brought the accusation against the French king that he planned 'to delete the English language throughout the land'. There were difficulties about a linguistic basis for patriotism, since Edward and most of his leading subjects spoke French as their first language (as did many of his Flemish allies), while Philip's own subjects in southern France spoke a language differing profoundly from French.

Despite the illogicalities of the situation, national feeling was

---

[1] Above, p. 40.　　　[2] *Inferno*, IX, 115: *De vulgari eloquentia*, I, viii, x.

now a powerful force, as may be seen from the attitude of the French clergy during Philip the Fair's dispute with the papacy. The contest for the loyalty of the clergy was crucial, both because these men were the educated class and because they had a rival allegiance to the supranational Church. In general they sided with the King, and it is notable that the religious houses which did not do so were those the majority of whose inhabitants were not French. The Franciscan house at Paris stood by the pope, but it is known that at the most seventeen of its eighty-seven friars were French, so that this is a true instance of the exception 'proving' the rule. The French clerics could have claimed with justification that Boniface was unworthy to be the representative of a spiritual cause but, whatever their outlook, their conduct contrasts strongly with the fidelity a century earlier to Innocent III of both the French and English clergy, in the time of the disputes with Philip Augustus and John. For some of them national loyalty was a more positive sentiment. When Philip IV attacked Flanders, a French priest preached a sermon in which he proclaimed that 'those who die for the justice of the king and the realm shall be crowned by God as martyrs', and a contemporary scholar at Paris, Henry of Ghent, even contended that to die for the community might be compared to Christ's supreme sacrifice for mankind.

If some of the French clergy were thus prepared to declare that 'God is on our side', this was in part the consequence of the high theoretical claims now put forward on behalf of the lay state by its propagandists. Philip IV was careful to justify his taxation in 1302 with the classical plea that it was required *ad defensionem natalis patriae* 'and the venerable antiquity of our ancestors ordained warfare on behalf of the Fatherland, putting its care before the love of descendents'. In the realm of unofficial propaganda, Philip's writers made use of Aristotle's doctrine concerning the moral purpose of society to claim self-sufficiency and independence for secular authority: they demanded for the state spiritual powers and absolute control over justice, legislation and the persons and property of the king's subjects. Such writings moved in a world of legal theory that had no influence on the ideas of the average man. But if the propagandists were to justify their employment they had to change the outlook of influential men.

Hence they did not merely elaborate logically contrived abstractions; they were forced to come down to earth. One sees this in the ironical descriptions of the clerics who scandalously failed in their role as Frenchmen, 'lying in the shade eating luxuriously, drinking joyfully, resting on their ornate beds, sleeping quietly and basking comfortably amid sensuous furnishings'.[1] In the same vein, the anonymous author of the *Antequam essent clerici* wrote that 'Just as any part refusing to give help to the body is a wicked part, and as it were useless or paralysed; so all those men, be they clerics or lay, nobles or villeins, who refuse to perform their required duties towards the head or the body of society, the king or the kingdom, show by their refusal that they are like useless or paralysed members.' [2]

The forces forging a strong central government in France were men and money, officials working to levy taxes which both paid for armies and in turn made possible the employment of more officials. This practical fiscal, administrative and judicial pressure on subjects was the primary and essential process of which a broader national consciousness, diminishing regional patriotism, was a secondary product. The military and political crisis with which this apparently robust state was confronted in the middle decades of the fourteenth century, a crisis which came close to nullifying all the labours of Nogaret and Philip the Fair, will be the subject of a later chapter.

Further Reading

E. LANGLOIS, *Le Règne de Philippe III le Hardi* (Paris, 1887)
R. FAWTIER, *The Capetian Kings of France* (London, 1960: and Papermacs)
J. R. STRAYER and C. H. TAYLOR, *Studies in Early French Taxation* (Cambridge, Mass., 1939)

[1] 'Disputatio super potestate praelatis ecclesiae' in M. Goldast, *Monarchia S. Romani Imperii* (Hanover, 1611), I, 16.
[2] P. Dupuy, *Histoire du Différend d'entre le pape Boniface VIII et Philippes le Bel roy de France* (Paris, 1655), pp. 21–2.

IV

DISINTEGRATION IN GERMANY

FRANCE in the early fourteenth century shows the potential strength of a medieval monarchical state in favourable circumstances, the Crown flourishing on the snowball principle that nothing succeeds like success. The German territories at the same time illustrate no less clearly the contrary process of disintegration, lack of central control fostering the institutions of local political independence and traditions of regionalism. The most obvious disadvantage suffered by the emperor was the elective nature of his throne. A strict rule of inheritance had not applied in the primitive period of the 'Germanic' kingdoms, when the leader had to be a strong man, and the people could not be exposed to the danger of rule by a child or an obviously incompetent weakling. The new king had to secure the acceptance of the leading men before he could enjoy power, and this situation was formalized in his 'election' or the recognition ('acclamation') of his succession (subtle distinction between these two concepts would be out of place in discussing primitive society). Normally the new king would be the eldest or most prominent son of his predecessor, but it was only slowly that more settled political conditions tended to make this common practice a constitutional rule, and even then agreement on such refinements as primogeniture was extremely slow: hence, for example, the dispute on the death of Richard I of England in 1199 as to whether the true heir was the youngest brother of the late king (John) or the son of an elder brother (Arthur). While the monarchies in France and England became in practice hereditary, the Empire remained elective—at times, under the Saxons and Ottonians, in theory only, but when there was no direct heir in practice also. At the end of the twelfth century Henry VI had striven energetically to

73

persuade the German princes to make the imperial succession hereditary, so that his son Frederick might follow him automatically in the imperial lands as he would in the Sicilian kingdom, but his efforts had met with no success. This was a decisive moment; the possibility of setting the Empire on a hereditary basis was not to recur for several centuries.

Elective kingship meant, above all, lack of continuity. This was a tremendous disadvantage in administration. Each time a new feudal family assumed the coveted burden of imperial rule, new officials took over and a new archive was set up; whatever resources this family enjoyed in the way of a bureaucracy embarked without the benefit of their predecessors' experience and records on the Sisyphean task of government. Whichever noble or royal house gained the Empire was dependent also on its own domain: by the mid-thirteenth century there was virtually no crown land and exceedingly little royal revenue from fiscal sources. The French monarchy had, it is true, advanced from a situation that in some respects was similar: until the mid-twelfth century the royal domain had been very small, and regional divisions in France remained extremely strong. But the Capetians had drawn prestige from the long duration of their house and the central position of their domain was an inestimable asset. Their initial weakness may have saved them from the attacks of other feudal houses, but in Germany the monarchy could not benefit even from this paradoxical advantage: its feebleness was such that nobles and towns were forced to make their own political arrangements, and there seemed no prospect of the monarchy acquiring the strength that would enable it to inherit these states in miniature, as the French had incorporated Normandy, Toulouse, Champagne and so much else.

In writing of Germany, however, there is a strong danger of interpreting that country's development in the light of anachronistic hindsight. We know that German unification was only achieved in the nineteenth century and hence tend to assume that in some way its medieval rulers failed to prepare the way for the 'unity' achieved by France, Spain and England in the early sixteenth century. Hence the whole of medieval German history is often looked on as the history of a political failure and each of its ages is interpreted by different writers as the era in which things went irreparably wrong. Yet Germany might well have been united in the sixteenth century if only Charles V had had to face slightly fewer problems outside Germany: the reasons for the failure to unify Germany at that time were not solely German reasons, and had they not existed there would be much less temptation to see the history of medieval Germany as a tragic tale of frustration. The tragedy, if there was one, should perhaps be ascribed to the sixteenth century, and in any case the history of the Italian peninsula should have made historians—even liberal nationalist historians—more sceptical concerning the blessings of unity and the evils of regionalism.

Some writers have regarded the late eleventh century as the decisive stage in Germany's development and have blamed the reforming papacy for supporting the German Church and lay nobility in their opposition to the Salian emperors. Others have emphasized the role of the Empire's expansion eastward and have attributed the strength of the princely houses to their ability to build up their power in these zones of new settlement untrammelled by the counterbalancing influence of a feudal baronage. But this is surely to put the decisive phases in Germany's political development too early: if there was a period when the German ruler's power shrank seriously in contrast with that of the other monarchies of the west it must be placed in the thirteenth century. Frederick II had disliked Germany, with its 'long winters, muddy towns, dark forests and rugged castles' and he regarded his Sicilian kingdom as both wealthier and easier to govern. He himself spent comparatively little time north of the Alps and was content for the most part to enjoy the title that Germany provided for him, while entrusting power there to the princes. These princes, both lay and ecclesiastical, were the beneficiaries of the two great privileges of 1220 and 1232, of which the latter (the *Constitutio in favorem principum*) gave them full control over justice and currency. Individual magnates also received valuable privileges— the Welf Otto, a former enemy of the Hohenstaufen, was bribed by the creation for him of the duchy of Brunswick—and domain territory was alienated on a considerable scale. Most paradoxical of all the features of Frederick's policy was his support of the feudal magnates against the towns, the obvious and traditional allies of the monarchy. This alignment was a cause of the revolt

of his son Henry, for Henry was more familiar with German conditions and hence less prone to his father's notion, based on
Italian experience, that towns were harder to manage than feudatories. When Henry turned traitor and was deposed and imprisoned, Frederick set up another son, Conrad, in his place, but
this time with the intention of keeping him under close control.
At this juncture, however, the emperor's Italian policy and his
consequent bitter struggle with the papacy were responsible for a
new and yet more serious deterioration in his position in Germany. Innocent IV, after deposing him, sought with considerable
success to deprive him of the vital support of the Church, and
Frederick found himself engaged in a competition to outbid the
pope's offers to the lay nobility. Another feature of the papal
offensive was the election of two successive anti-kings, Henry
Raspe, landgrave of Thuringia, a pious *rex clericorum* who was
prepared to surrender all control over the German Church to
Innocent's legates, and count William of Holland, chosen because there was little danger of his acquiring much political power
beyond the border territories of the Low Countries and Rhineland.

After Frederick II's deposition (1245), fate itself seemed determined that no one man should be granted time to face the problems of governing the Empire. Raspe, chosen to succeed
Frederick, died in 1247, only a year after his election. Frederick
himself died in 1250 and his son Conrad in 1254. William of
Holland was killed in battle in 1256. In the following year
imperial prestige declined to its nadir through the 'double
election' of Richard of Cornwall and Alfonso X of Castile.
Richard, earl of Cornwall was the younger brother of Henry III
of England and his appearance on the German scene was part of
the unsure and over-ambitious structure of scheming evolved by
Henry, which included the plan of gaining the Sicilian kingdom
for Edmund 'Crouchback'.[1] He also had the support of a party
in Flanders, whence he first received the proposal that he should
become a candidate for the throne. Well-directed bribes then won
Richard a following among the German nobility and some of his
backers crossed to England to persuade the justly suspicious
barons that Richard had already been elected. He in fact secured

[1] See above, p. 35.

—on conditions—the votes of the archbishops of Cologne and Mainz and of the duke of Bavaria. A little later king Ottokar of Bohemia was persuaded to add his support. The election of Alfonso of Castile, which took place some two months after Richard's (i.e. on 1 April 1257) came about in a very different fashion, but was in its essentials a similar product of 'vaulting ambition which o'er-leaps itself'. Alfonso had high schemes for extending his influence outside the Iberian peninsula (in Sicily as well as Germany) and he enjoyed the advantage of Hohenstaufen descent, his mother being a first cousin of Frederick II. The initiative which led to his election, however, came from Italy, where the Ghibelline city of Pisa turned to him as protector and announced its recognition of Alfonso as king of the Romans. A series of bribes in Germany procured for Alfonso the votes of the archbishop of Trier, the duke of Saxony, the margrave of Brandenburg, and the king of Bohemia. Ottokar of Bohemia had thus cast a vote for both candidates, and Alfonso's case was not assisted by the fact that the archbishop alone had voted in person, the other electors having appointed him as their proctor. Subsequent events in Castile were to reduce Alfonso's claim to an empty formality; he was never able to put in an appearance on imperial soil. Richard of Cornwall's performance was scarcely more substantial: he visited the Rhineland in 1257-9, 1260 and 1268, but was unable to institute any firm control even in that area.

The failure of both Richard and Alfonso to establish themselves in the Empire meant that for two decades Germany learned to do without a ruler. It also led to a more formal recognition of the existence of a fixed electoral college of seven princes, since each claimed during the subsequent proceedings in the papal court that the four votes that he had secured constituted a majority. In earlier periods the 'election' had been the concern of the greater lay nobles (as representatives of Germany's tribal divisions) and of the most powerful prelates: at times (as mentioned above) hereditary succession had made election a formality, but after the death of Henry VI and particularly during the subsequent struggle between the Hohenstaufen and the papacy it had been very much a reality. The limitation of the electoral college to seven assisted the worst of the abuses which had accompanied the events of

1257, for the number of principal recipients of bribes from those seeking election was now firmly fixed—at first the number only, not the names, since for a time the dukes of Lower Bavaria challenged the Bohemian kings for the seventh vote. Thus the choice of the Emperor[1] became, by fixed constitutional practice, the affair of seven magnates, and the man elected would be he whose choice was most compatible with the selfish interests of these seven princes.

The election in 1273 of Rudolf of Habsburg well exemplifies this generalization. In Rudolf the princes chose with care the representative of a house whose power could not compare with their own. The Habsburgs held land in Alsace, the upper Rhine, and what is now Switzerland; there was as yet no indication of the family's future greatness. Rudolf was so much the dependent of the electors that they were able to make him promise to alienate none of his domain except with their consent. His election was to a considerable extent the product of Gregory X's desire to raise up a northern counterweight to the overwhelming strength of Charles of Anjou, yet the man whom the electors chose was not powerful enough for the role. He was naturally forced to concentrate his attention on his own domain and the advancement of his family; his policy could not be an imperial one in the wider sense, but within its limits it was successful, for Rudolf gained Austria and Styria for his sons. Thus the family's territorial basis shifted further east: some of Rudolf's successors, indeed, were to be rulers of southern or south-eastern Germany only, though their control was not so strictly limited as that of William of Holland and Richard of Cornwall in the north-west.

This concentration on the south-east made possible friendly relations with the French monarchy, the interests of which had tended to clash with those of the Empire along the border, in the Carolingian 'Middle Kingdom'.[2] But the long struggle between France and England served to exacerbate disunity within the Empire, because each side attempted to recruit military support there. The Low Countries and Rhineland provided the most promising base for an English assault on the Île de France, while

---

[1] The emperor-elect was known as king of the Romans until he had been crowned by the pope.

[2] Above, pp. 61–2.

the French in turn exploited local disputes in the same region to build up a party favourable to them. Meanwhile growing nationalism in France and England made Germany's disunity still more pronounced in comparison, and the French crown was able to nibble away at imperial land in the no-man's-land of Franche-Comté, Lorraine and the Lyonnais.

Rudolf of Habsburg so frightened the princes by his territorial gains that on his death (1291) the electors rejected his son and instead turned again to a weak candidate, Adolf of Nassau. Adolf was soon deeply involved on the English side in the struggle for power in the Netherlands, was then challenged by Albert of Habsburg, and fell in battle (1298). Albert in turn was drawn into war, against the Bohemian dynasty; the weakness of his standing is well illustrated by Boniface VIII's attempt to persuade him to cede Tuscany and to recognize formally that any imperial election might be quashed by a pope.

Henry of Luxembourg, Albert's successor (1308), was a compromise candidate, chosen because he was neither a Capetian (French aspirations to the Empire now reappeared) nor a Habsburg, and because the comparative obscurity of his house made it likely that he would remain dependent on the princes who had elected him. By abandoning imperial claims in Thuringia and confirming Habsburg rights in Austria and Styria Henry conformed to the expectation that in his time Germany would remain without a strong ruler. Like his predecessors, however, he set out to strengthen the position of his own family and he secured the succession to Bohemia and Moravia through the marriage of his son John (1311). The main shift in imperial policy under Henry was his return to an ambitious policy in Italy. Initially the result of a natural wish to revive imperial claims south of the Alps, this policy benefited from the encouragement of the pope (Clement V) who saw it as a means of restoring some order to the peninsula and of counterbalancing the formidable power of France. Henry's intention was to stand above the Italian maelstrom as a neutral, but he had gone no further than Milan when he abandoned this attempt and was drawn into the struggle by the appeals of the Ghibellines. The high hopes that these men placed in Henry's role may be seen at their most extreme in Dante's letter saluting 'the successor of Caesar and Augustus' and begging him to fulfil his task throughout northern and central Italy, and in the same writer's fervently anachronistic *De Monarchia,* which founds the Empire's position on that of the ancient Romans, who ruled the world through God's will. Henry also discovered that Aragonese support compelled him to take sides against the Angevins, the other contenders for the south. Finally, after much hesitation, the pope himself declared against Henry, who thus came to dedicate the last three years of his short life to fruitless campaigning in Italy. Whatever Dante's hopes, Henry cannot be regarded as reviving the tradition of the Hohenstaufen, for he had the worst of both worlds and achieved dominance neither north nor south of the Alps.

Henry's death (August 1313) was followed by a disputed election, the rival candidates being the Habsburg Frederick and Lewis of Bavaria. The latter was the heir to the votes cast in 1308 for the house of Luxembourg; Henry's son John was young and, besides, papal pressure told against him. In the main Lewis was stronger than his rival, but he held only half of the old Bavarian duchy and the territorial basis of his power was inconsiderable. A bitter war between Frederick and Lewis caused great devastation and even Lewis's decisive victory at Mühldorf (1322) did not bring the struggle to an end, for the pope, John XXII, took advantage of the disputed succession to claim the imperial vicariate in Italy and, later, administration of the 'vacant' Empire. When the pope, after excommunicating Lewis, sought out a pro-French emperor among the Habsburgs and considered also reviving the candidacy of John of Bohemia, Lewis retorted by declaring himself joint emperor with his former rival Frederick: this arrangement lasted from 1325 till Frederick's death in 1330. Lewis salvaged some degree of prestige for the Empire by his intervention in Italy: he was never able to lay his hands on more than four thousand horsemen, but in the fragmented peninsula even this force counted for much. In any event Lewis, a practical man and an opportunist, was not aiming at an imperial restoration in thirteenth-century style. He saw Italy as a source of money and knew that if he could assert himself there even a little, the many tyrants who sought a constitutional basis for their *signorie* would pay him handsomely for the title of 'imperial vicar'. During his six years in Italy he was able to install an imperialist

anti-pope, but the main effect of his Italian policy was to keep
alive memories of the Empire's former greatness. Lewis never
visited northern Germany, but his dynastic policy gained for him
the Tyrol and the Brandenburg March and (by his marriage)
Hainault, Zeeland, Holland and Friesland.

Though able to play off Habsburg against Luxembourg, Lewis
never came close to achieving an imperial revival. Indeed such
a revival had never been practical politics during the century
which had passed since Frederick II's deposition. The strength
drained from the ruler had flowed continuously to the princes,
and the princes had affirmed their constitutional position by
declaring (at Rhens, in 1338) that the king elected by them had no
need of papal confirmation. It was also the princes who took the
lead at Frankfurt in 1346, when they chose Charles of Bohemia
(the son of John of Bohemia and grandson of Henry VII), to
supplant Lewis. Charles (born 'Wenceslas') was the candidate
brought forward by the strongly pro-French pope Clement VI
and was not unjustly known as 'the priests' emperor': he had been
educated at the French court, and had met Clement there. In the
history of the Empire the importance of Charles's reign lies in his
promulgation of the Golden Bull (1356) which gave official
recognition to the triumph in Germany of the particularist principle. This edict reaffirmed that the only necessary stage in the
choice of an emperor was election by the seven princes. The
electoral college was thus more formally constituted, and its
members were singled out by another clause which forbade them
to partition their territory. A number of special powers granted
to the princes ratified their position as virtually independent
rulers. Offences against them were to rank as *lèse-majesté* (treason).
No appeal was to lie from their law courts to the emperor's.
They were to have control over the currency of their lands.
The bull also prohibited the formation of leagues between towns
and among the nobles. In appearance a constitutional abdication
of a ruler in favour of seven powerful subjects—and a sensible
recognition of political realities—the Golden Bull was also an
invitation to the other great feudatories, secular and lay, to assume
similar authority, for it would be difficult to confine this virtual
independence to the electoral princes.

After the issue of the Golden Bull 'the history of German

internal development passes from the whole to the parts, and each separate principality requires individual treatment'.[1] There is only room in this book to deal with one 'principality' as an exemplar. The rulers that followed Charles IV call for no more than a brief mention, since their melancholy history is not the history of Germany. Charles's drunken and incompetent son Wenceslas (1378–1400) was tied to Bohemia by the struggle against Hussitism (see Chapter VI). Rupert of the Rhine replaced Wenceslas on his deposition, but achieved no hold outside his own lands during his rather brief reign (1400–10). On Rupert's death the electors turned to Sigismund, Charles IV's younger son, who had already acquired the crown of Hungary. Sigismund (1410–37) enjoyed some popularity in his lifetime and his knightly personality and his initiative in forwarding the Council of Constance perhaps did a little to revive royal prestige. Such power as he possessed, however, was based entirely on Bohemia and Hungary, and most of his reign was devoted to a series of unsuccessful Crusades against the Hussite risings. In the north he sold Neumark, conferred the duchy of Saxony on Frederick of Meissen and granted Brandenburg to Frederick of Nuremberg, thus assisting the foundation of Hohenzollern power. The Swiss Confederation also gained considerably in autonomy during his time. Sigismund's political ability was limited to a certain skill in exploiting the internal divisions of the towns. An instance may be given to illustrate this technique in action. In 1414 he promised a popular régime newly installed in Lübeck that for 25,000 florins he would give the city a 'privilege' whereby the former oligarchs were to remain in perpetual exile and the city's consuls to be recruited only from the lesser gilds; this handsome bribe was disguised as a loan, the privilege being valid only if repayment had not been made by a fixed date. Sigismund was of course powerless to prevent the return of Lübeck's exiles in 1416, by which time he was haggling for another gift of 16,000 florins. Even shamelessly cunning methods of this sort could come nowhere near to solving the problem of Sigismund's notorious insolvency. At times the king was reduced to wearing tattered clothes. In 1416, on his return journey from England, he had to pawn part of the insignia of the Order of the Garter, which he had recently received, and

[1] G. Barraclough, *Origins of Modern Germany*, p. 321n.

after the Council of Constance he was forced to leave some of his linen with the municipality: this proved unsaleable because it was stamped with the imperial arms. Sigismund's son-in-law and successor, Albert of Austria, reigned for a single year only (1438-9), but his cousin Frederick III was king till 1493. Under Frederick III, while the king struggled to retain control of his own Austrian duchy, much of Prussia was lost to Poland and Silesia and Moravia to Hungary; for a time, too, much imperial territory was in the hands of Charles of Burgundy.

In 1457 an Italian cardinal received a letter from his friend Martin Meyr, the chancellor of the archbishop of Mainz, lamenting the condition of Germany, which was being bled white by papal taxation. This cardinal, Aeneas Silvius Piccolomini, had travelled much in Germany during the previous quarter of a century and had indeed lived there for several years. He replied in a spirited work in which he described the wealth of many German cities and diagnosed the true sources of the woes of the Church in Germany as 'luxury and ambition'. The main trouble, however, was the political situation:

> You acknowledge the emperor as your king and lord, but he seems only to rule on sufferance, and his power amounts to nothing. You obey him only so far as you wish, and this is very little indeed ['tantum ei paretis quantum vultis, vultis autem minimum']. Liberty is pleasing to everyone and neither cities nor princes render to the Emperor what is due to him: he has no revenue and no treasury. Everyone wishes to be the manager and arbiter of his own affairs, hence the constant quarrels and perpetual wars which rage in your midst, from whence there arise pillage, slaughter, conflagration and a thousand other kinds of evil. How essential it is to intervene in such a situation, where there is not one ruler but many.[1]

The 'many rulers' were not merely princes, but also towns and those leagues of towns that had been condemned by the Golden Bull. Of the latter the most celebrated was the Hanseatic League, a loose association of German cities trading in the area between Russia and Scandinavia in the north and Flanders in the west. This Hanse was formed principally to protect the mercantile interests of the towns concerned and in particular to concert their relations

---

[1] Aeneas Silvius Piccolomini (Pius II), 'De ritu, situ, moribus et conditione Germaniae descriptio', *Opera Omnia* (Basle, 1571), pp. 1060-1.

with Scandinavian rulers and the other powers with whom they had dealings. Their co-operation achieved its greatest success in the Peace of Stralsund (1369) which gave them complete freedom of trade in Denmark. The *raison-d'être* of the League was the absence of any ruler capable of protecting the towns' own interests, but it was an *ad hoc* political entity and never evolved a firm constitution of its own. Lübeck was always the leader among the Hanse towns and the assemblies of the League were frequently held there, but attendance at the *Hansetäge* was slack and meetings were irregular. Many towns drifted into and out of the League, so that it is impossible to define its scope: at the greatest recorded gathering (1447) thirty-eight towns were represented. It was difficult for this amorphous body to bring pressure to bear on recalcitrant members, but at times it made use of the most obvious weapon available, 'unhansing', or deprivation of membership.

In its commercial motivation, its loose structure and its long duration, the Hanseatic League was untypical. The nature of a more characteristic league in the Rhineland is well described in some passages in a chronicle from Mainz:

> Around the year 1381 some powerful cities, to wit Ratisbon and Nuremberg and thirty-six Swabian towns in the Rhineland (Basle, Coblenz, Strasburg, Speier, Worms, Mainz and Cologne) and Frankfurt, Freiburg, Wetzlar and Gelnhausen in Wetterau and some other royal towns and cities, together with various barons, nobles, knights and squires (in particular Counts John and Rupert of Nassau) formed a league called *der stede bundt*.[1] They hired many lancers, paying them heavy wages. The purpose of the troops was to oppose vagrant robbers in those parts, for the barons there so encouraged these wicked bandits that it was unsafe for anyone to move between one town and another.

But the chronicler soon lost his enthusiasm for the league:

> At the same period [1382] the evil league called *der bund*, after capturing this town [Scholten], had become so arrogant that it entirely despised the princes, barons and knights of those parts and turned to the extirpation of the clergy. At Mainz it infringed ecclesiastical liberties in every way, and forbade its members under heavy penalties to work for the clergy as purveyors of salt or wine

[1] This phrase ('the league of cities') is in German in the chronicle, which is written in Latin.

Drapers selling their wares at stalls in Bologna
See Chapter V

Hawking: scene from a fresco in the Papal Palace at Avignon by
Matteo Giovanetti *See Chapter VI*

or in many other trades. The result of this was that for many years no services were said at Mainz,[1] which worried the citizens not at all, in fact they were happy about it, for heresy flourished.

In 1386 the citizens of Worms were cited a number of times by the clergy to the court of Wenceslas king of the Romans, on account of their violent actions against them [the clergy]. But the citizens persisted in their disobedience, refusing to appear in the court to defend their case because they were confident of the power of their confederation, *der stede bundt*. In consequence they were sentenced by the king to a fine of several gold marks.

Finally he was able to report with satisfaction that:

the cities in the confederation had spent tremendous sums of money on the payment of their army, for they had in their pay two hundred lancers, not to mention a vast throng of armed townsmen, artisans and peasants. These had done an enormous amount of harm and had served no useful purpose at all; also they were meeting defeat on all sides. Consequently Adolf archbishop of Mainz, the bishop of Babenburg and John of Venningen, the Master of the Teutonic Order, intervened and made peace after Whitsun [1389]: some of the cities had to pay large sums of money to lords as compensation for the harm done to the peasantry. They also had to endure the considerable shame and disgrace of these heavy payments. And so the whole conspiracy of the confederation of cities was annihilated and dissolved, and quiet restored in place of strife.[2]

This chronicler's grievances against the Rhenish League of 1381–9 were principally those of a churchman, but his account of the activities of the League's armies shows clearly enough that when this type of response to central weakness occurred the cure closely resembled the disease. Every German annalist of the fourteenth and fifteenth centuries has his own local version of this tale of brigandage and of warfare between towns and barons—often 'robber' barons whose castles were notorious as nests of thieves—as well as of violence and bitter class cleavages within the towns. At times princes granted jurisdictional and other powers to towns and town leagues. Thus in 1322, after Anklam, Demmin, Greifswald and Treptow had destroyed the castle of Bugewitz, the

---

[1] This is probably a hyperbolical statement, not to be taken literally.
[2] *Chronici Moguntini Miscelli Fragmenta Collecta* in J. F. Böhmer, *Fontes Rerum Germanicarum*, IV, 376–83.

duke of Pomerania gave these cities the authority to destroy any other castle within the duchy. These tactics could never provide a satisfactory solution to the problems of government, and in any case they were increasingly hindered in the fifteenth century by the general economic and political decline of the towns. Some places were rising in this period, particularly in southern Germany —Augsburg is an instance—and in the Lower Rhineland the cities continued to hold their own against the nobles, but this was exceptional. In the north-east the Hanse lost much of its Baltic trade to the Dutch and English. Many cities of this zone, enfeebled also by agrarian depression, forfeited their independence to the dukes of Pomerania and the Hohenzollern margraves of Brandenburg.

Contrasting with the general tale of the failure of the local leagues is the great success story of the rise of the Swiss Confederation. The emergence of a new state from the *débris* of imperial decentralization is not only of interest in its own right but serves also to illustrate the particular conditions under which local political institutions could consolidate and flourish.

Of the three different elements that made possible the growth of Switzerland, the most fundamental was perhaps the prior existence of the social and political institutions out of which the Confederation developed. Local *Landfrieden* could only become effective as means of joint action and judicial arbitration and co-operation if they involved communities already enjoying a certain degree of self-government. The communities of Uri, Schwyz and Unterwalden, forest valleys around Lake Lucerne, were already 'corporations' and the free peasantry, which comprised perhaps as much as two-thirds of the population, probably chose the 'judges' exercising rights of lower justice. Geographical factors were hardly less important. The Lake united the three cantons, facilitating communications between them. Their command of the northern approaches to the St Gotthard pass, which by the thirteenth century was the most important of the Alpine routes, gave them strategic importance, and its tolls yielded them considerable revenue. They thus had both lake and pass in common, and the aim of a good deal of their subsequent expansion was control over the southern approach to the St Gotthard. Another source of unity was the preponderance of the pastoral way of life, and the people also had in common their poverty: hence their willingness to take the career of a mercenary soldier as a means of escape. The medieval Swiss had a common language, for the area that came into the confederation early was entirely German-speaking.

These positive factors would not have brought about the crystallization of Switzerland without the decisive negative pressure of the Habsburgs. Imperial weakness made the threat of local noble control a real one when the ruler was not a Habsburg, and did nothing to remove it under the Habsburg kings. The first defensive league of the three Forest Cantons probably dates from the time when Count Rudolf IV, after his election as king of the Romans, sought to build up a really strong territorial state in south-western Germany. When this alliance was confirmed at the time of Rudolf's death (1291) it was described optimistically as a 'permanent league' and its constitutional basis was strengthened by a decree that judges within the cantons must be locally-born men. By the early fourteenth century the cantons were appointing their own 'headmen' and soon these *Landammänner* came to exercise higher justice.

Lewis of Bavaria's disputed election (1314) gave the Swiss the opportunity to assert their direct allegiance to this emperor against his Habsburg rival Frederick. When the Habsburgs launched their first war against the Swiss (1315), the troops of Frederick's brother Leopold were routed at Morgarten (for a contemporary account of the battle see below, pp. 91–4). This victory was followed by a new union (9 December 1315) proclaiming the open intention of mutual co-operation against the Habsburgs. One clause prescribed that the members

> should be as one person, like man and wife, and should be obedient in rendering reasonable services to their rightful lords, when their lord or lords use no violence against them and do not try to impose illegal demands by force. But they should perform no services so long as their lords act unjustly towards them.

Other clauses were directed towards giving the confederation greater cohesion: hence:

> We also agree that none of the members of the confederation

should take an oath or make an agreement with any outside power except after consulting the other members,

and

None of the members should have any negotiations with outside powers except after consulting the other members and securing their consent, so long as the members are lordless.[1]

The pact of 1315 was, however, only the beginning of the confederation's struggles. The emperor could never be a reliable ally against the Habsburgs, and the original territories had to expand if they were to achieve economic self-sufficiency. In the course of the fourteenth century they secured the adherence of the neighbouring rural zones of Glarus and Zug and of three towns, Lucerne, Zürich and Berne. The urban communities were valuable allies, but their interests, as municipalities and textile-producing centres, contrasted with those of the original rural cantons, and there could be no confidence that they had come to stay. Lucerne joined as a fellow-rebel against Habsburg lordship, but the circumstances that brought in the other towns were more or less ephemeral: Zürich turned to the Swiss when its tyrant, Brun, found that the exiles opposed to his regime had gone to the Habsburgs for support, while Berne was in need of allies to assist in the conquest of the surrounding rural area. The great asset of the Swiss during this period was the Habsburgs' concentration on their Austrian territories and the spasmodic nature of their attempts to assert overlordship further west. When the Habsburgs did at last wage determined war over Lucerne's adherence to the confederation (1385-9), the Swiss won another resounding victory, at Sempach (1386), in which Leopold of Austria, nephew of the Leopold defeated at Morgarten, met his death. Other successes in this war made it of decisive importance in the development of Swiss expansion and unity, but the 'confederation' was not yet a single organization, some of its members being linked with some but not all of the others. Antecedents of the firmer constitutional structure of later times are to be found by 1370 in a joint agreement concerning clerical privilege, and this trend is

---

[1] *Amtliche Sammlung der ältern Eidgenössischen Abschiede*, I (Lucerne, 1839), doc. 2.

still more marked in the *Sempacherbrief* of July 1393.[1] The most important clause of this statute laid down that:

> It is our unanimous opinion that henceforth no town or territory among us should enter upon a war . . . without giving notice in accordance with the sworn agreement linking all the towns and territories.

This was an important principle, though it was sometimes defied. Since the Swiss were entirely dependent for their position on the strength and prestige of their arms it was essential that some code should regulate the conduct of the confederation's forces. The *Sempacherbrief* not only forbade attacks on Church property and on women 'unless they are helping the enemy', but incorporated a clause concerning looting which is worth quoting for the light that it throws on the warfare of the age:

> Let it be known also that in this battle many of the enemy escaped . . . who would not have done so had our men pursued them instead of plundering before the battle was entirely won and finished, . . . so that those who were fleeing gathered together and won back command of the field and the bodies and possessions of the dead. We consider unanimously that, whenever the occasion arises, everyone should do his best as an honourable man to harm the enemy and hold the field, without plundering whether in fortresses, towns or the open countryside, up to the time when the battle has ended and been won, and the commanders permit plunder. Then all present may plunder whether they are armed or not and the loot is to be handed over to the commanders and it is to belong to them, and they shall divide it fairly among those of their men who are present, according to their number. And when they have divided the plunder among the men everyone should be content with his proper share.

A torrent of new accessions was inaugurated by the acquisition of the Valais as an ally in the early fifteenth century. Among these the Aargau was of particular importance for the confederation's constitution and for the growth of mutual interests among its members, since this formerly Habsburg territory was held in common between the confederates and taxed and governed by them jointly. By 1461, when the Thurgau, west of Lake Constance, was gained, the Habsburgs retained almost nothing of their former

[1] *Amtliche Sammlung der ältern Eidgenössischen Abschiede*, I, doc. 30.

lands south of the Rhine, and in the last two decades of the century there began another series of important accessions, Fribourg and Soluthurn joining the confederation in the 1480s and Basle and Schaffhausen around 1500. Between the late 1460s and 1476 the Swiss were threatened by the rise of the Burgundian duchy (see Chapter IX), and for a time they received money from both Sigismund of Habsburg and Louis XI of France to stimulate their opposition to the duke. When Charles of Burgundy invaded Switzerland in 1476 he was decisively defeated by the Swiss pikemen in the battles of Grandson and Morat. The Swiss could not always resist the temptation to indulge in military expeditions which were little more than large-scale looting forays into the Savoy and Franche-Comté, Vaud and the duchy of Milan. But a firmer agreement was reached concerning co-operation in foreign policy and military engagements (Compact of Stans, 1481) and further unity was conferred on the confederation by the ill-judged decision to neglect it in the constitutional reforms of the *Reichstag* of Worms of 1495.[1] Four years later the Swiss beat off the forces of Maximilian and the Swabian League and the Emperor was compelled to recognize the confederation as virtually independent.

The success of the Swiss is clearly attributable to their military strength and to the fact that the Habsburgs so rarely put this to the test in a prolonged war. The cavalry, conventionally the master of medieval battlefields, could make little headway in the mountains (see the account of the battle of Morgarten below, particularly p. 93) and the Swiss were hardy infantrymen, well-armed with halberds and pikes. They were carefully trained to maintain an unbroken formation even in difficult terrain and this made them formidable both when standing firm on the defensive against a ragged charge and when themselves advancing in slow-moving but implacable attack. Mercenary service helped to keep the Swiss in training and to gain them experience. By the end of the fifteenth century the prestige of their pikemen was unchallenged in western Europe. Machiavelli thought the Swiss the sole surviving heirs of Rome's military greatness. His *Art of War* is full of praise for their methods, and when he was charged with the organization of the newly-formed Florentine militia in 1506 he recommended that it should be drilled in the Swiss manner. Yet

[1] See below, p. 263.

the military power of the Swiss would not have been sufficient to win them independence had not the confederation evolved a constitution which bound the members sufficiently firmly in the face of opposition and which was yet sufficiently loose to allow for the inevitable strains of diverging interests. Around 1500 there were thirteen confederate 'cantons' which voted in the diets of the 'Great League of Upper Germany'; the cantons sent representatives with instructions to the meetings of the diet, the powers of which were undefined although it was the League's only federal authority. Membership was not yet a fixed and permanent affair, and in the mid-fifteenth century Zürich had deserted the League for a time and even fought some of its members. Outside the confederation stood a number of 'allies', two of which were groups of communities (Valais and Grisons), while others were country districts, towns and abbeys; many of the allies were still linked by treaty to some, but not all, of the cantons, and some of the cantons had their own subject territories, both singly and jointly. This complicated but flexible machinery worked successfully, and in the sixteenth century Switzerland was to show itself a power to be reckoned with in war and diplomacy, as well as in religion.

Further Reading

G. BARRACLOUGH, *The Origins of Modern Germany* (Oxford, 1946)

B. JARRETT, *The Emperor Charles IV* (London, 1935): pp. 33–68 are an abridged translation of Charles IV's autobiography

F. L. CARSTEN, *Origins of Prussia* (Oxford, 1954)

E. BONJOUR, H. S. OFFLER, G. R. POTTER, *A Short History of Switzerland* (Oxford, 1952)

H. S. OFFLER, 'Aspects of Government in the late medieval Empire' in *Europe in the Late Middle Ages* (ed. Hale, Highfield and Smalley, London, 1965)

P. DOLLINGER, *The German Hansa* (London, 1970)

Appendix

The Battle of Morgarten. 1315.
(Translated from the Chronicle of John of Winterthur, ed. Baethgen, 1924, pp. 77ff.)

In the year of our Lord 1315 a certain rustic people living in the valleys called 'Swiz', which are almost surrounded by high mountains, denied Duke Leopold the obedience and payments and customary services that they owed him: they prepared to resist him, trusting in the

well-fortified strength of their mountains. Duke Leopold was enraged
at this and made no secret of the fact that he was assembling an army
which was to be ready by St Martin's Day [10 November]. He is said
to have mustered no less than twenty thousand men from the places
subject to him and from friendly-disposed neighbours: this army was
raised to defeat, despoil and subjugate the rebellious mountain folk.
The force collected by the Duke was a strong, determined body of
specially chosen well-trained troops, met together as one man to sub-
due and humiliate these rustics gathered within their wall of mountains.
To make certain of utterly defeating, capturing, destroying and des-
poiling the region, the Duke's soldiers were provided with cord and
ropes to assist them in carrying off sheep and cattle. When the news of
these preparations was known the inhabitants of the weaker places
were very frightened and they strengthened their defences with walls
and ditches and in every other possible way, and commended themselves to God by prayer, fasting and litanies. They 'possessed themselves beforehand of all the tops of the high mountains' [1] and the men
in those parts where the army was likely to pass were ordered 'to keep
watch where the way was narrow between the mountains'. They did as
was 'commanded them' and 'every man cried to God with great fer-
vency and with great vehemency did they humble their souls' in fasting
'both they and their wives' and they 'cried to God all with one consent
earnestly that he would not give their flocks for a prey and their wives
for a spoil, and their villages to destruction and their honour and virtue
to profanation'. They 'cried unto the Lord with all their power, that
he would look upon their people graciously', saying 'O Lord God of
heaven and earth, behold their pride, and pity the low estate of our
nation and show that thou forsakest not them that trust on thee, and
that thou humblest them that presume of themselves, and glory in their
own strength'. They also did penance and begged with all their might
for peace and forgiveness for their disobedience: this they did through
the offices of a certain Count of Toggenburg, a man noble both in body
and mind, who acted as arbiter and tried to make peace between the
two parties and to put an end to the quarrel. This Count worked hard
and faithfully in the interest of both sides, but he could make no headway with Duke Leopold, who was 'very wroth' with the Swiss 'and
his anger burned in him': he was unwilling to accept the humble terms
that they offered him through the Count of Toggenburg, as it was his
intention to destroy them and to scatter them with his forces. When
the Swiss heard this 'they were struck with great fear and trembling'.
And so the Swiss 'took up their weapons of war' and they remained

---

[1] Many phrases in this passage are biblical quotations or reminiscences, particularly from the book of *Judith*: these phrases are indicated by inverted commas.

'in those places where the passage was strait and they took mountainous paths, and watched all day and night'.

On St Othmar's Day Duke Leopold tried to advance with his army
into the area between a certain mountain and a lake called the *Egeri
See*, but was hindered by the height and steepness of the mountain.
Almost all the knights had thrust themselves eagerly to the fore in the
hope of gaining loot but, however daring their advance, it was completely impossible for them to climb the mountain on horseback;
indeed it was impossible even for the infantry to find a footing there.
The Swiss knew beforehand, through the Count, that this was the
direction from which the attack was coming and they realized that this
part was particularly difficult of access. They were much heartened,
and they now came down from their hiding-places, surrounded their
enemies till they were like fish caught in a net, and put them to slaughter
without meeting any resistance. They had no difficulty in finding a
footing on even the steepest slopes, where neither the enemy nor his
horses could stand at all, with the aid of certain iron contrivances with
chains[1] which they attached to their feet, as was their custom. Also the
Swiss were armed with a lethal kind of battleaxe which is called
'halberd' in the vernacular: with this terrifying weapon they could cut
up even well-armoured opponents as though with a razor, slicing them
in pieces. This was not a battle but rather, for the reasons that have
been given, it was a massacre of Duke Leopold's men who came 'like
sheep for the slaughter' to fall at the hands of the mountain folk. These
spared nobody and took no prisoners but 'smote them all until they
were dead'. Those who were not killed were drowned in the lake into
which they had plunged in the hope of swimming to the other side.
When the infantry heard their valiant knights being struck down in
such terrifying fashion by the Swiss some were so frightened and
driven out of their wits by fear of this horrifying death that they too
threw themselves into the lake, preferring to fling themselves into the
deep waters rather than fall into the hands of so dreadful an enemy. It
is said that fifteen hundred men fell 'by the sword' in this battle, apart
from those who were drowned in the lake. So many knights from the
territories around were killed that for some time afterwards there was
a lack of knights: almost all those who were killed were knights and
nobles who had been trained to arms from childhood. The troops who
were going into the attack by other approach routes avoided the blood-
stained hands of their enemy, because they 'fled for their lives' when
they heard of the ferocious slaughter that had taken place. A number of
men from the surrounding cities, towns and villages were killed, and
everywhere 'the voice of mirth and gladness' was silent and the only

[1] Crampons.

sound to be heard was 'lamentation and weeping'. From the town of Winterthur one man only was killed and he was one who had become separated from his fellows and had the misfortune to be with the cavalry: all the others returned home unharmed. Duke Leopold on his retreat was to be seen among these, looking half dead in his great distress. I saw this with my own eyes, for I was then a schoolboy away from home and I and the other schoolboys ran happily to watch from the town-gate. And indeed Duke Leopold had cause to look melancholy and afflicted, for he had lost the flower and strength of his army. All this happened on 15 November 1315 on St Othmar's day while the Duke's brother Frederick was in Austria. After the battle the Swiss took the weapons of the men who had been killed and drowned and whatever booty they could recover, so that they were greatly enriched in money and arms. They also proclaimed that the day was to be celebrated annually as a feast and holiday in perpetuity, on account of the victory granted them by God.

V

ECONOMIC SETBACKS AND DEVELOPMENTS
IN THE LATER MIDDLE AGES

ECONOMICS is the science of wealth and economic historians like to pose the all-important question of 'how much wealth?' Unfortunately this question, when asked of a medieval archive, will receive at the very best a murmured and ambiguous reply. This is in part the explanation of the fact that historians who have despaired of a reliable answer to this query have preferred instead to ask 'how?' and have come away with answers about such economic institutions as the manor and the gild.

The sources available for quantitative research into economic movements in the medieval period can only provide a discontinuous picture, a little clearer for some areas and periods than for others, but never really distinct. Occasionally statistics can be gained from Customs accounts—many of these are extant for English and Hanse ports for part of the fourteenth and fifteenth centuries—and some of the contemporary estimates of industrial production and of exports were probably based on official sources. Even the official evidence is difficult to interpret, particularly since it normally refers only to overseas trade in certain commodities. As the evidence for medieval prices and population is no less spasmodic than that for production and trade, the economist has none of his essential preliminary data in a secure form. This is not to imply that full statistics would eliminate controversy or that economic aspects are a particularly tenebrous and frustrating region of medieval history; on the contrary, the need to work from inadequate sources is the very essence of the study of these centuries, the only possible justification for the conventional division between 'medieval' and 'modern' history.

The specific difficulty, to come to the fourteenth century, is to decide whether the impression, gained by many who have investigated this period, that Europe's economy went through a time of serious, widespread and prolonged depression, is based on particular information that is indeed characteristic of a general situation. To end the long catalogue of preliminary cautions, one must emphasize the extreme rashness of generalizing about the economy of 'Europe', particularly at a time when the typical activity was the production of food for a local market. Regional conditions were all-important and, on the whole, difficulties, particularly of transport, caused different regions to be less interdependent than they were to become later.

The central period of the Middle Ages presents so clear-cut a picture of economic expansion that the warnings given above can easily be forgotten. It is evident that between the eleventh century and the thirteenth the population of Europe grew very considerably. New land was colonized and brought under cultivation on a very large scale, most notably in the 'frontier' territories of Germany east of the Elbe, but also on soil hitherto s purned as too densely wooded, too marshy or liable to flood, or in some other way too poor in quality to justify the expense of initial labour and capital. In the west the greatest areas were gained in low-lying Flanders, in the valley of the Po where a tremendous work of dyking and embanking was initiated, on the Atlantic coast of Gascony, and perhaps in the parts of Spain reconquered by the Christian kings. Whilst these *villes neuves* and colonized lands provided one outlet for the increasing population, many of the older towns were also growing rapidly. There are plentiful indications of the widespread extension of the practice of producing food and textiles for sale, rather than for local or seignorial consumption, expanding population having contributed to a considerable rise in the price of grain and other food. The boom did not, however, necessarily imply a rise in individual standards of living. More people survived, but they did so for the most part in extreme discomfort and poverty, on a diet that was little above subsistence level. Many of the peasants produced wheat that went to make bread for their lord—or for him to profit by its sale for consumption in a town—while they themselves ate coarser bread made from rye, barley or oats. In a bad year even this might be a luxury and acorns, normally valued as food for pigs, were not unaccustomed diet for humans in some parts of western Europe.

In the age of expansion long-distance maritime trade came to flourish on a considerable scale in both south and north. In the Mediterranean, Venice, Genoa and Pisa dominated western Europe's commercial link with Byzantium, Syria, Egypt and the lands beyond. In the North Sea the most active route lay between Bruges, London and the other English and Flemish ports of the 'narrows' in the south, while at the farther end of this axis were the Hanse towns of the Baltic and North Sea, exporting mainly the fish, furs, timber, wax and honey of the north, and east German grain, and receiving cloth from the west. The principal link between these two zones of maritime trade was by land, over the Brenner Pass from Venice or (for a larger proportion of goods) across the Alps and through eastern France, where lay the normal meeting-point for the merchants and financiers of the two regions, at the fairs of the Champagne. By the end of the thirteenth century this connection by land was coming to be superseded by the sea-route through the Pillars of Hercules, which was regularly employed by Genoese galleys from the year 1298. The main industry feeding long-distance commerce was cloth manufacture, situated principally in the Low Countries and Tuscany, and dyes concerned with this industry, as well as alum, the essential mordant for them, were other commodities of major importance. Other textiles (silk and cotton) and metals (in particular iron) were wares of note, and the foodstuff that ranked second only to grain was wine, much of which was shipped along a route lying outside those mentioned above, the export area being Gascony (with Bordeaux as its principal port) and the main recipient England, which was French in tastes but too northerly to have many vineyards of its own.[1]

These major trade-routes are those most easily investigated and they have tended to monopolize the attention of historians. It by no means follows that they occupied the energies of more men at the time or even that more money was made from them. There was a great deal of local trade by land, centred on fairs and

[1] Froissart reports the men of Bordeaux as saying: 'We have more commerce with the English than French, in wool, wines, and cloth, and they are naturally more inclined to us.' (*Chronicle*, trans. Johnes, IV, 677.)

markets dealing mainly in agrarian produce and craftsmen's wares, and trade by sea also was not confined to the great convoys of the Levant and Baltic. Local 'coasters' plied down and across the Adriatic, based on Venice and elsewhere, and the Tyrrhenian ports—less conveniently placed for oriental commerce—did much of their trade between Provence in the north (with an occasional extension into Catalonia) and Sicily in the south. Thus Porto-venere, a small place between Genoa and Pisa, traded entirely within the Tyrrhenian, principally with Sardinia, sometimes with Corsica, Pisa, or the small grain-ports north-west of Rome, more rarely farther south to Naples and Sicily. Sicily, an exporter of grain and other food (see above, p. 47) was a considerable importer of textiles, and around the middle of the thirteenth century an enterprising Pisan, Lazario Talliapanis, made a considerable fortune largely through the export of hats to Sicily. Lazario was farmer, industrialist and merchant; the hats were manufactured by him from the wool of his own sheep. Men such as he were famous for their business acumen and the speed with which they became rich, and the *Novellino*, a thirteenth-century collection of stories, preserves one far-fetched tale from the many that must have been told about the methods of these parvenu millionaires:

> A merchant was voyaging with hats. They got wet and he laid them out to dry. A lot of monkeys appeared and each one put a hat on its head and ran up into the trees. This seemed a grievous matter to the merchant. He went back and bought breeches and thus he regained the caps [presumably the monkeys put on the breeches, which made them less agile] and made a good profit on them.[1]

A man like Lazario Talliapanis, however, would not normally have travelled with his own wares. It is characteristic of a great change in commercial and financial methods that by the thirteenth century the 'merchant' himself was normally no longer peripatetic; he left the conduct of his affairs in distant markets to representatives. These might be factors employed solely by him, like the men paid by the Tuscan and other bankers to staff their various branches; the Bardi of Florence alone had twenty-five branches in the early fourteenth century, and such employment was a common way to start on a business career. On the other

[1] *Il Novellino*, n. XCVIII (adapted from the translation of E. Storer).

hand it was also habitual for a merchant to make use on a commission basis of the services of an agent residing abroad who was
also acting for a number of other men or firms. The introduction
of bills of exchange facilitated the technique of the 'sedentary'
financier by obviating the need to move currency in specie. This
development, as well as the increasing use of the sea-route through
the Strait of Gibraltar, played a part in the rapid decline of the
Champagne fairs after about 1320. Earlier, these fairs had been
primarily occasions for dealing in commodities; now that their
business was mainly financial and that the Italian bankers had
branches established at Bruges it was no longer necessary to have
a meeting-place halfway between Europe's two zones of maritime
trade.

During the first half of the fourteenth century the movement of
economic expansion was checked in many parts of Europe. The
process of extending the area of land under cultivation may have
come to an end in France and southern England as early as the
middle of the previous century, but clear signs that a depression
had set in in some sectors of the European economy date from
about a quarter way through the fourteenth. Malthus-fashion,
the population of certain parts of Europe had so out-stripped food
supplies that a series of poor harvests brought about appalling
famines. These were followed by epidemics of bubonic plague
(of which the most serious was the 'Black Death' of 1348-9), and
recovery was further hampered by widespread warfare associated
with the dislocation of economic life and with heavy taxation.
Evidence, particularly concerning the movements of Swiss
glaciers, suggests that there may also have been climatic deterioration, with colder weather.

The story should perhaps begin with the famines of 1315-17,
which affected all northern and eastern Europe and parts of the
Mediterranean region. Three successive bad harvests (1314-16)
led to a disastrous shortage of grain in Scandinavia, the Slav
countries, Germany, Flanders, France, Britain and northern Italy.
The price of grain in England rose from five shillings a quarter in
1313 to 26s. 8d. in 1315 and at Antwerp the price tripled in a
period of seven months. Animals became scarce and sober
chroniclers record appalling stories of cannibalism. The situation

was most acute in the Low Countries, where the numerous towns were normally dependent on grain imports from northern France and eastern Germany. During the summer of 1316 more than three thousand people—about one-tenth of the population—died in Ypres alone.

All the chronicles of the time record the same story, and two may serve as exemplars:

> In the year of Our Lord 1316 famine, hunger and great mortality prevailed. A *modius* of spelt was then worth 4 of the large, old shillings (*solidi*) or more.

> So great was the universal pestilence that many corpses of poor people who had died of hunger or plague were to be found lying in the roadways, and a number of towns had general pits dug in the cemeteries and fixed the dues to be paid for burial of such corpses in these.[1]

Plague and famine were allies, for fields and flocks were neglected in time of epidemic (see below, pp. 113–14), while undernourishment weakened resistance to disease. Both were in turn assisted by war, which is the hardest to assess of all these factors. There seems to be a consensus of opinion that warfare was more continuous in Europe during the fourteenth century and the first half of the fifteenth than during the preceding two centuries, and that the wars of this period were more ruinous in their economic consequences. But these things cannot be measured and such an impression is not susceptible of demonstration; the evidence is so piecemeal that it must be presented merely as an impression. Campaigns were normally brief and confined to the summer months, but companies of unemployed mercenaries lived off the land even in peace. The most usual way to harm an enemy was to damage his crops—no misconception about the past is so fatuous as the belief that military action against civilians is an invention of the twentieth century—so that even a short campaign might mean a year of starvation. The Hundred Years War certainly involved larger bodies of troops and wrought enormous destruction in parts of France between the early fourteenth century and the mid-fifteenth, and the belief that the quantity or

---

[1] *Die Chronik der Grafen von der Mark von Levold von Northof*, ed. Zschaeck, Mon. Germ. Hist., N.S., VI, p. 67: *Gesta Trevirorum*, ed. Wyttenbach and Müller, II, 235.

Excavation on the site of the battlefield of Aljubarrota (1385) in
Portugal, showing pits probably dug by English archers
See Chapter VII

A tournament. From an illustration to Froissart's *Chronicle*
See Chapter VII

volume of warfare increased at this time is based mainly on that prolonged struggle and on the Hussite and other wars in eastern Europe. The appalling condition of France during the Hundred Years War and the despair to which it gave rise can be seen in this extract from the diary of a Frenchman for 1422:

> *Item*, the King of England was at this time before Meaux and he spent the New Year and Epiphany there. His men were all over the region of Brie and were pillaging everywhere, so that on account of them and the others [Burgundians] it was impossible to till the soil or sow anywhere. Many were the complaints to these lords [the English], but they only mocked and laughed, and their men behaved worse even than before. Most of the peasants abandoned work in the fields and were in despair. They left their wives and children and said to one another: 'What shall we do? Let us give everything over into the hands of the devil, for it cannot matter what becomes of us. To do our worst will profit us as much as doing our best. The Saracens would treat us better than the Christians do, and we may as well do our worst, they cannot do more than kill us or make us prisoners. Thanks to the false government of traitors we have had to leave our wives and children and flee to the woods like lost animals. This has not lasted one year or two; the tragic dance began as long as fourteen or fifteen years ago. . . .[1]

Moving from the north-east of France to the south-west, to consider the effects of the hostilities in the area around Bordeaux, one finds that much land was abandoned at times, particularly in the zone of the French-Gascon frontier, whence many peasants fled to the towns. There were severe epidemics in Gascony in 1348, 1362, 1410–11 and 1414. The first of these was preceded by campaigning and famine, and by 1349–50 wine exports from Bordeaux had diminished to a quarter of the average figures for the first third of the century. A recovery followed in the 1350s and '60s, but 1373 was another year of famine and 1374–9 a period of intensive fighting, during which much land was deserted. When the war ended in the mid-fifteenth century the frontier zone of the Entre-deux-Mers (the wine-growing region between the Garonne and the Dordogne) had declined greatly, and here in particular many houses and fields were abandoned.

[1] *Journal d'un Bourgeois de Paris sous Charles VI et Charles VII*, ed. A. Mary (Paris, 1929), pp. 154–5.

H

Most of the seignorial families of the area had suffered through
the loss of land by confiscation (even a general willingness to
change sides did not make it possible to be always on the side that
was winning), and through the need to alienate land to supporters
and to diminish the services of the hard-pressed peasantry. Con-
fiscations meant frequent changes of ownership, and a general loss
of confidence must also have served to discourage enterprising
cultivation. Even after the end of the war recovery was slow, and
Gascony was treated by the French monarchs as a defeated colony
rather than as a recovered province. In that region the greatest
change wrought by the war was the decline of the nobility, but
this was probably untypical of France as a whole. There may
have been some truth in the view of the Englishman Fortescue
(expressed in 1465) that the French peasants lived in misery 'in
the most fertile kingdom in the world'.

The case of Gascony shows clearly how a single wave of
devastation was not by itself the cause of serious economic
decline: permanent setback followed only when a prolonged
series of campaigns and military occupations deprived an area of
the means or even the will to restore ravaged fields and to rebuild.
Probably the loss of a year's harvest, appalling though its effects
may have been, was less lasting in its consequences than loss of
livestock. Medieval soldiers, living admittedly off the land, were
likely to take every opportunity of supplementing their 'rations'
off the hoof. It would have been difficult to keep armies adequately fed by any other means, and a meal could be made off
local livestock far more quickly and easily than off local stores of
grain. Enormous damage must have been done in this way, and
the soldiery, it may be supposed, gave no thought to the problem
of the priority of chicken or egg, but made away with the
chickens at the expense of their own future consumption of eggs.
The countryside had to bear the burden not only of soldiers
employed in campaigns against the forces of an enemy, but also of
temporarily unemployed bands of 'adventurers' organized to exploit the possibilities of a parasitic way of life. The consequences
of such a situation may be studied in Froissart's account of the
activities of Marcel in south-western France during the period
midway between Edward III's and Henry V's French campaigns
(below, pp. 114–15).

Heavy taxation was another consequence of war, but this would not necessarily fall on the areas in which fighting was taking place —indeed the sufferings of these regions and the need of governments to retain their loyalty meant that the burden was likely to be heavier elsewhere. Nor is it easy to judge who was ultimately the poorer through heavier taxation. England's expenditure on the Hundred Years War was met to a considerable extent by heavy Customs duties on the export of wool. In the early phases of the war the burden of these seems to have fallen mainly on the English graziers, but after the middle of the fourteenth century the price of English wool on the Continent rose considerably, and it appears that Flanders was by then paying much of the cost of England's war.

Whatever the sequence of causes may have been, it is clear that the period of demographic growth had come to an end in many parts of Europe before the Black Death of 1348–9 and that this disaster merely accentuated an existing trend. Conservative estimates suggest that in the worst-hit areas the population was diminished by more than a quarter by this epidemic, and that later outbreaks prevented the achievement of a significant recovery during the next twenty years. Gascony's deserted villages had their counterparts in many other places at this time. It is never possible to be certain to what extent this phenomenon represents migration to other places—in particular to towns—for we have extremely few figures for population at this time, but it is surely significant that in the fourteenth century, for the first time since the later Carolingian period, there is much evidence of rural depopulation, coming from widely separated areas in Scandinavia, Germany, France, England and Italy.[1] The figures in table 1, relating to some of the few towns for which we possess estimates, suggest that depopulation in the countryside cannot be explained in terms of migration into the cities.[2]

[1] One example from central Italy will serve as an instance. A tax register of 1426 concerning the 'district' (the area within 100 miles radius of the city) of Rome records 105 villages as 'destroyed and uninhabited'. (*Archivio della Società Romana di Storia Patria*, XLIX (1926), 331–54.)

[2] Sources: *Cambridge Economic History of Europe*, II, 339. P. Wolff, *Commerces et Marchands de Toulouse*, pp. 68–86. For Barcelona *v.* J. Vicens Vives (ed.) *Historia Social y Economica de España y America*, II, 51–2: these figures are affected by the revolution of 1477 and by the growth of Valencia from a city of *c.* 40,000 in 1418 to *c.* 75,000 in 1483.

Table 1

	1335	1350	1367	1379	1385	1385-6	1398	1405	1468	1500
Freiburg im Breisgau	—	—	—	—	9,000	—	—	—	—	6,000
Zürich	—	12,000	—	—	—	—	—	—	5,000	—
Montpellier	—	—	22,500	5,000	—	—	—	—	—	—
Toulouse	30,000	—	—	—	—	26,000	24,000	22,500	—	—

	1326	1338	1351	1379	1380	1462	1477	1482	1497	1526
Perpignan	—	—	—	18,000	—	—	—	—	15,500	—
Modena	22,000	—	—	—	—	—	—	8,000–9,000	—	—
Florence	—	110,000	45,000–50,000	—	70,000	—	—	—	—	70,000
Barcelona	—	—	—	38,500	—	38,000	20,000	—	29,000	—
Lerida	—	—	—	6,000	—	—	—	—	3,500	—
Tarragona	—	—	—	5,500	—	—	—	—	4,500	—

In some well-documented sectors the nature of Europe's economic setbacks is at least clearer than their causes, though even here the evidence is often ambiguous. After the famines of 1314–16 the price of grain fell in France and England to a level considerably lower than that prevailing in the early years of the century. The fall in prices was in turn reflected in manorial profits, and the value of land naturally fell in sympathy.[1] Such a decline is recorded in various parts of England and France and Scandinavia and was probably widespread, as grain-farming for the market was increasingly abandoned. Again it must be emphasized that collective contraction did not necessarily imply individual impoverishment. Men who might otherwise have worked for wages took up farms, and the consequent relative shortage of wage-labour caused a marked rise in wages. In agriculture, as in industry, there is no evidence of a fall in output per head, and it was on this that standards of living depended.

Cloth production in Flanders is another instance of fourteenth-century decline. This major industry was largely dependent on exports of raw wool from England, which fell fairly steeply in the second half of the century, as may be seen from the following table:[2]

1350–60 : (average in sacks *per annum*) over 30,000
1380–90 : *c.* 20,000 sacks *p.a.*
after 1393: never above 20,000 sacks *p.a.*

Exports of English cloth rose considerably during the same period (the average for the 1390s being roughly treble that for the years 1360–80) and it seems clear that the main explanation of the decline of the Flemish industry lies in the growth of cloth-making in England. It is not, however, possible to tell whether there was an overall decline in English wool production, as there are no reliable figures for the amount of English cloth consumed in the home market during the fifteenth century. The Flemish had to compete with the Italians for English wool, and suffered from

---

[1] For English corn prices see *Cambridge Economic History of Europe*, II, 205. For English examples of declining manorial profits and land values, E. Miller, *The Abbey and Bishopric of Ely*, p. 105, and F. G. Davenport, *The Economic Development of a Norfolk Manor*, pp. 55 and 78–9.

[2] *Cambridge Economic History of Europe*, II, 192: cf. E. M. Carus-Wilson, *Medieval Merchant Venturers*, p. xviii and graph.

English fiscal policy, which alternated embargoes on export to north-western Europe with high export duties. English exploitation during the French wars of Flemish dependence on English wool involved rapid fluctuations for the textile industry and, in particular, periods of disastrous unemployment. The Flemish craftsmen reacted to this by attempting to wrest political and industrial control from their employers—the anti-French revolution of 1302 has been mentioned above (pp. 58–9) and there were further serious risings in 1324–8 and 1379–82—and this unrest must in turn have affected unfavourably Flemish ability to compete with Italy and England. The textile industry of the Low Countries is typical, however, in that it presents no simple picture of all-round regression: the decline of the Walloon towns, such as Arras, Lille and Douai, coincided with the rise in Brabant of Brussels, Louvain and Malines, and increased exports from Bruges to both north-eastern Europe and the Mediterranean may have offset the decline of the French market.

Italy also experienced some marked industrial and commercial setbacks during the fourteenth century. Florence suffered severely in the 1340s through the bankruptcy of the Bardi and Peruzzi, involving the fall of almost all the other important Florentine banking companies, and in the ensuing period the Italians were to lose the near-monopoly in European finance that had been gained by their commercial advantages and precocious techniques. Local bankers appeared and sapped the position of the Italians in many parts of Europe, particularly in economically advanced areas such as Flanders, England and France. At the same time Florentine cloth manufacture, which had enjoyed primacy in the peninsula in the production of high-quality materials for export, began to experience change. Giovanni Villani, who was not an official writer but probably made use of official sources, puts Florence's annual output of cloth at the beginning of the fourteenth century at 100,000 pieces. Thirty years later, he says, the quantity of the city's production had fallen by about one-quarter, but owing to the use of better wool—from England—the *value* of the output had greatly increased.[1] But the Florentine clothiers, like the bankers, were challenged by new rivals, this time in the peninsula

---

[1] G. Villani, *Cronica*, Bk. XI, ch. 94. (It is of course possible that Villani's is not the true, or full, explanation of this change.)

itself. Local industry developed in other Tuscan towns, in Venetia (particularly at Padua), and in Lombardy. The rise of these Italian centres was probably largely responsible for a marked decline in Florentine production in the century after Villani's later figures: by the early fifteenth century output had fallen to about 30,000 pieces a year, and no firm recovery was made after that time.

This age of economic setback and change was also an age of popular unrest, of revolts by the 'blue-nails' in Flanders and the *Ciompi* at Florence, of *Jacqueries* in France and the English Peasants' Revolt. There is clearly a connection between the developments described above and these democratic movements. The weakening of manorialism and consequent demands for the end of villeinage lie behind the English revolt of 1381, while the French risings were directly connected with that country's sufferings during the Hundred Years War. As for the movements of the clothmaking proletariat, these had led to violence in Flanders and some parts of Italy well before the close of the thirteenth century. Serious troubles at Siena (in 1329 and 1342) preceded the first momentous impact of democratic feeling on Florentine politics, the achievement of a temporary tyranny with popular backing by the Frenchman Walter of Brienne (1342–3). Brienne gave the textile workers, or *sottoposti*, some share in the city's government, but after his fall they lost this position. The Black Death led to an improvement in their pay, thanks to the drastic decline in Florence's population, but an expensive war against the papacy in the mid-1370s aggravated fiscal grievances and discontent with the narrow oligarchic régime of the Albizzi. This was a time of popular movements in a number of central Italian towns: the *popolo minuto* came to power at Lucca in 1369, at Siena in 1371, at Perugia in 1372. The programme of the Florentine *Ciompi* in 1378 shows clearly enough what the textile workers wanted. The right to organize their own gilds ranked first in their list of demands, followed by freedom from prison-sentences for small debts of the type that they were liable to contract to money-lenders during periods of unemployment. They asked for a lower rate of interest on the *Monte* (the state funds) probably in the hope of stimulating investment in industrial plant as well as diminishing 'unearned income'. For a time the Ciompi gained control in

Florence and new gilds were formed of dyers, shirt-makers and the undifferentiated *popolo minuto*, but the employers were later successful—partly through a lock-out—in effecting a division between the moderates of the movement and the extremists. In this classic dilemma the now isolated Ciompi lost their control of the city, and the position of the Florentine workers worsened considerably in the ensuing period. Both in urban Flanders and at Florence the root of the troubles was the existence of a large body of proletarian labour, employed by the day and therefore utterly at the mercy of fluctuating economic conditions, and denied the right to organize in its own interest by masters who held the reins of political power. There were indeed a very few Italian towns, such as Venice and Verona, which permitted the formation by *sottoposti* of *scholae* or confraternities. Normally, however, any institution of this sort was regarded with fear and horror by the authorities. There is a parallel between the struggle of these workers for the right to organize against town merchant oligarchies and the conflict of the English trade unionists with a national trading oligarchy between the First and Third Reform Acts.

The greatest difficulty in attempting to decide whether or not to accept the thesis of a 'secular slump' is that a story of success can be set beside almost every story of decline, and that there is inadequate information to measure the two against each other. Just as Brabant gained at the expense of southern Flanders, so Antwerp came forward to take the place of Bruges, now affected by silting as well as by the decline of its industrial hinterland. When the German Hanse lost its near-monopoly of Baltic and Scandinavian trade the beneficiaries from the later fourteenth century were the English, and in the mid-fifteenth the Dutch, both of whom exploited skilfully the conflicting interests of the Hanseatic ports. New towns were also coming to the fore in south Germany and Switzerland as industrial and commercial centres, notably Augsburg and Nuremburg, and Pisa's sharp decline was connected with the rise of Marseilles and of Barcelona, which in turn lost ground to Valencia. In England Lincoln and some other wool-marketing towns fell on hard times, but Hull advanced as a cloth port, and new industrial areas emerged in East Anglia, in Gloucestershire, Wiltshire and Somerset, and at Coventry. In

Italy Lucca and the south lost their quasi-monopoly of silk manufacture at the same time as the Florentines were yielding their unrivalled primacy in cloth: Milan, Venice, Genoa, Bologna and Florence all had considerable silk industries by the end of the fourteenth century. In Florence itself new banking houses came to the fore after the collapse of the Bardi and Peruzzi, among them that of the city's future rulers. In 1373 Foligno dei Medici wrote pessimistically of his family's decline from its former greatness: 'so great were we once', he records, 'that there used to be a saying "You are like one of the Medici"; every man feared us'. In Foligno's day the many branches of the family were concerned principally with agriculture, but Veri di Cambio (who retired in 1392) was a wealthy financier. He it was who trained Giovanni di Bicci, who founded the fortunes of the Medici Bank in Rome in the 1390s. Early in the following century the Bank had its headquarters at Florence, with branches at Rome and Venice, and by the time of Giovanni's death (1429) the Medici were the papacy's principal financiers. Until the mid-1470s they normally retained this position, which brought them immense prestige and gained for them the task of organizing the housing and financing of the many ecclesiastical Councils of the period. Under Cosimo, Giovanni's son, there were also permanent branches at Pisa, Milan, Geneva, Avignon, Bruges and London. This international structure was of immense assistance to the Medici when they became, after 1434, *de facto* rulers of Florence; they were able, for example, to obtain rapid news from all parts of Europe through the firm's own channels. Nor were Cosimo's commercial activities confined to banking; he was involved in the textile industry and he dealt in commodities, particularly alum. In the diversity of his interests Cosimo was a characteristic figure. Specialization in economic activity dates from a much later period, and at this time it was normal throughout Europe for such men with predominantly urban backgrounds and interests to enjoy at the same time considerable agrarian incomes. Only in Italy, however, were these sources of revenue supplemented by interest derived from holdings in government stock.

The history of the Medici is an important part of Europe's political and cultural history, and as such we shall have to return to it in a later chapter (Chapter XI). A glance at the careers of two fifteenth-century Venetian businessmen may illustrate better how enterprising people could flourish in an age when the total volume of Mediterranean commerce may well have been contracting. Andrea Barbarigo (1399–1449) came of a family which had connections and estates in Crete, but his recorded dealings relate mainly to trade in other parts. At one stage he is to be found buying cotton through an agent at Acre, but he quarrelled with this agent and then suffered through a dispute with the Sultan which interrupted trade with Syria. After this affair Andrea turned to Valencia, whence he shipped Spanish wool and olive oil to Venice. Shortly after this he was doing business in England, where he sold gold thread and pepper and bought cloth. At the same time as he suffered by the Sultan's embargo he experienced similar difficulties in southern Germany, where political troubles led to the closing of the main land-route between Venice and the north of Europe. These problems and Andrea's readiness to switch his interests rapidly from one foreign market to another illustrate both the advantages of Venice's position as a centrally-placed 'universal middleman' and the knowledge and judgment required to make correct decisions involving distant countries in times of great economic and political fluctuations. It was the very essence of the methods of such men that they were not specialists and that they could shift their interests constantly while retaining the support of the system of galley convoys organized and controlled by the Venetian state.

Barbarigo's descendants drew out of mercantile affairs and lived mainly on the proceeds of the estates bought by Andrea on the Italian mainland near Treviso and Verona. It was a time of constant warfare between Venice and Milan, and they suffered heavily when these lands underwent enemy occupation. Nor was the later fifteenth century a good period for holders of government bonds, and this was another source of worry to the Barbarigo, though some of the family benefited from salaries earned as state officials in Venetian territories overseas and in the expanding empire on the *Terraferma*.

The activities of Barbarigo's contemporary Guglielmo Querini (*c*. 1400–68) show a close resemblance to those of Andrea. Like Barbarigo, he himself played a sedentary role in Venice, at least from his adult years. He, too, did much business in Italy, some of it almost locally. When he ranged farther afield, it was sometimes to Spain, sometimes to England and Flanders, sometimes to Greece and the Levant. The pattern is not entirely the same, however: Querini traded at Geneva and in southern France, and his most original line was the sale of Sicilian grain at Tunis and on the island of Djerba. These men benefited immensely from their city's Mediterranean empire (see above, Chapter II) and a policy which insisted that all export from that empire must be to Venice and on Venetian vessels. The city probably drew about one-fifth of its own grain supplies from its dominions, as well as wine, honey, cheese and oil, cotton, alum, iron, wax and timber. Most of its imported grain came from non-Venetian territory such as Southern Russia and Thrace, and through the Levant came silk, spices, dyes and slaves. Thus the main role of the ports of Venice's empire, even of Candia, was to serve as *entrepôts*, and bases and points of call for the galleys. They constituted a defensive system for the maritime routes thanks to which these versatile Venetian patricians were able to retain their prosperity.

In the final analysis the problem of Europe's wealth in the later Middle Ages should be judged in relation to agriculture, for this was the pursuit of by far the biggest element in the population. Yet here we return to the difficulty that changes in organization are far more certain than changes in wealth. It is clear that in most parts of Europe there was a decline in seignorial authority, that lords tended increasingly to become *rentiers*, particularly when labour shortage, after the Black Death, made domain farming dearer. In western Germany this change was accentuated by unsettled political conditions, for lords frequently alienated their lands to pay for soldiers or else lost them to bailiffs. However the *rentier* solution characteristic of England, France and western Germany was not universal, and in the corn-exporting areas of east Germany and Prussia the knightly class was building up its domains and turning to farming in earnest, while many of the peasantry suffered eviction. If the period was marked by an increased proportion of payments in money, there was certainly no abandonment of payments in kind, indeed one form of this, *métayage* (share-cropping) was becoming more common. When payments were made in money, much depended on the frequency with which dues could be increased in times of rising prices; the impoverished nobles were those who could not change rents often enough. Their decline must have been made more conspicuous by the ascent of the most assiduous and fortunate among the peasantry.

Some historians have seen the fourteenth century as a time of economic tragedy, the fifteenth as one of recovery. The rise of the Lombard textile industry provides one clear instance. By the 1420s Venice was importing more cloth from Lombardy than from Florence. Moreover the cultivation of rice and of mulberries was now first undertaken on a large scale in the Po valley, where a great deal of land was reclaimed. Between 1439 and 1475 fifty-five miles of canals, with twenty-five locks, were constructed in the plain south of Milan, and this is but one of many striking instances of fifteenth century technological progress, to be found in both southern and northern Europe, in shipbuilding, in the use of water-power and in the mining and processing of metals. Nor were the successful financiers of fifteenth-century Italy all Florentines: apart from the Genoese, one may mention the Sienese Chigi and the Borromeo, Tuscans turned Milanese. Yet the peninsula had owed its economic primacy above all to its position in the Mediterranean, and it is unlikely that in the fifteenth century the total volume of sea-trade in the Mediterranean increased. That this was the situation is strongly suggested by the failure of the Pisan galleys. Florence acquired this long-coveted port in 1406 and soon attempted to organize convoys of galleys there after the Venetian model. The scheme took twenty years to get under way, it was immensely subsidized, and yet by 1480 it had been virtually abandoned.

It seems unlikely that the fifteenth century marked a general recovery in the north. The misery of Prussia in this period has already been noted, as has the general decline of the German Hanse in the face of the challenge of the English and Dutch. In England land values continued to fall and the enclosure of land for sheep farming brought a new form of unrest. One northern area to achieve a very marked advance in maritime trade during the last quarter of the century was Normandy, and this development is significant both because it signalizes France's recovery after the Hundred Years War and because Normandy soon began to look to the west, to Spain and the New World, rather than to the north.

Are we, then, to accept the view that the economy of Europe in the later Middle Ages underwent a 'secular crisis'? The evidence discussed above suggests that it should rather be considered as passing through a series of set-backs and changes—troubles that may indeed also have marked the ill-documented earlier centuries of expansion. For all the calamities of famine and disease, there was never a breakdown in the fabric of commercial interdependence. That local specialization could make new advances in this age is shown by the gains of the salt trade of the Bay of Bourgneuf, on the Atlantic coast of France, which now achieved the leading position in the English market, at the expense of native English salt. Historical research has illuminated great changes in Europe's economy in the first half of the fourteenth century. Further investigation may make it possible to decide whether or not this was followed by a long period of general economic contraction.

Further Reading

The Cambridge Economic History of Europe, Vols. I, II, III (Cambridge, 1952–66). Vol. I is concerned with agriculture, Vol. II with trade and industry, Vol. III with organisation and policies.

G. LUZZATTO, *An Economic History of Italy* (London, 1961)

R. DE ROOVER, *The Medici Bank* (New York, 1948): a fuller version by the same author is *The Rise and Decline of the Medici Bank* (Cambridge Mass., 1963)

E. POWER and M. POSTAN (eds.), *Studies in English Trade in the Fifteenth Century* (London, 1933)

G. DUBY, *Rural Economy and Country Life in the Medieval West* (London, 1968)

(Studies of particular towns include H. VAN WERVEKE, *Gand,* Brussels, 1946; J. SCHNEIDER, *La Ville de Metz aux 13e et 14e siècles,* Nancy, 1950; D. HERLIHY, *Pisa in the early Renaissance,* New Haven, 1958 and *Medieval and Renaissance Pistoia,* New Haven, 1967; J. HEERS, *Gênes au 15e siècle,* Paris, 1961; G. A. BRUCKER, *Renaissance Florence,* Wiley paperbacks, N.Y., 1969)

Appendix

The Black Death in Tuscany, 1348.

(Boccaccio, *Decameron,* Introduction to the First Day: partly taken from an anonymous translation of 1620.)

Now, because I would wander no further in every particularity concerning the miseries happening in our city, I tell you that, extremities running on in such manner as you have heard, little less spare was made in the villages round about; wherein (setting aside enclosed castles which were like cities in little) poor labourers and husbandmen, with their whole families, died most miserably in out-houses, yca in the open fields also; without any assistance of physic or help of servants; and likewise in the highways, or their ploughed lands, by day or night indifferently, yet not as men, but like brute beasts. By means whereof they became lazy and slothful in their daily endeavours, even like to our citizens; not minding or meddling with their wonted affairs, but as a waiting for death every hour, employed all their pains, not in caring any way for themselves, their cattle, or gathering the fruit of the earth, or any of their accustomed labours; but rather wasted and consumed even such as were for their instant sustenance. Whereupon it so fell out that their oxen, asses, sheep and goats, the swine, poultry, yea their very dogs, the truest and faithfullest servant to men, being beaten and banished from their houses, went wildly wandering abroad the fields, where the corn still grew on the ground without gathering or being so much as reaped or cut. Many of the foresaid beasts (as endued with reason) after they had pastured themselves in the day time would return full fed at night home to their houses, without any government of herdsmen or any other.

To leave the country now and return to the city, what more can I say? Such was the cruelty of heaven, and perhaps in part that of men too, that between March and July, owing to the illness itself and the abandonment or neglect of many of the sick by those who were afraid to approach them, it is thought that certainly more than a hundred thousand people died within the walls of Florence. Before the plague many might not have known that the population of the city amounted to so many.

How many fair palaces! How many goodly houses! How many noble habitations, filled before with families or lords and ladies, were then to be seen empty, without any one there dwelling, without even a silly servant? How many kindreds worthy of memory! How many great inheritances! And what plenty of riches; were left without any true successors? How many good men! How many worthy women! How many valiant and comely young men, whom not even Galen, Hippocrates, and Aesculapius (if they were living) could have reputed any way unhealthful; were seen to dine at morning with their parents, friends and familiar confederates, and went to sup in another world with their predecessors?

Aymergot Marcel in the Rouergue, 1391.
(From Froissart's Chronicle, Book IV, chapter 15: based on Johnes' translation).

Aymergot Marcel was sore displeased with himself in that he had

sold and delivered the strong castle of Aloise: for he saw his own
authority thereby greatly abated, and perceived well how he was the
less feared. For all the season that he kept it he was doubted and
feared, and honoured with all men of war of his part, and had kept
great state always in the castle of Aloise: the composition of countries
that he held under subjection was well worth yearly twenty thousand
florins. When he remembered all this he was sorrowful; his treasure he
thought he would not diminish; he was wont daily to search for new
pillages, whereby he increased his profit, and then he saw that all was
closed from him. Then he said and imagined that to pillage and to rob,
all things considered, was a good life, and so repented him of his good
doing. On a time he said to his old companions: Sirs, there is no
sport nor glory in this world among men of war, but to use such life
as we have done in time past; what a joy was it to us when we rode
forth at adventure and sometimes found by the way a rich prior or
merchant, or a troop of muleteers of Montpellier, of Narbonne, of
Limoges, of Fougans, of Béziers, of Toulouse, or of Carcassonne,
laden with cloth of Brussels, or leatherware, coming from the fairs, or
laden with spicery from Bruges, from Damascus, or from Alexandria,
whatsoever we met all was ours, or else ransomed at our pleasures;
daily we got new money and the villeins of Auvergne and of Limousin
daily provided and brought to our castle wheat meal, bread ready baked,
oats for our horses, and straw, good wines, beef and fat mutton,
poultry and wildfowl: we were ever furnished as though we had been
kings: when we rode forth all the country trembled for fear, all was
ours going or coming. . . .

. . . Then Aymergot viewed the place to see if it were worth the
fortifying thereof: and when he had well viewed the situation thereof,
and the defences that might be made there, it pleased him right well.
Thus they took it and fortified it little by little, before they began to do
any displeasure in the country: and when they saw the place strong
sufficiently to resist against siege or assault, and that they were well
horsed, and well provided of all things necessary for their defence, then
they began to ride abroad in the country, and took prisoners and ransomed them, and provided their stronghold with flesh, meal, wax, wine,
salt, iron and steel and of all other necessaries; there came nothing
amiss to them without it had been too heavy or too hot. The country
all about, and the people, thinking to have been in rest and peace by
reason of the truce made between the two kings and their realms, they
began then to be sore abashed: for these robbers and pillagers took them
in their houses, and where soever they found them, in the fields
labouring; and they called themselves adventurers.

VI

THE TROUBLES OF THE ROMAN CHURCH

THE domicile of the papacy beyond the Alps between 1305 and 1377 marks no sudden break. Since the 1240s residence in Rome had been exceptional and the sojourns at Lyons of Innocent IV (1244-51) and Gregory X (1273-5) had shown that the pope could continue his functions outside Italy. The Avignon papacy does, however, mark with topographical incontrovertibility the triumph in the Curia of the French element which had become so powerful since the election of Urban IV and the triumph of Charles of Anjou (see above, pp. 37-40).

On 5 June 1305 the conclave gathered at Perugia elected as pope Bertrand de Got, a Gascon who was archbishop of Bordeaux. Four days later the cardinals wrote to Bertrand in terms which reveal their realization that Clement V might wish to reside outside Italy. 'There can be no doubt', they argued, 'that the see of Peter will be a stronger residence for you and that you will shine there more resplendently, and will be able to live more tranquilly in his territory. If you are farther from kings, princes and their subjects, they will think more highly of you and you will gain greater devotion and obedience from them, for everyone is stronger in his own house than elsewhere and finds sweeter repose in his own church. The part of the sword that cuts deepest is that which is furthest from the hilt: what is seen often is despised and what is easily reached and attained is little esteemed. Come, then, and we pray you again that your benignity should yield on this point to our prayers.' Clement was reminded that Clement IV and Gregory X, the last two popes to be elected when outside Italy, had rapidly made their way to the peninsula, and yet again asked 'to prepare yourself for the journey to the apostolic see'.[1]

[1] Mansi, *Sacrorum conciliorum nova et amplissima collectio*, XXV, cols. 125-8.

The terms of the cardinals' letter show their implicit acceptance of the fact that relations with Philip IV of France would take precedence on the new pope's agenda. The main reason for this was the unresolved conflict which had reached its climax at Anagni in 1303; the cardinals of 1305 were sharply divided between protagonists of Boniface and Philip, and the latter still awaited a reply to his request for the calling of a General Council which should pronounce on Boniface's deeds and his doctrines. But there were also important secondary considerations. The French crown, by far the greatest power in the west since the decline of imperial strength, was involved in an endless dispute with the English monarchy over the English king's tenure of Gascony. The quarrel implicated Flanders and Scotland as well, and so long as it lasted there could be no hope of mounting a successful crusade, although the urgent need for such an expedition had been recognized ever since the fall in 1291 of Acre, the last Christian stronghold in Palestine. Moreover Clement V, as a Gascon subject of Edward I of England, was in a promising position to effect a pacification between the English and French kingdoms. There were also negative reasons, as the cardinals well realized, which might persuade Clement to remain for the time being north of the Alps. South of Rome a war raged between the dispossessed Colonna and the Caetani, the family of Boniface VIII, for domination in the Campagna. In the rest of the Papal State central authority since the 'outrage of Anagni' had been even weaker than usual. Thus Rome seemed out of the question as a base and Umbria, where the conclave had met, scarcely more inviting.

Finally it was pressure from the French king which prompted in Clement the fateful decision to postpone his journey to Italy. Threatening a posthumous trial of Pope Boniface, Philip insisted on the transfer of the coronation from Vienne (in imperial territory) to Lyons. The king's further intention, of inducing Clement to settle in France, was frustrated, but Clement remained beyond the Alps, postponing his departure till he should have made a thorough recovery from his chronic state of ill-health. After four years of peregrinations he settled at Avignon, which was an Angevin enclave in the papal territory of the Comtat-Venaissin; the halt was intended to be a temporary one and much of the machinery of administration, such as the archive, still remained in

Italy. In 1310, however, Clement took the step of appointing a vicar to represent him at Rome. The city on the Rhone was never thought of as a permanent base, and schemes for a move to Italy were more or less constantly under discussion. In 1332 detailed plans were worked out for a move to Bologna, though it is very doubtful whether this independent and turbulent city, adjoining the still more turbulent Romagna, was really a practicable compromise between Avignon and Rome. The decision of Benedict XII (1334–42) to build a palace at Avignon marks a belated acceptance of the fact that the 'captivity' was something more than a passing visit. Not until 1367 was a return made to Rome, by Urban V, and this proved abortive, for three years later Urban deserted the city once more. It was left to his successor, Gregory XI, to make an Italian journey, in 1377, from which there was no return. As well as the predilections of the preponderant French element in the Curia, inertia, the old age and illness of successive popes, and the tempting strength of Avignon (which in 1348 was purchased from the Angevins) all played a part in this prolonged sojourn of seven decades.

Urban V met so much opposition from the cardinals when he began preparations for his move to Rome that he is said to have had to overcome it by threatening to 'swamp' the objectors by a wholesale creation of new cardinals. This episode, if true, is characteristic of the strife within the college between French and Italians, which led to a curious war of pamphlets regarding the respective merits of Avignon and Rome. While Frenchmen depicted the horrors of a malarial Eternal City, decayed and desolate, and vaunted the delectable vintages of the Languedoc, Italians deplored the abandonment of the Church's time-honoured home. Periodically embassies came from the widowed city to implore the popes to return and rescue it from obscurity and economic collapse. As early as 1308 Italians wrote of the papal *captivatio*, and a succession of patriotic writers, of whom Dante was one of the first and Petrarch the most fervent, denounced 'carnal' Avignon as the new Babylon. In a conversation with Clement VI Petrarch told the pope that it was unfortunate that he did not know Italy as well as he knew France and England, and later he addressed two long and eloquent hortatory letters on the subject to Urban V.

Your see is wherever you wish [says the poet], but the only one that
is your own true see of old, for the benefit of the faithful and the
advantage of all, is Rome, that place grateful to God, venerable to
men, the desire of the pious, the terror (when you are there) of
rebels. That is the see fitted to reform the world, to rule over monarchs,
the see that till now has known no equal and, unless I am misled by
the wishes of my heart, will know none in future. . . . All other
cities have their spouses, subject to you but ruling over their own
churches; Rome alone has none but you. Though you are the
superior in all others, in the city of Rome you are the only Pontiff,
the only spouse.[1]

In Italy all the Avignon popes were regarded with extreme
suspicion as patriotic Frenchmen. It was even rumoured that when
the cardinals elected Clement V they thought him already dead,
while a story was current in Germany that a papal official had
accepted a bribe of 16,000 florins to hand over the whole of
Benedict XII's treasury to Philip VI.[2] This view would not have
been that of the French kings. Clement V, as we have seen, was
a Gascon, and none of his Avignonese successors was born north
of the Loire: John XXII was from Quercy, Benedict XII from
Foix, Clement VI, Innocent VI and Gregory XI from the Limousin, Urban V from the southern part of the Massif Central. No less
than 113 of the 134 cardinals created by these popes came from
greater France, but their court was Languedocian, rather than
'French'. Their native tongue differed from the Languedoïl as
much as it did from Italian and, with the partial exception of
Clement V, they were certainly not puppets of the French kings.
Clement V was terified by the threats of a posthumous trial for
Pope Boniface into a humiliating participation in the shameful
Affair of the Templars. Clement VI, once keeper of the Seal to
Philip VI, made enormous loans to his former master; between
November 1345 and February 1350 these totalled no less than
592,000 florins and 5,000 crowns. Apart from this, there is no
reason to accept the contemporary Italian view of the Avignon
popes. The belief of most of them that they could hope, as true
neutrals, to end the Hundred Years War, was genuine, and—
unlike the Italians—they rightly saw in this war the greatest

---

[1] *Senilia*, VII, 1 (see also IX, 1).
[2] Heinricus Dapifer de Diessenhoven in *Fontes Rerum Germanicarum*, ed. J. F.
Böhmer, IV, 34 (*ad* 1340).

political problem of western Europe. Moreover their principal preoccupations—war for their Italian lands, relations with the Empire, the crusade, ecclesiastical taxation, theological controversies—were their own, not those imposed by an external authority.

In a way their very independence of the French was a source of weakness to these popes in their Italian policy, which was the most pressing of their temporal concerns. The Neapolitan kingdom was neutralized, first by war with Aragonese Sicily, then by economic decline and political collapse. The Empire was weak and was in any case still inconceivable as an ally. Finally, France became so involved in the war with England that the popes found themselves facing alone the intolerable double burden of anarchy in the Papal State combined with the enmity of the immensely powerful Visconti of Milan. When these men are blamed for their failure to return to Italy, it must be remembered that a series of crises faced them in the peninsula with a relentless recurrence just when circumstances might seem to have made the transfer possible. In 1310–13 it was Henry VII's Italian expedition, then the growth of Ghibellinism in Tuscany and the challenge of the Visconti, followed by Lewis of Bavaria's invasion of 1327–1330, which in turn gave way to the quasi-imperialist schemes of John of Bohemia. After a brief interlude, the Visconti war was renewed in 1341, coalescing later with the long-standing revolt in Romagna. Only in the 1350s did it become possible for the popes to think in terms of a positive Italian policy and, later, Albornoz' achievements were immediately followed (in 1370) by renewed opposition from the Visconti, with support from within the Papal State, and by the Florentine 'War of the Eight Saints' (1375).

Throughout this time the papacy had lost almost all authority in central Italy, which was in a condition of endemic lawlessness. Revenues from papal territory fluctuated enormously in these circumstances, but they can rarely have attained half of the sum nominally due, and expenditure—particularly on mercenary armies, now predominantly German—was enormous. Warfare in Italy was the financial haemorrhage that necessitated the notorious fiscality of these popes, whose total revenues were often insufficient to meet this source of expenditure alone. The most interesting of a number of governmental experiments tried at this time in papal Italy was the vicariate, an institution taken over from imperial practice and first employed by the papacy in 1329. The essence of the vicariate was a bargain with local rulers, who now gained official recognition of their jurisdiction in exchange for certain obligations—mainly financial—which they by no means always fulfilled. There was much to be said for this realistic semiabdication of rule, less for appointments to offices in the Papal State which alternated between French relatives or protégés and local men who were often feudal magnates. Nepotism did enormous harm, particularly in Clement V's time, when central Italy became a rich pasture for the d'Albret and other Gascon relatives, but it was not always an improvement when such a man was succeeded by an Orsini or a Farnese, while Italians who lacked any local standing might secure no obedience at all. The common belief was that prelates were less likely to be rapacious than lay men, but Tavernini, an ecclesiastic who was treasurer of the Tuscan Patrimony for many years, was so unpopular as to provoke riots and left a fortune of over 35,000 *l.*

The first papal envoy to attempt a general appeasement in Italy was Cardinal Bertrand du Poujet, legate from 1320 to 1334, who conducted a strenuous struggle against the Visconti, but failed to gain reliable allies and was finally overcome by the strength of local tyrants. Cardinal Gil Albornoz, a Spanish archbishop who was appointed legate in Italy in 1353, accomplished with weak resources and little backing the immense task of pacifying the papal lands. In achieving this Albornoz made cunning use of the disunity of his antagonists. His method was to work his way up gradually from the south, tackling first his opponents in the neighbourhood of Rome and eventually reaching Romagna, where in 1356–9 he fought a successful war against the Ordelaffi thanks to the alliance of the Malatesta. After this he was able to fight the Visconti, first at Bologna and then father north. Albornoz was a statesman who knew when to compromise with his adversaries and a legist who never failed to make very precise terms when he compromised. He was in command of considerable mercenary armies at times, but neither Innocent VI nor Urban V gave him wholehearted support; he was removed from his legation in 1357 and, though he returned the following year, he was finally superseded in 1364 by a legate who was prepared to come to terms with

the Visconti. Albornoz has been regarded as 'the founder of the
Papal State', mainly on account of the impressive code of laws
which he promulgated in 1357, but his achievement was bound
to disintegrate. By 1375 Florence was at war with the papacy and
stimulated revolts in many major towns of the Papal State by
calling them to arms against the French 'whose ambition has left
no honour to the Italians and whose insatiable avarice has left
nothing unravaged'. The papacy was only able to return after a
new series of notable concessions to its subjects, and whatever
remained of Albornoz' work was undone in the anarchy of the
next thirty years.

Although the Avignon popes were compelled to keep Italy in
the forefront of their minds, they were not condemned to purely
negative political and military activity. All were active in seeking
to put an end to the Anglo-French conflict, and attempted to
forward the Crusade. All but John XXII were notable theologians,
and Benedict XII, Urban V and Gregory XI were men of outstanding piety. Even John XXII, who quarrelled with the
Franciscans and drove the extreme 'Spirituals' into the imperialist
camp, entered the realm of theology and condemned the doctrine
of the absolute poverty of the disciples, a move welcomed by the
Dominicans, some of whom are said to have repainted their
crucifixes to depict Christ taking money with one hand. Assisted
by the conveniently central position of Avignon, which was admirably situated to facilitate communications with France, Flanders
and England to the north and the Empire and Spain to the east and
west, as well as with Italy, the popes greatly strengthened the
financial and general administration of the papacy. The chancery
was reorganized in seven offices and the judicature in four tribu-
nals. Under the pressure of Italian requirements, the fiscal organization was also systematized, special regional collectors being
regularly used, while a new source of revenue, the annates, was
exploited with great success. The Church throughout western
Europe was brought more strictly under central control than
hitherto, not only in financial matters, but in appointments to
benefices: the number of cases in which 'provision' was automatically made by the papacy was now greatly increased.

The greatest organizational change of the time, however, probably lay in the increasingly independent status of the college of

cardinals. The role played by these dignitaries and their house-holds in the Curia's notorious luxury was visible enough: Clement VI spent 8,000 florins a year on clothes for his household, and the cardinals, one of whom entertained Clement at a banquet of twenty-seven courses, were not to be outdone in conspicuous consumption. One cardinal required ten stables for his horses, another fifty-one houses for his entourage, and a characteristic expression of their outlook is perhaps to be found in the will of Cardinal Pierre Bertrand (d. 1361), who bequeathed 100 florins to the papal see, the same amount to his cook, and only a little less to his falconer, baker and butler respectively.[1] Many of these prelates were papal relatives, a fact which in part explains their determination not to be outshone by their fortunate and benevolent patron; John XXII appointed nine new cardinals from Quercy, of whom five were related to him, while twelve of Clement VI's fifteen appointments were Limousins. But the new element in the situation, growing invisibly but inexorably, was the tendency of each cardinal to conduct his own policy and intrigues as a semi-independent magnate and—more important still—for the college to regard itself as a separate institution, having its own interests, which were not necessarily those of the pope. This development was encouraged by the independent financial organization of the college, which had its own chamber and after 1289 was supposed to receive half of various forms of papal revenue. In the conclave following the death of Clement VI the cardinals' oligarchic pro-clivities came into the open for the first time. Almost all the cardinals present then swore an agreement to bind the future pope: no major decisions concerning papal territory or papal taxation should be taken without the consent of at least two-thirds of the cardinals, and the same majority would be required for the appointment of a cardinal, while the members of the college were never to number more than twenty. Innocent VI, who was elected in this conclave, was among those who had added a 'saving clause' when consent-ing to this 'compromise', and he proceeded to annul it on the grounds that it contravened canon law, though some of its terms in fact constituted no radical departure from existing law. The events of 1352, though they had no immediate effect, reveal the

[1] F. Du Chesne, *Histoire des Cardinaux françois de naissance*, II, 345–68 (the text of Cardinal Bertrand's will).

cardinals very clearly in their baronial role. The wider results of this development in Church government were to appear a quarter of a century later, on the death of Clement's nephew, Gregory XI.

Gregory, the man who brought the 'exile' to an end, disembarked from his galley opposite S. Paolo, outside the gate of Rome, on 17 January 1377. He lived in the city for a year, though even this residence was broken by more than five months of *villeggiatura* Anagni. On 27 March 1378 he died. Ten days later the conclave gathered in the Vatican, while, in the *piazza* outside, the throng vociferously expressed its wishes: 'Romano lo volemo, o al manco italiano' ('We want him to be a Roman, or at least an Italian'). The sixteen cardinals present, of whom seven were Limousins and another four Frenchmen, proceeded to an election on the very first morning of the conclave. The man on whom their choice fell was a Neapolitan, Bartholomew Prignano, a pious and learned legist who had served as papal vice-chancellor under Gregory XI and was now archbishop of Bari. The noisy behaviour of the crowd was later used to justify the claim that undue pressure prejudiced this election and made it invalid, but it seems certain that Urban VI was elected 'in fear, but not through fear'. The original choice was rapidly confirmed, to banish any possible doubts, by thirteen of the electors, the six cardinals who had remained at Avignon hastened to convey their homage, and in the early days of the pontificate no cardinal refused Urban his recognition.

The new pope's position, however, was not an easy one. A man of violent and tactless temperament suddenly found himself raised above the cardinals whom he had long served in a subordinate capacity. To make matters more embarrassing, Urban was a man of relatively humble birth who lacked the social polish of the prelates whose gracious living he saw as an insult to his schemes for radical reform. St Catherine of Sweden was later to explain the sequence of events by attributing them to 'the rigorous justice of the pope, who was not gentle to the cardinals when they made requests, but attempted to reform them'. One of these cardinals put it in similar terms: 'if the archbishop of Bari had been a prudent man and had had *savoir-faire* he could have been a pope . . . but he was in no way fitted to govern the Church', and the future Benedict XIII complained that 'he turned everything upside-down through his violence'. Urban's forthrightness and refusal to compromise showed from the very start. He ordered the cardinals to have only one course at each meal and to abandon the time-honoured custom of accepting retaining 'pensions' from lay rulers. He had flaming rows with the Cardinal of Limoges, whom he once struck in a consistorial assembly. In another consistory he launched a tirade against the Cardinal of Amiens, whom he accused of accepting bribes from both the French and English when engaged in peace negotiations with these two nations. He rejected angrily suggestions that the Curia should return to Avignon, and when a 'whispering campaign' began to hint at the possibility of his resignation he said to the bishop of Todi: 'They don't know me well: if they pointed a thousand swords at my neck, I still wouldn't give up.'[1] All this serves as a reminder that the 'constitutional' issue between pope and cardinals was no mere paper dispute over legal principles; it was the outcome of a series of bitterly-felt grievances against autocratic monarchs.

Intrigues against Urban had started soon after his election. The messenger despatched to announce the election to Charles V of France cast some doubt on his legal position, and a second embassy to Charles mysteriously failed to arrive. An ambassador to Castile and Portugal played an equally ambiguous role. The bishop of Amiens, Jean de la Grange, who was a former councillor of Charles V, had not been present at the conclave. It was he who set out to organize Urban's downfall. By June (1378) he had gathered at Anagni a number of cardinals who proceeded to declare Urban's election invalid and to demand his deposition. These cardinals then moved to Fondi, south of the Neapolitan frontier, where they received a letter from Charles of France encouraging them to go ahead with their plans. Two days later, on 20 September, they met in conclave and thirteen cardinals gave their vote to Robert of Geneva, bishop of Cambrai. Robert, who was the brother of the Count of Geneva and whose mother was a cousin of Charles V, took the title of Clement VII, thereby expressing his allegiance to the Avignonese tradition.

Since France was already committed to the cardinals' party, it was natural that Charles (with the support of the university of Paris) should proceed to recognize Clement. The summer after

[1] E. Baluze, *Vitae Paparum Avinonensium* (ed. G. Mollat, Paris, 1927), II, 758.

his election (1379) Clement was forced by rioting to leave Naples, and in June he took up residence at Avignon. Thus, less than three years after Gregory XI's departure, Avignon was again opposed to Rome, but this time with a rival pontiff, not merely as a rival tendency within the Curia. Each side created its own cardinals—Urban twenty-nine in September 1378, Clement nine that December—and soon the schism was reflected throughout western Christendom. There was a general topographical pattern in this division, with most of France, the Iberian kingdoms, and Scotland declaring for Clement, while the other areas were predominantly Urbanist, yet each pope had his supporters in 'enemy' territory, and the rift came to bisect even the smaller subdivisions of the Church. Religious orders sometimes had two rival masters, sees two bishops and chapters, monastic houses two abbots. Adversity made Urban no more tractable, and the cardinals adhering to him were driven to consult a lawyer about what action could be taken against a pope who showed himself incapable of governing the Church. Learning of this, he had the five prelates involved imprisoned and tortured, and only one of them survived. When Urban died in 1389 he was at once succeeded by a less unpopular Italian, Boniface IX. Clement lived on till 1394, and it is possible that his death failed only by a few hours to put an end to the schism: the slowness of medieval communications may for once have played a decisive part in events, since Charles VI of France wrote to the cardinals on hearing of Clement's death, ordering them not to proceed to an election—but the conclave had opened just before the king's letter arrived, and the cardinals agreed that it should be read only after an election had been made. Clement's successor, the Aragonese Peter de Luna (Benedict XIII), was an elderly cardinal who had played the leading part in winning over the Iberian kingdoms to the Clementist cause. Like his fellow-participants in the conclave Benedict had agreed to renounce the papacy if this was necessary to end the schism, but he proved to be a character of extraordinary tenacity. France was the power most likely to be able to bring the contest to an end by exerting pressure on both popes, but French action was at the mercy of ducal intrigues for Charles VI was frequently insane. Only in 1398 did the French Church withdraw its obedience from Benedict XIII, and this action proved indecisive and was abandoned after five years. Boniface IX was succeeded by two more Italian popes, Innocent VII (in 1404) and Gregory XII (in 1406). The participants in the conclave which elected Gregory XII made an agreement that, if elected, they would resign on condition that Benedict XIII did the same. After almost thirty years some progress was at last made towards healing the schism, but it was a slow and painful business. A meeting between the two sides was planned, but Gregory failed to appear. The French again withdrew their obedience from Benedict, and a number of other states, including the Empire, now declared their neutrality. In 1409 a Council at Pisa was attended by cardinals previously in either camp, but both popes boycotted its proceedings and held councils of their own. Anxious to retain the initiative, the Council of Pisa perhaps acted precipitately in failing to secure the representation of all the major lay powers and in accusing both popes of heresy. Its only immediate effect was to secure the election of a third pope, Alexander V, who survived less than a year and was then succeeded by the Neapolitan John XXIII, a 'great man in temporal matters' and a worthy antagonist of Benedict XIII.

The new Council which met at Constance in 1414 was at last able to bring the schism to an end. John XXIII was deposed, Gregory XII resigned, and Benedict XIII was eventually condemned as a heretic and schismatic. A decree ('Frequens') was promulgated ordaining that a General Council of the Church should be held at intervals of not more than ten years. Any future papal schism was to be settled by a Council within a year of its occurrence. In November 1417 a new pope was elected by a special body of twenty-three cardinals and thirty prelates, representing the six 'nations' into which the Council was divided: the man on whom their choice fell was Cardinal Oddo Colonna, who became Pope Martin V.

Inevitably the schism had given rise to much discussion in ecclesiastical circles about the constitutional method to be used in bringing it to an end, and a voluminous literature was compiled on the subject. Even before Clement VII was elected some Italian cardinals had mooted the idea of a new Council to decide whether Urban's election was valid, and a little later opinion in the University of Paris came to favour a council as the most practicable solution to the schism, in preference to the appointment of arbitrators ('compromise') or a mutual agreement to abdicate ('cession'). The commonsense argument in favour of the conciliar method (as framed by Henry of Langenstein), was this:

> New and dangerous emergencies which arise in any diocese are dealt with in a council of that particular diocese or a provincial synod, and therefore it follows that new and arduous problems which concern the whole world ought to be discussed by a General Council. For what concerns all ought appropriately to be discussed by all, or by the representatives of all.[1]

From such a view there was a natural progress to the extreme claims put forward by theorists of conciliar authority, that the pope was subject to a General Council in matters of faith; if the only infallible body on earth was the universal Church, it followed that a council should have the power to judge and condemn a pope's doctrines and to depose him if he proved obstinate. Such theories found support by analogy from two secular classical concepts, of the lawfulness of resistance to an unjust ruler, and of mixed government (advocating a judicious combination of monarchy, aristocracy and democracy). These ideas lie behind the famous decree of the Council of Constance which has been called 'the most revolutionary official document in the history of the world'. This decree proclaimed that:

> This holy synod of Constance . . . declares, being legitimately met in the Holy Spirit and a General Council which represents the Catholic Church, that it holds its powers directly from Christ, and that everyone, of whatever status or dignity he may be, even if he is the pope, is bound to obey it in matters pertaining to faith, to the extirpation of this schism and to the reform of the Church in its head and members.[2]

After the ending of the schism the tide of conciliarism rapidly receded from this highwater mark. Martin V certainly feared the institution that had elevated him, but the events of the following thirty years were to show the difficulties in normal circumstances of holding together a composite institution against an individual

---

[1] Henry of Langenstein, 'Consilium Pacis', in J. Gerson, *Opera Omnia* (Antwerp, 1706), II, 823 (cited by J. N. Figgis, *From Gerson to Grotius*, ed. 2, p. 205).

[2] C. Mirbt, *Quellen zur Geschichte des Papsttums und des Römischen Katholizismus* (ed. 3, 1911), p. 169.

and the manifold advantages enjoyed by an ecclesiastical autocrat. Martin had to convoke a Council, which met in 1423 at Siena, and his forebodings seemed justified by the radical nature of the measures proposed by the French reforming party, but such was the dissension within the Council that it accomplished nothing and concluded ignominiously in dissolution by the papal legates. The next council met at Basle in 1431, again with the pope's reluctant consent, though Martin died before the opening session was held. His successor, Eugenius IV (1431–47), soon quarrelled with the Council, mainly over its willingness to open negotiations with the Bohemian Hussites. For a time the Council seemed to have triumphed over the pope, but the reforms proposed in 1435 (which included the abolition of annates) were radical and probably unrealistic, and later Eugenius contrived to take into his own hands the negotiations for reunion with the Byzantine Church (1438 9). This was, of course, *par excellence* the sort of field in which a great assembly was handicapped by the difficulty of formulating an agreed policy and conducting prolonged bargaining. In 1439 the Council, with some support from France and the emperor, took action against Eugenius and formally deposed him. The conciliar anti-pope was Amadeus, the pious duke of Savoy, who took the name of Felix V, but a conciliarist pope proved—as might have been foreseen—a paradox more unfeasible than a Ghibelline pope. Felix resented his treatment by the Council, achieved little recognition, and at last (in 1449) abdicated. One of the last acts of the venerable Council was to 'elect' as pope Nicholas V, who two years earlier had succeeded to Eugenius.

The background to the immediate occasion of the Schism had been the constitutional issue between pope and cardinals, but the main cause of its prolongation arose from political developments in western Europe. The long-standing dispute between French and Italian in the Curia, going back to the period of the papacy's struggle with the Hohenstaufen, was both protracted and re-moulded by the increasing power of the nation-state. Political alignments crystallized the schism, and the Council, the institution which brought the Schism to an end, could only be effective if it was organized in a manner which recognized nationalism—while at the same time this recognition served in turn to harden nationalist feeling.

The situation which shaped the alignment of the two sides during the Schism was the long French struggle to resist domination by England. Thus French leadership of the Clementist cause involved the participation on Urban's side of Flanders and Gascony, the two French fiefs which fought with England in the war. With the same inevitability France's ally Scotland was drawn to Clement's party—with the by no means negligible consequence that Scots no longer went to study at Oxford or Cambridge and hence universities had to be founded in Scotland at St Andrews, Glasgow and Aberdeen. When local ecclesiastical councils were held in the Iberian kingdoms, the German parts of the Empire, Bohemia and Hungary, each made its choice by virtue of its diplomatic relations *vis-à-vis* France rather than by a consideration of the legal merits of the cases presented by the rival popes. Portugal was at first hesitant, but in 1385, thanks to the intervention of John of Gaunt, it came within the English sphere of influence and thus henceforth Portugal was Urbanist. The kingdom of Aragon was also slow to decide its allegiance, but in 1387 it declared for Clement and the election in 1394 of an Aragonese successor brought this kingdom to the fore as a zealous supporter of Benedict XIII. Eventually it became clear that the Schism could only be ended by efforts to cut across diplomatic loyalties; hence the French secured the support of England, Castile and the emperor before the 'withdrawal of obedience' of 1398. The same spirit shows in the willingness of most states to accept the pope named by the Council of Pisa; after this Council only Castile, Aragon and Scotland still held out for Benedict XIII, while the kingdom of Naples, Poland and a few parts of the Empire persevered in their allegiance to Gregory XII.

The Councils had to recognize the nature of the Schism and to assume the only form of organization which was adapted to healing it: *de facto* they were gatherings of discordant nations, and if agreement was to be effective their structure had to reflect this. At Pisa most of the major lay powers—France, England, the Empire, Poland and Portugal—were represented, though the king of Aragon confined his intervention to an embassy asking that Benedict XIII's representatives should be heard. This was the first Council to be divided into four 'nations' (France, England, Germany and Italy); the institution was based on one already existing in that forcing-house of xenophobia, the medieval university. At Constance the voting for the first time took place by nations, the Spaniards being added as a fifth nation after 1416. Each nation met separately in the initial phases of discussion, having its own president; laymen were permitted a vote. Measures agreed on by the 'nation' were then proposed, *nationaliter*, in a general congregation of the nations, and if they secured acceptance at this stage were further considered, *conciliariter*, in a general session wherein each nation remained a voting unit. At Siena again, in 1423-4, voting was by nations, and each nation was instructed to draw up its own programme of reform—an unlikely recipe for securing agreement on reform. The Council of Basle was not organized by 'nations', but national feeling was prominent in its deliberations and had to be recognized by an arrangement whereby each of the nations was represented on the four 'deputations'—concerned respectively with heresy, pacification, reform and ecclesiastical organization—through which the Council transacted its business. It was impossible to ignore the tendencies which were turning the oecumenical assembly into an international conference.

The medieval Church rightly saw heresy as a serious threat only when it had the support of lay authorities, as in the county of Toulouse in the early thirteenth century. The history of the Schism illustrates clearly the strength in the later Middle Ages of those secular loyalties which might cut across loyalty to the universal Church, and subsequent events were to show how they could give new force to theological heresy. This occurred on a large scale for the first time in Bohemia.

In the kingdom of Bohemia there existed all the necessary ingredients for a precocious growth of national consciousness. This Slav territory, bounded to the west by the 'Bohemian Forest' and to the north by the Erzgebirge and Riesengebirge, had considerable geographical unity, and German proximity and German settlement in the towns had made of it a frontier zone highly conscious of its ethnic personality. As early as the twelfth century a Czech chronicler had written bitterly of 'the innate arrogance of the Germans, who in their puffed-up pride always hold in contempt the Slavs and their language'. Czech sentiments were particularly strong in the towns, where German merchants and craftsmen monopolized most of the wealth, and strongest of all in the capital, Prague.

Under the long regency and rule of Charles IV (1334–78) Prague had acquired a 'new town'—populated entirely by Czechs, many of them peasants who had moved in from the surrounding countryside—as well as an archbishopric and a university. Feeling ran high in the university between German and Slav, the latter elements gaining ground as new *studia generalia* were founded in Germany. Prague's first archbishop was Charles's chancellor, Ernest of Pardubice, a scholar, lawyer, ascetic and patron of learning and the arts. He was the leading figure in Charles's attempts to make the Prague court a prominent centre of culture. One of Charles's main interests was the promotion of historical writing tending to enhance the prestige of his family and to foster loyalty to it, and a consequence of these activities was the growth of a school of patriotic Czech erudition. Beneš of Weitmil, the author of the *Cronica ecclesie pragensis*, was virtually Charles's official historiographer, and the king himself assisted Beneš in collecting material. He also commissioned Přibik Pulkava's Bohemian chronicle as well as the *History of Bohemia* of the Italian Giovanni da Marignola, and himself finished a life of the royal saint, King Wenceslas. Charles also encouraged writing in the vernaculars, both Czech and German; chronicles and lives of saints, as well as the Bible, were translated into Czech, and a Czech encyclopaedia and Czech–Latin dictionary were compiled.

When Charles IV persuaded his friend Clement VI to free Prague from its ecclesiastical subordination to Mainz he was insisting on the independence of his own country. He and his archbishop rebuilt the cathedral and Prague became a centre of religious reform as well as cultural activity. The leaders of reform in Charles's day were Conrad Waldhauser and John Milič. Hymns sung in the vernacular, the denunciation of ecclesiastical corruption and of excessive reverence for images and relics, and the advocacy of daily communion were a central part of this movement, which gained strength through the grievances felt during the papal Schism. Such grievances were increased by the territorial wealth of the Church, which held no less than half of the land in Bohemia. The Crown held approximately one-third of the remainder, but the estates gained considerably in power in Charles's time, and under his son and successor Wenceslas aristocratic opposition was even more effective. The king's authority was circumscribed by a permanent council, and for a time Wenceslas was imprisoned. These movements gave the Bohemian baronage increased cohesion at a time when a nationalist element was entering into Czech religious fervour. The contrast drawn between 'native' religious feeling and the luxurious and rapacious Church of Rome naturally tended to become intertwined with anti-German feeling. To contemporaries the two were inseparable, as may be seen from the words of a chronicler who wrote that 'in Prague the people got very infuriated against some priests and monks and against the Germans, and they drove them out of the town, and others fled on their own account. For at that time it was common for Germans to be on the council and in the town offices'.[1] The later 'crusades' against Bohemia by predominantly German armies merely served to strengthen a tendency in Hussitism which was strong from the very start.

John Huss began his studies in the university at Prague as a young man around 1390 and had a distinguished career there as a student of theology. In 1401 he became the dean of the faculty of arts, and the following year he began to preach (in Czech) in the new Bethlehem chapel, a centre of the reforming religious movement which could house a congregation of four thousand. Huss was a student of the English scholastic theologians and his affinity to Wyclif was to prove a matter of some embarrassment to him, for in 1403 the university condemned a number of Wyclif's opinions. Still more dangerous to his position was Huss's constant criticism of the clergy, concerning which serious complaints were first raised in 1408. During the Schism in the Church it was always likely that disputes over doctrine would lead to differences in papal affiliations and this now occurred at Prague, where the archbishop remained loyal to Gregory XII at a time when Huss had already accepted the decisions of the Council of Pisa. The quarrel was intensified after 1409 when Huss became the rector of the university: the archbishop now ordered him to cease preaching and placed him under excommunication. In 1412 the circumstances of the Schism were again decisive in driving Huss and his

---

[1] Trans. from 'The Very Pretty Chronicle of John Žikža', in F. G. Heymann, *John Žižka and the Hussite Revolution* (Princeton, 1955), p. 4.

K

supporters towards the defiance of authority which was to lead to a struggle lasting a quarter of a century. In that year John XXIII declared a 'crusade' against his enemy king Ladislas of Naples and indulgences were sold in Bohemia to raise funds for the campaign. Some of Huss's supporters were executed for their protests, Prague was placed under interdict, and Huss himself was now excommunicated by the pope and summoned to his Curia. For two years Huss abandoned the capital, but in 1414 he agreed to the suggestion of Sigismund, king of the Romans, that he should accept a safe-conduct and attend the Council at Constance. Soon after his arrival there he was imprisoned, despite the terms of the safe-conduct, and accused of holding heretical, Wycliffite opinions. Huss refused to recant his doctrines unless they could be proved erroneous by evidence from the Scriptures, and on 6 July 1415 he was condemned and burned.

A fifteenth-century Bohemian writer tells us that Huss

> began to preach, and to castigate the people for their sinful life. . . .
> But then he began to preach also against the sinfulness of the clergy, sparing neither the Pope on his throne nor the lowliest priest, and he preached against their haughtiness and their greed, against simony and concubinage, and he said that priests should not wield worldly power nor have worldly estates, and he preached also that in the Holy Communion the Body of Christ and also the Blood of Christ should be given to the common people.[1]

The main burden of Huss's preaching, in fact, as with the earlier Prague reformers, was clerical corruption. Ecclesiastical morals occupied much more time than theology, and even the theology was by no means whole-heartedly Wycliffite. It was a case of affinity rather than influence, for Wyclif was a fellow scholastic with the same preoccupations: both men were opponents of nominalism and, what is more important, both felt doubts about the authority of a worldly papacy and the claims of a Church which had great possessions. Huss rejected Wyclif's doctrine concerning transubstantiation, he even felt doubt about the Englishman's view that priests who sinned forfeited their priestly status; although he sympathized with this position, he considered it too absolute and preferred to regard such priests as unworthy rather than illegal.

---

[1] Quoted from the contemporary biography of Žižka (above, p. 133 note) in Heymann, *op. cit.*, p. 3.

He agreed, however, on the fundamental point that 'the Church' consisted of Christ and all the elect, not of the pope and cardinals. It was this democratic ecclesiology which led logically to the view that the laity should receive the Communion in the same form as the clergy, that is in the 'two kinds', the wine as well as the bread. This symbolic levelling of priest and people, which was to give the Hussites their most cherished liturgical idiosyncrasy, was first practised in Prague about 1414, after Huss's departure, by two of his followers, Jacoubek of Stříbo and Nicholas of Dresden. The chronicler quoted above erred in ascribing 'utraquism' to Huss himself, but Huss was informed of this development and expressed his approval. In rejecting erring priestly authority he had no intention of installing in its place religious anarchy: there was still a supreme authority, and this was the Bible. All disputes could be settled by reference to the Bible, and obedience was due to the Church, as Huss insisted at his trial, only when this was in conformity with the Bible.

When Huss was put to death the story of Hussitism as a social and political force was only at its beginning. In the face of great 'crusading' invasions by foreign forces the Hussites were to perform extraordinary military feats—all the more extraordinary because of the constant tension within the movement between extremists and moderates. The men who had rejected the Church's authority were free also to reject traditional religious practice, and soon after Huss's death there were important developments in this direction: Hussite priests married, auricular confession and the Latin liturgy were abandoned, 'images' fell into complete disfavour. In the fortress of Tabor, which was founded in 1420, Hussitism became a popular movement. Leaders were elected and property was held in common. The Taborites held the millenarian belief, characteristic at various times of the religion of the poor, that 'the end of the world is approaching, resplendent castles shall fall into ruins, proud cities shall perish, magnificent monasteries crumble into dust, all existing society is to be destroyed'. Soon Christ would descend, 'place supreme power in the hands of the people' and 'faith will blossom forth and justice flourish.'

Some extracts from the 'Articles' of Tabor will make clear the nature of the religious and social ideals of the extremist party:

First, that in our time there shall be an end of all things, that is, all evil shall be uprooted on this earth.

That this is the time of vengeance and retribution on wicked men by fire and sword so that all adversaries of God's Law shall be slain by fire and sword or otherwise done to death.

So that in this time whoever will hear the Word of Christ, then let them that be Jews (*sic*)[1] flee to the mountains, and those that will not leave the towns, villages and hamlets for the mountains or for Tabor shall all be guilty of mortal sin.

Everyone that will not go to the mountains shall perish amidst the towns, villages and hamlets by the blows of God.

In this time nobody can be shielded from God's blows but on the mountains.

The Taborite brethren are in this time of vengeance the messengers of God sent to purge away all offences and evil from Christ's kingdom, all wickedness from good people and from the Holy Church.

The Taborite brethren shall take revenge by fire and sword on God's enemies and on all towns, villages and hamlets.

Every church, chapel or altar built to the honour of the Lord God or of any saint shall be destroyed and burnt as a place of idolatry.

Every house of a priest, canon, chaplain or other cleric shall be destroyed and burnt.

In this time of vengeance only five towns shall remain and those who flee to them shall be saved. . . .

As in Hradiště or in Tabor nothing is mine and nothing thine, but all is common, so everything shall be common to all forever and no one shall have anything of his own; because whoever owns anything himself commits a mortal sin.

Debtors who flee to the mountains or the aforesaid five towns shall be acquitted of paying their debts.

Even now, at the end of the ages, all shall see Christ bodily descend from Heaven to accept His kingdom here on earth. . . .

In this time no king shall reign nor any lord rule on earth, there shall be no serfdom, all dues and taxes shall cease, nor shall any man force another to do anything, because all shall be equal, brothers and sisters.

Holy Mass shall not be sung or read in the Latin tongue, but only in the language of the people.

Missals sung in Latin, prayer books and other books, priestly vest-

---

[1] Evidently the intention was to quote Mark 13:14 'let them that be in Judaea . . .'

ments, surplices, silver or golden monstrances and chalices, silver or golden belts, ornamented or richly embroidered garments, finely made or costly robes: all these things shall not exist and must therefore be spoilt and destroyed.

Priests shall have no payments nor hamlets nor cattle nor estates nor houses in which to dwell nor anything of the like, even if they were given such things as alms, even if they held them by secular law and governance.[1]

It may seem strange that the Bohemian baronage ever co-operated with the men who proclaimed such a revolutionary political and social programme. That they did so at times can only be attributed to the increasingly strong patriotic element in the movement. In 1419 the 'Taborites' acquired a great military leader in the person of John Žižka, a squire who had previously served as a mercenary captain in his own country and in Poland. The spirit of the ensuing struggle between the Hussites and the forces of King Sigismund is typified by the terms in which Žižka called for support from the inhabitants of Domažlice: 'Defend yourselves bravely against the misdeeds which the Germans commit against you and follow the example of the Czechs of old who, having made ready for the march, defended not only God's cause but their own also.' Žižka, who was an original military thinker, based his tactics on the use of mobile fortress-camps; the perimeter was held by waggons, the crews of which were organized like modern tank-crews, and the fortress was normally sited on a hilltop. Žižka's infantrymen were often armed with flails, but his force was no mere mob of peasants. He possessed quite powerful artillery and learnt to use his guns tactically in the offensive; he was the first European commander to make effective use of artillery other than in siege warfare. This unorthodox general also knew the advantage of surprise and employed it ingeniously: he was to have a profound influence on later warfare in Germany and Hungary. Nor did he fail to understand the importance of morale, and he neatly expressed the religious bellicosity of his army by adopting the chalice, the symbol of ultraquism, as his emblem.

Sigismund raised an invading army and in 1420 the religious struggle became a national war.

---

[1] Slightly adapted from the translation in J. Maček, *The Hussite Movement*, pp. 130-3.

The Germans [says Žižka's early biographer] sought the lives of the Czechs and the Czechs of the Germans . . . when the Germans got hold of a Czech, even if he was of their own party in his creed, they did not even ask him about that, but as soon as they laid eyes on him they took him and burned him. And this went on until even those Czechs who were of the king's own party grew indignant against him.

In 1420 Žižka achieved the extraordinary feat of holding Prague against the invaders. The following year he became completely blind, but the greatest of his campaigns, which brought about the defeat of Sigismund's new crusading armies, was fought in 1421–2.

The German electors invaded the land [says *The very pretty Chronicle of John Žižka*] with a very strong army, and with them there were many princes, counts, bishops, and also the Margrave of Meissen. And they committed many cruelties, and whenever they got hold of a Czech they killed or burned him. . . .
. . . Then the Hungarian King came with a vast army to Bohemia, having with him Turks and Wallachians, Croatians and Hungarians, Cumans and Yassyans, Germans and other people from many different countries.[1]

Whether or not the atrocities of this heterogeneous army are exaggerated by the chronicler, his account confirms that the Czechs were now involved in a national struggle against an external foe. The invaders were routed and driven from Bohemia, but inevitably the passing of the crisis led to renewed discord between the moderate Hussites and the chiliastic extremists. Žižka's last opponents before his death in 1424 were the Catholic nobility, but by then he had already been involved in warfare against the radical Taborites.

After Žižka's death the Hussites found a new commander in Prokop the Bald, under whose generalship the struggle continued until 1433, defence against the crusading forces of Cardinals Beaufort and Cesarini alternating with raids into Austria, Silesia, Slovakia and Hungary. By this time Hussitism had permeated into neighbouring territories, particularly to Brandenburg and to southwestern Germany, where there was a hierarchy of four Hussite bishops. The last acts of the drama saw Hussites negotiating with the Council at Basle and with its representatives at Prague

---

[1] Quoted from the translation of F. G. Heymann, *op. cit.*, pp. 7–8.

at the same time as Prokop was fighting on behalf of the Taborites and the 'Orphans' of Žižka against a league of Bohemian barons. After the league's capture of Prague and Prokop's death the less extreme party among the Hussites agreed to the 'Compactata' of 1436, a compromise which permitted the continuation of utraquism. In the same year Sigismund was at last accepted as king of Bohemia and soon Hussite resistance was at an end. In one sense the compromise of 1436–7 marks the beginning of the Reformation, but a group among the Hussites refused to accept it and exists today as the Moravian Church, the survivor, with the Waldensians, of the medieval protestant movements. The most profound consequences of this great upheaval, however, were social and political. The entire structure of the Bohemian feudal Church was dismantled, the principal beneficiaries being the nobles and gentry. Once the Church lost its estates the gains, in the absence of a powerful monarchy, were bound to go to the local magnates. A typical story concerns the estates of the monastery of Zlata Koruna in southern Bohemia, which were confiscated in 1419–20 by the Hussite supporter Oldřich of Rožmberk. A few years later this baron went over to the crusaders, but he contrived to retain the monastery's lands by becoming its 'Catholic protector'. While the lords gained, the peasantry suffered: the famines and epidemics that accompanied the wars bore particularly heavily on them, and in general the status of the villein was depressed. Lastly, the long struggle had sharpened Bohemian nationalism and given it a 'myth'. Consciousness of being Czech was stronger than before, particularly in the towns, and thus religious war had served to strengthen the rival loyalty that challenged the Church, in Prague as in the Councils and in the papal Curia itself.

Further Reading

R. W. SOUTHERN, *Western Society and the Church in the Middle Ages* (Penguin Books, 1970)

G. BARRACLOUGH, *The Medieval Papacy* (Thames & Hudson Library of European Civilization, 1968)

G. MOLLAT, *The Popes at Avignon* (Edinburgh, 1963)

Y. RENOUARD, *The Avignon Papacy* (London, 1970)

J. MAČEK, *The Hussite Movement in Bohemia* (Lawrence and Wishart, London: Orbis, Prague)

F. G. HEYMANN, *John Žižka and the Hussite Revolution* (Princeton, 1955)

VII

FRENCH DEFEATS AND CHIVALROUS IDEALS: THE HUNDRED YEARS WAR

A PREVIOUS chapter described the strength of the French monarchy at the beginning of the fourteenth century, and some mention has already been made of the economic effects of the prolonged struggle with England which dictated the course of French history from that time till the end of the following century. The main *casus belli* was the old and insoluble dispute concerning Acquitaine, the remaining fief of the English kings in the French kingdom. As the power of the French monarchs increased it became both more intolerable to them that much of south-western France should be held by another sovereign and more conceivable that firm administrative and military action might dispossess the English crown of Acquitaine.

The question remained dormant during the brief reigns of Louis X and Philip V (1314–22), but Charles IV (1322–8) was confronted by less baronial opposition than they and was encouraged by the contrast with the deteriorating internal situation of Edward II of England. Moreover the worsening relations between Edward and his Queen, who was Charles's sister, removed one of the brakes on French action. The conventional methods of the French in Acquitaine had been to exploit to the full the inextricably complicated legal status of the duchy by transferring lawsuits from its courts to Paris and instigating intervention by French officials on the ground that the duke's failures to secure justice justified intervention by the overlord. Disputes over action of this sort combined with commercial rivalry in the Channel, French support of the Scots and English involvement with Flanders to keep Anglo-French relations in a state of perpetual hostility. Despite the appointment of numerous commissions of reform and constant changes in official personnel, English administration in Gascony was unsuccessful and expensive. A seneschal was appointed to rule the whole duchy in 1323, but he was handicapped by the lack of an appellate court in the duchy (itself an encouragement to the French in their tactics of citing cases to the royal court), and Gascony, which needed financial aid from England, was expected to run at a profit.

In 1324 war broke out over an incident at the disputed village of St Sardos. Charles IV declared the duchy confiscated to the French crown on account of Edward II's failure to perform homage for it, and French forces advanced, meeting little effective resistance. By 1326 only a small coastal strip remained in English hands. Edward II was too occupied with the unsuccessful attempt to retain his own crown to organize a systematic defence of Gascony or of Ponthieu, the area round the mouth of the Somme which he had inherited from his mother and which now also fell to the French. In 1327 an agreement gave the French a solid return for their victories by assigning them most of the disputed frontier territory.

When Charles IV, Philip the Fair's youngest son, died in 1328 there was no direct male heir: after three and a half centuries the Capetians had at last come to the end of their genealogical luck. The line was not extinct, however, and there was a fairly obvious successor in the person of Philip of Valois, the son of Philip the Fair's brother Charles. A case could be made for the claim of the new king of England, since Edward III was the son of Charles IV's elder sister, but there was almost every conceivable practical objection to this candidate; he was the king of England, he was only fifteen years old, and he was under the control of his disreputable mother Isabella and her lover Mortimer. It was natural that the assembly of peers and prelates should declare for Philip, who had a firm base in France's feudal structure as Count of Valois, Anjou, Maine, Chartres and Alençon.

Although Philip was a man of thirty-five he had not yet had much experience of political affairs. He had not been educated in the expectation that he would become king of France, but his father, Charles of Valois, had once been claimant to the throne of Aragon (see above, p. 57) and was to be the son, brother and father of kings. Charles was sufficiently optimistic to have a special history text-book compiled for his son, designed to instil in him the wish to emulate the virtues and deeds of the Jews, Greeks, Trojans and Romans. Philip VI was a pious man, able and willing to take on the pope in an argument about the Beatific Vision, and an enthusiast—too much of an enthusiast from the viewpoint of French interests—for the crusading ideal. The papacy was favourably disposed towards him (above, p. 119) and granted him valuable powers in appointing to benefices and taxing the French clergy. He also had a close ally in King John of Bohemia, whose daughter was later to marry his son. Philip shared the conventional chivalrous outlook of his day, but he was not a popular character. He had the good fortune to begin his reign with an overwhelming victory at Cassel over Flemish insurgents, but the ferocity of his reprisals against these clothworkers and peasants is sufficient to explain his unpopularity in that region.

The change of dynasty of 1328, even though it took place in circumstances which gave the English king a claim to the throne, disturbed France far less profoundly than England was unsettled by the revolution of 1326–7 and the subsequent supersession of his mother and Mortimer by Edward III (1330). Philip VI can hardly be blamed for failing to foresee the extraordinary tenacity and success of the English onslaught on France in the following decades. As the ruler of a monarchy enjoying unrivalled political and cultural prestige in Europe and possessing perhaps three times as many subjects as those of Edward III, he had no strong reasons for fearing a house which had recently seemed much more likely to lose all of Acquitaine than to gain new territory in France.

Anglo-French relations came to a crisis in 1337 when Philip VI retorted to Edward's claim to the French throne by declaring Gascony confiscated. By this time both sides were recruiting allies in the Low Countries. An English mission, well supplied with money, purchased the support of Brabant, Hainault, Berg, Juliers, Limburg, Cleves and Marck; finally they triumphantly bought the alliance of Lewis IV, and Edward became the emperor's vicar-general in imperial Flanders. The French king's feudatory, the Count of Flanders, and his allies, Luxembourg, Liège and Cambrai, made a less impressive showing. The stage was set for what would clearly be a crucial trial of strength.

This is not the place for a chronological account of the campaigns which have gained the rather misleading name of the 'Hundred Years War'. The military successes won by the apparently weaker power require explanation and some suggestions may be offered concerning advantages enjoyed by the English. In the first place, the strategic initiative lay with them, in that they could select the direction from which assaults were launched against the Île de France and could synchronize or coordinate assaults from more than one base. Acquitaine and the Low Countries provided the original bases, but after 1341 the English gained a third *pied-à-terre* by supporting Jean de Montfort, one of two rival claimants to the duchy of Brittany. Moreover, French provincialism made it possible for the English cause to gain some sympathy in other regions, notably in Normandy. The war was fought almost entirely on French soil, its characteristic strategic feature being the *chevauchée* (cavalry raid) launched from friendly territory by the English across France. In the intervals between the regular campaigns France was plagued by marauding companies of unemployed mercenaries (above, pp. 100 ff.); for the civil population a truce rarely signified peace. So long as she could launch her armies from secure bases against the heartland of France, England was a formidable adversary, and the vigour with which her commercial wealth was mobilized to keep her armies in the field meant that the French were challenged powerfully and frequently. Finally it was a disadvantage to the French that they had no zone which acted as a permanent training ground. The English were able to employ the well-tried manoeuvres which had won successes in the frequent hostilities in Wales and Scotland, where the lessons of the longbow had been learnt. These theatres of war to some extent occupied the position that centuries later was to be held by the Indian north-west frontier.

The phase of the war which opened in 1337 and concluded in 1361 with the Treaty of Brétigny was marked by two disastrous French defeats, Crécy (1346) and Poitiers (1356). A brief account of these two battles will make it clear that weaknesses in the French methods of conducting war were no less critical than French strategic disadvantages. Edward III's campaign of 1346 was based on Normandy, an exiled feudal lord of the Côtentin having persuaded him of the advantages of this approach. Edward struck south as far as the walls of Paris, then turned north-east. Near Abbeville he was caught by the French pursuit, and each side felt strong enough to risk an engagement in the open field, though the English numbered only some 2,500 heavy cavalry and the same number of horse-archers. Horse archers had been used to bring the Scots to battle as long as fifty years before, and these tactics had been employed with success at Falkirk (1298), Dupplin Moor (1332) and Halidon Hill (1333). The English victory at Crécy was due to the rashness of the French in assaulting a very strong position. The tactics of the English were to extend their wings forward, so that the advancing cavalry met fire from three sides. The assault of the French, launched through their own crossbowmen, who suffered heavily, was ill-disciplined and appallingly costly, as attack always is when directed against a well-armed and well-positioned enemy. The English archers and horsemen had been trained to fight together and the longbow, the principal English weapon, had a rate of fire at least three times as great as that of the French crossbow: it was almost as though machine-gunners were fighting riflemen. Despite the tremendous casualties, this French defeat was not decisive: the English were too weak to exploit their victory, and for the next twelve months they were occupied with achieving the submission of Calais.

For several years after 1347 there was little fighting in France. During this time Philip VI died (1350) and again fortune favoured the English, for Jean le Bon, though an amiable man, was an incompetent ruler, whereas the English king was a capable and experienced general backed by a son whose military ability was no less than his own. In 1356 one English force attacked Normandy from Brittany, while another, under Edward's son the Black Prince, broke out of Acquitaine in a northerly direction. The Prince had no more than 2,600 horsemen and the ensuing battle near Poitiers was a much more close-run thing than Crécy. The French commanders made the mistakes that had been made ten years before. In a preliminary council of war Marshal Clermont, who recommended caution, was accused of cowardice, whereupon he walked out and launched a rash assault. Eventually the French were defeated when attacked from the rear by the

Gascon Captal de Buch. This time the inability of the English to attempt a territorial exploitation of their victory was of little importance, for they already held the trump card: the French king had been taken prisoner. Jean's captivity was all the more disastrous in that the young Dauphin was faced by risings in Paris and elsewhere and by a formidable enemy in the person of his cousin Charles of Navarre. The subsequent Treaty of Bré-tigny, which was never fully effective, granted the English three million crowns as a ransom for the French king, together with a greatly enlarged Acquitaine (now including all the disputed borderlands on its eastern frontier) as well as Ponthieu and Calais. The French were to be compelled to pay heavily indeed for the military ineptitude which had twice led them into the trap laid by their experienced adversary.

The financial burden of war fell heavily on the English too, but success, which reconciles men to military expenditure, in this case also helped to diminish it, since large ransoms were paid for the captive French nobles. Meanwhile the fiscal problems of the French were increased by the dislocation of their trade; customs receipts were down by one-third in 1344 as compared with 1332. Apart from clerical taxation and debasement of the currency, the French king had to rely mainly on loans. For these he turned everywhere, to the pope and the French clergy, to towns, feudatories, royal officials and the communities of Italian and Jewish merchants.

It might be supposed that the great defeats of 1346 and 1356 should have cost the French crown heavily in prestige and constitutional standing as well as in money, but this was not the case. Even during the early critical years of King Jean's captivity the French estates failed to strengthen their position. The assemblies called to give consent to taxation were normally local ones, and although they did not fail to demand reforms and to seek control over the distribution of the subsidies and even over the troops themselves, they made no solid gains in this sense. The very fact of the king's captivity may have hindered those seeking effective concessions from the Crown. Certainly it strengthened sentiment concerning the monarchy; there was a feeling of national mourning after Poitiers, as is witnessed by the decision that no minstrels or *jongleurs* should perform in the Languedoc. Demands for radical constitutional 'reform' were indeed put forward at this juncture. It was proposed that twenty-eight counsellors, from all three estates, should temporarily take control in France, that in future some counsellors should always be nominated by the estates, and that the estates themselves should decide when meetings should be held: the local assemblies were to be discontinued. In 1357 nine 'reformers' were actually appointed. Yet all schemes for reform foundered because the different discontented elements failed to collaborate. Étienne Marcel's movement of 1357–8 in Paris was entirely local and the rural *Jacquerie* was also independent.

Jean le Bon returned from his captivity in 1360, but soon afterwards the Duke of Anjou, who was hostage for the payment of the remainder of the king's ransom, broke his oath and fled to France. Rather than allow the honour of his house to be tarnished, Jean returned voluntarily to his English prison and died as a captive.

His son and successor Charles V (1364–80) was an able man whose comparatively early death was to cost his country very dear. Charles, who had a considerable library, took an interest in the theory as well as the practice of kingship; experiencing difficulty in reading Aristotle in Latin he had a French translation of the *Politics* made for his own use. He realized that fiscal embarrassment might restrict the constitutional powers of the French monarchy, and hence was careful to evade consultation with the estates; moreover he was singularly successful in levying taxes which had hitherto required consent. He approached warfare in a much more business-like spirit than his grandfather and father, appointing as his principal commander Bertrand du Guesclin, an unpolished Breton knight who defied the traditions of chivalry in that he cherished his men and attempted to avoid engagements in the open field.

By 1380 there seemed every reason to suppose that France had weathered the storms of the English onslaught. Edward III, the initiator of the war and the hero of its early phase, was dead and England was under the rule of a mere boy, Edward's grandson Richard. That France underwent a second and far more dreadful crisis was the consequence of a series of misfortunes, beginning with the early death of Charles 'the Wise' and the succession of his incompetent son Charles (VI) at the age of eleven. The tragic tale of Charles VI's relations with his uncles and of the family quarrel which drove the powerful Burgundian duchy into alliance with the English cannot be related here, though in part it will form the theme of a later chapter (Chapter IX). After 1392 Charles underwent recurrent periods of mental illness, and later he became incapable of carrying on the business of government. The length of his life (he died in 1422) was as unlucky for his country as was the brevity of his father's.

Even this combination of calamities might have been ineffective had it not coincided with the succession to the English throne in 1413 of a king resolved to be the reincarnation of Edward III. Henry V's first attempt to win glory in France began unpromisingly with a lengthy siege of Harfleur, and looked like ending disastrously when the six thousand English archers making for Calais were intercepted by a much stronger French force. But at Agincourt (25 October 1415) the story of Crécy and Poitiers was repeated. The French cavalry was handicapped by the wet conditions and a narrow front did not permit the horsemen to deploy and thus benefit from their superior numbers. Again the stationary archers were victorious. Some seven thousand Frenchmen were killed. Agincourt had no decisive strategic consequences, but its effect on English opinion helped Henry to renew the war in 1417 with ambitious plans for the capture of Paris. At first progress was not rapid, but the murder of Jean sans Peur, duke of Burgundy, carried out at the instigation of the French Dauphin, drove Burgundy into alliance with the English (December 1419). After this Charles VI and his advisers saw no hope of further resistance and the following spring they agreed to the humiliating terms proposed by the English. By the Treaty of Troyes the Dauphin was disinherited, the French king recognized Henry as his regent and heir, and Henry agreed to marry Charles's daughter, Shakespeare's 'plus belle Catherine du monde'. Henry still had to reduce to terms the very considerable area of France (approximately from Paris southward) which now supported the Dauphin, but this did not appear to be an impossible task. The French estates duly ratified the Treaty of Troyes, Paris itself fell to the English before the end of 1420, and the Dauphin lacked a formidable governmental machine to control the zones which acknowledged him. 1356 had been disastrous enough, but 1420 marks the very nadir of French fortunes.

In eighty years the apparently powerful French kingdom had been brought to its knees. There seemed every likelihood that within the next decade the king of England would also in fact be king of France, though there was as yet no intention of merging the two monarchies. How had this extraordinary situation come about?

In order to attempt an answer to this question it is necessary to return to the military methods of the two sides, and this in turn involves a discussion of attitudes towards the conduct of war in the later Middle Ages. We must consider, in fact, the outlook and institutions comprised by the abstraction 'chivalry'. 'Chivalry' means, literally, 'horsiness'; it was the code of the men who fought on horseback, the knightly class. It owed its existence to the pride of this class in what differentiated it from its social inferiors, and to the deep-seated human desire to formulate and define distinctions within society. Manners softened in this age of late feudalism, but they also crystallized and became more formal. Pride of 'birth' was felt and displayed by the medieval nobility with a confident directness denied to later aristocrats. What these men had in common was a certainty of superiority over the socially ineligible, and particularly over those whose ways of life brought them closest to what birth denied them, the wealthy bourgeois and the non-noble cavalry sergeant.

This certainty of pertaining to a privileged and higher category of humanity emerges clearly in three episodes recounted by Joinville in his *Life of St Louis*. The first concerns a discussion between Joinville himself and Robert de Sorbon, the king's confessor and founder of the college which gave its name to the university of Paris. Sorbon had rebuked Joinville for being more nobly dressed than the king. The retort that he drew on himself was as follows:

> Master Robert, with your permission, there is nothing to blame in me if I wear fur and green cloth; for this is the clothing that my father and mother left me. On the contrary, it is you who are doing something blameworthy, for you are the son of villeins and you have

given up the clothing of your father and mother and are wearing richer cameline cloth than the king is.[1]

The next story is of an episode which occurred in Palestine, during St Louis' first crusade:

One of the king's sergeants, a man named Goulu, laid his hand on one of the knights of my *corps de bataille*. I went and complained to the king. The king told me that he thought I might well let the matter drop, as the sergeant had only given the knight a push. I told him that I would not allow it to drop, and that if he did not grant me justice I would leave his service, since his sergeants pushed knights about. He granted me justice and the justice [verdict] was thus, in keeping with the usage of the country: the sergeant came to my tent, barefoot and wearing only his underpants, carrying his drawn sword, and he kneeled down before the knight, took hold of the sword by the point and held out the pummel to the knight, saying 'Sire, I make amends to you for having laid my hand on you, and I have brought this sword so that you may cut off my hand if you wish.' And I asked the knight to pardon the sergeant's offence; and he did so.[2]

Joinville's other tale concerns Henry 'the Generous', Count of Champagne:

Artaud of Nogent was the burgher in whom the Count trusted most of all the burghers in the world, and he was so rich that he built with his own money the castle of Nogent l'Artaud. Now it happened one Whitsun that Count Henry was going out of his rooms at Troyes to hear mass at St Stephen's. At the foot of the staircase there was kneeling a poor knight, who said to the Count: 'Sire, I beg you for the love of God to give me money, so that I may marry these two daughters of mine whom you see here.' Artaud, who was walking behind the Count, said to the poor knight: 'Sire knight, it is not courtly to ask of our lord, for he has given away so much that he has no more to give.' The generous Count turned to Artaud and said: 'Sire villein, you are not telling the truth when you say that I have no more to give; I have something, for I have you. Take him, sire knight, for I give him you, indeed I will guarantee him to you.' The knight was not taken aback but got hold of Artaud by his cloak and told him that he would not let go until they had come to terms. And by the time Artaud got away they had come to terms to the tune of five hundred pounds.[3]

[1] Joinville, *Life of St Louis*, ch. VI.   [2] *Ibid.*, ch. XCIX.   [3] *Ibid.*, ch. XX.

All three of these stories illustrate the essentially exclusive nature of chivalry; the pleasure in being a member of an *élite* comes solely from the contrast between one's position and that of the non-elect. Above all, this class mystique was nourished by the contrast between the code or conduct of the nobles and those of the rich but 'low-born' merchants, the Artauds of the world. This shows clearly in the verses addressed by a fifteenth century poet, Jean Molinet, to the bourgeoisie, lines obviously intended to be acceptable to a noble reader:

> You lead a comfortable life, peaceful, secure,
> While they endure mortal suffering in the fray.
> You sleep warm in the city, restfully,
> And they out in the fields, still armed.
> You dream of adding to your rank,
> And they are dying for you and your inheritance.[1]

Bertrand de Born, the Provençal freebooter of an earlier century, emphasized the same contrast in a poem celebrating the delights of war:

> And it will be a happy time, for the usurers will be robbed of their property and pack-animals will no longer be able to journey in peace on the roads, nor will the townsmen and the merchants on the road from France travel in safety. He who takes willingly will become wealthy.[2]

This bellicose ideology was the prerogative of those who had been inducted or 'dubbed' as knights by being struck a blow with a sword by one who was already a knight. The symbolism involved in this magical transmission of special powers is a reminder that the occasion was essentially a quite primitive initiation ceremony, though the Church worked strenuously to 'infiltrate' chivalric ideas by adding religious and social obligations to the list of the knight's duties, and dubbing became a sacrament whereby the knight and his arms were consecrated. When he was admitted to the chivalrous class the warrior was expected to train seriously as a cavalryman: the tournament was the peace-time form of exercise in which he learnt and practised the skilled art of fighting on horseback in close formation. So profound was the

---

[1] Jean Molinet, *Chroniques*, I (1827), 83–4.
[2] M. de Riquer (ed.), *La Lírica de los Trovadores*, I, 427.

division between the man who waged war on a horse and he who fought on foot that it was felt by some nobles to be unfitting that a knight should be killed by an infantryman; indeed the duke of Julliers hanged one of his foot soldiers who was so rash as to claim responsibility for the death in battle of the duke's enemy the count of St. Pol.

The virtues most prized by the chivalrous were military prowess, loyalty to a feudal overlord, and 'courtesy'—considerate manners, that is, towards other members of the chivalrous class. The 'romance' literature of the Middle Ages elaborated on these qualities as they had been displayed by the knights of King Arthur's court and by Charlemagne's paladins, and to the men who set the tone of the chivalrous society of the later Middle Ages these were very real heroes. 'We had great need to-day of the good knights of the Round Table', said John I of Portugal at the siege of Coria, 'for surely, if they had been here, we should have taken this place.' [1] Charles the Rash of Burgundy, later in the fifteenth century, was a great reader of Arthurian literature, and used to speak of his desire to emulate the knights of chivalrous romance and the heroes of antiquity; 'he was great of heart', says Chastellain, 'in his desire to be known and highly regarded for his outstanding deeds'. Imitation of the great men of the past was the way to glory, it was believed, and Charles had his court at Dijon decorated by tapestries depicting the siege of Troy, the labours of Hercules and the voyage of the Argonauts, Trajan and Caesar, Alexander the Great and Charlemagne, King Arthur, Godfrey of Bouillon and the rest of the Nine Worthies. Similar collections of noble exemplars were to be found depicted at any court, and may still be seen, for instance, at the ducal palace of Urbino. But the modest opinion, characteristic of the earlier Middle Ages, that the men of latter, degenerate days could never rival the heroes of antiquity, was lacking. Instead, attempts were made to inaugurate a sort of cult of those contemporaries who showed to perfection the virtues of chivalry. Such an attitude is strongly marked in a number of laudatory biographies, particularly those of Du Guesclin, of Marshal Boucicaut and of Jacques de Lalaing, the Burgundian *bon chevalier* whose knight errantry is

---

[1] Fernão Lopes, *Crónica de D. João I*, Pt. II, ch. LXXV (ed. Almeida and Basto, 1949, Vol. II, 187).

described in the *Livre des faits*, and who was fair as Paris, pious as Aeneas, wise as Ulysses and passionate as Hector—and yet *courtois*, *débonnaire* and even *humble* towards his opponents. As for Boucicaut, the eulogistic biography published in his lifetime tells us that beside accomplishing imperishable feats of arms, he was so devout that he daily prayed for three hours and heard two masses, and never failed to wear black each Friday.

So much for the ideals of chivalry. It is now time to come to the difficult question of their influence on the conduct of the war. Exponents of chivalric theory saw warfare as a series of equal engagements conducted in such a manner as to test and show the prowess of the individual knightly participants. As late as the sixteenth century it was normal to propose the settlement of wars by individual combat. Such schemes were never effective, although the elaborate plan to resolve the Sicilian dispute by a personal combat at Bordeaux between Charles of Anjou and Peter III of Aragon (1283) was not entirely insincere and came somewhere near to fruition. Similar proposals were sometimes made for contests between small teams representative of the two sides; thus Marshal Boucicaut suggested during the siege of Al-Mahdiya (1390) a combat of either one, ten, twenty or forty representatives of the king of Tunis and of the crusaders, who were to advance on each other from the two sides of a closed field. This view of warfare also entailed the elimination of any form of unjust advantage which might vitiate the verdict of battle as a test of military prowess. It was by some considered unfair to set ambushes or even to make use of side-roads in campaigning. A head-on clash was the most impartial trial, and during the English siege of Calais (1346–7) William of Hainault suggested that a truce should take effect for three days while a bridge was built which would conveniently enable the English and French armies to meet in battle.

The chivalric virtue of 'courtesy' implied kind treatment of knightly prisoners of war, and the well-known passage in which Froissart describes the Black Prince's generosity towards the French nobles after Poitiers shows that this could be effective in practice:

> The same day of the battle at night the prince made a supper in his lodging to the French king and to the most part of the great lords

that were prisoners. The prince made the king and his son, the lord James of Bourbon, the lord John d'Artois, the earl of Tancarville, the earl of Estampes, the earl Danmartin, the earl of Joinville and the lord of Partenay to sit all at one board, and other lords, knights and squires at other tables; and always the prince served before the king as humbly as he could, and would not sit at the king's board for any desire that the king could make but he said he was not sufficient to sit at the table with so great a prince as the king was. But then he said to the king: 'Sir, for God's sake make none evil nor heavy cheer, though God this day did not consent to follow your will; for, sir, surely the king my father shall bear you as much honour and amity as he may do, and shall accord with you so reasonably that ye shall ever be friends together after. And, sir, methink you ought to rejoice, though the journey [the result of that day's battle] be not as ye would have had it, for this day ye have won the high renown of prowess and have passed this day in valiantness all other of your party. Sir, I say not this to mock you, for all that be on our party, that saw every man's deeds, are plainly accorded by true sentence to give you the prize and chaplet.' Therewith the Frenchmen began to murmur and said among themselves how the prince had spoken nobly, and that by all estimation he should prove a noble man, if God send him life and to persevere in such good fortune.[1]

The Black Prince's courtesy was of course assisted by his fluency in French, which remained the first language of the English court, and was in a sense the international language of chivalry. Moreover, this generous treatment of fellow-aristocrats in the hour of victory should not be taken as a typical occasion. The Black Prince and the English nobles would naturally have felt generous after gaining a decisive victory which put the French kingdom at their mercy and promised to win fortunes for many of them in ransom money; yet the very fact that many went to war to seek financial gain rather than glory was incompatible with chivalric ideals. Treatment of the non-noble classes was quite another matter. The Black Prince himself was responsible for the sack of Limoges in 1370, when the city was burnt and more than three thousand of its people put to death. Infantry taken in battle were entitled to none of the consideration granted to the nobility and no ransom could be expected for

[1] Froissart, *Chronicle* (trans. Berners), ch. CLXVIII.

them; they were often slaughtered rather than being suffered to become a burden on the victor's food resources.

In so far as it affected warfare, then, the chivalrous outlook detracted from the efficient conduct of war; its emphasis was on the manner of accomplishment rather than the thing accomplished, on glory rather than 'results'. To be chivalrous was to be unbusiness-like in the matter of achieving victory, and thus to be handicapped. We have seen that the French met defeat in the three great actions of Crécy, Poitiers and Agincourt because they employed the conventional chivalric mode of attack, the cavalry charge, against armies whose strength lay in a non-noble weapon, the longbow. Does it follow from this that the English won their victories over the French because they were more sceptical of the noble mirage of chivalry and, specifically, were less inhibited by chivalric notions of warfare?

Certainly the English were unashamed to proclaim the un-aristocratic longbow as their characteristic weapon. By Edward I's Statute of Winchester (1285) it became an obligatory weapon for English foot-soldiers and Edward III made compulsory the holding of archery contests on holidays. The great folk hero of later medieval England, Robin Hood, was a renowned archer with the longbow, a man who could 'slice the wand' again and again from a range of many hundred yards:

> I was counted the best archèr
> That was in merry Englond.[1]

If the English archery and tactical combination of archers with other arms suggest a professional approach to war which contrasts with French dilettantism, the explanation of this must be sought in the constant wars of the English with their Celtic neighbours, from whom, indeed, the use of the longbow had been learnt. Frequent campaigning in difficult terrain against the Welsh and Scots compelled the English to give much thought to strategy, tactics, weapons and the other problems of war; the consequences of military conservatism for them would have been expensive and humiliating and there was constant need for inventiveness. Throughout the eighty years of war the English had their eyes on the serious proposition of gaining the French

[1] 'A Little Geste of Robin Hood and his Meiny' in *The Oxford Book of Ballads*.

kingdom rather than the pageantry of chivalric pomp: it is symbolic of this that Henry V, when he married Princess Catherine in June 1420 (see p. 147), refused to hold any tournament but instead hurried off his knights to besiege Sens.

The French had indeed had opportunities to learn the dangers involved in launching knights against well-disciplined infantry— as witness their defeat by the Flemish in 1302 at Cambrai—but the lesson had not been learnt. In all the three major engagements the French cavalry was unleashed in a courageous but rash charge, and such tactics were not confined to their wars with the English. It was the French and Burgundian element which insisted on a headlong assault against the Turks at Nicopolis in 1396, despite the warnings of the king of Hungary who was accustomed to warfare against the Ottomans and refused to commit his own troops to mass suicide. Du Guesclin was able to show that successes could be won if only battle was not made the occasion of an undisciplined display of valour, but in opposition to him was a strong and respected tradition which reasserted itself at Agincourt. Such a tradition is exemplified by the reported refusal of the French to accept the services at Agincourt of six thousand archers offered by the city of Paris: 'what need have we of these shop-keepers?' they proudly enquired, and it was suggested that the principles of knightly honour would be contravened if the French army thus came to outnumber the English. It is not altogether just to adopt Froissart, who was a native of Valenciennes in Hainault and spent several years at the English court, as the characteristic representative of the French chivalric attitude to war, yet nowhere outside his pages are these campaigns depicted in such chivalrous colours as a series of knightly deeds in which the nobles of the contending sides were joined by a common devotion to valorous and 'courteous' enterprise. For Froissart, who set out to describe feats of arms and wondrous deeds as an encouragement to valour, the bowmen who actually won the decisive battles were an insignificant rabble of boors. Yet Froissart's stupid snobbery must not blind one to the nobler side of chivalry, the side that is seen in King Jean's decision to return voluntarily to imprisonment in England when his hostage absconded.

A difficult question remains to be answered. Should the French reliance on cavalry and preference for bravery over tactics be ascribed to mere military conservatism, or is this anachronistic emphasis on the aristocratic arm symptomatic of a more profound difference between the two countries? Did the French suffer merely from bad generalship or was their exaggerated respect for the horse-soldier and contempt for the infantryman indicative of a more hierarchical society? Certainly the English governing class was more content to recruit assistance in war from the lower ranks, a fact which suggests that class differences were less profound in England, while co-operation in war would in turn tend to foster a stronger feeling of community. Probably the French defeats were to some extent the result of France's social structure, but since the sort of historical sources which throw light on a country's social structure and the feeling between different ranks of society are almost entirely lacking for the medieval period it is not possible to give any confident answer to this intriguing and important problem.

A case could be made for the statement that the war was embarked on in a spirit of chivalry on both sides and that this view of warfare prevailed for a whole generation—until the Peace of Brétigny or perhaps the death of Edward III (1377)—to perish thereafter except in its disastrous revival by the French at Agincourt. King Edward, the founder of the Order of the Garter, was the very soul of chivalry and would have been puzzled at the argument that the English waged war less chivalrously because they relied to a greater extent on archery. For Froissart the great days of knightly feats of arms ended with this phase of the war, and when he returned to England in 1395 he found that there were Englishmen who shared his point of view and asked

> What has become of the great ventures [*entreprises*], the valiant men, the fine battles and the fine conquests? Where are the knights of England now, to accomplish such things? In those days the English were feared, and spoken of everywhere. Since good King Edward's death things have gone from bad to worse . . . and now King Richard of Bordeaux only seeks rest and pleasures. . . .[1]

It must be remembered, of course, that the sentimental Froissart was then an elderly man who would easily fall prey to nostalgia.

[1] Quoted by Kervyn de Lettenhove, *Œuvres de Froissart, Chroniques*, t. 1 (Introduction), pt. I, 418-19.

By the time that Richard II ruled England (1377–99) the French had begun to reflect on the causes of their defeats. Honoré Bonet's *Arbre des Batailles* (issued in 1387) is a practical handbook on war, not a treatise on chivalry and honour; it advocates defensive tactics in battle and suggests that the French should make more use of their peasantry, who are accustomed to a rigorous life. By the middle of the following century such views were commonplace, and similar warnings against indisciplined impetuosity and advice in favour of reliance on infantry and defensive warfare are to be found in Jean Juvénal des Ursins' *Remontrances* (1453) and Jean de Bueil's *Le Jouvencel*. The latter work (*c.* 1466) went directly against chivalric doctrine by forbidding any form of fraternization with the enemy : the author makes his hero reject a suggestion from the enemy commander that twelve knights from each side should pick out a convenient and impartial site for battle, on the ground that 'there is a common saying, and it is thought to be a very old one, that one should never do anything on the enemy's initiative'.[1]

In the 1370s an anonymous author presented to Charles V of France a weighty book of advice in the form of a dialogue entitled the *Somnium Viridarii* or *Dream in the Pleasure-garden* (better known under its French title as *Le Songe du Verger, qui parle de la disputacion du clerc et du chevalier*). The cleric who is a participant in this dialogue remarks sarcastically that 'The knights of our day have foot-battles and cavalry engagements painted on the walls of their rooms, so that through their eyes they may take delight in imaginary battles, which they would not dare to witness as members of an army, or even to be present at in person.'[2] This suggestion that there was now a strong vicarious element in chivalry, that its reality was a thing of the past, contains much truth. Every such ideal must look back to a golden past that can never have existed in reality, but it is particularly true of chivalry that the less of it there was the more it was talked about and the more strenuous were the attempts to revive it. Characteristic of this late, formalized, self-conscious chivalry is the highly-organized and pedantic pageantry of heraldry, with its learned glorification of

---

[1] Jean de Bueil, *Le Jouvencel*, ed. L. Lecestre (1889), I, 210.
[2] 'Somnium Viridarii' in Volume 2 of *Traitez des Droits et Libertez de l'Eglise Gallicane* (1731), I, 3.

noble descent, and such chivalric foundations as Edward III's Order of the Garter (*c.* 1348) and Philip the Good of Burgundy's Order of the Golden Fleece (1429). The Golden Fleece was inaugurated by Duke Philip

> from the great love we bear to the noble order of chivalry, whose honour and prosperity are our only concern, to the end that the true Catholic Faith, the Faith of Holy Church, our Mother, as well as the peace and welfare of the realm may be defended, preserved and maintained to the glory and praise of Almighty God our Creator and Saviour, in honour of His glorious Mother, the Virgin Mary, and of our Lord, St Andrew, Apostle and Martyr, and for the furtherance of virtue and good manners.

Membership of this Order was restricted to twenty-four (later thirty) noble knights. Four officers and a chancellor, secretary and treasurer served under the Master and Sovereign, who was always the reigning duke. Naturally France was most prolific of these Orders. Among the French foundations may be mentioned King Jean's Order of the Star (1352), whose three hundred members took an oath never to flee in battle (and which ceased to exist after only one year when more than a quarter of the knights were killed in a single engagement), and Boucicaut's Order of the White Lady, founded in 1398 for the defence of ladies and maidens in distress.

Sir Thomas Malory, the author of *Le Morte Darthur*, who flourished in Yorkist England, was convinced that chivalry was decadent in his day:

> O ye Knights of England, where is the custom and usage of noble chivalry that was used in those days? What do ye now but go to the baths and play at dice? And some not well advised, use not honest and good rule, against all order of knighthood. Leave this, leave it! and read the noble volumes of Saint Graal, of Launcelot, of Galahad, of Tristram, of Perseforest, of Perceval, of Gawain, and many more. There shall ye see manhood, courtesy, and gentleness. And look in latter days of the noble acts since the Conquest, as in King Richard's days Cœur de Lion, Edward the First and Third and his noble sons, Sir Robert Knolles, Sir John Hawkwood, Sir John Chandos and Sir Walter Manny; read Froissart, and also behold that victorious and noble King Harry the Fifth and the captains under him, his noble brethren, the Earls of Salisbury, Montagu, and many others

whose names shine gloriously by their virtuous noblesse and acts that they did in the honour of the order of chivalry. Alas! What do ye but sleep and take ease, and are all disordered from chivalry?[1]

Not all Malory's heroes, it will be noted, came from the distant past. It has already been suggested that attempts were made in their own lifetime to raise on to a chivalric pedestal such figures as Marshal Boucicaut (1366–1421) and Jacques de Lalaing (1421–53), the latter of whom was denied a knightly end in that he was killed by a cannon-ball. In the following century the same treatment was accorded to Bayard, the chevalier *sans peur et sans reproche* who met his death from arquebus fire in Lombardy in 1524. In Bayard's day the Emperor Maximilian strove hard to revive chivalry, writing a verse autobiography (1517) in which his adventures in the tourney and chase were recounted in the tradition of chivalrous literature, and assisting in the preparation of *Der Weisskünig*, a similar work on his father Frederick III and himself. Throughout the sixteenth century, jousting, though it had lost much of its utility as a form of military training, remained the aristocratic sport *par excellence*. King Henry II of France was killed jousting in 1559 and in the half-century after this the English court fêted its Queen in the annual accession-day tilts.

The brief account given here of the splendours and miseries of chivalric warfare has no claim to constitute a description of the phenomenon 'Chivalry'. Almost nothing has been said of chivalry and 'courtoisie' as literary *genres*—or one should perhaps say as a literary *Zeitgeist* witnessing to a *Zeitgeist* general among the classes of society who read or were read to. *The Adventures of Don Quixote*, that 'light and mirror of all knightly chivalry' (1604–14), bear witness to the fact that the valour of knights and their 'courtesy' to ladies remained the favourite topic of Europe's fiction-readers long after the armoured knight had disappeared from the battlefield. Don Quixote, it will be remembered, 'filled his mind with all that he read in his books, with enchantments, quarrels, battles, challenges, wounds, wooings, loves, torments and other impossible nonsense; and so deeply did he steep his

[1] W. Caxton, *The Book of the Ordre of Chyvalry* (ed. A. T. P. Byles, E.E.T.S., 1926: modernized here), pp. 122–4. Caxton continues: 'How many knights be there now in England that have the use and the exercise of a knight, that is to wit that he knoweth his horse and his horse him?'

imagination in the belief that all the fanciful stuff he read was true, that to his mind no history in the world was more authentic'. And so it came about that Don Quixote repaired his ancestors' rusty armour and fitted it with a pasteboard visor because 'he thought it fit and proper, both in order to increase his renown and to serve the state, to turn knight errant and travel through the world with horse and armour in search of adventures, following in every way the practice of the knights errant he had read of, redressing all manner of wrongs and exposing himself to chances and dangers, by the overcoming of which he might win eternal honour and renown'.[1]

Don Quixote is not merely a satire on chivalry but also the great prose poem of the sunset of chivalry. In Elizabeth I's England, Cervantes' contemporary Edmund Spenser was writing in his *Faerie Queen* of another 'gentle knight', 'for knightly giusts and fierce encounters fitt'. As in architecture there was no clear break between the last of 'true' Gothic and the beginning of the Gothic revival, so in literature there was no interruption between this prolongation of medieval romance and the Romantic revival of medieval taste as witnessed in the ballad collections of Bishop Percy and J. G. Herder and the European popularity of Macpherson's *Ossian* and Scott's *Ivanhoe*.

Even today international law enshrines the chivalric notion of warfare in the clauses of the Geneva Convention which govern the treatment of prisoners of war. The terms of these provide that 'other ranks' who are captured may be forced to work for the imprisoning power, but it is illegal to compel officers to work; they are the heirs of the nobles who dined with the Black Prince after Poitiers.

Further Reading

E. PERROY, *The Hundred Years War* (London, 1951)
K. FOWLER (ed.), *The Hundred Years War* (London, 1971).
E. PRESTAGE (ed.), *Chivalry* (London, 1928)
J. HUIZINGA, *The Waning of the Middle Ages* (Penguin Books)
S. PAINTER, *French Chivalry* (Great Seal Books)
FROISSART, *The Chronicles* (trans. G. Brereton, Penguin Classics)

[1] *Don Quixote*, ch. I (translation by J. M. Cohen).

VIII

THE EARLY RENAISSANCE

CONSIDERATION of military events in fourteenth-century France in the previous chapter led on to a discussion of the role of 'chivalry' in the social and literary culture of later medieval Europe. This discussion was almost entirely confined to Europe north of the Alps, and we must now turn to the culture of the wealthiest and most advanced region in western Europe, the Italian peninsula. Although this chapter is prefaced by the time-honoured abstract noun, 'Renaissance', its subject is perhaps better defined as the intellectual and cultural history of Italy in the fourteenth and the earlier part of the fifteenth centuries.

This culture differed from that of contemporary northern Europe in that its tone was set as much by town-dwelling merchants and lawyers as by feudatories from courts and castles, and more by all these than by clerics. The chief element in the contrast between Italian civilization and that of Europe north of the Alps was secular education. The lay schoolmaster had never disappeared from medieval Italy. By the thirteenth century he was to be found even in the smaller towns, and in the great cities he was ubiquitous. The mercantile classes sent their children to receive an education that was at least in part professional—there was a strong emphasis on mathematics—and in the towns of northern Italy the literacy rate must have been high. Giovanni Villani reports that at Florence in the 1320s some 8,000 to 10,000 children were in attendance at elementary schools at any one time. The total population of the city at that time was in the region of 90,000. Owing to the high death-rate, the age structure of the population was very different then from now, but if 10 per cent of the population was indeed attending elementary school it is likely that a majority of the male citizens received some schooling. The proportion of Florentines that went on to receive further education was less considerable. More than 1,000 boys attended the six mathematical schools and the four grammar schools had a total of 600 pupils, but probably a good many boys and girls were taught at home by a tutor at this stage.[1]

The tone of the Italian culture of this period is markedly urban in the most direct sense. Collections of amusing stories, like the *Novellino*—from which one tale has already been quoted (p. 98) —were immensely popular, and a theme that ranked in favour with the quick-witted merchant and his prompt retorts was his rustic counterpart, slow of understanding and easily imposed upon. The satirists made no attempt to spare the feelings of the peasant, for he was not part of their public; and without the stock figure of the credulous, gullible yokel, Boccaccio and Sacchetti would be deprived of much of their subject-matter. But, if the countryman was a mere figure of fun, the countryside itself was the object of a new admiration. This revolution in the history of sensibility is directly connected with the urban quality of the culture of the time. The man who appreciates the beauty of the rural landscape is the man who visits it for his summer holiday (the fourteenth-century Florentine merchant usually spent four months a year at his villa) or to picnic and to hunt, not he who struggles to wrest a living from it. No doubt it was partly their reading of the Latin poets which made them see beauty in rural scenery, but its effect went deep, and men now not only read pastorals but again wrote pastoral poetry with sincerity of feeling. Shepherds and shepherdesses had come back to decorate the literary scene for many a century. In no one is this feeling for the country stronger than in Petrarch (1304–74), whose joy in scenery even shines through his self-conscious literariness. It was typical of his time that Petrarch should contrast the 'convenience of the city' with the 'leisure of the country'. His letters contain many descriptions of scenery and in one he declares that 'I have always felt, from my earliest childhood, a hatred of cities, implanted in me by nature, and a love of sylvan life.' [2]

If the countryside was an escape from town and business,

---

[1] G. Villani, *Cronica*, Bk. XI, ch. 94.
[2] Petrarch, *Familiarium Rerum*, X, 4.

there was another world of escape into the imagination provided by that very literary tradition, native to France, which was described in the preceding chapter. For the merchant nothing was more delightful than to sit comfortably in his chair and to read of the perilous, valiant and exhausting deeds of chivalrous knights. Thus he took his risks and his exercise vicariously, and as his modern counterpart sails with the *Kon-Tiki* or climbs Everest so he in his mind's eye fought with Hector and King Arthur and Charlemagne, or mingled with such chivalrous heroes of a more recent age as the 'Young King' (the son of Henry II of England) and Saladin. Dante himself confessed attachment to memories of such reading of:

> the ladies and the knights, the toils and ease
> which roused in us both love and courtesy
> where now so evil have all hearts become.[1]

And when Folgore of San Gimignano, also writing in the early fourteenth century, composed a series of sonnets on the months, his April was 'the gentle countryside all flowering with fresh grass' and his May pure chivalric nostalgia, a picture of horses, banners, trappings, shields, jousting-spears, lances and garlands.[2]

These men were also patriotic citizens of precarious city-republics and normally they played an energetic part in the political life of their state. Coluccio Salutati, who served Florence as chancellor in the later fourteenth century, was one of a number of literary men who defended the 'active life' which was contrasted in time-honoured controversy with the religious and philosophical 'contemplative life'. Again and again it was urged that a 'complete man' should play an active part in public affairs (Cicero was often quoted to this effect) and that he should have a family. Before the middle of the fifteenth century such a view was a commonplace. Giannozzo Manetti (1396–1459) attacked Pope Innocent III's ascetic work on *Contempt of Worldly Things*, and quoted with approbation the tag from Terence 'I am a man and I think nothing human alien to me.' Matteo Palmieri's *Della Vita Civile* (finished in 1439) attacks 'idle men who live in solitude away from all public affairs, contributing nothing to the

---

[1] *Purgatorio*, XIV, ll. 109–11 (tr. A. L. Money).
[2] *Sonetti Burleschi e Realistici dei primi due Secoli*, ed. Massèra (Bari, 1940), pp. 159–60.

common good of other mortals and concerned only with their own health . . . Mere sanctity does no good to anything but itself.' [1] L. B. Alberti's *Della Famiglia*, written in the same years, teaches the same doctrine: 'the true citizen will love tranquillity, but his own less than that of other good men; he will delight in his own leisure, but not less in that of the other citizens; he will wish for unity, quiet, peace and tranquillity in his own household, but still more for these in the affairs of his city . . . Wise men say that good citizens should undertake the affairs of the republic and bear the burdens of their *patria* . . . to maintain the general well-being of the citizens.' [2] In these phrases concerning the 'common good', we return, it will be noted, to Aristotle, the fountain-head of political writers (see above, p. 10).

The civic patriotism that received this theoretical justification was a powerful force which had no need of literary backing. *Campanilismo*—a man's narrow preference for his native town—is still a strong sentiment in Italy, and was far more potent in an age when towns were independent republics having their own political traditions and a long history of warfare against their neighbours. The *palazzo comunale*, the outward sign of the commune's personality, had to be worthy of the town's prestige, as did its other ecclesiastical and municipal monuments. The patronage of the republics was thus an important influence in 'Renaissance' artistic achievement. A city would pay well a man who could enhance its beauty, but the worker in the visual arts was still an 'artist' only in the sense that he was a member of an *arte* (gild); he had no great pretensions and as yet he was vexed by no problems concerning his 'role in society'. Versatility was expected of him as a conscientious craftsman—not as an 'all-round personality'—and he had to be able to turn his hand to the design of fortifications and acqueducts and fountains, as well as being ecclesiastical architect, sculptor and painter. By the early fourteenth century the successful Florentine artist could already hope to enjoy a certain prestige. In 1300 the Council called Arnolfo di Cambio, the master of works at the cathedral and the campanile, 'the most famous master and greatest expert in church building known in these parts', and in 1334 they were proud to

---

[1] M. Palmieri, *Della Vita Civile*, Bk. 1.
[2] L. B. Alberti, *Della Famiglia*, Bk. 3.

appoint Giotto to 'the honourable and worthy mastership and governorship of the work at the church of S. Reparata and of the construction and perfection of the walls of the city of Florence . . . and the other connected works of the said city'.

At the beginning of this chapter it was stated that its theme would be Italian culture in the fourteenth century, yet the time-honoured phrase 'Renaissance' has already been brought into use many times. How has it come about that the civilization of the period has received this highly adhesive label, and can the use of this abstraction be justified? The answer to the first of these questions is comparatively straightforward: it is, in brief, that influential writers in Florence, from the fourteenth century to the sixteenth, believed themselves to be living in an age of cultural 'rebirth'. Soon after the middle of the fourteenth century Boccaccio proclaimed that the muses had long been banished from Italy, but Dante had opened the way for their return and Petrarch restored them. He praised Giotto in similar terms as 'one of the lights of Florence's glory', who 'brought painting back into the light after it had been hidden for many centuries under the errors of those who aimed to please the eyes of the ignorant rather than the understanding of the wise'.[1] In his own day, he thought, individuals not unlike the men of antiquity were seeking immortality, and the tiny spark of their efforts raised a hope that the lost light of antiquity might be restored. Giotto had already figured in Giovanni Villani's *Chronicle* as 'the most sovereign master in painting of his day and the one who could best depict people and their movements in a lifelike way',[2] but only rather later, in the writings of the chancellor Salutati and Villani's nephew Filippo, can this view be seen to have crystallized as an agreed (but highly Florentinocentric) version of cultural history. Salutati says that the study of 'letters' declined from late classical times, but emerged again with the Paduan Mussato and with Dante, Petrarch and Boccaccio. Filippo Villani in his *Lives of Famous Florentines* (*c.* 1400) echoes his uncle's view of Giotto but names Cimabue as the first restorer of artistic standards. The first post-classical poet whom he notes is Dante and he mentions six more recent 'moderns'.

[1] *Decameron*, Day VI, nov. 5.
[2] *Cronica*, XI, 12.

M

In the 1430s the same interpretation is to be found in Matteo Palmieri who proclaims that:

> before Giotto painting was dead and pictures of people risible; he raised it up and his followers have maintained this. Carving and architecture for an extremely long period produced only stupid marvels, but in our time they have risen again and come back into the light after being polished and perfected by many masters. As for letters and liberal studies, it would be better to be silent than to say little. The principal leaders and true masters of men in every good attainment were so forgotten for more than eight hundred years that there was no one who had any true knowledge of them.

But 'Latin elegance' and 'the sweetness of the Latin tongue' were restored by Leonardo Bruni (1370–1444), and now men should thank God that they have had the good fortune to be born in an age when 'the excellent arts of skill are flourishing more than they have for a thousand years'.[1] The same tremendous confidence appears in Leon Battista Alberti's dedication—addressed to Brunelleschi, the designer of the dome of Florence cathedral—to his work *On Painting*:

> I believed that it was as many people told me, that nature, the mistress of things, had now indeed grown old and weary, and, just as she no longer brought forth giants, so with talents, which in her younger and more glorious times, so to speak, she brought forth plentifully and wonderfully.
>
> But after I was brought back here to this city of ours [Florence], adorned above all others, from the long exile in which we Alberti have grown old, I realized that in many, but especially in you, Filippo, and in our dear friend Donato [Donatello] the sculptor, and in those others, Nencio [Ghiberti], Luca [della Robbia], and Masaccio, there was talent for every noble thing not to be ranked below any who was ancient and famous in these arts.[2]

This was the sort of optimism that in 1464 caused Giovanni Rucellai to thank God in all sincerity for having made him a Christian born in Italy, 'the most worthy and noble part of Christendom', in Tuscany 'esteemed one of Italy's most worthy provinces' and, above all, at Florence, 'the most beautiful city not

[1] M. Palmieri, *Della Vita Civile*, Bk. 1.

[2] L. B. Alberti, *De Pictura*, Dedications (translation from E. G. Holt, *A Documentary History of Art*, Vol. I (Doubleday Anchor Books, N.Y., 1957), 205–6).

A Renaissance ruler and his son: Federigo and Guidobaldo da
Montefeltro *See Chapters VIII and XI*

Chancellor Rolin, adviser to Philip the Good of Burgundy
By Van Eyck *See Chapter IX*

only in Christendom, but in the whole world'—and for the fact
that his lot had fallen 'in the present age, which all who understand aright know full well transcends in splendour every age that
has passed since Florence was first built'.[1] This Florentine certainty of existing in a great time of rebirth was finally incorporated
and crystallized in Giorgio Vasari's immensely influential *Lives of
the most excellent Painters, Sculptors and Architects* (1550), and it
secured acceptance by Michelet, John Addington Symonds, and
Burckhardt, who in the nineteenth century popularized the idea
of the Renaissance in French, English and German. The concept
of an age of the Renaissance, then, was the product of the age
itself—indeed it states the period's estimate of itself.

To decide whether the concept of a 'Renaissance' is justified by
the culture of fourteenth- and fifteenth-century Italy is much
more difficult. There is certainly no clear break in the continuity
of Italian culture. The classical studies of the fourteenth-century
'humanists' (the word implied a contrast with 'divine', or theological, learning) were in the tradition of a rhetorical education
which had never been abandoned. Lawyers had long studied the
art of writing and speaking eloquently in accordance with classical models. The Paduan lawyer Mussato (1261–1329), mentioned
by Salutati, and his contemporary Lovato, may have seen Roman
civilization as a living thing because their studies of Roman Law
gave it reality, but their taste for reading Latin authors was
nothing new. They were exceptional only in their extension of
the principle of classical imitation: Mussato composed a drama,
Eccerinis, on the model of the classical tragedies, concerning the
thirteenth-century Ghibelline tyrant, Ezzelino da Romano. The
corpus of classical literature known to Mussato differed little
from that available to thirteenth-century scholars, but he was
acquainted with some books of Livy's *History* which had long
been unread. The circle of humanists at Padua was not unique:
others existed at the same time at Verona—where the Chapter
library housed many little-known classical works—at Naples and
in the papal court at Avignon.

One resident of Avignon was Petrarch (1304–74), the most
important figure in the literary culture of fourteenth-century
Italy. Petrarch, a Florentine by descent, had been sent to study

[1] Giovanni Rucellai, *Zibaldone* (ed. A. Perosa), pp. 117–18.

law at Montpellier and Bologna, but neglected his studies and conceived a fanatical admiration for the works of Cicero. He even addressed ardent letters, couched in his best Ciceronian Latin, to the long-dead author, and behaved in so unbalanced a manner that his enraged father burnt some of his books, though he eventually spared Cicero's *Rhetoric*. Abandoning the legal career, Petrarch took minor orders and, thanks to the patronage of the Colonna, received several prebends and a priorate. He visited Paris, the Netherlands and the Rhineland, and once undertook a mission to Naples on behalf of the pope, but for many years resided mainly at the papal court, living on his unearned ecclesiastical income as a self-consciously literary figure, a sort of fourteenth-century Jean-Jacques Rousseau, an author in several *genres* and a scholar. In middle age he returned to Italy, living at Parma, Padua, Milan, and finally in and near Venice.

Petrarch's writings serve admirably as a reminder of the high degree of continuity in fourteenth-century Italian culture. There was little change in legal or medical education, and philosophy and theology continued to be studied in the scholastic tradition, based on Aristotelian logic. The theme of Petrarch's *Secretum*, which is perhaps his most deeply-felt work, is the preference which should be given to virtue over glory. In form the book is a dialogue, in which Petrarch holds a discussion with St Augustine, the greatest of the fathers of the Church, and there is nothing in his conclusions which would have shocked the readers of the intervening medieval centuries. 'Some people in their pride', he says, 'have sought to secure by force the secrets of nature and the high mysteries of God, which we receive with humble faith.' He goes on to quote with approval (from Romans 11 : 34) 'For who hath known the mind of the Lord?' and 'But what is commanded thee, think thereupon with reverence; for it is not needful for thee to see the things that are secret. Be not curious in unnecessary matters: for more things are showed unto thee than men understand.' (Ecclesiasticus 3 : 23–4). It would scarcely be possible to be more 'medieval' than this and more antagonistic to that spirit of enquiry which is often considered the very essence of 'the Renaissance'. Moreover, another of Petrarch's works, the *De Vita Solitaria*, is an essay in one of the most popular of all medieval *genres*: far from being a protagonist of the civic and family virtues, he wrote a defence of the monastic life. In one of his letters Petrarch describes an ascent of Mont Ventoux (near Avignon), and both this gratuitous undertaking and his account of the climb and of the view from the top—which is perhaps fictitious—have been held to mark an epoch in the evolution of human sensibility. But the significant point is Petrarch's reflection after the climb that St Augustine is right, and that 'men admire mountains and sea, river, oceans and stars' but 'nothing is truly wonderful except the soul'. Nor is Petrarch exceptional among the early humanists in the closeness of his adherence to traditional ways of thought. His friend Giovanni Boccaccio (1313–75), also a scholar and a versatile author, in many respects followed the footsteps of the writers of medieval romances and *fabliaux* in both style and content, while such works as his *De viris illustribus* (*On famous men*) had French analogues in writings of the same century which advocated imitation of the virtues of the ancient Romans (above, p. 142).

So much for the element of continuity. But the 'Renaissance' is not a mere delusion; there were new cultural threads interwoven with the old. Some of these are connected with the rediscoveries of classical writings already mentioned. Petrarch himself, who was a good textual scholar, found an unknown work by Cicero at Liége and a better text of Livy at Chartres. A friend of Petrarch's made similar discoveries in the monastic library at Monte Cassino, and Boccaccio was responsible for putting back into circulation, as it were, the great historian Tacitus and some works of Cicero, Seneca and Ovid. In certain moods of Petrarch one may detect a new confidence in his attitude towards intellectual authority. He defiantly mocks those who accept every word of Aristotle as true: 'I think he was a great man,' he says, 'but he was a man . . . and I do not doubt that he was totally wrong about some things . . . even important ones.' Yet his deference towards Cicero and St Augustine perhaps tended to substitute a Roman for a Greek authority. 'Among the many subjects which interested me,' he says, 'I dwelt especially upon antiquity, for our own age has always repelled me and, had it not been for the love of those dear to me, I should have preferred to have been born in any other period than our own.'[1] The belief that imitation of Roman

[1] *Posteritati* (trans. by J. H. Robinson).

virtues could restore the great days of classical Italy shows clearly
in Petrarch's account (not necessarily an entirely veracious one)
of his meeting with the Emperor Charles IV at Mantua in 1354.
He promised to present the emperor with his still unfinished
Lives of Famous Men when Charles had become distinguished not
only by his title 'but also by your deeds: and when, by the greatness of your character, you shall have placed yourself upon a level
with the illustrious men of the past. You must so live that
posterity shall read of your great deeds as you read of those of the
ancients.'

> Following up the opportunity afforded by my words, I presented
> him with some gold and silver coins, which I hold very dear. They
> bore the effigies of some of our rulers—one of them a most lifelike
> head of Caesar Augustus—and were inscribed with exceedingly
> minute ancient characters. 'Behold, Caesar, those whose successor
> you are,' I exclaimed, 'those whom you should admire and emulate,
> and with whose image you may well compare your own. To no one
> but you would I have given these coins, but your rank and authority
> induce me to part with them. I know the name, the character, and
> the history, of each of these who are there depicted, but you have not
> merely to know their history, you must follow in their footsteps; the
> coins should, therefore, belong to you.' Thereupon I gave him the
> briefest outline of the great events in the life of each of the persons
> represented, adding such words as might stimulate his courage and
> his desire to imitate their conduct.[1]

The influence of Greek antiquity on fourteenth-century Italian
culture was small. Throughout the medieval period there had
been many in the formerly Byzantine territory of southern Italy
who knew Greek; both Petrarch and Boccaccio had sought assistance from natives of this region, but neither managed to acquire
a good knowledge of the language. Before the end of the century
a number of Greeks, such as Manuel Chrysoloras, left Byzantine
soil and taught Greek in Italy, and at this time the direct influence
of Plato's own works began to be felt. Earlier, his impact had
come only through the *Timaeus*, an uncharacteristic book, and,
more strongly, through neo-Platonic writers. Far more influential than Greek writings, however, was the contribution of
France, and in particular of French imaginative literature. This

---

[1] *Familiarium Rerum*, XIX, 3 (trans. by J. H. Robinson).

went back to the chivalresque epics and to romance poetry—the *Roman de la Rose* was much read in Italy—and above all to the Provençal troubadours, who were the delight of St Francis of Assisi and did much to form the *dolce stil nuovo* ('sweet new style') of Dante's predecessors in Tuscany. Dante himself pays tribute to the troubadours in the *Divine Comedy* when he breaks into eight lines of Provençal (*Purgatorio*, XXVI, lines 140-7). Nor was it uncommon for Italians to write works in French, though this became rarer in the course of the fourteenth century. Brunetto Latini—placed by Dante in his Inferno—compiled in the 1260s a sort of encyclopaedia in French (the *Livre dou Tresor*) and Marco Polo's *Travels*, dictated by Marco during his Genoese captivity in 1298-9, also first appeared in the French of his fellow-prisoner Rustichello of Pisa, the author of a number of French romance works. The strong French element in the writings of Boccaccio, who was probably born in France, has already been mentioned.

To complete this attempted answer to our second question—how valid is the concept 'Renaissance'?—we must return to the *milieu*. The civilization of a period requires consideration in terms of its volume (to express it crudely) as well as its content, and these need to be seen in the light of contemporary patronage. The achievements of Italy in learning and the arts in the fourteenth and fifteenth centuries would have been impossible without the wealth of the traders and financiers of the time, and in an infinite number of ways they reflect the outlook of these men. Boccaccio's *Decameron* has been called a 'mercantile epic' and most of his tales derive their setting and action from the world of the cosmopolitan merchant of his day. Much of the contents of the *Decameron* could be defined as stories written about commercial travellers for commercial travellers, and more than two-thirds of the surviving early manuscripts are known to have belonged to merchant families. The importance to the visual arts of the patronage of these families is evident. One has only to recall the names of the chapels in which are to be found frescoes by Giotto (or attributed to him). These are the chapels of the Bardi and Peruzzi (both great banking houses, which together lent Edward III of England £125,000 in 1338-9) in S. Croce (Florence) and at Padua the chapel of the Scrovegni founded by the wealthy

Paduan merchant Enrico Scrovegni. Contemporaries of course realized that the wealth and the cultural achievements of their time were connected. Giovanni Rucellai—whose gratitude for being born a fifteenth-century Florentine has already been recorded—has another striking passage in his Notebook (*Zibaldone*), in which he lists the various aspects of Florence's greatness in his day (he is writing in about 1458). The Italians, he says, are now pre-eminent in arms; literary style has reached a level unapproached since Cicero; Florence has added greatly to its subject-territory; the appearance of the city has been wonderfully improved by the skilful architects of churches, palaces and other buildings; there have been notable painters and workers in the other arts; people are now dressed and their houses decorated with greater luxury, and they have many more slaves than formerly;[1] the manufacture of new types of costly textiles has begun; the Florentines now trade (from Pisa) in heavy galleys; dowries have been increased, thanks to the ingenious invention of dowry funds as part of the city's public debt; and Florence has seen recently four 'notable citizens worthy to be remembered'. These are Palla Strozzi, happy, learned and wealthy; Cosimo dei Medici, 'perhaps the richest Italian there has ever been', an extremely able man who 'controlled the government of the city as though he had been its lord'; Leonardo Bruni, scholar and eloquent writer; and Filippo Brunelleschi, the greatest architect since Roman times. 'The revenues of the commune of Florence are greater than ever before', churches are wealthy and religious observance flourishing. There is a possibility that all citizens may be exempt from taxation for ten years. Even the middle ranks of society now dress in the best quality cloth and 'the city is richer than ever in ready money, merchandise, property, and holdings in the public funds, and therefore tourneys, weddings and other feasts have become richer and more magnificent than they ever were in the past'. Rucellai ends, as a true merchant, with some statistics. Among these are his estimate of the wealth of Florence's citizens in specie and commodities alone at a million and a half florins: the same figure, he thinks, would have held good thirty years before, but in 1418-23, before the expensive cam-

---

[1] These were mostly oriental and Circassian slaves shipped to Italy from the Levant.

paigns against the Visconti, it might have reached two million florins.[1]

Rucellai, it will be observed, deals with economics and the arts together, but he does not imply a simple relationship between wealth and cultural achievement of cause and effect. It has been argued that this causation in a sense worked in reverse because merchants tended to spend more money on artistic patronage when the returns from mercantile ventures diminished. This hypothesis supposes an extreme degree of rationality in the merchants and it receives little support from parallel circumstances, but it serves as a useful reminder of the truism that there is no simple equation whereby greater wealth creates greater artistic and intellectual achievement.

Although Rucellai dwelt on the wealth and flourishing condition of the Florentine church, the culture of his day had a secular tone which contrasted strongly with the characteristically medieval culture of European scholasticism. For the first time since the classical period the educated layman was not an exceptional figure. Italy, with its considerable class of lawyers and notaries, had increasingly constituted an exception, but, *grosso modo*, the educated men of western Europe for a millennium were clerics and therefore had no children—or were supposed to have no children.[2] The genetic effects of clerical celibacy, though quite imponderable, must be taken into account in discussing the social background to Renaissance culture. By depriving of posterity a high proportion of the most able men, this institution almost certainly diminished the average intellectual ability of the population as a whole.[3] Furthermore it prevented any direct continuity of intellectual achievement within the family; the home was never an environment within which intellectual traditions could be handed down from generation to generation, although certain monastic houses came near to substituting for this the nurture of a religious 'family'.

When fathers who were merchants or lawyers began to take an interest in the upbringing of their sons a new form of cultural

---

[1] *Zibaldone* (ed. A. Perosa), pp. 60-2.

[2] In practice there was little attempt to enforce celibacy among the lower clergy until the eleventh century.

[3] Cf. Francis Galton's attribution of the 'Dark Ages' to the compulsory celibacy of 'gentle natures' (*Hereditary Genius*, Pt. 3).

transmission came into being, and pride in family traditions ensured that this new force should be a powerful one. The same spirit of family pride and loyalty played a direct part in encouraging cultural patronage, since no distinguished family wished to be outshone in the fashion of expending its money on the 'right' artists and men of letters. No work illustrates the strength of these family traditions better than L. B. Alberti's dialogue *Della Famiglia*, although (or because?) Alberti's father was an illegitimate descendant of this illustrious Florentine house. Again and again Alberti returns to the family's great past, its military deeds, its distinction in the law and in administration:

> Our family, the Alberti, which has always been most honest in all its undertakings, has long conducted its commercial transactions in the West and in many other parts of the world, with such honesty and integrity that we have won universally no inconsiderable or undeserved fame. There was never a single man amongst us who permitted any dishonest practice in trading. All observed the terms of every transaction with entire, scrupulous probity, and thus we became known as great merchants in Italy and abroad in Spain, in the west [England and Flanders], in Syria, Greece and indeed in every port. Moreover the Alberti have been of no little assistance to the state. Of every thirty-two *danari* spent by the state [Florence] in those days, one at least had been provided by our family. A great sum indeed this, but our goodwill and affection towards our State and our furtherance of its interests have always been yet greater! And so we have won fame and reputation with all, but more good feelings and love from strangers than from our own fellow-citizens.

The purpose of this harangue, addressed to two young members of the family by Lionardo Alberti, is to ensure 'that you should always continue as devoted as you are to our family, and equally desirous of increasing its dignity, authority, fame and glory in every way that is open to you; for it would be shameful should you fail to preserve the reputation won by our ancestors'. The Alberti have been considered among the wealthiest of Florentine families for more than two hundred years; no other family has had so long a history of prosperity, for the Cerchi, Peruzzi and many others have fallen into distress. The Alberti have always kept their word, and their continuing affluence must be a divine reward for this. 'I have tried to show you', Lionardo adds, 'that not a few occupations by which wealth may be gained are praised and are honest ones, and that one of these is the merchant's profession.' [1] Elsewhere Lionardo gives his views on education. 'I should wish to see a young noble with a book in his hand more frequently than a hawk on his fist; I never liked that common saying that it is sufficient to know how to write your own name and add up the money due to you. I prefer the old custom of our Family. Almost all we Alberti have been considerable men of letters. . . .' He then expatiates on the distinction of no fewer than seven Alberti in theology, mathematics and other fields. 'Any family, but particularly one like ours, should bring up its boys so that with age they increase in wisdom and knowledge, not merely to conform with this ancient and admirable custom of ours, but also on account of the other advantages that a family derives from its men of letters.' [2]

The same atavistic version of the Renaissance principle of *imitatio* figures prominently in another dialogue of the same period, Matteo Palmieri's *Della Vita Civile*, which is dedicated to Alessandro degli Alessandri, 'born of a noble line, begotten by an excellent father, and brought up to study the arts' in the hope that in him 'the glory of the perfect virtue of Ugo, your excellent father, and of your other most renowned and glorious ancestors, may achieve its climax'. In Book I Palmieri deals with education, and throughout he assumes that a boy's father will be directly concerned with his upbringing. 'A father to whom a son has been born should above all have ideal hopes for him and should expect him to grow up a virtuous and worthy man . . . the father would not be willing to weary his mind on the education of one for whose future he cherished no hopes.' When the child emerges from babyhood 'the father should start to observe his son closely, for this is the age when the boy first thinks that he already knows things, and when he begins to be free to make decisions and to live in his own way'. 'It is unnecessary to say anything of grammar [Latin], for every father should know positively that without that foundation any learning that may be built up is bound to tumble into barren ruin.' Beyond this, the father should hope that his son will acquire some special talent displaying 'a reverent readiness of the body or a worthy employment of the mind which is an adornment to life'.

[1] *Della Famiglia*, Bk. 2.   [2] *Ibid.*, Bk. 1.

The greatest of Florentine mercantile families, the Medici, have not been discussed in this account of Renaissance culture and families—there will be some mention of them in a later chapter—but Rucellai, Alberti and Palmieri were all Florentines, and it is probable that this chapter has been concerned too exclusively with Florence. By definition the greatest centre of Renaissance culture is not the most characteristic centre, and some wealthy Italian cities were far less concerned with the arts and learning. At this period, Genoa, for example, did not acquire a tradition of patronage, though it is noteworthy that some Genoese showed a stronger enthusiasm for contemporary Flemish painting than was normally found elsewhere in Italy. This taste was certainly acquired through Genoa's trading links with the Flemish textile cities and with Bruges.

It is worth remembering that the emphasis—perhaps exaggerated here—on the *bourgeois* nature of the Renaissance *milieu* would have been indignantly denied by many of the most characteristic figures of the time. Dante thought of himself as a town-dweller of noble, rural descent, and many Florentine thinkers and writers of the fourteenth and fifteenth centuries (those for instance who were members of the intermarried Strozzi and Acciauoli families) considered themselves in the same light. This was in part the consequence of the general permeation of chivalrous, aristocratic ideas, while the snobbery of merchants who made good naturally took the form of hankering after noble status. Yet there was much justification for this attitude, since such families drew much of their income from landed property. The merchants of Florence and Venice cannot be contrasted with rural property-owners because the former retained their connection with the countryside and invested their profits by purchasing more land: this generalization, however, does not hold true for Genoa, whose merchants had little taste for buying land, while the aristocratic landowners of Liguria played scarcely any part in the city's business life. Moreover—to leave the business-men altogether—Courts did not cease to be important centres of culture and patronage (see below, Chapter XI). Early *signori* such as the Scaligeri of Verona and Carrara of Padua were patrons respectively of Dante and Boccaccio, and much later, in the fifteenth and sixteenth centuries, a dominant role was played by more aristocratic and even feudal *milieux*. This phase of the Renaissance is mirrored in the frescoes executed by Mantegna for the Gonzaga at Mantua, in the *Orlando Innamorato* of Boiardo and the *Orlando Furioso* of Ariosto, whose patrons were the Este of Ferrara, and best of all in Castiglione's exquisite *Courtier*, of which the setting is the Montefeltro court at Urbino.

We must now return to our central problem: is the culture of this time aptly described by the epithet 'Renaissance'? Questions concerning the applicability of generic terms are not, of course, answerable in terms of straight positives and negatives. Historians accept or reject such concepts by subjective pragmatic criteria; they arrive at a judgment on the utility to them in considering and describing cultural developments in fourteenth- and fifteenth- century Italy of employing the concept 'Renaissance'. In practice the term is so generally used that its complete rejection in either thinking or writing seems unattainable. The idea of a Renaissance cannot now be abolished, but there remains the danger that, through illogical thinking, it may be accepted as something more than a label or generalization. The 'Renaissance' was not a 'thing' or 'force', to which consequences may be attributed. Nothing caused 'the Renaissance', nothing resulted from it, nothing was part of it and nothing lay outside it. Some aspects of the cultural development of the time are characteristic of humanism (in the restricted sense of classical learning), but to describe any of them as characteristic of 'the Renaissance' is another dangerous abuse of language. The term must be applied to that development in all its manifestations, not confined to supposedly new trends within an indivisible cultural complex.

Further Reading

J. BURCKHARDT, *The Civilization of the Renaissance in Italy* (many edns.)

F. CHABOD, *Machiavelli and the Renaissance* (Harper Torchbooks), Chapter IV ('The Concept of the Renaissance')

P. O. KRISTELLER, *Renaissance Thought* (Harper Torchbooks)

D. HAY, *The Italian Renaissance in its Historical Background* (Cambridge, 1961)

M. BISHOP (ed.) *Letters from Petrarch* (Bloomington & London, 1966)

D. THOMPSON (ed.), *Petrarch: an Anthology* (Harper paperback, N.Y.)

BOCCACCIO, *Decameron* (many translations)

IX

BURGUNDY, THE GREAT DUCHY OF THE WEST

THE crisis of the French monarchy in the early fifteenth century has been mentioned above (Chapter VII), and reference has been made to France's disunity during the reign of the mad Charles VI and the emergence of a powerful and quasi-independent duchy of Burgundy.[1] Between the first onset of the king's insanity (1392) and the death in battle of Duke Charles the Rash (1477), the course of French history was largely dictated by the policy of successive dukes of Burgundy. Burgundian abandonment of the English cause (1435) was the turning-point in the Hundred Years War, and forty years later the downfall of the duchy was equally decisive in the revival of the French crown between the close of the war and the French campaigns in Italy. This long and vital role in the history of France seems to justify the allocation of a chapter to the great period of Burgundy's history.

Burgundy emerged as a duchy, from a combination of counties, during the time of Carolingian decay. It fell to the Capetian house in the eleventh century, was granted by Robert the Pious to a younger son, and descended in this cadet line of the royal house for over three hundred years. The power of the dynasty, which often intermarried with the direct royal line, increased greatly during this long period. The advance of the duchy in cohesion and wealth was a gradual achievement, dependent on purchasing land and vassals, gaining from escheats, increasing revenue from judicial, monetary and ecclesiastical rights, and benefiting from the towns of the duchy, with their tolls, fairs and markets, their desire for privileges and willingness to provide

[1] See Map II and Genealogical Table.

THE VALOIS DUKES OF BURGUNDY

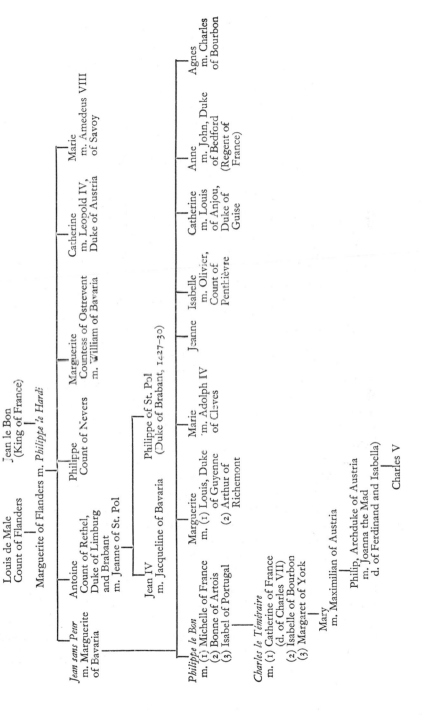

loans. The greatest territorial gain, the acquisition of the imperial county of Burgundy (Franche-Comté) was made by duke Eudes IV (1315–49) who was brother-in-law of Louis X and Philip VI and son-in-law of Philip V.

In 1361 the direct ducal line came to an end on the premature death of Philip de Rouvres, grandson of Eudes IV. The duke's cousin, King Jean le Bon, hastened to Dijon and took over the duchy, claiming it as next of kin. He made no attempt to gain the Franche-Comté, which went, with Artois and Champagne, to Margaret, the widowed countess of Flanders, while some of Philip's other lands were allotted to the house of Boulogne. Thus a number of possible claimants were satisfied. The king's decision to grant the duchy in appanage to his youngest son Philip, duke of Touraine, rather than annexing it to the Crown, perhaps requires explanation. The later consequences of this action were so unfortunate that it seems obvious to condemn it; but it must be remembered that Jean, after Brétigny and his first period of imprisonment, was beset with potential enemies—of whom the chief was Charles of Navarre—and felt unable to add to his own immediate responsibilities. The award to Philip, attributed by popular report to the youth's courageous bearing at Poitiers, was only made public on his father's death in 1364.

During the reign of Charles V, Philip the Bold of Burgundy ranked, with his other brothers Louis, duke of Anjou and John, duke of Berry, as one of the three great royal feudatories. His principal preoccupations were the pursuit of the war against the English and the giving of counsel to his royal brother. When Charles VI acceded in 1380 at the age of only eleven, Philip's duty of counselling his nephew became a yet more pressing obligation. Although the first moves in the process that was to build up the duchy to greatness took place in Philip the Bold's time, there was as yet no hint that these gains could be disadvantageous to the French crown. Indeed the intention of Philip's marriage to Margaret, daughter and only surviving child of Louis de Male, count of Flanders, was to bar English pretensions in the Low Countries. Margaret had been betrothed to Edmund of Langley, a son of Edward III, but Pope Urban V had given aid to the French cause—and perhaps to that of peace—by refusing a dispensation for this marriage within the prohibited degrees.

The Entry of Ferdinand and Isabella into Granada
See Chapter XIII

The Pope as the Whore of Babylon in Luther's Bible
See Chapter XIV

Her marriage to Philip took place in 1369, her father having finally given his consent in return for a considerable money payment and the return to Flanders of the territories lost to France in 1305. When the Count died in 1384 Philip succeeded him in Flanders, Artois, Franche-Comté and the smaller counties of Nevers and Rethel.

The great acquisitions of 1384 were the beginning of the fortunes of the Burgundian house (see Map II). These gains could certainly be reckoned an extension of French power, hence Charles VI's readiness to assist Louis de Male and then Philip in subjugating Ghent, and to arrange marriages for Philip's children which spread his sphere of influence still further to the east: a son and a daughter married into the Bavarian ducal house (which was also heir to Hainault, Holland and Zeeland), the other two daughters into the houses of Austria and Savoy. Nevertheless Philip was clearly exploiting his hold over his nephew, and doing so to such effect that between 1382 and 1403 he received one and a third million *livres* from Charles in 'gifts' alone. Towards the end of his life nearly half Philip's revenues were drawn from the French crown in the form of pensions, gifts and grants of royal taxation.

Philip quarrelled with his brothers the dukes of Anjou and Berry, and for a time lost much of his dominance through Charles VI's decision, in 1388, to take over the government of the kingdom. Four years later the king's madness brought to a head the struggle for control between Philip and Louis, duke of Orléans, Charles's younger brother. The pathetic king was at times so hopelessly insane that it was necessary to disguise as black-faced devils the strong men who had the task of changing his clothes. Meanwhile the bitter division which prevailed at the French court prevented France from exploiting the English civil disputes of the last part of Richard II's reign and the dynastic change of 1399.

Philip the Bold died in 1404, and was succeeded both in his duchy and dissensions by his son John 'the Fearless'. John made skilful use of demagogy to win over the people of Paris to his side. When an armed gang murdered the duke of Orléans in November 1407, John was almost at once forced to confess his responsibility for the deed, but the king took no action against

N

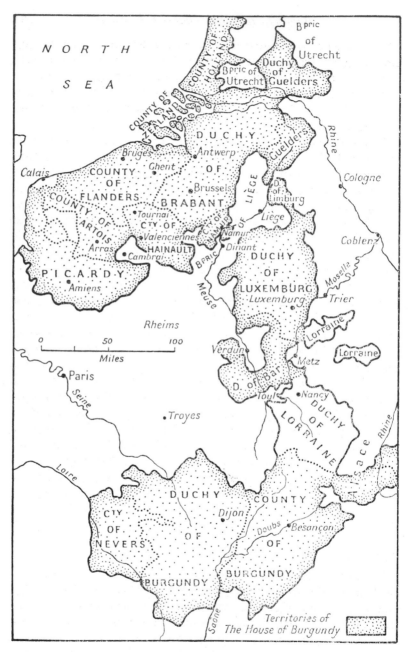

II. The Duchy of Burgundy in the fifteenth century

him. John was even permitted to present a justification through the theologian Petit, who defended the murder as a case of 'tyrannicide', the killing of an infamous tyrant or traitor in accordance with morality and with natural and divine law. Three years passed between the murder and the outbreak of civil war, during which time the leadership of the Orleanist cause came to be shared between the duke's son and successor Charles and the latter's father-in-law, the count of Armagnac. When the fighting began the two sides inevitably competed for English support. The English hesitated between Burgundian and Armagnac; it was clear that either side could do much to re-establish English power in France, but Henry IV could wait to see which would offer the most handsome terms. There is not room to describe here the disastrous civil wars and disturbances of this period, which culminated in the Agincourt campaign of 1415. Henry V, long a supporter of the Burgundian alliance, secured the duke's neutrality and thus John, now virtually an independent power, stood aloof while France suffered overwhelming defeat. Later he was to regret his absence from Agincourt, in which battle both his younger brothers were killed, but for the time John's feelings against the Armagnacs were too bitter. Meanwhile Agincourt greatly strengthened John's situation as well as Henry V's. In 1417 he came to an agreement with Queen Isabel, Charles VI's discarded wife, and the two of them governed much of northern France from Troyes; he also reached a secret understanding with the English king whereby he accepted Henry's claim as heir to the French throne. The following year Duke John's party gained Paris, and from this immensely strong position he embarked on negotiations for an agreement with the Dauphin. On 10 September 1419, when the two leaders met on the bridge at Montereau, where the Yonne flows into the Seine, John the Fearless was assassinated.

Whether or not the Dauphin was personally responsible for this murder, the crime would inevitably serve to drive the duke's heir into a new alliance with the English. This heir, Duke Philip the Good (1419–67), was married to the Dauphin's sister. He was entirely French by education, and he could feel his cause to represent French patriotism better than that headed by a king who was mad and a prince whom he thought a murderer. He hesitated before reaching a rather humiliating *entente* with Henry V, but his urgent wish for revenge and Henry's already dominant position in northern France sufficiently explain his decision— and do something to justify the alleged *mot* of a monk who a century later showed John's skull to Francis I with the words 'This is the hole through which the English made their way into France.' Philip the Good's acceptance of Henry as regent in France and heir to Charles immediately preceded the peak of Henry's achievement, the Treaty of Troyes of May 1420 (see above, p. 147).

Not till fifteen years after Troyes did Philip abandon the English, but the story of the relations between these two powers, whose interests differed radically, is one of increasing coldness. This was due both to the general decline of the English cause and to direct diplomatic conflict in the Low Countries. Philip soon found that he had no say in the government of France, that his own subjects were reluctant to accept Henry as the French heir, and that Henry's promises of a marriage alliance and more land meant little. As it turned out, Henry V was to die shortly before Charles VI, in August 1422. John, duke of Bedford, who then ruled in northern France on behalf of his infant nephew Henry VI, had to make considerable concessions to retain Philip's friendship: Philip had indeed been offered the regency, but refused it as a doubtful blessing. Bedford married Philip's sister (1423) and offered him more territory—on condition, however, that he conquered it for himself, from the Dauphin. When Philip lost influence in France his eyes turned further east, and it was there that he and the English clashed, thanks to the foolish policy of Bedford's younger brother, Humphrey, duke of Gloucester. The Burgundian house had long had an interest in Brabant and Limburg, which had passed through marriage to Anthony, son of Philip the Bold, and thereafter to his son, John IV. This duke John was married to Jacqueline, countess of Hainault, Holland, Zeeland and Frisia, but the match, a great success for John the Fearless on the diplomatic plane, was a failure on the human level. Jacqueline left her husband and gained the protection of Gloucester, who married her (her first husband being still alive), and by his ambitions in the Low Countries wrecked his brother Bedford's hopes of a continuing Burgundian alliance. For several years Philip of Burgundy campaigned intermittently against Gloucester, till the latter at last withdrew, and Jacqueline finally resigned to Philip the counties of Hainault, Holland and Zeeland and the lordship of Frisia (1433). Philip had already gained Brabant through the death without heirs of Duke John's younger brother, the count of St Pol.

Throughout these years, when the war in France was beginning to swing in favour of the Dauphin, Philip had given little assistance to the English, with the notorious exception of the handing over of the captive Joan of Arc (1430). By the beginning of 1435 the strength of Charles VII (the former Dauphin) was such that Philip prepared to abandon neutrality and move over to the French side. A preliminary peace was concluded in February 1435 and formal terms promulgated at Arras in September of the same year. The French were compelled to pay heavily—or so it appeared on paper—to secure Burgundian withdrawal from the struggle. Charles sought Philip's forgiveness for the murder at Montereau, offered to establish many pious foundations for the repose of the soul of Philip's father and promised to search out and punish the murderers. Philip was exempted from the obligation of doing homage to Charles as king of France, and even received the right to appoint twelve counsellors at the Paris *parlement*. His more substantial gains included the towns and counties of Mâcon, Auxerre and Boulogne, and the domains of the French crown on either bank of the Somme and between that river and Flanders. These 'towns of the Somme', however, were liable to compulsory repurchase by the French king if he could produce a sum of 400,000 gold crowns. Other clauses promised Philip an enormous revenue from fiscal rights in these territories and the county of Artois.

In practice Philip was to receive a good deal less from Charles VII than he had been offered by the terms of Arras. His perpetual hope that he might be accepted by Charles as a leading counsellor, the greatest of France's feudatories, was frustrated: the murders of 1407 and 1419 and the bitter opposition of the following years had inevitably made the relationship a deeply suspicious one. On the other side the murderers were never punished, the pious foundations were never forthcoming, and Charles did much to impede Philip's enjoyment of the fiscal and judicial rights ceded to him by the agreement of 1435. During the last five years of Charles's reign (1456–61) his relations with Philip were further poisoned by his quarrel with his son, the future Louis XI, and the latter's flight to Philip's territory.

For all these disappointments, Philip remained a great figure in Europe. Again failure in the west was counterbalanced by acquisitions in the east. Philip acquired the governorship of the duchy of Luxembourg from his aunt, Elizabeth of Görlitz, and he was able to extend his influence into the bishoprics of Utrecht and Liége by securing the election to these sees of a bastard son and a nephew. But, like his old enemy, Philip was saddened during his last years by serious disputes with his heir. One of the points at issue was the desire of Louis XI, Charles VII's successor, to buy back the 'Somme towns' under the terms of 1435. It was primarily in order to pay for a crusade that Philip accepted this repurchase, to which his son Charles was firmly opposed. Philip, whose father had fought in the heroic and disastrous crusade of Nicopolis (1396), was not least a Frenchman in his devout and anachronistic attachment to crusading schemes.

Under Philip's son and successor, Duke Charles the Rash (1467–77), Burgundy came to play a different role in French history, both on account of the duke's own ambitious temperament, and because England's withdrawal from France and involvement in her own civil war gave Burgundy the position of an independent challenger rather than the weight in the Anglo-French scales. This is not the place to recount the involved story of Charles's relations with Louis XI of France. While still count of Charolais he joined in alliance with various feudatories and challenged Louis in the ill-named War of the Common Weal (1465: see below, p. 237). Later he had Louis in his power at Péronne, but finally allowed the king to go free, probably on grounds of expedience rather than morality (below, p. 238). The same year (1468) he married Margaret, sister of Edward IV of England, and his support played a big part in the Yorkist restoration of 1471, achieved at the expense of the French-aided Lancastrians.

Charles's greatest efforts, however, were reserved for his attempt to gain Lorraine, Alsace and Champagne, the wide corridor which divided the Burgundian Low Countries from Bur-

gundy proper (see Map II). In 1469 he achieved his first success
in this endeavour when he received Alsace from the Archduke
Sigismund as a pledge for repayment of a loan of 50,000 florins,
needed by the archduke to raise an army against the Swiss Confederation. Sigismund's lordship over Alsace was little more than
nominal, but the title was worth acquiring, and it must have
seemed unlikely that the debt would be repaid (as stipulated) in a
lump sum. Despite difficulties in securing control in Alsace and
Guelders (which he annexed in 1473), Charles now turned against
the French in a frenzied attempt to destroy the structure of
Louis XI's kingdom. Already his debts to towns, bankers and
his own officials amounted to an enormous sum, so that by 1473
of the Italian bankers in Flanders only the Medici were willing to
lend him money; the others had recently been charging him rates of
interest rising to 48 per cent and even 55 per cent. Portinari, the
Medici's manager at Bruges, became a councillor of Charles, and
his unauthorized commitment to the duke was responsible for
heavy losses leading to the belated withdrawal of the Medici from
the branch in 1480–1. The armies raised with this money were of
very considerable size and De la Marche, who was present as
commander of the ducal guard, tells us that in 1474 at the siege of
Neuss Charles had 18,000 cavalry (including the archers brigaded
with the horsemen), 300 cannons, and an unspecified number of
infantry companies of 300 men each.[1] But Charles was now
detested by his overtaxed subjects, that year the Flemish estates
refused him an *aide*, and several of his officials had already deserted
to the service of Louis XI.

Meanwhile an astonishing agreement with Edward IV (Treaty
of London, 1474) provided for what was virtually a division of
France. Edward was to be king, but would have little territory
in eastern France—though Charles graciously allotted him
Rheims, for the day of the coronation ceremony only! By now
Charles's pigeons were coming home to roost in inconveniently
large numbers. Alsace was in revolt and Louis XI giving aid to
the rebels, new enmities were being stirred up by Charles's expansion into Germany, and Sigismund unexpectedly produced
(thanks again to Louis) the money which gave him the right to

[1] O. de la Marche, *Mémoires* (ed. H. Beaune and J. d'Arbaumont, 1883–8), IV,
82–94.

resume his lordship in Alsace. From the end of 1474 Charles's downfall was rapid. Louis XI, 'the universal spider', was already an ally of the Swiss and in close touch with Sigismund of Austria. In December 1474 he signed the treaty of Andernach with Frederick III. Soon the duke of Lorraine was brought into the alliance. Louis at last attacked Burgundy directly in the spring of 1475, by which time Charles had no money to pay his troops except those serving on the French frontier. When Edward IV's invading army landed, toward midsummer, it received so little of the support promised by Charles that Edward permitted himself to be bought over by the French. This treacherous abandonment was achieved at a cost to France of 75,000 crowns down, a pension of 50,000 crowns a year, and a dowry for the Dauphin's marriage to Edward's daughter Elizabeth (who was in fact destined to become the Queen of Henry VII). After this treaty (Picquigny, August 1475), Louis was able to follow the slightly less expensive policy of signing a truce with Charles and fighting him through parsimonious subsidies to the Swiss and the duke of Lorraine. Unwisely attempting a winter campaign against the Swiss, Charles was defeated by their pikemen at Granson on Lake Neuchâtel (March 1476). Three months later he lost still more decisively at Morat, on the route to Berne. Finally, now without money or allies, and with a much smaller army, he challenged duke René's reconquest of Lorraine, but was overwhelmed and killed at the battle of Nancy (5 January 1477).

This renascent Middle Kingdom of Lotharingia was made possible above all by Anglo-French rivalry, which allowed the dukes to play off the two sides against each other, but also by the particular circumstances of Charles VI's insanity and his son's lack of spirit. The English required the goodwill of Burgundian Flanders if they were to conquer northern France, and this area derived much of its economic importance from its proximity to England. Yet, skilfully though they used their initial strength to achieve territorial expansion to the north and east—and their marriage policy was greatly favoured by fortune—the Burgundian dukes never entirely transcended the status of 'over-mighty subjects'. The sumptuousness of their Court and the intricate formalities of its etiquette were famous throughout the west.

No chivalric order surpassed in prestige Philip the Good's foundation of the Golden Fleece. From the time of John the Fearless's leadership at Nicopolis the Burgundian house was recognized as the natural director in every scheme for a Crusade. Philip the Good's protection of the Dauphin Louis emphasized still further Burgundy's position as a sort of Third Force. Yet the dukes fatally lacked 'the sweet fruition of an earthly crown'.

There was talk of a royal title for Philip the Good in 1447, during his negotiations with Frederick III, but Philip was thinking in terms of something more grandiose than the kingdom of Brabant that Frederick was willing to consider. In 1473 Frederick III approached Charles the Rash with a new scheme for the erection of the duchy into a kingdom, which again came to nothing, presumably because the duke asked for too much—perhaps for a new Middle Kingdom that would include Provence. The dukes liked to recall the barbarian Burgundian kingdom 'usurped by the Franks', but contemporaries seeking complimentary names for Philip or Charles were constrained to call them 'the great Dukes of the West'. One fundamental difficulty about their position, and about schemes for their recognition as kings, was that, although their heterogeneous subjects spoke a variety of tongues approximating to French and Dutch, the dukes thought of themselves primarily as Frenchmen. They liked to be described by court writers as *bon et entier Franchois*, and Philip the Good, even after the murder of 1419, was accustomed to bemoan his own absence from Agincourt. Only Charles the Rash departed from this tradition and expressed anti-French feelings, a sign of the way in which a Burgundian national tradition might have been forged had not Burgundy undergone disaster through Charles's ambition, and later absorption into the imperial state of Charles V. Charles the Rash, it should be remembered, was one-eighth English by descent (his mother, Isabella of Portugal, was a grand-daughter of John of Gaunt and Blanche of Lancaster) and his third wife was English. He spoke Flemish, and also English, as appears from Commynes' account of his agonized discussion with his brother-in-law Edward IV after the latter had deserted him at Picquigny: 'the Duke talked in English and spoke of some of the great deeds performed by kings of England who had crossed to France, and of the sufferings they had undergone in order to gain honour there; he complained strongly of the truce . . . but the King of England took his words very ill'.[1]

When the Anglo-French war ended at last—and this momentous discussion on the road between Péronne and Picquigny perhaps marks its true conclusion—Burgundy could no longer be parasitic on the flank of a mutilated France. Charles's fall was sudden and complete owing to his folly in antagonizing too many of his neighbours at the same time, but the doubt remains whether his state could otherwise have survived as a considerable power. Its role in European diplomatic affairs had been great, far transcending its relations with France and England. The dukes were a factor in Iberian affairs, as allies of Aragon and Portugal, and in Italy as allies of the king of Naples and would-be rulers of Genoa. Further afield still Burgundy exerted influence through its constant preparations for the Crusade and, less notably, through the feeble and ineffective campaigning which ensued from them. Yet the loose bundle of territories gathered together by the four dukes—primarily through their marriage policy— lacked all unity, and no time was granted for consolidation. The duke's subjects, wrote Georges Chastellain, the official historiographer of Philip and Charles, are 'of various countries and various conditions, and their temperaments [*natures*] also are various as are their ancient loyalties [*affections*]'.[2] North was divided from south by a wide corridor, and for long Luxembourg constituted an isolated enclave to the east. There was no true capital. The dukes, who were constantly on the move, tended increasingly to become involved in the urgent affairs of their northern territories: Philip the Good never visited Dijon, the capital of the old duchy, after 1455, and Charles the Rash never resided as duke in either French or imperial Burgundy.

There was not much progress in the direction of administrative centralization, but it must be remembered that provincial institutions had the advantage of guaranteeing contact with local potentates. From the time of Philip the Bold there were two *chambres de conseil* for the transaction of judicial and financial business, one at Dijon for Burgundy and the Franche-Comté, the other at

---

[1] Commynes, *Mémoires*, IV, 8.

[2] G. Chastellain, 'Exposition sur Vérité mal Prise', *Œuvres* (ed. Kervyn de Lettenhove), VI, 369.

Lille for Flanders and Artois. John the Fearless then subdivided the latter of these, taking the judicial part first to Audenarde and later to Ghent. After 1447 another financial chamber at Brussels covered a very wide area, taking in Holland, Zeeland and Frisia as well as Brabant and Limbourg, while the *chambre* at Lille dealt with the Somme towns and the other lands of the western Low Countries as far as Hainault, as well as with Flanders and Artois. The dukes naturally possessed a chancery and counsellors of their own, drawn from the different parts of their lands; their 'civil service' was probably the best in Europe. Fundamental departure from the principle of ruling each territory through its own existing institutions is only to be found under Charles the Rash, who levied a general tax on all his lands in the Low Countries in 1465 and later (1473) set up a single court for the same region. Apart from this, taxes were demanded of the various provincial estates, and the areas retained their own *bailliages* and other units of local administration, their own councils and sometimes chanceries. Representatives or relatives of the duke often acted as provincial governors, as Charles did in Holland before his accession, and Corneille—one of Philip the Good's fifteen acknowledged bastards—in Luxembourg.

The territories in the Low Countries inevitably preoccupied the dukes most because they provided most of their revenues. In the time of the last two dukes (1419–77), *aides* accounted for one-third of the extraordinary revenues, and 75 per cent of the ducal income from *aides* was derived from the Low Countries. 'Ordinary' revenue was a small and diminishing proportion of the total, but it is notable that under Charles the Rash only 5 per cent of this was yielded by the 'two Burgundies' (the duchy and Franche-Comté). Receipts from domain and customs, as well as from direct taxation, increased enormously as the dukes acquired new lands. The following table[1] compares annual averages of receipts and expenditure under Philip the Bold and Charles

	Average annual revenue	Average annual expenditure
Philip the Bold (1364–1404):	340,000 *l.*	324,000 *l.*
Charles the Rash (1467–77):	773,000 *l.*	761,000 *l.*

[1] See M. Mollat, 'Recherches sur les Finances des Ducs Valois de Bourgogne', *Revue Historique*, CCXXIX (1958), 285–321.

the Rash, and illustrates the great expansion achieved in less than
a century.

The main financial asset of the dukes was the prosperity, and in
particular the commerce, of the Low Countries. The countryside was scarcely less valuable than the sea-coast, which included
the mouths of the Scheldt and Rhine, and its industrial hinterland.
When Philip the Bold took possession of Flanders in 1390 he
found it wretched and depopulated after six years of wars and
floods; the ports had been damaged (the Hanseatics had abandoned
Bruges) and Ghent and Ypres had suffered equally. During the
next half-century an enormous improvement in conditions came
about, thanks largely to peace and good administration. Monetary unification facilitated commerce and regulations carefully
fostered the gold currency, though a deflationary policy may have
had adverse effects on banking and industry. Communications
improved, and in general there was greater security. The rural
areas profited most because they benefited also from the declining political power of the towns and the increased willingness
of burghers to sink their capital in schemes for reclaiming
flooded land. Bladelin of Bruges, Philip the Good's last financial
adviser, reclaimed a vast area of marshland on which the new
town of Middelbourg was built. Farming methods improved,
and the population increased, certainly up to about 1464—when
Philip the Good probably had some two million subjects in the
Low Countries—after which period there began a slow decline.

The wealth of Holland, Zeeland, Hainault and Brabant was
predominantly agrarian, but Flanders was severely affected by
industrial decline. Competition from the English industry and
the increasing tendency for Italians to import their wool in
galleys direct from England brought the Flemish cloth manufacture to its knees (see above, p. 105). Ghent at least had its grain
market, but Ypres, which had no other source of wealth, dwindled
to a skeleton. Cloth production for local consumption continued
in the countryside and a linen industry began to grow up, but the
overall loss was severe. Commerce, a more important source of
revenue, underwent great changes but no general decline. In the
fourteenth century Bruges was the greatest financial and trading
town of Europe north of the Alps. Until late in the following
century it lost none of its importance as a banking centre and still

presented the appearance of a flourishing city. Louis of Bruges, lord of Gruuthuse, built a superb *hôtel* (now the Musée Archéologique) between 1420 and 1470, and the visits of the dukes were celebrated with undiminished splendour. But Bruges was no longer a great entrepôt for trade between the Netherlands and England. Its commercial importance was coming to lie mainly in its relations with the Iberian countries: of 75 vessels known to have called at the port in 1486–7, 33 were from Spain and 6 from Portugal. By then the Zwin was already badly silted up, and early in the following century carts were able to cross the river at low tide. A survey of 1494 mentions between four and five thousand ruined houses at Bruges.

The sharp decline of Bruges provides an instance of circumstances in which the dukes' economic policy could not benefit all their subjects. When Charles the Rash aided Bruges—in return for a grant of taxation—mainly with assistance in dredging works, he did so in the face of appeals from Ghent and Ypres, and the direct opposition of Antwerp. It was a case of directly contrasting interests, and the duke was compelled to take sides, though he could play a double game by turning a blind eye to Antwerp's flouting of the regulations against importing English cloth. In such circumstances no general policy was possible; Flanders and Brabant had to be allowed to make their own, independent commercial treaties. Antwerp was growing as Bruges declined, and largely at Bruges's expense. It was already a centre of some importance for the transit trade of Germans from the Rhineland and Italians in the early fourteenth century, and throve by an exceptionally liberal policy of encouraging alien traders. The Hanse merchants turned to Antwerp from Bruges in the fifteenth century, as did the English from the 1440s, and the visits of the Venetian galleys began in 1459. The Antwerpers themselves owned few ships, but the population figures[1] bear witness to the rapid advance of their town as a centre of commerce:

Number of 'hearths'

1435	3,440
1480	5,689
1496	6,801
1526	8,785

[1] H. Pirenne, *Histoire de Belgique* (ed. 2, 1908), II, 435.

In comparison with the Low Countries, Burgundy was of small economic importance, yet Dijon grew with the power of its dukes —its population doubled between 1436 and 1460—and the area already had a significant export trade in wines.

The wealth of their lands enabled the Valois dukes of Burgundy to display a courtly luxury which was perhaps a compensation for their unattained kingship. Every form of patronage which could enhance their prestige was considered to be worth lavish expenditure. Guests were entertained at banquets of unparalleled splendour (see below, pp. 196-7), and a series of official historiographers recorded the deeds of the dukes, who took their last rest in the superb tombs of the Charterhouse at Champmol near Dijon. Claus Sluter, the great sculptor of Champmol, was a Dutchman who was Philip the Bold's 'ymagier et varlet de chambre'. The 'peintre et varlet de chambre' of Philip the Good was Jan van Eyck, who was taken into the duke's employment in 1425 at a retainder of 100 *livres* per annum, and rendered him service both as a painter and diplomat. Van Eyck travelled to Portugal for the duke to paint for him a portrait of the princess Isabel, during the negotiations for their betrothal, and the duke stood as godfather to one of the painter's children. Many aspects of the life of the duchy's greatest days survive in Van Eyck's pictures, such as the portraits of Philip's greatest minister, the chancellor Rolin, of Cardinal Albergati, who helped to negotiate the peace with France, and of Giovanni and Giovanna Arnolfini, the Tuscan merchant family trading at Bruges. One regrets the more the loss of all the paintings he executed for the duke himself, including the portrait of Isabel, the portraits that he must surely have executed of the duke, and a spherical map of the world. Duke Philip's patronage was not the mere outcome of his determination to be outshone by no king, but reflects his miscellaneous personal tastes: a typical page from his account-books records payments to an illuminator, a bookbinder, three jesters, several minstrels, heralds and trumpeters, and the keeper of his dromedary.[1] Much money was spent on tapestries—one famous series depicted the deeds of Jason, the model of the Order of the Golden Fleece—and on illuminated manuscripts, another characteristic taste of the time. The ducal library included at least nine

[1] Comte de Laborde, *Les Ducs de Bourgogne*, Pt. II (*Preuves*), Vol. I, 249.

hundred works at the time of Philip the Good's death, and was added to by Charles, who had a passion for reading about the heroes of antiquity and commissioned translations of Caesar and Xenophon.

Charles's irremediable lack of wisdom and the sagacity of Louis XI brought Charles to destruction. It is easy now to see his history as a model tragedy of overwhelming pride punished by fate. So it fell out, not merely because Charles was monstrously ambitious but also because it was unrealistic, in the face of French opposition, to attempt to enlarge dominions that had not had time to acquire cohesion. What the dynastic matchmakers had joined together men could very easily put asunder.

After the collapse of Charles the Rash's power, Louis XI gained for France the old French duchy of Burgundy, Picardy and Artois, and later Franche-Comté. But Flanders and the Low Countries, the richest share of the Burgundian legacy, passed to Mary, Charles's only child, and she became the wife of the emperor Maximilian and grandmother of Charles V. Moreover, Artois and Franche-Comté receded to Maximilian in 1493. To a sixteenth-century historian the role of the dukes was that of 'founders of the Belgian empire', for their marriage policy had brought together the lands which composed Charles V's greatly-valued 'Circle of Burgundy'. Burgundian rule in the Low Countries left its mark in England, where the anachronism of referring to those lands as 'Burgundy' long continued: in *Richard III* Shakespeare makes Clarence recount his fearful dream:

> Methought that I had broken from the Tower,
> And was embark'd to cross to Burgundy. . . .

England, through its war, had done much to bring Burgundy to greatness. The fateful failure of France and success of the house of Habsburg in the struggle to become its principal legatee will be discussed in a later chapter (p. 240).

Further Reading

J. CALMETTE, *The Golden Age of Burgundy* (London, 1962)
O. CARTELLIERI, *The Court of Burgundy* (London, 1929)

R. VAUGHAN, *Philip the Bold: the Formation of the Burgundian State*
(London, 1962); *John the Fearless* (London, 1966); *Philip the Good*
(London, 1970); *Charles the Bold* (London, 1973)
P. DE COMMINES, *Memoirs* (tr. M. Jones, Penguin Classics)

Appendix

Philip the Good's Banquet at Lille. 1454.
(Translated from Olivier de la Marche, *Mémoires*, Bk. I, ch. 29).

. . . The second table (which was the longest) had a pie in which were
twenty-eight live people who, when it came to their turn, played
musical instruments. The second set-piece at this table was a castle,
representing Lusignan; at the top of its highest tower was Melusine, in
the form of a serpent, and from two of the lower towers orange-water
flowed into the moat. The third was a windmill on a mound, and on
the highest sail of the mill was perched a magpie; around were people
of all ranks, with bows and crossbows, all aiming at the magpie, to
show that shooting magpies is an occupation common to all sorts of
men. The fourth was a barrel in a vineyard containing two different
wines, of which one was sweet and good, the other bitter and nasty;
on the barrel was a finely dressed figure holding in his hand a notice
saying: 'Help yourself'. The fifth represented a desert in which a
wonderfully life-like tiger was engaged in a struggle with a large
serpent. The sixth was a wild man mounted on a camel which appeared
to be wandering through the countryside. The seventh included a man
on a perch beating a bush full of little birds, while nearby, in a charm-
ing orchard hedged by climbing roses, a knight and his lady sat at
table eating the little birds from the bush; the lady pointed with her
finger to the man beating the bush, to indicate that he was working in
vain and wasting his time. The eighth was a madman on the back
of a bear, amid strange mountains and rocks from which there
dangled fine mirrors. The ninth scene was a lake on the shores of
which stood towns and castles; on the lake sailed a handsome vessel,
fully equipped and in constant movement.

The third table (which was the smallest) had a marvellous forest, like
an Indian forest, within which were strange beasts, moving as though
they were alive. The second set-piece at this table portrayed a lion tied
to a tree in the middle of a meadow, and nearby a man beating a dog.
The third and last was a merchant passing through a village, carrying
a basket full of all sorts of haberdasher's wares.

. . . Half-way down the hall, near the partition and facing the long table, was a high pillar on which was carved a naked woman. Her hair was so long that it covered her back to below her waist, and she wore a very fine hat. She was wrapped in a loose cloth on which there was Greek writing, and throughout the meal hippocras wine flowed from her right breast. Nearby a live lion was tied to another large pillar by an iron chain; the lion was the guard over the woman, and this pillar bore a buckler on which was written in letters of gold: 'Do not touch my lady.'. . .

X

THE TURKISH CONQUEST OF SOUTH-EASTERN EUROPE

THE role of the Burgundian dukes as the great protagonists of the crusading movement in their day can only be understood in the light of the events in south-eastern Europe which are the subject of the present chapter. The diminishing coastal strip of Palestine which remained in the hands of the western Christians in the thirteenth century finally disappeared with the fall of Acre (1291). Its history since the days of Saladin and Cœur de Lion had been so discouraging that one can sympathize with the disillusioned Knight Templar who wrote after the loss of Arsouf in 1265 that 'he is mad who seeks to fight the Turks since Jesus Christ does not deny them anything. . . . God, who used to keep watch over us is now asleep, but Mahomet works with all his might.' [1] Meanwhile the restored Byzantine state of the Palaeologi was, as we have seen (Chapter II), a mere skeleton, the relic of a body politic whose flesh had been consumed by Bulgars, Franks, Venetians and Genoese, not to mention such separatist Greeks as the Despots of Epirus. An account of military and political developments in Byzantine and formerly Byzantine Europe will make it clear why crusading triumphs filled the dreams and daydreams not only of the Avignon popes and the Burgundian dukes, but of Henry IV of England (1399–1413), who dreamt that he would die at Jerusalem, and of his son, Henry V, who liked to think of his French victories as mere preliminaries to greater exploits performed against the 'malignant and turban'd Turk'. Indeed, for all the great warrior-kings of the west the Turk came to figure as a sort of 'last enemy', the supremely formidable

---

[1] Ricaut Bonomel, in V. de Bartholomaeis, *Poesie provenzali storiche relative all' Italia,* II, 222–4.

opponent who took his place at the end of a queue of more
immediate minor foes: even Charles VIII's invasion of Italy in
1494 was presented as the prelude to a great Turkish campaign.

The weak condition of the Byzantine Empire at the beginning
of the fourteenth century under Andronicus II (1282–1328) is well
illustrated by the story of his employment of a body of Catalan
mercenaries. The conclusion of the War of the Sicilian Vespers in
1302 meant that a great number of professional soldiers were out of
work. Roger of Flor, a German mercenary commander who had
served under Frederick II of Sicily, received permission to seek
terms with Andronicus: it was known that a ruler who had lost
'more than thirty days of land' to the Turks would be grateful for
the aid of Catalans and Aragonese, and particularly those who had
been fighting against the hated Angevins. When Roger reached
Constantinople he seems to have had no difficulty in gaining a
contract. Pay was fixed for his followers at rates varying from
four gold ounces a month for a fully-armed cavalryman to twenty
tarins for a crossbowman. Roger himself was to be the emperor's
'Megaduke' and to marry his niece. His men, numbering some
6,500, reached Constantinople in the autumn of 1302, and their
deeds over the next eight years have been recorded by one of their
number, Ramon Muntaner, in his *Chronicle*.

The Catalans began satisfactorily by crossing to Anatolia and
fighting the Turks, but were bitterly resentful when (in 1304) they
were asked to fight the Bulgars. Disputes arose over pay and other
matters, and in 1305 the Greeks themselves attacked the Catalans
and murdered their leader. During the next phase of its activity
the company, hitherto based on Gallipoli, occupied most of
Thrace and fought a number of campaigns against the Byzantines.
Muntaner himself held Gallipoli against the Genoese in 1306, and
the same year the Catalans accepted reinforcements from a new
quarter:

> And so the Turks came before Gallipoli, and one of their chiefs,
> Xemelic by name, came and asked to have speech, and said that if
> we agreed he would enter Gallipoli and talk with us. And I sent an
> armed ship and he came on it with two knights who were both
> relations of his. He announced to Rocafort and Ferran Xemenis and
> myself [Muntaner] that he was prepared to come over to us with all
> his company and their wives and children. They would take an oath

and perform homage, promising to stand with us like brothers, he and all his company. They would stand against all the people in the world, would entrust their wives and children to our power, were willing to be under our command in all things and for all things as the lowest men of our company, and they would give up one-fifth of all their gains.

The Catalans were not the men to refuse an offer of this sort:

> And so we ruled and rode up and down the Empire in our own way, and when the Turks and Turcopols went on cavalry campaigns those of our men who wished to go went too, and the Turks treated them most honourably and saw to it that they came away with twice as much gain as themselves. And so there was never any trouble between us and them.[1]

Later the Catalans fell out among themselves, pillaged Phocaea in Asia Minor with a ferocity that was exceptional even for them, and, after fighting both with and against all the other variegated despoilers of Byzantium, turned at last to their old enemy and swore an oath of fealty to Charles of Anjou. After moving into Thessaly they took service with the Frenchman Walter of Brienne, duke of Athens (1310). At the end of six months, however, the Catalans had received only two months' pay. The duke made liberal promises in an attempt to retain a small body of two hundred cavalry and three hundred infantry, whom he hoped to detach from the rest of the company. But the Catalans refused to be divided and a bitter battle was fought when the duke attacked them on the river Cephisus in Boeotia (March 1311):

> And the battle was very fierce [says Muntaner], but God, who always aids the just, gave our Company his aid, so that of all the seven hundred [Frankish] knights, only two escaped. The rest were all killed, the Count [Walter] and all the barons of the principality of Morea, who had all come to destroy the Company. . . . And so all the cavalrymen of the whole country were killed there, as well as more than twenty thousand infantry. And thus the Company quitted the field, having won the battle and the whole Duchy of Athens.[2]

The Catalans offered their Turks several places in the duchy, but the Turks refused, saying that 'God had done well for them, and they were so rich that they wanted to go back to their friends in

---

[1] R. Muntaner, *Cronica*, §228.   [2] *Ibid.*, §240.

III. The eastern Mediterranean, *c.* 1340

the kingdom of Anatolia'—an unfortunate decision, since the Genoese killed or captured most of them on the Hellespont, and the remainder were killed near Gallipoli by the Byzantines. As for the Catalans themselves, they ruled the duchy (Attica and Boeotia), and in 1318 extended it far to the north, into Thessaly. They lost these northern lands to the Serb Dušan in 1349, but held the duchy itself till dispossessed by Neri Acciauoli, lord of Corinth, in 1388.

The tale of the Catalan Company has been related only as an instance of the manner in which parasites, Frankish, Italian, Greek and Turkish, settled on hitherto Byzantine soil and brought about the political fragmentation of the southern parts of the Balkan peninsula. Dissension within the Palaeologan house itself was rarely lacking, nor was there any unity in the Slav regions farther north, which were divided between Bulgars, Serbs, and Bosnians. The whole of south-east Europe was so segmented in race, religion and rule that warfare was constant, and warfare—as we have seen above—inevitably involved appeal to the powerful military support of the Turks.

It is now time to turn to the principal protagonists of the achievements described in this chapter, the Ottoman Turks. The Ottomans were a small emirate imbued with a strong spirit of religious militarism; they saw themselves as a community of *Ghāzīs*, warriors of the Mohammedan faith. They first figure on the historical scene in the early fourteenth century when, with the assistance of warriors from other emirates, they began to make slow territorial progress against tenacious Byzantine resistance in western Asia Minor. They were sufficiently powerful to rank as attractive allies and to benefit by Greek disunity in 1345, when John VI Cantacuzenus called them in to aid him in Thrace against John V Palaeologus. The emir married John VI's daughter, while John recognized Ottoman control of Bithynia. The Ottomans then seized Gallipoli from another emirate, and by 1354 occupied the whole of this strategically important peninsula. At about the same time they gained Angora (Ankara) and other territory in Asia Minor. As the only intensely active *Ghāzī* state, they received much assistance from volunteers from the other emirates, and by 1360 they had begun to expand into the Balkans.

Ottoman advance in south-eastern Europe originally took the

form of suzerainty, but gradually vassal dynasties were eliminated and direct Ottoman control replaced overlordship. During the 1370s the rulers of Bulgaria and Serbia and the Byzantine emperor himself became tributaries, to be joined soon by many lords in Greece and Albania, as well as in Anatolia. Under Bayezid I (1389–1403) direct rule was inaugurated, in Anatolia and Bulgaria, and this abandonment of the more cautious method of amassing overlordships may have been in part responsible for the disastrous defeat suffered at the hands of the great conqueror Timur ('Tamburlaine', 1336–1405). Timur's kingdom, a powerful amalgam of Turkish and Mongol elements, was transitory, while Ottoman direct rule survived and proved immensely effective. Newly-conquered territories were the subject of elaborate statistical surveys (the *defters*), and these Domesday Books were both bases for fiscal exploitation and records establishing legal claims to land. Certain districts were specially appropriated to the military fisc, and the *defter* was used to assign revenue to the army as well as to regulate taxation. Thus Ottoman military, fiscal and legal arrangements came to supplant those of the conquered lands, but the transition was eased by the fact that there was no radical substitution of a new governing landed class. Christian *seigneurs* and *voyvods* often retained much of their estates by entering the Ottoman army as *askeri* or securing feudal rank as holders of *timars* owing cavalry service.

Ottoman government offered efficient rule, improved communications, tolerably light taxation and even a fair degree of religious toleration. Yet there could be no doubt that this was conquest. The subject population had to submit to the periodic levy of the *devshirme*, the tribute of children taken to serve as soldiers, administrators and pages. Equally characteristic of absolutist rule was the employment of mass deportation. Albanians, Serbs and Greeks were transferred in vast numbers to Anatolia and—after 1453—to Constantinople, while Anatolians (often nomads) were transplanted to Thrace, Bulgaria and the border zones of the Balkans. The purposes of compulsory migration were of course fiscal and military as well as political. The Ottomans' unsurpassed infantry of janissaries recruited from their Christian subjects and excellent system of cavalry service due from feudatories (timariots) presented a formidable picture of organization and unity, which contrasted with the piecemeal resistance of their European victims.

Only at one moment did it seem possible that a powerful Christian kingdom in the Balkans might halt the progress of Ottoman conquest. This was during the reign of Stephen Dušan (1331–55), 'Emperor of the Greeks and Serbs'. Rascia, which later became Serbia, was one of the inland Balkan states owing vassalage to Byzantium which emerged from semi-independence in the time of Byzantine decline after the late twelfth century. Serbia's first king, Stephen, a Slav by birth but Byzantine by education, was crowned in 1217. The history of Serbia's brief hour of hegemony begins a century later with a decisive victory over the Bulgars at Küstendil (1330). Stephen Uroš III, the victor of Küstendil, was deposed, and probably killed, in the following year by his son Dušan, who allied himself with a weakened Bulgaria, kept the peace with Hungary and Bosnia, and set as his aim the conquest of Constantinople, no less. Making use, as did the Ottomans, of the disputed Byzantine succession of 1341, Stephen gained Albania and Macedonia, and in 1346 ambitiously inaugurated a 'Serbo-Roman Empire'. As the self-styled successor to the Byzantines he was crowned *Imperator Rasciae et Romaniae* and his archbishop was made a patriarch. Turning his forces against northern Greece, he reached Volos on the Thessalian coast by 1348, and proposed to the Venetians a scheme for a joint conquest of Constantinople. Undeterred by Venice's refusal, he proceeded with plans for an unassisted assault on the city, but died in the year before that which he intended to mark the fruition of his career.

Dušan's empire broke up on his death (1355), and it is not easy to estimate whether his achievement would have lasted had he been spared. Certainly his dominion was a makeshift affair, for with virtually no central administration or judicial system he had little control over his own nobility. Nor did he rule a wealthy country, though he derived a considerable revenue from the mining of gold, silver and iron, and there was a lively trade with the eastern Balkans in the mining towns and with Italy through Dubrovnik (Ragusa) and other Dalmatian ports. These coastal cities rendered certain dues which no doubt facilitated the employment of a cosmopolitan mercenary force. Dušan had a personal guard of three hundred Germans, and his paid troops played a considerable part in his military triumphs.

After the collapse of Dušan's empire the Ottoman advance in Europe began to gain momentum. Murad I (1360–89) conquered Thrace, making Adrianople his capital, then annexed Macedonia and much of southern Serbia. The ruler of Bulgaria became his vassal, as did the emperor John Palaeologus (1373). Niš and Sofia were captured by 1386 and Salonika in the following year. A tardy alliance between Bosnians and rebel Serbs and Bulgarians met defeat in June 1389 at Kossovo; this battle, in which most of the Serb nobility was killed, was decisive for the fate of south-eastern Europe. Early in the present century the Montenegrins still wore a black border to their caps as a sign of mourning for the day of Kossovo.

The end of resistance to the Ottomans in Albania, northern Serbia and Bulgaria was to provoke energetic, though belated, action in the west. The Turks were in fact halted by Mongol armies from the east, not by the Christians from the west, but the 'Crusade of Nicopolis' of 1396 is an event of sufficient significance to justify a brief excursus on the history of crusading thought in the century after the disappearance of Christian rule in Syria. Throughout this period there was much discussion concerning the methods to be used to regain the territory now lost to Christianity. The ideas of the Catalan Ramon Lull (1232–1315/16) are of interest for their originality, though they had no practical effect. Lull had plans for military reconquest, but his most novel recommendation, a sort of medieval 'Hayter Report', proposed the foundation of chairs of oriental languages in western universities. Moslems were to be converted by what would now be called 'brain-washing'. Special linguist-preachers should 'hold disputations with prisoners to convert them to the Holy Catholic faith', and they should read certain books which prove that Mahomet was not a true prophet.

> Afterwards the ruler-commander [under whom the military religious orders were to be unified] should release these captives. He should pay them their travelling expenses with a fair and friendly expression on his face, and send them off to the Saracen kings and other rulers . . . so that they should make clear to them (the rulers) what we believe concerning the most holy Trinity . . . and this will be

a way of converting the Infidels and of spreading our most holy faith.[1]

The most fundamental of the many disadvantages of this scheme was that the Christians very rarely succeeded in taking Moslem prisoners.

It was natural that the most active propagandists of the Crusade should be those who were most closely threatened by the Moslem advance. Pierre de Thomas, a French Carmelite friar, went to the eastern Mediterranean around 1350 and spent the remaining fifteen years of his life as papal legate in Crete and Cyprus. Among Thomas's disciples was Philippe de Mézières, who became chancellor of Peter I of Cyprus, planned to found a chivalrous order (to be called 'The New Order of the Passion of Jesus Christ'), and wrote a number of works on the Crusade after returning to France in 1369. King Peter (a Lusignan) was a close friend of both these men, and with their energetic encouragement and assistance he raised a fleet of 165 vessels and launched an expedition of which the anticlimactic outcome was the capture—for a single week—of the city of Alexandria.

The assault on Alexandria (1365) was the issue of three years' preparatory work, including a visit by King Peter to the west, where he held discussions with pope Urban V, John II of France, Edward III of England, the emperor Charles IV, and the kings of Hungary and Poland. It took its place in a long and uninterrupted series of military failures, a list that includes Clement VI's league of 1343 (which did, however, capture Smyrna) and Peter's own earlier expedition against Asia Minor, which also captured a solitary port, Adalia. It was followed by the 'Crusade' of Count Amedeus VI of Savoy, who took fifteen galleys and several mercenary companies to the east in 1366, but was diverted into fighting against the Christian Bulgarians on behalf of the Byzantine emperor.

Almost a generation passed before the next ambitious scheme, the joint Franco-Genoese Crusade of 1390 against the Tunisian port of al-Mahdiya. A hundred galleys sailed on this enterprise under the command of Louis II de Bourbon, uncle of Charles VII of France. The attack on al-Mahdiya, like all crusading ventures,

---

[1] Lull, *Liber de fine*, in A. Gottron, *Ramon Lulls Kreuzzugsideen* (1912), pp. 64–96 (this passage is p. 88).

was the product of mixed motives, motives which affected both the composition of the force involved and the outcome of the operations. The Genoese—who supplied 1,000 crossbowmen and 2,000 cavalrymen as well as the shipping—were principally concerned with al-Mahdiya as the home of corsairs who hindered their valuable north African trade. The French were sincere crusaders, benefiting from the respite afforded by the pacific policy of Richard II of England; they were indeed reinforced by English, Flemish and Aragonese elements. The siege proved a difficult undertaking, the Genoese were naturally the first to feel discouraged, and negotiations soon resulted in their agreement to a ten-year truce which offered them all they really wanted. The reluctant French were compelled to follow suit and after three months the siege was abandoned.

The last of the major crusading ventures was the outcome of the great Ottoman victory of 1389 (see above, p. 205). Like the al-Mahdiya expedition, the Crusade of Nicopolis was made possible by the long lull in the Anglo-French war. In 1395 negotiations led to the formation of a great league involving France, England, Hungary, Venice and Burgundy: Duke Philip the Bold was the principal promoter and his son John of Nevers (the future *Jean sans Peur*) commanded the Franco-Burgundian element. More than half of the very large Christian force involved were Hungarians. In the summer of 1396 this army advanced from Buda along the Danube and besieged Nicopolis. Sigismund of Hungary, experienced in warfare against the Ottomans, favoured cautious tactics, but the French could only think in terms of the headlong chivalric assault which had cost them so dear at Crecy and Poitiers. When Bayezid broke off the siege of Constantinople and came to the aid of Nicopolis the French at once launched an attack (25 September 1396). After winning ground in the early stages of the engagement, they were defeated with the loss of almost their entire force. The Ottomans then turned against the Hungarians, who had held aloof from the French battle, and they too were overcome. Most of the French prisoners were put to death, but Bayezid spared the nobles, who were later ransomed for a fee of 200,000 florins. Among these was John of Nevers, who reached home the following year.

The great military undertaking of 1396 had failed to halt the

Turkish advance and Constantinople would almost certainly have
fallen within a few years but for the defeat of Bayezid by Timur
in 1402. Throughout the preceding century the western Christians
had compared unfavourably with their opponents—whom they
had consistently under-rated—in every respect. Their tactics and
discipline had been inferior and they had fought in unsuitable
armour. Above all, their efforts had been spasmodic and had been
frustrated by internal divisions and conflicting motives. As an old
man, Philip of Mézières, the great crusading propagandist of the
age, learned the news of the crushing defeat of his hopes at
Nicopolis. In these last, sad years of his life he was accustomed to
write of himself ruefully as a *vieil abortif*.

Bayezid's defeat and capture near Ankara in 1402 postponed
Ottoman domination throughout south-eastern Europe for several
decades. During this period both Venice and the kingdom of
Hungary were sufficiently powerful to dispute the relics of the
Eastern Empire with the Turks—though inevitably they were
rivals and not allies. After the death of Sigismund (1437) Hungary
lost much of its cohesion, and the eventual successor, Ladislas of
Poland, had to struggle for control in Hungary as well as fighting
the Turks in Serbia. The campaigns of 1442–4, which probably
saved Constantinople from conquest by Murad II, were fought
under the virtual leadership of John Hunyadi of Transylvania, a
Wallachian noble who had come into prominence in the service of
Hungary. Hunyadi was also involved in the attempt to exploit
Murad's absence in Asia during 1444, which culminated in the
disastrous defeat of Varna, in which King Ladislas was killed.
Surviving this battle, Hunyadi became regent in Hungary for
Ladislas Postumus, the grandson of Sigismund and heir to
Ladislas III. Hunyadi in his turn became preoccupied with internal factional strife, and in the following years the main role in
opposing the Ottomans was assumed by the Albanian Scander
Beg (b. *c.* 1405). Scander had been taken by the Turks in youth as
a hostage and, as a Moslem, served them for many years before he
fled to his native land and set up as the leader of resistance there
in 1443.

As early as the 1420s western visitors to Constantinople were
startled to find its population much under the influence of
Turkish ways. The honour of suppressing the shrunken vestige

of the empire founded by Augustus fell to Mahomet II 'the Conqueror' (1451–81). The man who achieved the success so long promised by God to the champions of the Islamic faith, and so long denied them, was in every respect worthy of his triumph. Mahomet was born in 1432, the son of Murad II by an unknown slave. An elder half-brother was murdered and Mahomet became heir presumptive as a young child; indeed, his father abdicated in his favour in 1445, but had second thoughts and resumed power in the following year. Mahomet's first campaign was probably the victorious one against Hunyadi which culminated in the second battle of Kossovo (1448). Murad died three years later, and Mahomet marked his succession by putting to death a young half-brother who was a potential centre of opposition. The same fate was later to befall a series of Grand Viziers, but Mahomet must be given credit for his punctilious observance of etiquette in such matters: when an important dignitary was executed his head was exposed on a silver plate, whereas that of a lesser official was only granted a plate of wood. The Sultan's favourite method of execution was to order men to be sawn in half, and his whimsical sense of humour permitted him to claim that he had been true to his word when he had three hundred Italians killed in this way at Mytilene in 1462 after promising that 'they might keep their heads'. His methods did little to distinguish him from his Christian opponents, and Mahomet's campaign against the Vlachs in the same year had involved a ghastly march through a 'forest' of 20,000 impaled Turks and Bulgars.

Mahomet was steeled by an unlimited faith in his own destiny. From childhood he had believed that Constantinople would be his, and later he was to dream of the conquest of Hungary and even of Rome. He had a great taste for Greek and Roman history, as well as for what we should now call medieval chronicles; these works were read to him presumably in Greek (for he knew this language, as well as 'Slav'), by Italians. A particular favourite was Alexander the Great, and there can be little doubt that Mahomet saw himself as the new Alexander, called by destiny to repeat in reverse the deeds of the old. 'The times have changed now', he is reported to have said, 'and I shall go from east to west as formerly the westerners penetrated the East.'

Mahomet's best-known military achievement, the conquest of

Constantinople, was not his greatest feat of arms. This was merely the last symbolic act in the extinction of an Empire which had long servived only by consent of the Turks. On the death of the emperor John VIII Palaeologus in 1448 the rival claimants, John's brothers Constantine and Demetrius, invited Murad to decide the succession. Not unnaturally Murad declared for Constantine, the despot of Mistra, who two years earlier had become his tributary. The city that Mahomet set out to subjugate in 1452–1453 had long been encircled, but he took care to occupy the forces of the Emperor's two brothers by launching a diversionary campaign in the Morea. The final siege began on 6 April 1453. Since the Byzantines were able to muster only some 9,000 men (of whom one-third were Genoese and Venetians) to hold four miles of wall, the outcome of the siege was a foregone conclusion once the Sultan had turned his full might against the city. Nevertheless, tribute must be paid to the ingenuity which enabled the Ottomans to drag seventy ships across land from the Bosphorus to the waters of the Golden Horn, thus circumventing the chain which was supposed to protect the harbour against naval assault. The walls were at last breached on 29 May. The emperor Constantine died courageously among his men, and within hours the entire city was in Ottoman hands; inevitably there were appalling scenes of massacre and looting.

Mahomet fought an almost ceaseless series of campaigns in Europe and Asia. To chronicle them would be tedious, but without doing so it is difficult to give a sufficient impression of Ottoman military power at this period. In Asia the emperor of Trebizond, another beneficiary of Byzantine decay, was overthrown, as were a large number of Anatolian rebels and Persian challengers. To the north, naval and military campaigns made of the Black Sea a Turkish lake, with disastrous consequences for western European traders. Mahomet's onslaught on Europe was checked in 1456 by the heroic relief of Belgrade by Hunyadi and the crusaders of the friar Capistrano. Belgrade was long to defy the Turks, but by 1459 Mahomet had regained all Serbia and within three years of this he held Athens and the Morea. To his conquests in mainland Greece he soon added Mytilene (Lesbos) and various other islands, though the Venetians were able to retain Euboea ('Negroponte') till 1470. By that date Bosnia had

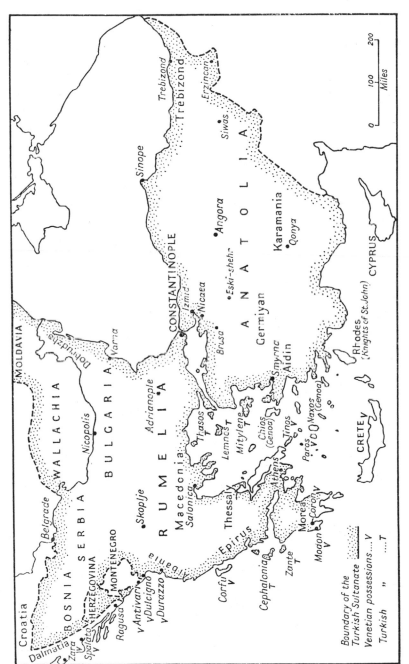

IV. South-eastern Europe, 1481

fallen and resistance in Albania almost come to an end with the death of Scander Beg (1468). From Bosnia marauding Ottoman irregulars launched annual raids as far to the north-west as Styria and Carinthia, and in 1477 a force pressed so far into Italy that the fires caused by its depredations could be seen from Venice. Three years later the Ottomans attacked southern Italy, captured Otranto, massacred every male in the city, and held it for over twelve months.

When Mahomet died in 1481, at the age of forty-nine, Ottoman strength was still checked in the Balkans by the resistance of Belgrade and in the Mediterranean by that of Rhodes.[1] The growth of Turkish sea-power under Selim I (1512–20) made possible the conquest of Syria and Egypt. Only under Suleiman II (1520–66) was the advance into Europe resumed, while Charles V warred with Francis I of France. Then the king of Bohemia and Hungary was killed in the decisive battle at Mohacz (1526) and, with the acquisition of Hungary, the Ottoman Empire became a greater power in Europe than its Byzantine predecessor had been, even in its heyday before the First Crusade. Not only had the territorial problems set by Byzantine decline been settled for centuries, but the western European states had to reckon with a mighty neighbour whose weight was to count for much in the balance of power diplomacy of the 'early modern' period. By splitting Christian Europe, the Reformation served to make the domination of the Turks yet more secure. The crusading ideal lived on strongly in the ideas of the Counter-Reformation, but even the naval victory of Lepanto (1571) failed to check the Ottoman advance: a century after this the Turks captured Crete and besieged Vienna. The replacement of a stricken Christian empire by an aggressive Islamic autocracy was certainly the greatest change in the map of Europe between the thirteenth century and the early years of the sixteenth.

Further Reading

G. OSTROGORSKY, *History of the Byzantine State* (Oxford, 1956)

A. S. ATIYA, *The Crusade in the later Middle Ages* (London, 1938)

P. WITTEK, *The Rise of the Ottoman Empire* (London, 1938)

F. BABINGER, *Mahomet II le Conquérant et son Temps* (Paris, 1954)

[1] See Map IV.

XI

THE TYRANNIES IN ITALY

THE institutions of the Italian city-republics (see above, Chapter I) were constantly re-shaped and at last effaced by the interplay of the forces of social and aristocratic faction, combined with frequent external crises and the pressure of individual ambition. Before the end of the thirteenth century a number of towns had fallen to the rule of a despotic dynasty and by the middle of the fifteenth Venice alone among the greater cities had maintained its independence and preserved a genuinely republican constitution.

The triumph of tyranny constitutes the pragmatic criticism of Italy's free communes. These republics had existed in an atmosphere of continual instability and the normal outcome of endemic political disequilibrium is of course dictatorship. The communes suffered not only the normal constitutional handicaps of democracy—slow decisions, lack of secrecy and hamstrung diplomacy —but also the disadvantages of a discontinuity in personnel and policy which was in part imposed by the shadow of the fate which ultimately befell them. The executive officials of the republics held power for periods which rarely exceeded six months and were often as brief as two; longer periods in office would have failed to ensure a proper rotation among those regarded as eligible, and have facilitated the schemes of any man set on suppressing the commune to his own advantage. Constant changes in the executive can be palliated by the existence of a permanent civil service— as was the case under the French Third and Fourth Republics— but the Italian cities had few permanent officials and none of high rank, until in the later fourteenth century the chancellor in some cities began to provide a certain element of diplomatic continuity.

By that time, however, it was normally too late. The perpetual struggle of the states within the state, 'popular', Guelf and Ghibelline, encouraged these factions to entrust leadership to an individual, and what began as a measure of defence usually resulted in the overthrow both of republicanism and of the faction itself. The leader of the successful party became lord of the city, and those most likely to be 'purged'—as Machiavelli noted[1]— were the very men who had helped him to power. The occasion for the grant of special, unconstitutional powers to an individual was frequently an external crisis. Warfare between the towns, particularly between neighbours, was almost continuous, and was exacerbated by the periodic intervention of external powers, in particular the Empire. Military crisis was of course normally accompanied by fiscal crisis, and failure in war was the most propitious of all circumstances for a potential tyrant.

The overlordship at Florence of Walter of Brienne, titular duke of Athens, in 1342–3, followed the city's humiliating defeat at the hands of the Lucchese, and was untypical only in that the initiative came mainly from the citizens. More commonly the tyrant accomplished his own ascent to power through a carefully planned *coup d'état*. However recognizable such a *coup* may be to the eyes of historians, it was usually possible at the time to disguise and minimize it. The city commonly in the first instance granted special powers to an individual for a fixed period only—alleging the need in a time of crisis to suspend for a while the normal workings of the constitution—but both the duration of the grant and the width of the powers were often extended later. Even when full powers had been made over, it was usual for the commune to maintain its own legal existence, its former institutions surviving though they came *de facto* under the control of the tyrant. Many *signori* (lords) regularized their position by securing a grant of special powers from a 'parliament' held to represent all the citizens, this anachronistic assembly having never formally lost its position as the commune's sovereign body. Commonly such an election continued to be made in each successive generation, the heir sometimes even taking an oath to protect the well-being of the commune. Normally *signori* came to acquire the power of appointing their successor—usually a son or nephew—and sometimes they associated him in office when they became elderly. A

---

[1] *The Prince*, cn. XX.

formal agreement on hereditary succession was likely to be a quite late development; it is only found at Verona, for example, after 1359, when the Scaligeri had been lords of that city for almost a century.

In seeking recognition of his status the despot had a double task, however. A constitutional *entente* with his nominal superior was desirable, as well as with those whom he ruled. The title of 'vicar' had long been held by local representatives of imperial power and the vicariate proved a convenient method for conferring respectability on tyrannical rule. Thus in 1311 Henry VII recognized Matteo Visconti as imperial vicar of Milan, Cangrande della Scala as vicar of Verona, and Rizzardo de Camino as vicar of Treviso. The vicariate, a useful juridical *modus vivendi*, was soon adopted widely. It granted to lords powers that they already normally enjoyed in practice, giving them a recognition for which they were willing to pay. In consequence the institution flourished most under those emperors (from Charles IV onwards) who enjoyed least authority in the peninsula, and were content to part with paper rights in exchange for much-needed revenue. As lords extended their dominions, new grants extended the areas of their vicariates. In theory vicariates were granted usually for the lifetime of the grantor only, but the successor was willing to extend the arrangement, and clauses making these grants revocable in case of rebellion were ineffective in practice, as emperors discovered when they attempted to enforce them against the Visconti. Naturally the vicariate was of equal utility to the empire's frail twin-brother, the papacy, always ready 'to make a bad bargain, sooner than no bargain at all, with powerful subjects'.[1] The Estensi became papal vicars of Ferrara in 1329, the Malatesta were granted the same status at Rimini in 1355, and by the end of the Great Schism (1417) the Montefeltro of Urbino and the tyrants of many other towns in Romagna, the March of Ancona and Umbria held vicariates of the papacy.

One imperial title was more impressive than that of vicar, and the lords of Milan gained a unique position in 1395, when, for 100,000 florins, King Wenceslas conferred on Gian-Galeazzo Visconti the proud style of duke. This rank was transmitted both to Gian-Galeazzo's hereditary successors and to the Sforzas who

[1] For an earlier version of this policy, see p. 53.

ruled the city after 1450. A good deal later there were to be dukes of Urbino, Ferrara and Florence.

The general defeat of republican institutions in Italy was a very long process, extending over some two hundred years. For the most part it occurred sooner in the plain of Lombardy and Venetia than in the hilly landscape of Tuscany and the Papal State. The earliest firm tyrannies in important towns were achieved by feudatories who owed their position in part to alliances with Frederick II. Of these Ezzelin da Romano held Verona from 1232 and added Padua in 1237, while by the time of the emperor's death (1250) Hubert Pallavicino was lord of Cremona and Pavia. With the dissolution of Frederick's authority all northern Italy went into the melting-pot, and soon after the mid-century a number of new *signori* emerged. From 1258 mastery at Milan alternated between two rival families, the Della Torre (Guelf) and the Visconti (Ghibelline). At the same period a 'popular' family, the Della Scala, was gaining a control in Verona which received formal recognition in 1277 when Alberto della Scala was elected Captain General of the city for life. In the first half of the following century the Scaligeri built up a considerable empire, acquiring Vicenza, Padua, Treviso and even, for a time, Parma, Reggio and Lucca. By then tyranny was already the norm in Lombardy, Venetia and Romagna and was becoming common in Tuscany, Umbria and the March of Ancona.

The first Tuscan *signorie* were the work of mercenary commanders, Uguccione della Faggiuola (lord of Pisa and Lucca from 1314 to 1316) and Castruccio Castracane (lord of Lucca, 1320-8). In the particularly unsettled era which followed the death of Henry VII (1313) Tuscany was a prey to constant warfare between Ghibelline and Guelf powers: the lordships of Uguccione and Castruccio arose from this situation, as did the more circumspect grants of special powers in Florence to the Angevins—Robert of Naples (1313-22) and Charles, duke of Calabria (1325-8). These abortive Florentine *signorie* which were followed by a brief taste of sterner Angevin rule (under Walter, duke of Brienne in 1342-3), illustrate well both how often the origins of tyranny lay in an external crisis and how difficult it was for a despot to retain control when he lacked local roots.

In some cases a great feudal family almost overshadowed the

commune from its very origin. At Ferrara, for instance, the house of Este disputed control over the town with a rival dynasty, the Salinguerra, from the very early thirteenth century, if not before, and many smaller towns never fully escaped the mastery of a feudal castellan. The force which usually proved too strong for republican institutions was the old-established family having a deeply-rooted territorial position, a powerful military retinue, and allies linked by marriage and interest: these provided the financial and social means which could break its enemies and make its friends. Often the commune was heavily in debt to such great men before they became its lords, and above all they could over-awe opposition by a show of armed force and by the wealth which could 'corrupt' the *popolo*.

To discuss the scores of tyrannies which developed throughout northern and central Italy is inevitably to generalize and thus to be misleading, for the régimes of different lords and cities differed greatly from each other. Characteristic instances have already had to be selected in the foregoing treatment of tyrannical origins, and in dealing with fully-grown despotism it will also be necessary to select examples, and to confine the discussion to Milan, Florence and Bologna.

The history of tyranny at Milan involves two celebrated names, those of Visconti and Sforza. The Visconti—whose name bears witness to their feudal origin—ruled Milan for nearly two centuries and much of northern Italy for a considerable time, but their acquisition of power was not rapidly or easily accomplished. The Guelf Della Torre controlled the city from 1258 to 1278, and the subsequent régime of archbishop Ottone Visconti and his nephew Matteo was ended by a Della Torre reconquest in 1302. In 1311, however, with the support of the emperor Henry VII, Matteo Visconti regained power, and this time Visconti rule lasted until 1447. Their recognition as imperial vicars and dukes has already been mentioned. The story of their immensely successful expansionist policy is too involved to be recounted here at length. Matteo Visconti, inheriting earlier Milanese ambitions, embarked on the conquest of Lombardy and forced several neighbouring cities into submission. This first Visconti empire crumbled, but was reconstructed and enlarged by Azzo and Luchino Visconti in the 1330s and 1340s. In 1350 Giovanni Visconti secured a foothold in papal territory by acquiring Bologna, and for a time (1353–6) the Visconti held the vastly more valuable prize of Genoa. The greatest age of Visconti imperialism came under Gian-Galeazzo, who between 1385 and 1402 was perhaps within reach of setting up a north Italian state. Within a few years he overthrew the Scaligeri to gain Verona and Vicenza and the Carraresi to win Padua, and was thus in a position to thrust further south. From 1399 his pressure on Tuscany was very strong: Pisa and Siena fell to him, he became protector of the lord of Lucca and to the south-east he won Perugia and other places in Umbria. But Florence remained as an immensely energetic leader of the opposition to Gian-Galeazzo and the duke died in 1402 with his conquests incomplete. The Visconti then lost their more southerly territories and the Venetians combined with the Florentines to keep Milan in check.

The triumphs of the Visconti were made possible by an efficient and strictly-controlled internal administration. Two small councils and two committees concerned with finance were the main institutions of government. The old 'great council' of 900 lost all real power and after 1396 its members were nominated instead of being elected. Milanese municipal affairs were directed by a 'vicar', with the Twelve of the 'Office of Provisions'. Subject communes kept their local institutions; but, naturally, political and financial policy were under Viscontean control. Despite their centralizing ambitions, the Visconti were obliged to reach compromises with the strong traditions of particularism: Gian-Galeazzo's special council at Verona for the territories east of the Mincio represents the only serious attempt to make inroads into local multiformity.

When the Visconti descent in the male line came to an end in 1447 the Milanese proclaimed a republic, but municipal revolts and war with Venice persuaded the republic's leaders to turn for salvation to a *condottiere*, Francesco Sforza. Francesco, himself the illegitimate son of a mercenary commander, had served Filippo Maria Visconti and after a long and chequered engagement married his illegitimate daughter Bianca Maria. At one time he had carved out a state for himself in papal territory, but later had been dispossessed of this. Francesco won victories for the republic, but after Pavia made him its lord he was regarded with much suspicion, and ultimately he justified this by going over to the Venetians. The Milanese decision to make peace with Venice failed to save the republic from having to capitulate to Sforza, who became duke of Milan in 1450. Marriage to the late duke's illegitimate daughter gave Francesco no strong claim to the duchy, but he was extremely successful in his diplomatic policy. Medicean Florence and the kingdom of Naples became loyal allies to Francesco, enabling him to survive Venetian hostility and the difficult years of the Sforza régime's infancy. Within the duchy he attained a stronger position of autocracy than that won by any of the Visconti. He kept a characteristically tight hold over the Church, retaining the revenues of all vacant benefices and winning from the papacy *de facto* control over nominations to bishoprics and abbacies; indeed, under Pius II (1458–64) all ecclesiastical appointments within the duchy were the concern of a special office which was under Sforza influence. From 1454 Francesco's brother was Milan's archbishop. Immunities and private jurisdiction were whittled away, and foreign affairs conducted by the duke with the assistance of his secretary Cecco Simonetta.

An unsettled period for the Sforza followed Francesco's death in 1466, and the family had difficulty in retaining the duchy. Gian-Galeazzo Sforza was aged only seven on his accession in 1476, and after a long factional struggle between his uncles, he fell under the control of one of these, Ludovico 'il Moro', who kept him a virtual prisoner and executed Simonetta. Ludovico came to be haunted by his lack of a rightful claim and by the opposition of the Neapolitan royal house, the king's grand-daughter having married the lawful duke. His fear of the Neapolitans persuaded him to encourage Charles VIII of France to invade that kingdom in 1494, and his formal accession to the duchy after his nephew's death in the same year did nothing to increase his popularity. Contemporaries believed—probably wrongly—that Ludovico was guilty of this death, and when a new French invasion, directed against the duchy, occurred in 1499, he had very little support from his subjects. The following year he lost his state and he died a prisoner in France. His sons Massimiliano (in 1512–15) and Francesco II (in 1522–35) returned as nominal dukes under imperialist protection, but Ludovico was the last true *signore* of Milan.

The Medicean tyranny at Florence presents many contrasts with that of the Visconti and Sforza, notably in the long co-existence of republican forms of government with the practice of *signoria*. Moreover, Cosimo di Medici's initial power was based upon money as undeniably as Francesco Sforza's upon arms, and this great banker won his lordship not as a single victor over a republic but as the leader of a successful party among competing factions.

After the defeat of the popular rising of 1378, power in Florence became the preserve of a fairly narrow oligarchy. The dominant clique was for long headed by Maso degli Albizzi, but after his death (1417) control was shared between Maso's extremely autocratic son Rinaldo and Niccolò da Uzzano. Though Florentine publicists contrasted their city's *libertas* with the tyranny of Milan, this was a 'liberty' that had nothing to do with democracy. In the time of Rinaldo degli Albizzi and Uzzano there were many dissatisfied elements in Florence, and the story of Medicean rule begins with the alliance formed between these malcontents and the *nouveau riche* banker Giovanni di Bicci dei Medici (see above, p. 109).

Giovanni (who died in 1429) was recognized as head of the opposition to the prevailing oligarchs, and in this position—as well as in control of the Medici Bank—he was succeeded by his son Cosimo. Cosimo was then aged forty. He was not perhaps entirely a politician by temperament, but it was accepted that men of rank in the city should play an appropriate role in politics, and to withdraw from this was to accept serious social and financial disadvantages. 'It is not a good life in Florence for the rich unless they rule there', said Cosimo's grandson Lorenzo, referring to the heavy taxes levied on those who could afford to pay and had failed to win a say in the city's fiscal arrangements. When the moderate Uzzano died in 1433, Rinaldo degli Albizzi's fear of Cosimo led to the latter's arrest and banishment for one year, a sentence later increased to ten years' exile. The accusation brought against Cosimo—that he was planning a *coup d'état*—was probably intended to provoke a death sentence, and may have failed to do so only because Cosimo was careful to keep pace with Albizzi in his bribes to the officials. Meanwhile Albizzi, by his increasingly tyrannical methods, was alienating some of his leading supporters, and in the autumn of 1434 Cosimo was recalled by an unexpectedly recalcitrant set of *priori*. There was not room in the city for both Albizzi and Medici, and the banishment of the former was decreed at the same time as the recall of the latter.

Cosimo had achieved no easy position of complete control: 'conspiracies' against him were foiled in 1444, 1457, and 1458. His great advantages were the reputation of the Medici as a 'popular' family and the wealth of his Bank, then the most famous house of all Europe. The Bank gave Cosimo a voice in the affairs of external powers as well as rapid news of foreign events and a valuable link with the papacy. Together with his many commercial and industrial interests, it provided him with an immense fortune.

Cosimo's system of rule—he rarely held office in person—involved dependence on a body of supporters, some of whom were powerful men in their own right. Constitutional methods of distributing office, which involved the use of the 'lot', had to be manipulated to secure the choice of safe Mediceans. It would have been too blatant to abolish the 'lot', but Cosimo could not risk being overthrown, like Albizzi, by a single unfavourable *priorate*. The choice of priors, however, was often admittedly made deliberately ('by hand') rather than being entrusted to chance. From 1458 the system of choice 'by hand' became permanent, and a surviving petition to Cosimo's son asking for the leading position in the next *priorate* illustrates the reality of Medicean control. Also taxation bore far more heavily on Cosimo's opponents than on his supporters. Cosimo's friendship with Francesco Sforza was responsible for a great diplomatic revolution which aligned Florence with its traditional enemy, Milan, in opposition to its old ally, Venice. This daring defiance of Florentine republican convictions led to an unpopular war, but the ensuing Peace of Lodi (1454) gave Florence a decade without hostilities.

Cosimo's description of a man as having 'a ready money sort of mind' ('il cervello in danari contanti') might well be applied to himself. Remembering the origins of his family's popularity, he was careful to avoid ostentation in dress and to be noted for his friendliness towards the peasants. He was business-like even in his patronage of learning and the arts, and his assistance in reorganizing the Florentine *studium* certainly had the object of bringing students and money to the city as well as of forwarding education.

Cosimo died in 1464 and for five years the reins of power were held by a far less formidable figure, his semi-invalid son Piero. The next quarter-century (1469–92) was the age of the greatest of all the Medici, Lorenzo the Magnificent. At the time of Piero's death his son Lorenzo was a young man of twenty-one. In practice the city's *signore*, in law he remained an ordinary private citizen. The paradox was of course remarked by contemporaries, including Lorenzo, who regarded his republican mask as an advantageous disguise and warned his own son that on diplomatic missions he should not take precedence over his elders, for 'you are but a citizen of Florence, as they are'. 'Lorenzo made himself master of the *essence* of government while he left the *appearance* of it entirely to the officials', said a writer of the time,[1] and this duality had a curious effect on the conduct of external relations. Florentine ambassadors might be compelled to seek pardon 'both on behalf of the city and of Lorenzo', and they had to conduct correspondence with Lorenzo himself as well as through 'official channels'. Lorenzo normally appointed ambassadors and they were in reality dependent on him and tended increasingly to write to him only, though he sometimes passed on their letters to the officials of the republic. Foreign powers also found themselves compelled to conduct a double correspondence, and at times were puzzled to find some contradiction between the 'line' taken by Lorenzo and that of the officials. They must have realized that the former was the one which really mattered, for they could see that even ambassadors were accompanied and watched by 'chancellors' appointed by Lorenzo.

Lorenzo could afford to leave no aspect of Florentine life unsupervised. Since there was always a potential opposition among the powerful families and alliances between these could be forwarded by marriage unions, marriages within this class came to require Lorenzo's consent. In the law-courts, particularly those of the dependent towns, Medicean supporters had preferential treatment. Fiscal favouritism was less glaring than under Cosimo now that the Medici were more firmly in the saddle, but men who wrote to petition for a less heavy assessment took care to mention

[1] B. Pitti, *Cronaca* (1905), p. 25.

that they were faithful Mediceans. Moreover, Lorenzo occasionally secured special exemptions from taxation for himself and it
was generally believed that he laid hands on a great deal of public
money. The Bank was now much less flourishing than in his
grandfather's time, and a vast source of expenditure was the purchase of a cardinalate for his son Giovanni, later Leo X. Yet a lot
of Lorenzo's own money was spent on diplomacy, entertaining
and a 'secret service', and it was not iniquitous that this should be
recouped from the public purse.

If there was a check on Lorenzo's power, it was provided by the
need to retain the support of his own men. Decisions were often
made in small gatherings of trusted Medicean partisans, the resolu-
tions of this caucus being passed later in formal committee-
meetings. The names of steadfast Medicean families, often linked
by marriage, commercial partnership or employment, recur constantly in the lists of council members, and such supporters could
be sure of advancement to well-paid office, particularly to gover-
norships in the towns of the Florentine *dominio*. Behind these were
arrayed the devoted officials made by the Medici and dependent
on them, the 'low-born men' whose position was resented by the
patricians, particularly in the case of those whose origins lay not
in the city but in its subject-territory. Normally the machinery of
control by secretaries and supporters worked smoothly enough,
but any institution which acted without Medicean consent felt at
once the grip of the iron hand. In 1491 one Cambi, then *Gonfaloniere di Giustizia*, acted on his own initiative in depriving certain councillors of office for absenteeism: he paid for his rashness
by himself suffering permanent deprival of office, while the men he
had deposed were immediately restored.

Although content with his own position as a 'private citizen',
Lorenzo found it convenient to adjust the institutions of the
republic to facilitate his autocratic rule. In 1471 he deprived the
Council of the Commune and the Council of the People of much
of their competence, and thenceforth governed through a single
council, the Hundred. Seven years later he had to face the one
severe crisis of his régime, the Pazzi conspiracy. The principal
parties in this plot were the wealthy anti-Medicean Pazzi, pope
Sixtus IV with his family, the Riarii, and the king of Naples.
Their plan was to kill Lorenzo and his brother Giuliano in the

cathedral of Florence during the celebration of High Mass (26 April 1478). At the agreed moment, that of the elevation of the host, two assassins set on Giuliano and killed him, but the men to whom Lorenzo had been allotted bungled their assignment, and he was able to make his escape. The intended *coup d'état* was abortive, and Lorenzo, the survivor, was accorded a great demonstration of popular support—as well as being freed, as the cynical remarked, from the possible rivalry of his brother. Lorenzo's enemies attempted to press home their attack by two military campaigns which drove Florence to the verge of defeat, and from which Lorenzo was only able to emerge thanks to the skill with which he persuaded the king of Naples to withdraw from the hostile alliance. After he had brought back 'peace with honour' from Naples, Lorenzo put through a more radical constitutional reform (April 1480) which geared Florence's conciliar and executive machine yet more closely to the Medicean regime. A new body of 70 now became the principal Council, and the chief executive committees were to be chosen from its members or by them.

To the Italians of his day Lorenzo the Magnificent was pre-eminently the skilful diplomatist who maintained contact between the rulers of the peninsula and did much to keep the peace in a time of threatened catastrophe.[1] Of the other Italian powers, Venice and the papacy were always on the alert for possibilities of expansion at the expense of their neighbours, while the two 'satiated' states, Naples and Milan, were threatened both by internal dissensions and by fear of French claims (see below, p. 244). By appealing for co-operation against the Ottoman and French menaces, particularly to the unreliable Ferrante of Naples and Ludovico of Milan, Lorenzo did much to preserve the peninsula in a condition of comparative peace, and it became a commonplace to refer to him as 'the balance' that preserved Italy from upset and disaster. Luca Landucci, who kept a chemist's shop, spoke for all the Florentines when he noted in his diary on Lorenzo's death that 'he was a wise head, and everything he attempted turned out well. . . . He ennobled not only his family but the whole city.' A more formal writer thought that 'We have lost the splendour not only of Tuscany but of all Italy. Every day

[1] See Map V.

we shall learn more what we have lost . . .', and Ferrante of Naples wrote prophetically that 'this man has lived long enough for his own immortal fame, but not for Italy'.[1]

In later times Lorenzo the Magnificent has been celebrated less as a ruler and statesman than as a delightful poet and a highly intelligent patron of learning and the arts. Something will be said of him as a patron below, but we may note, before turning briefly to the later period of Medicean rule, that posterity may have pardoned too readily this many-sided man's failure to supervise adequately the Bank which had gained the Medici their rule in Florence. In this respect there is a clearly-marked distinction between Lorenzo's personality and that of his grandfather Cosimo. A fictional parallel may be found in the theme of *Buddenbrooks*, Thomas Mann's novel of burgher life in nineteenth-century Lübeck, for the Buddenbrooks too turned towards the arts, their money-making urge diluted after several generations of fiercely energetic success.

Lorenzo the Magnificent's death in 1492 marks the beginning of a forty-year crisis for the Medici. His son and successor Piero fled from Florence in 1494 when a coalition of anti-Medicean magnates proved more adept than he in coming to terms with the French invaders. For eighteen years the city reverted to genuine republicanism, and the new régime was overturned only when disaster befell the French cause in Italy (1512) and the republic's own malcontents allied with Medicean exiles and sympathizers. From 1512 till 1527 Florence again came under the Medici, but the family was restored in circumstances that brought about a complete change in the nature of its rule. Lorenzo's son Giovanni and later his illegitimate nephew Giulio became popes (as Leo X, 1513–21, and Clement VII, 1523–34), and hence Florence was almost an 'annexe' of the papacy. Control there was entrusted to a series of Medici relatives, lay and ecclesiastical, and ultimately to a Cardinal, Passerini, in whose time the Medici name was represented by two young bastards, one of them the son of an oriental slave.

Clement VII's disasters in 1527, when an imperialist army sacked Rome, were the occasion of a new republican revival, and

[1] L. Landucci, *Diario Fiorentino*, ed. I. Del Badia (Florence, 1883), p. 65; Janet Ross, *Lives of the Early Medici as told in their Correspondence*, pp. 306 ff. and 341–3.

for three years Florence defied empire and papacy. After his defeat of the French at Pavia (1525), however, the Emperor Charles V was the real master of Italy, and when he was able to turn his attention to Florence the republic came to realize that for all its commercial wealth it was an anachronism in a new world of great powers. Clement wanted Florence back for the Medici, and in Charles's eyes the papacy was a more weighty ally than the Florentine republic. When a papalist-imperialist army besieged the city in 1529 the 'last republic' was doomed. It capitulated in 1530 and the Medici returned once more. In 1532 the old constitution was abolished and Alessandro, the illegitimate son of a grandson of Lorenzo the Magnificent, became the first of the line of Medici dukes which lasted into the eighteenth century.

The history of Milan and of Florence illustrates quite well the development of the *signoria* in the peninsula as a whole. There are no significant general differences between the tyrants of the papal lands and those of imperial Italy, and indeed the chronology of the *signoria* of Bologna, the greatest city of the Papal State, resembles closely that of Florence. After an abortive fourteenth-century tyranny (that of the Pepoli in 1337–50), Bologna fell to the control of a single dynasty, the Bentivoglio, who ruled the city, with some interruptions, from 1401 until 1512. Like the Medici, the Bentivoglio never formalized their status as tyrants. Like the Visconti they gained recognition as vicars—of the pope. Bologna, however, was a less powerful piece on the Italian chessboard, and hence its lords were more dependent on external favour than those of Milan and Florence. Thus Giovanni Bentivoglio ruled in 1401–1402 with the support of the Visconti, Sante from 1446 to 1463 with that of Cosimo di Medici and, for a time, of Francesco Sforza. In the sixteenth century the *signori* of the Papal State became victims of papal centralization, and the extinction of Bentivoglio rule by Julius II (1512) was a salient episode in the downfall of tyranny in the State.

Much has already been said about patronage in Chapter VIII, but the Italian tyrants are so closely linked with this topic that we must return briefly to their share in fostering art and learning. For them it was a matter of prestige to be surrounded by handsome buildings and works of art and to be known as the patrons of distinguished artists, writers and thinkers. It came to be believed that this was a race in which no tyrant, whatever his temperament, could afford to lag behind; to do so would have been a confession of avarice, of petty-mindedness, perhaps even of poverty. For the same reasons it was important to keep pace with changes in taste; patronage of a genre which was no longer fashionable was almost as bad as no patronage at all. Inevitably such patronage grew snowball-wise, like the acquisition of Old Master paintings by American millionaires in the days of Duveen and Berenson. Artists and humanist writers dictated swings in fashionable taste and enjoyed their own new-found prestige. No longer mere 'artists' (craftsmen), they revelled in the sellers' market which brought to men like Michelangelo and Raphael grovelling letters from rulers beseeching them to accept their patronage.

There is not room here to discuss even the leading centres of Renaissance court patronage. It will perhaps be convenient, since their rulers have already been mentioned, to deal with Milan, Florence and the papacy, omitting such important patrons as the Montefeltro of Urbino and the Este of Ferrara. A letter from Leonardo da Vinci to Ludovico 'il Moro' of *c.* 1482, illustrates well the nature of Sforza patronage. In it Leonardo urges on Ludovico his skill as a military and naval engineer, offering to construct tanks ('covered cars') and other ingenious weapons: apart from this, he is skilful as an architect, in designing both houses and systems for conveying water, he is a painter and a sculptor in marble, clay and bronze, who longs to take in hand the proposed equestrian statue in bronze of Francesco Sforza.[1] Unfortunately no evidence has survived to reveal whether Leonardo's employment produced the practical military advantages that he promised.

The two greatest Medici rulers were both distinguished as patrons. Cosimo gave encouragement to Marsilio Ficino, the teacher of Lorenzo, and to other Neo-Platonic philosophers, besides subsidizing Niccolò Niccoli in the collection of classical manuscripts which later came to his own library and to the public library he founded, the Marciana. Cosimo showed comparatively little interest in the visual arts, but his son Giovanni ordered the famous Gozzoli frescoes in the chapel of the Medici palace and his other son Piero, an invalid, spent many hours with his collections

---

[1] For a full translation see below, p. 229.

of gems and illuminated manuscripts. Lorenzo was another con-
noisseur who probably spent more money on antiques—medals,
precious stones and jewellery were his speciality—than on contemporary art. He certainly devoted much time to the plans for
his new villa at Poggio a Caiano, but painting does not seem to
have been among his principal enthusiasms. He was often consulted by other rulers about Florentine artists and the effect of his
advice was to disperse rather than to employ them, for Da Vinci,
as we have seen, moved to Milan, and Verrocchio to Venice and
then to Rome, where he worked, like many other Florentines, for
Pope Sixtus IV. As a fine poet himself, as the close friend of the
philosopher Ficino and of the classical scholar and poet Poliziano,
Lorenzo stands apart from other Renaissance patrons. He could
well afford to indulge in the Maecenas' budget which reflected his
individual tastes.

The greatest of fifteenth-century Italian patrons in terms of
mòney was the papacy. The proud tradition was firmly founded
by Nicholas V (1447–55), himself a classical scholar and virtually
the originator of the Vatican library. In Nicholas's chancery were
such humanists as Poggio Bracciolini, Leon-Battista Alberti and
Lorenzo Valla, and he encouraged Valla and the Greek Cardinal
Bessarion to undertake translations of the works of Plato and
Thucydides. He employed as painters Fra Angelico, Piero della
Francesca and Andrea Castagno, and he formulated ambitious
schemes for rebuilding. His fulsome biographer, Manetti, likens
his buildings to those of Athens, to Solomon's Temple, the
Colossus of Rhodes and the Pyramids, but his greatest contribution was the decision to build a new St Peter's. Nicholas's successor, Pius II, though himself a humanist—or perhaps *because* he
had been a humanist—was no enthusiastic patron of letters, nor
was his successor Paul II. The tradition, however, was resumed
with enthusiasm by the Franciscan Sixtus IV (1471–84), who began
the alterations at St Peter's, built the famous chapel which bears
his name (the 'Sistine'), employed Botticelli, Ghirlandaio, Perugino, Signorelli and other noted artists, and chose as his librarian
the papal biographer Platina. His successors, Innocent VIII and
Alexander VI, gave work to Mantegna and Pinturicchio, but the
greatest products of papal patronage, the building of a new
St Peter's, the addition of many suites of rooms to the Vatican

palace, and the re-planning of much of Rome, were to be the work of the sixteenth century.

To emphasize their rank, which placed them above the merely temporal rulers of Italy, the popes determined to outshine all others as patrons. Their activities came to a peak when princely and pontifical pride joined together in the Medici popes Leo X and Clement VII. But there was no slackening under Clement's Farnese successor (Paul III) nor under the popes of the Counter-Reformation. The building of the new St Peter's proceeded throughout the sixteenth century, and only in that century did Rome become—what Florence had been since the time of Brunelleschi—a 'Renaissance' city, bearing the marks of the classical theories of proportion and harmony which were restated by Leon-Battista Alberti. By the later sixteenth century Rome was the only Court in Italy that remained a centre of artistic patronage, but 'Renaissance' traditions had been taken up in the courts of the monarchies. Tastes were inherited as well as traditions, and the Queen of the greatest of English royal collectors, Charles I, was by descent a Medici.

Further Reading

P. J. JONES, 'Communes and Despots', *Transactions of the Royal Historical Society*, 5th. s., vol. 5 (1965)

D. M. BUENO DE MESQUITA, 'The Place of Despotism in Italian Politics' in *Europe in the Late Middle Ages* (ed. Hale, Highfield and Smalley, London, 1965)

C. M. ADY, *Milan under the Sforza* (London, 1907)

C. M. ADY, *Lorenzo dei Medici and Renaissance Italy* (London, 1955)

J. BURCKHARDT. *The Civilization of the Renaissance in Italy* (Mentor Books; and many other edns.)

E. F. JACOB (ed.), *Italian Renaissance Studies* (London, 1960), particularly E. H. Gombrich's chapter on 'The Early Medici as patrons of Art': the same author's *The Story of Art* (London, 1953) provides an excellent introduction to the art of the period dealt with in this book

Leonardo da Vinci writes to offer his services to Ludovico 'il Moro' of Milan. Circa 1483.
(From *Selections from the Notebooks of Leonardo da Vinci*, ed. I. A. Richter, The World's Classics, Oxford, pp. 294–6).

Most illustrious Lord. Having now sufficiently seen and considered the proofs of all those who count themselves masters and inventors of instruments of war, and finding that the invention and working of the said instruments do not differ in any respect from those in common use, I shall endeavour without prejudice to anyone else to explain myself to your Excellency, showing your Lordship my secrets, and then offering at your pleasure to work with effect at convenient times on all those things which are in part briefly recorded below.

1. I have plans of bridges, very light and strong and suitable for carrying very easily, and with them you may pursue, and at times flee from, the enemy; and others secure and indestructible by fire and battle, easy and convenient to lift and place in position; and plans for burning and destroying those of the enemy.

2. When a place is besieged, I know how to remove the water from the trenches, and how to construct an infinite number of bridges, covered ways and ladders and other instruments having to do with such expeditions.

3. Also if a place cannot be reduced by the method of bombardment either owing to the height of its banks or to its strength of position, I have plans for destroying every fortress or other stronghold even if it were founded on rock.

4. I have also plans of mortars most convenient and easy to carry with which to hurl small stones in the manner almost of a storm; and with the smoke of this cause great terror to the enemy and great loss and confusion.

And if it should happen that the fight was at sea I have plans for many engines most efficient for both attack and defence, and vessels which will resist the fire of the largest cannon, and powder and smoke.

5. Also I have means of arriving at a fixed spot by caves and secret and winding passages, made without any noise even though it may be necessary to pass underneath trenches or a river.

6. Also I will make covered cars, safe and unassailable, which will enter among the enemy with their artillery, and there is no company of men at arms so great that they will not break it. And behind these infantry will be able to follow quite unharmed and without any hindrance.

7. Also, if need shall arise, I can make cannon, mortars, and light ordnance of very useful and beautiful shapes, different from those in common use.

8. Where the operation of bombardment fails, I shall contrive catapults, mangonels, *trabocchi*, and other engines of wonderful efficacy and in general use. In short, to meet the variety of circum-

stances, I shall contrive various and endless means of attack and defence.

10. In time of peace I believe I can give perfect satisfaction, equal to that of any other, in architecture and the construction of buildings both private and public, and in conducting water from one place to another.

Also I can carry out sculpture in marble, bronze or clay, and also I can do in painting whatever can be done, as well as any other, whoever he be.

Moreover, the bronze horse may be taken in hand, which shall endue with immortal glory and eternal honour the happy memory of the Prince your father and of the illustrious house of Sforza.

And if any of the aforesaid things should seem impossible or impracticable to anyone I offer myself as most ready to make trial of them in your park, or in whatever place may please your Excellency, to whom I commend myself with all possible humility.

XII

THE FRENCH RECOVERY

THE Treaty of Troyes of 1420 (above, p. 147) and its
ratification by the French estates marked the lowest tide in
the fortunes of France. The English, assisted by Burgundy,
held most of northern France, and their king had been accepted as
heir to the French throne. The finances of France were in a disastrous condition. The extravagance of the royal household was
notorious; the 'Remonstrances' of Paris in 1413 claimed that the
expenditure of the Queen's household alone had recently risen
from 36,000 to 154,000 *livres* a year. Even more serious were the
financial consequences of the pressure exerted on the demented
king by both Orléans and Burgundy during the years of their
struggle for power; Louis of Orléans, besides an annual pension
from the Crown of 12,000 *livres*, received 500,000 for renouncing
his claims to Genoa, the same amount on the occasion of his son's
marriage to the widow of Richard II of England, and much else.
The currency of the unoccupied zone was chaotic—and at Rouen
groats were minted bearing the menacing legend 'Henricus rex
Angliae heres Franciae'. In Paris the population was for the most
part more bitterly anti-Burgundian or anti-Armagnac (according
to individual sympathies) than anti-English. Henry V of England
was joyfully received in the city in 1420 and the following year the
birth of his son was fêted. This desertion of the French cause was
not, of course, unanimous; when the Parisians took the oath of
loyalty to the English in 1423 it was noted that 'some did so with
a good heart, others most unwillingly'.[1] The effect of the Treaty,
in fact, was that the French were no longer clear where their
allegiance lay.

After the Treaty and the fall of Paris the disowned Dauphin was

[1] *Journal d'un Bourgeois de Paris* (ed. A. Mary, 1929), p. 171.

able to carry on the war from Bourges, with other centres of support at Poitiers and Toulouse. The death of Henry V in 1422 brought some hope to the Dauphin, and a few months later that of his father gave him a claim to the royal title, but France's dilemma was reflected in the very serious dissensions within his own party. These led to a series of campaigns between the chamberlain La Trémouille and the Angevin house supported by the constable Richemont amounting to a civil war within the framework of the greater struggle.

In 1429 the war at last took a favourable turn for the Dauphin with the relief of Orléans, on the Loire. Not only was this fortress a key position for the defence of central and southern France, it was also the town of the captive duke Charles d'Orléans, and some held that in these circumstances the English were transgressing the rules of war in besieging it. French indignation at this action is mirrored in the decisive intervention of Joan of Arc, the symptom and at the same time the agent of French national sentiment. Joan's passionate patriotism was that of frontier-territory; her village, Domrémy, lay on the boundary of the pro-Burgundian duchy of Bar, and it had once been destroyed by Burgundian troops. Her talk was as much of 'French blood' as of the saints, and the very words of her 'voices' are characteristic: 'Go to France, you will relieve Orléans.' Joan persuaded the Dauphin of his legitimacy, then played a prominent part in the relief of Orléans. It is hard to assess her share in determining strategy and even to decide to what extent she ranked as a military commander, but her contribution to morale was great and vitally important in this turning-point of the war. The English issued a proclamation against 'the captains and soldiers who have abandoned their posts, influenced by the incantations of a maid', and the letters of Charles of France announced her successes as a miracle. After the relief, Joan took part in the further victory of Patay, then set the seal on her triumph by escorting the Dauphin across France to Rheims, where he was crowned as Charles VII.

It was natural that Joan's achievements and her influence at Court should make her enemies. La Trémouille in particular was jealous of her prestige and helped to rouse doubts concerning her when she met failure in an ill-prepared sally against Paris, in the course of which she was wounded for the third time. When she fell into the hands of the Burgundians at Compiègne (May 1430) the English paid 10,000 crowns for her to her captors. Her subsequent trial by the Inquisition was aimed, by implication, at Charles also, for if she could be discredited, so was his coronation. Yet the French court now virtually disowned her and nothing was done to save Joan when she was sentenced to be burnt after being tricked into abjuring her errors. After her death (May 1431) she was remembered among the French people, but the monarchy did not obtain her official rehabilitation until a quarter of a century later. Recent writers, in reaction against the view which ascribes all historical developments to the deeds of outstanding individuals, have minimized the importance of Joan's intervention. Contemporary testimony leaves no doubt that her role was an enormously important one and chroniclers as far afield as Lübeck[1] recorded her deeds and her death.

The momentous consequence of Charles VII's military revival was the gradual detachment of Burgundy from its English alliance. This was assisted by the dissolution by death of the marriage alliance—Anne, duchess of Bedford, sister of the duke of Burgundy and wife of the English regent, died in 1432 and Bedford himself in 1435—but essentially it was the product of the shift in the balance of military success. At Arras in 1435 the Burgundians at last came to terms with the French crown. The terms were humiliating for Charles, and in view of his circumstances they could not be otherwise: he had to yield the Somme towns, to excuse duke Philip homage, and to express contrition for the murder at Montereau. Nevertheless, the crisis in the struggle was now over. The following year Paris was reoccupied, and France entered the slow and painful process of recuperation. With England beset by internal dissension and France by bands of parasitic mercenaries, both sides were extremely weak. By 1439 Charles was able to begin a series of military reforms, asserting royal control of recruitment to the mercenary Companies. After the truce of Tours (1444) there followed more effective military reorganization, with the formation first of a regular cavalry force, the Compagnies d'Ordonnance consisting of 1,500 'lances' of six men each, then of a similar infantry force, the Francs-Archers, recruited by the provision of one archer from every fifty 'hearths'.

[1] Hermann Korner, *Chronica Novella* (ed. J. Schwalm, 1895), pp. 509–10.

In time of peace the Francs-Archers were to be remunerated by exemption from tax. There was also some reform in financial organization, four local receivers-general being appointed. Perhaps as influential in restoring order as these formal measures was Charles's success in the 1440s in loaning the baneful mercenary companies for employment by Frederick III and the duke of Lorraine.

In mid-century the last decisive campaigns of the war were fought. Profiting by English political disunity and financial embarrassment, Charles recovered Normandy in 1449–50 and Guyenne between 1449 and 1453 after a temporary set-back due to Gascon resentment of rule by Frenchmen. Charles lived on until 1461. Despite his unimpressive personality, his achievements were immense. In some ways the most important of these was his success in bringing the monarchy out of the war with its hold over its noble subjects greatly strengthened. He checked the acquisition of new fiefs and the construction of new fortifications, limited seignorial taxation, and increased the scope of royal jurisdiction at the expense of the nobility. More nobles were taken into royal employment as officials and in office they enjoyed power *qua* officials rather than *qua* nobles. Three times Charles had to face noble 'conspiracies', but only the *Praguerie* of 1440, which involved the Dauphin as well as the dukes of Brittany, Alençon and Bourbon and the count of Anjou, was a serious threat: it was perhaps frustrated only by the refusal of the English to participate. The next reign was to show that the monarchy had by no means cowed the greater feudatories. The falling-back of the lesser nobles and their tendency to become aligned with the Crown was an essential element in the extraordinarily rapid recovery of the French monarchy. Their recession is usually attributed to impoverishment by the war and inability to increase their incomes to meet the rising cost of fighting on their own account, but such explanations of general social changes are hard to establish, and this one cannot yet be regarded as proved.

Louis, son and heir of Charles *le Bien Servi*, had long been in opposition to his father, and for the last five years of the reign had lived under the protection of the duke of Burgundy. The curious and interesting personality of Louis XI had much to do with France's continued recovery. He was a hard man and a hard worker, authoritarian, unscrupulous and expecting no scruples in others. Pious, jovial, and in manner unassuming and unimpressive, he had no interest in ceremony, and at his coronation banquet he took off his crown, because he found it uncomfortable, and put it on the table. He had a passion for information and for diplomacy. Louis spoke Italian and admired the Italians, but in the opinion of Europe he had nothing to learn from them of diplomatic subtlety; certainly his comment on Francesco Sforza that 'he was never so great as when he was up to his neck in water' could be applied with equal truth to himself. The historians of his defeated rival, Burgundy, admiringly called him 'the universal spider', and Commynes, the servant and adviser whom he lured from the Burgundians, spoke from close acquaintance when he called him 'the cleverest man I have known at extricating himself from an adverse situation' and the one 'who worked hardest to win over a man who could serve him or do him harm'.

There is no room here to deal with Louis' diplomacy at length, and we must renounce, for example, the tale of his tangled negotiations in the Iberian peninsula, which occupied much of his time and energy. In his three principal aims, the overthrow of the virtually independent Burgundian duchy, the curbing of the other great French feudatories, and the elimination of English intervention in France, he achieved success. These three themes are so interrelated that they cannot be treated in isolation. Philip the Good of Burgundy was the greatest of the feudatories, a fact he emphasized tactlessly at Louis' coronation by attending with a suite of four thousand which greatly outnumbered the king's. Others were not far behind. The duke of Brittany almost ranked as an independent ruler, with his own administration and army, his own diplomacy and an agreement with the papacy which gave him very considerable authority over the dioceses of his duchy. Further south the Angevin descendants of Charles V's brother Louis held the middle Loire as well as Anjou and Maine and the isolated county of Provence; moreover, René of Anjou was claimant to the kingdom of Naples, his sister was the widow of Charles VII and his daughter the wife of Henry VI of England. In central France the duke of Bourbon dominated the upper Loire and Auvergne, thus completing a potentially hostile chain which terminated in the east with the duchy of Burgundy. Only a little after these greatest of nobles ranked the houses of Orléans and Alençon, and those of Armagnac and Foix in the south-west.

'On his accession he thought of nothing but revenge', says Commynes, and the dismissed officials of Louis' father played a leading part in the organization of the great alliance of malcontents which was formed in 1464. The claim of this coalition to stand for the Public Weal (*le Bien Public*) bears witness only to the imagined persuasive strength of the tritest of all political commonplaces, and one to which the king himself subscribed when he advised his successor to rule *pour le bien commun*.[1] The Parisian writer who dated his poem from 'the year in which everyone put his own interest first' (*l'an que chacun à son profit tendait*) made the aptest comment on these pretensions. The chief characters in the conspiracy were Charles, count of Charolais (the heir of Philip of Burgundy), the duke of Brittany, René of Anjou's heir John of Calabria, the duke of Bourbon and the count of Armagnac, the king's brother Charles was its figurehead. Louis had the support of Normandy, Picardy and Champagne, of two of his uncles, the majority of the towns, and a mercenary force provided by his ally Francesco Sforza, but his enemies were able to put well over 10,000 men into the field and his hopes of salvation lay mainly in their dissensions. In action the coalition proved a very piecemeal affair. The first attack was launched from Brittany in the spring of 1465 by the king's brother. Thereafter Louis was able to confront his opponents one by one, first defeating John of Bourbon, then checking Charolais at the indecisive battle of Montlhéry. By the autumn Charles of France had lost his enthusiasm for the war, but Louis was only able to extricate himself from the crisis by distributing sops to the principal plotters. By the Treaty of St Maur (October 1465) Burgundy received Boulogne, Guines and the recently ceded Somme towns, Bourbon the lieutenant-generalship of Languedoc and a gift of 100,000 crowns, Louis' brother Normandy, and the duke of Brittany and John of Calabria lesser rewards. A 'commission of reform' was appointed, but no reform followed. Soon afterwards Louis drove his brother from Normandy, which as a possible base for future English reconquests was a sensitive point; by then all Charles's former allies had forgotten the Public Weal, for none came to his defence.

[1] *Le Rosier des Guerres*, ch. 3.

Only once after the *Bien Public* did Louis have to face an acute crisis. This occurred after Charles of Charolais' accession to the Burgundian duchy (1467), when through over-confidence Louis enmeshed himself in the tortuous coils of his own diplomatic intrigue. In 1468 he pressed for a meeting with Charles the Rash which took place at Péronne. But he had recently completed negotiations for a rising of Charles's subject city of Liége, and the news of this rebellion, together with Louis' evident complicity, reached the duke when the king, with almost no entourage, was on his territory and at his mercy. For three days the angry duke held Louis virtually as a prisoner; the king was 'fort effrayé', says Commynes, who goes on to recount how

> that night, the third, the duke never took off his clothes. He only lay down on his bed two or three times, then started to pace up and down, as was his way when he was worried. I slept in his chamber that night and sometimes I walked up and down the room with him. In the morning he was in a greater rage than ever, he was making threats and was ready to carry out a great deed [*à exécuter grande chose*]. Nevertheless he decided to reduce his demands; he would be content if the king swore to keep peace [with him] and went with him to Liége to aid him in his revenge against the bishop of Liége, who was a close relative of the king's. And so he abruptly went off to the king's room to tell him this decision.[1]

The episode of Péronne and the subsequent campaign against his Liégeois allies were a humiliation for Louis, but the duke had realized that international politics is not a game that ends with the capture of the king. In the event his gains were comparatively meagre. Louis yielded some jurisdictional rights and more territory. This time he granted his brother Champagne and Brie, which were dangerously adjacent to Burgundy, but later Charles was persuaded to accept instead Guyenne, tenure of which almost precluded friendship with England. Meanwhile an assembly of notables freed Louis from his engagements to the duke of Burgundy on the ground that these had been extorted under pressure.

As England early in the century had hesitated between support of Burgundian and Armagnac, so Louis now hesitated between Lancaster and York. During the 'Public Weal' he had been Yorkist and was fortunate in that Burgundy was then linked with

[1] Commynes, *Mémoires*, Bk. II, 9.

the failing fortunes of Henry VI, whose brother-in-law John of Calabria was prominent in the League. Soon after this the Burgundians turned Yorkist, but Warwick the Kingmaker's quarrel with the Woodvilles and flight to France gave Louis the opportunity to plan a Lancastrian restoration. He contrived to reconcile Henry's queen, Margaret of Anjou, with the man who had done so much to bring about her husband's deposition. In 1470 he assisted Warwick's invasion, and triumphed when Edward IV fled to the Low Countries and Henry VI was released from the Tower of London and restored to the throne. This success had its logical continuation when Louis sent an embassy to England to propose a joint attack on Burgundy; the duchy was to be carved up, England receiving the Low Countries.

But Louis had backed the wrong horse. Edward, with support from Burgundy, the Hanse and Brittany, invaded England and put an end to the Lancastrian restoration after less than a year. Now it was Burgundy's turn to prepare an attack on France, and the cycle of events became complete in 1474 when, by the Treaty of London, Charles of Burgundy came to terms with Edward IV for a partition of the kingdom of France (see above, p. 187).

The following year Edward landed a large force at Calais, but he was disappointed to find that the promised aid from the dukes of Burgundy and Brittany did not materialize. Louis took his chance, arranged a personal meeting with Edward at Picquigny and bought him off for 75,000 crowns down, to be followed by an annual payment of 50,000. Charles of Burgundy was bitterly indignant at his ally's defection, but it was his own fault that he had committed himself to expansionist schemes in too many directions at the same time and was involved with his army in the Rhineland when he should have been assisting Edward: 'God had troubled his senses and his understanding', says Commynes. Picquigny marked the end of any serious English claim to the French throne and thus the liquidation of the Hundred Years War. It was characteristic of Louis that this should be achieved by money. As he explained in the *Rosier des Guerres*: 'To fight is the most dangerous thing in the world. . . . If one errs in anything else, one can amend it later, but when one has lost a battle there is no way of making amends.' [1] This preference for financial

---

[1] *Le Rosier des Guerres*, ch. 6.

methods shows, too, in the handsome pensions later allotted by
Louis to Edward's councillors, which were intended to secure
English support for his Burgundian schemes after the death of
Charles the Rash. Lord Hastings, the chamberlain, was the most
favoured of these, at 2,000 crowns per annum—for which he was
unwilling to furnish a receipt since he was also a pensioner of
Louis' rival, Mary of Burgundy.

After Picquigny, Burgundy was by far the most important of
Louis' preoccupations, but Charles who 'would not have been
satisfied with half Europe', did much to bring about his own
destruction. The story of Louis' organization of an alliance including the Swiss, Frederick III and the duke of Lorraine, and of
Charles's frantic campaigns and downfall has been recounted
above. Louis' exploitation of Charles's death, however, cannot
be ranked among his successes. The vital element in the situation
was the future of Mary of Burgundy, Charles's only daughter, who
was nineteen when her father was killed at Nancy. Essentially
Louis had to opt between supporting the heiress or opposing her:
yet he fell victim to his characteristic fault of over-subtlety and,
by attempting to reap the advantages of both courses, he gained
little from either. He annexed Picardy, Artois, the towns of the
Somme and—in the face of a good deal of opposition—the 'old'
duchy (of Burgundy). These conquests by force were not easily
reconcilable with Louis' plans for marrying Mary to his seven-
year-old heir, and thus gaining the greater prize of the Low
Countries. Mary was able to choose as her husband the obvious
alternative, Maximilian the son of Frederick III, and this marriage,
possibly the most momentous in the entire history of Europe,
took place in August 1477. The matter of the Burgundian lands
was only settled, after some fighting, by the Peace of Arras of
1482. By the terms of Arras Louis gained Picardy and the Burgundian duchy. The intention was that Artois, the Franche-
Comté and some other territories should also come to France, as
the dowry of Mary's daughter Margaret, who was betrothed to
the Dauphin, but this marriage did not eventuate, and the lands
proved untenable and had to be restored. All the rest of the great
Burgundian inheritance was also gained by the hitherto weakly
house of Austria. In the pragmatic test Louis' diplomatic expertise
had not shown up well.

Nevertheless this was on the whole an era of continued monarchical recovery. We hear of Louis returning happy from a successful boar hunt 'singing a song written about the rout of the duke of Burgundy', and by the end of his reign there was a good deal else about which he could feel content. René of Anjou was survived by none of his male descendants, and after his death (1480) the Crown came into possession of the Angevin lands, including Maine, Provence and the county of Bar. One of Louis' daughters married the heir of John de Bourbon, another Louis of Orléans, and thus two of the great noble dynasties were more closely linked with the monarchy. More welcome still were the confiscated estates of Armagnac, St Pol and Nemours. Brittany was now the sole remaining quasi-independent fief, and even Brittany was not long to maintain this position.

If Louis preferred expenditure to war, he was fully aware that such a policy entailed a special care for his country's financial productivity. His attitude is reflected with striking clarity in his advice to his son, which breaks off strangely from the flow of political and military platitudes to culminate in some down-to-earth (if debatable) economics. The last words of this work are:

> If all gilding was forbidden, this would be a good thing: for a lot of gold is lost in this way. Also no one should wear or use silk. And the old fairs of the kingdom should be revived. Thus all would be wealth.[1]

Louis' attempts to foster French fairs are seen at their most energetic in his support of Lyons, which he built up as a rival to Geneva—so overtly that its fairs were held on the same dates as Geneva's—with considerable success. Indeed, he experimented with almost every possible form of economic *étatisme*. In the Mediterranean he backed a series of monopolistic ventures in state galleys, based first on Aigues-Mortes and other ports in the Languedoc, then, after its acquisition in 1482, on Marseilles. These however were unsuccessful, perhaps because the French were too accustomed to importing Levantine goods by land from other ports, such as Genoa. The small state arsenals set up originally at Tours, Rouen and Paris, and later at eighteen other centres, were a rather less ambitious and more effective undertaking. Cannon-

[1] *Le Rosier des Guerres*, ch. 7.

foundries were also inaugurated at Tours, Rouen and Orléans. In the winter of 1480-1, requiring 5,500 pikes, 14,500 halberds and 18,500 daggers for the forthcoming campaign in Flanders, Louis was delighted to receive the total order within two months.

Typical of Louis' methods was his treatment of Arras when the burghers proved hostile to French rule after the occupation of Artois (1477). He had many of the inhabitants exiled, and in 1479 set out to repopulate the city by the compulsory settlement there of 3,000 families, drawn from every zone of France and each designated to follow a particular trade. For three years immense efforts were made to make the colonization of Arras work. New families were drafted in, entailing tremendous administrative exertions at the recruiting end, economic privileges were lavished on Arras (now rechristened 'Franchise'!), royal officials organized the setting-up of cloth firms, and other towns were forced to purchase their produce at artificially high prices. Yet this impressive display of Colbertism *avant la lettre* proved ineffective. The peace terms of 1482 permitted the return of the former inhabitants, and two years later such of the new colonizers as had remained were expelled.

Another enterprising but unsuccessful attempt at regulation was the plan to draw business from the great Burgundian fairs at Bruges and Antwerp. It was hoped to attract English trade away from them to newly founded fairs in Normandy—originally at Caen and later Rouen. In essence this scheme was one of Louis' many attempts at economic warfare, attempts which included military attacks on Burgundian crops and naval ones on the Flemish herring-fleet, and which are seen at their most ambitious in the great embargo on trade with Flanders in 1470. The latter was a serious measure of blockade which attempted to deny the Flemish towns the French grain on which they were dependent, in the hope that the starving population would rise against Charles the Rash in revolt. Louis' economic interventionism was significant rather for what it attempted than for what it achieved, but he had inherited a very formidable fiscal machine. There were already 'receiving' offices, each under a *receveur général*, at Paris, Tours, Rouen and Montpellier, beside that for the Dauphiné, and to these Louis added *recettes* for Burgundy and the Somme towns (1477) and for Provence (1484). Extraordinary taxation, which came under a central office of *généraux*, was organized by local units known as *élections*, and another network to ensure the collection of the salt-tax (*gabelle*) covered most of the kingdom. The ultimate fiscal court, the *Chambre* or *Cour des Aides*, had both judicial and administrative functions. The extent of France's recovery shows in the fact that the average annual revenue from taxation of his country rose from about 1,800,000 *livres* at the start of Louis' reign to about 4,800,000 at the end,[1] though he may have inflicted hardship by excessive taxation, particularly in the countryside.

Louis' heir, Charles VIII, was only thirteen on his accession in 1483, and not a very intelligent thirteen at that. He was under the guardianship of his elder sister Anne and her husband Pierre de Beaujeu, the heir to the duke of Bourbon, but the authority of this pair was challenged by the duke of Orléans, who was husband of the king's second sister Jeanne, and himself a cousin of the king. To maintain their control the Beaujeu made use of parliamentary institutions: the meeting of estates summoned to Tours, the first to be styled *États généraux*, was in substance merely a successful manœuvre to confirm the regency. There was no strong demand for central estates in France, probably because regional feeling remained strong (and, indeed, some local estates continued to meet), and because the nobles, being exempt from taxation, took little interest.

The great political problem of the early years of the reign was that of Brittany, whose duke, Francis II, had no male heir. The duchy was the last great survival of feudal independence (its ruler no longer owed liege homage to the Crown), and there was always the danger that the English might again use it as the gateway to France, as they had done in the previous century. As with Burgundy a few years before, everything hinged on the marriage of the heiress, Anne. A prominent pretender to her hand was the duke of Orléans, who was seeking a divorce from his wife Jeanne. When Orléans rose in rebellion in 1485 (*La Guerre Folle*) he had some support from Brittany, as well as from king Maximilian and the king of Navarre. Duke Francis's death (1488) was followed

---

[1] R. Gandilhon, *La Politique Économique de Louis XI*, p. 295. In the mid-seventeenth and late eighteenth centuries France was to demonstrate again how rapidly a nation can recover from financial and political disaster.

by negotiations for a marriage between the heiress Anne and Maximilian, now a widower, and a proxy ceremony took place in 1490, but Maximilian lacked the means to intervene strongly in French affairs. The war in Brittany went in favour of the French crown and in 1491 Anne was married to Charles VIII. Thus the last of the great fiefs lost its independence, and a new immense accession of domain was added to the recent gains of Anjou, Provence, Alençon and Armagnac. The very strong control over the French Church recognized by the Pragmatic Sanction of Bourges (1438) and the Concordat of Amboise (1472) rounded off for the monarchy a position of strength that would have been unimaginable during the long agony of Charles VI's reign.

Charles VIII had no difficulty in finding an arena within which to display this strength. The story of French interest and intervention in the Italian peninsula can be traced back without interruption to the conquest of Charles of Anjou in the 1260s. By the middle of the fifteenth century this tradition had been strengthened both by the claim of the new Angevin house—recognized by Queen Joanna II (d. 1435)—to the throne of Naples, and that of the Orléans line to the duchy of Milan, based on the marriage of Charles VI's brother Louis of Orléans to Valentina, daughter of Gian-Galeazzo Visconti. By Charles VIII's time the former of these claims had passed to the French crown. The acquisition of Marseilles made Tyrrhenian Italy a tempting zone for nascent French naval power, while Asti, Valentina Visconti's dowry, would serve as a convenient French base south of the Alps. Long before 1494 Lorenzo de Medici had realized the strong danger that the rivalry between the main Italian powers, and in particular the unstable régimes of Ludovico Sforza in Milan and of the feudalized Neapolitan kingdom—the two states to which the French monarchy possessed claims—might bring in the French and upset the precarious balance of the peninsula. Charles VIII was not the man to resist the temptation to win military renown. Diplomatic precautions came first, in the form of agreements to secure the neutrality of England (Étaples, 1492), Spain (Barcelona, 1493) and the Empire (Senlis, 1493). There followed the military preparations which make it possible to explain Savonarola's 'prophecy' of forthcoming invasion (December 1493) as no more than well-informed prediction.

This is not the place in which to recount the story of how, in 1494-5, 30,000 Frenchmen conquered Italy, as it was said, 'with chalk' (the chalk with which they marked the billets for their troops), or of the Italian wars which continued, with interruptions, up to the Peace of Cateau-Cambrésis of 1559. The first French invasion ended in 1495 when Charles was frightened from Naples by an alliance including Spain and the Empire, as well as most of the Italian powers. In 1499 Charles's cousin and successor, Louis XII, renewed the struggle, dispossessed the Sforza of Milan, and reached an agreement with the Spanish which promised him half the Neapolitan kingdom as well. Later, however, he too was driven out of southern Italy and at the end of his reign he lost Milan also, but this was regained by his successor Francis I (1515).

The experiences of Charles VIII and Louis XII showed that Spain and the Empire were formidable opponents who were linked closely with the southern and northern parts of the peninsula respectively, and were unwilling to tolerate French supremacy in Italy. When a single ruler, in the person of Charles V, came to the throne of both Spain and the Empire (1519), the days of that supremacy were numbered. French power in Italy was shattered at the battle of Pavia (1525) and rarely reasserted. Direct rule in the south (Sicily and Naples) and the north-west (Milan) and predominance over the rest of the peninsula passed to Charles V and later to his son Philip II of Spain. This was the culmination of a series of campaigns which brought home to the Italians the strength of the great states who were their neighbours and whose battlefield they now supplied. The effect of this confrontation, which made some Italians see their own states as anachronistic survivors in a new world, will be discussed in the last chapter of this book.

Further Reading

E. PERROY, *The Hundred Years War* (London, 1951)
P. S. LEWIS (ed.), *The Recovery of France in the 15th century* (London, 1971)
P. M. KENDALL, *Louis XI* (London, 1971)
P. DE COMMINES, *Memoirs* (see above, p. 196)

R

XIII

THE UNIFICATION OF SPAIN

ACCEPTED generalizations concerning the history and temperament of Spain and the Spaniards (their pride, their poverty, religious faith, reluctance to engage in commerce and industry, and so on) are so current both in Spain and outside that it is necessary to emphasize that Ferdinand and Isabella ruled not one kingdom but two, and that Castile and Aragon differed from each other profoundly in their political and social traditions and their economic foundations.

The history of Castile, the senior of the two partners, was essentially that of the 'Reconquest' and the accompanying Christian settlement of lands previously held by the Mohammedans. The first great period of Reconquest, during which Toledo and central Spain were recovered, occurred in the eleventh century. Another vast advance in the first half of the thirteenth won Seville and much of Andalusia, but Granada remained to the Muslims. When invited by Louis IX of France to join him on Crusade, Ferdinand III of Castile (1217–52) had retorted with complete truth: 'There is no lack of Moors in my own country.' Medieval Castile was in fact Christian frontier territory, a land in which crusading mentality—but not crusading activity—was unceasing. The task of settlement was an immense one, for the defeated Muslims normally withdrew from the areas gained by the Castilians: in particular the towns were almost deserted. Although the thirteenth-century Reconquest added to the territory of Castile by 50 per cent, the addition to its population has been estimated at a mere 10 per cent. Nevertheless the kingdom's total population, which was probably about four million at the time of these victories (*c.* 1212–48), had perhaps doubled by the end of the fifteenth century.

The most striking feature of medieval Castilian institutions is the weakness of the Crown, which was frequently enfeebled by minorities and disputed successions, and rarely benefited from tenure by really able and effective men. The kings struggled ahead on inadequate revenues, there was little wealth from trade or industry for them to exploit, and inevitably they lived off their capital by alienating the royal domain. Nor did they allow their ambitions to be held in check by their meagre resources, for they embarked on schemes for the conquest of Portugal and Aragon and even (in the case of Alfonso X) the Empire. Anarchy was at its worst during the long war between two rival contenders, Peter the Cruel (1350–69) and his half-brother and successor Henry of Trasta-mara (1369–79), during which time Portugal, France and England were also drawn into the struggles of Castile. No period of recovery from this civil war was granted. Henry's son and successor, John I (1379–90), who sought to check the nobles by means of the peace gilds (*Hermandades*) and a regular army, died young. His son, Henry III (1390–1406), came to the throne after a long minority and died at the age of twenty-seven. Then Henry's infinitely less able son, John II (1406–54), succeeded, again after a minority, and Castile, like contemporary France, was haunted by the long survival of the unfittest. At times during this reign Castile was kept in some degree of order by the king's favourite, Alvaro de Luna, but, after several outbreaks of opposition to de Luna, and even civil war, he fell from power through the enmity of John's second queen, Isabella of Portugal, and was executed in 1453. The position of the monarchy was in no way strengthened by the accession of John II's feeble son, Henry IV 'the Impotent' (1454–1474), the troubles of whose reign will be mentioned below. Through a whole century of disputed successions and civil war Castile's rulers struggled for recognition and support by conferring land and offices on newly aggrandized magnates, into whose possession fell the pastures which were the country's principal source of wealth.

With the political and financial weakness of the Castilian monarchy went a correspondingly decentralized institutional structure. The nobles were powerful, not so much in formal feudal jurisdiction—which they could enjoy without requiring royal approbation—as in exemptions, and in the right to raise their own troops.

Similar exemptions were enjoyed by the military Orders and other religious corporations. The towns, too, inevitably had a high degree of formal independence, because during the Reconquest they could only be settled with adequate numbers of Christian inhabitants if their privileges were tempting. New frontiers had to be held, and hence the towns had to be granted considerable rights over the surrounding countryside, as well as much self-government. The standing of the towns in the kingdom shows in their early representation in the Cortes (above, pp. 14–16), and in times of royal weakness—particularly in the late thirteenth and early fourteenth centuries—it was further strengthened by the formation of imposing Leagues of towns.[1] In the fifteenth century, however, the towns tended to be drawn as dependents into the struggles of the greater feudatories. Toledo, for example, which was virtually the capital, was frequently rebellious, but never in its own municipal interests. It is symptomatic of this situation that in the Cortes of 1442 the towns should have petitioned the Crown that men having more than two hundred vassals should neither inhabit towns nor hold office in them.[2] So pronounced was the dominance of the nobles over the insignificant *bourgeoisie* that the *Hermandad general* of towns was prevailed upon to declare that civil war lay beyond its jurisdiction (1467).

The organs of central control, though withered through desuetude, were not lacking. The Crown still legislated, it exercised some influence over local jurisdiction through the institution of *corregidores*, and it possessed revenue from the trade-tax (*alcabala*). There was no conciliar opposition, nor were the nobles—accustomed to sufficient independence in practice—in the habit of expressing opposition within the Cortes. The means were to hand, then, but the reality—during the two centuries before the accession of Ferdinand and Isabella—had normally been chaos.

The setting of Castilian history was the arid central plateau of the Iberian peninsula. Aragon differed fundamentally from Castile in that it possessed a window on to the Mediterranean, whence it drew most of its wealth and strength. The Aragonese kingdom had its own Reconquest, culminating in the thirteenth century

---

[1] These Leagues were known as *Hermandades* (brotherhoods), but were quite distinct from the peace-gilds which went by the same name.

[2] *Cortes de los antiguos Reinos de León y Castilla*, III, 410–11.

with the capture of the Balearics and Valencia, and since fewer of the Moslems had fled from these places their contribution to its population (which they increased by some 30 per cent) was much greater than that gained by the Castilians from their conquered territories. Much of Aragon lay inland and this was not fertile country, but it was the Catalans, with the assistance of the Valencians, who determined the nature of Aragonese achievements by their commercial and military expansion in the Mediterranean in the thirteenth and fourteenth centuries. Something has already been said about this expansion in connection with the Aragonese role in the 'Sicilian Vespers' of 1282 (above, pp. 45–7). The conquest of Sicily (1282–1302) was followed by that of the duchy of Athens (1311–88) (see above, pp.199 202), Sardinia became a dependency after 1326, and at times tribute was paid by the rulers of the Tunisian littoral. The trade that 'followed the flag' was mainly one in Sicilian grain and Sardinian silver, which were exchanged for Aragonese cloth. Further afield the Catalans had commercial links in the Adriatic (with Ancona and Ragusa), and above all in the eastern Mediterranean in Cyprus and Rhodes, at Alexandria, at Pera (the transpontine suburb of Constantinople) and in the Crimea. Barcelona's recession in the second half of the fifteenth century –in part offset by the continued expansion of Valencia—did not prevent the survival of its traditions of independence, as is evident from its leadership in the Catalan revolt of 1461 72. Aragon's eastward outlook shows most clearly in the policy of Alfonso V (1416–58), who undertook the conquest of the kingdom of Naples and when he had accomplished this task (1442) made Naples his normal residence. After his death Naples passed to a bastard son, and was again divided from Aragon and Sicily, but the link remained a close one. In this southern point of ingress and Aragonese connection there was already much that prefigured the eventual Spanish domination in Italy.

Aragonese political institutions in the later Middle Ages differed from those of Castile mainly in that prolonged constitutional opposition had gained more formal privileges for the nobility. The 'great' privileges of 1283 and 1287 promised 'due process of Law' and no forfeiture of fiefs except by decision of the Council and *Justicia*, no military obligations overseas for the upper nobility, annual meetings of the *Cortes* and the representation of all classes in the Council. In 1287 the king was forced to offer sixteen castles as security for his observance of these terms and to accept the right of the nobles to depose him if he failed in this. The struggle of the Aragonese feudatories against their king—the towns enjoyed less independence than those of Castile—is witnessed also by the striking terms of the coronation oath quoted above (p. 8). A particular point of dispute was the office of the *Justicia*, the supreme judge appointed to watch over the observance of the Law and to settle suits between nobles and the Crown. It is significant that around the middle of the fourteenth century the long struggle for control of this office was resolved in favour of the king. At the same period the privileges of 1287, which were the outcome of the circumstances following Peter III's death and had never been fully effective, were formally annulled.

The history of the monarchy itself was rather less disturbed in Aragon than in Castile. The direct male line of the royal house came to an end in 1410 on the death of Martin I, but two years later the matter of the succession was satisfactorily settled by the choice of Ferdinand of Antequera, who was Martin's nephew and a son of John I of Castile. The accession of a Castilian was of great importance for the future of the kingdom, yet it did nothing to alter Aragon's Mediterranean orientation; indeed, Ferdinand's son Alfonso V earned unpopularity with his Aragonese subjects by his desertion of them in favour of Naples. The continuance of profound differences between the two countries in the fifteenth century shows clearly in their contrasting literary traditions, that of Castile being strongly idealistic and religious, whereas Aragonese writing was more 'down to earth', practical and humorous, influenced less by French notions of courtly love and more by Boccaccio, Petrarch and the Italian schools.

The all-important marriage of Isabella of Castile and Ferdinand of Aragon, the product of the policy of Ferdinand's father, John II, led to unification only because Henry IV of Castile had no un-disputed heir. Henry himself, during a chaotic period of civil war, veered between accepting as his heir his queen's daughter Joanna (b. 1462), whose father was generally believed to be Beltran de la Cueva, and his own half-brother Alfonso; after the latter's death in 1468 he declared for Isabella, Alfonso's sister. The Castilian nobles foresaw the consequences for them of unification and strongly opposed the marriage project. Meanwhile John II, who was dogged by the threat of intervention by Louis XI and had to cede Roussillon and Cerdagne to the French, acquired the throne of Navarre, but was then compelled to face a full-scale revolt in Catalonia. His schemes came to fruition when the marriage ceremony was at last performed by the archbishop of Toledo on 19 October 1469, without the consent of Henry IV and with a forged papal dispensation: Ferdinand himself had reached Valladolid disguised as a muleteer. Henry now indignantly pronounced against Isabella as his successor, declaring again for Joanna *la Beltraneja*.

When Henry IV died in 1474, Isabella, who was convinced of Joanna's illegitimacy, had herself crowned at once. She faced a serious threat from the Portuguese king, Alfonso V, who invaded Castile in 1475, secured the support of some of the nobility, and became engaged to marry *la Beltraneja* (who was his niece). For a time they styled themselves king and queen of Castile and held court at Madrid. In 1476, however, Isabella's forces won a decisive engagement at Toro, and finally by the Treaty of Alcaçovas (September 1479) Alfonso abandoned his claims, as did Joanna, who became a nun. The end of the crisis in Castile coincided with the death of John II (January 1479) and the accession of Ferdinand in Aragon. It was fortunate for him that for four years he and Isabella had been able to concentrate on the menace of the Portuguese. As it was, he felt insufficiently strong to claim Navarre, which passed to his sister Eleanora, and he made no attempt to evict Louis XI from Roussillon and Cerdagne. For the time being the government of Castile and Aragon was a sufficiently heavy task for the dual rulers of the two kingdoms.

Ferdinand's Castilian descent did much to facilitate the unification. He seems to have thought of himself—and the revolt of the Catalans may well have emphasized this sentiment—as a Castilian rather than Aragonese. Indeed he went so far as to claim the throne of Castile in his own right on Henry IV's death, in competition with his wife, but there is no sign that he was dismayed when this claim was rejected. The arrangements for the dual monarchy set up a sort of loose confederation, within which Castile was the dominant partner. There was no 'kingdom of Spain' and each of the kingdoms retained its own political institutions, laws and law courts, fiscal and financial organization and armed forces. Ferdinand had promised before his marriage that Castile would keep its own laws, and that he would not alienate Castilian royal domain or make appointments in Castile; he also pledged himself to live there and to complete the Reconquest by ending Muslim rule in Granada. Isabella, in fact, administered in Castile, but Ferdinand was more than a consort, and both signed letters and decrees. Any attempt to impose identical institutions in the two kingdoms would have been entirely impracticable, and presumably never occurred to Ferdinand or Isabella as a possibility.

Not least among the advantages of the *reyes catolicos* were their complementary qualities, their conscientiousness and their mutual loyalty and co-operation. Isabella was hard-working, pious and a willing participant in the pomp and majesty of kingship, while Ferdinand provided the cunning and parsimony so necessary to the success of their partnership. Each, too, had received a suitably stern political education, for Ferdinand's childhood had been spent in the successive crises of the Catalan revolt (when still very young he had been besieged, with his mother, at Gerona by the rebellious forces) and Isabella's most impressionable years had been those of the struggle against *la Beltraneja*.

The elements of weakness in the royal situation were essentially those prevailing in Yorkist and Tudor England and in France after the Hundred Years War—powerful feudatories, fragmented jurisdiction and meagre financial means. In Spain, however, these were accentuated by two special difficulties, the contrasting nature of the two kingdoms and the presence of religious disunity owing to the existence of large communities of Mohammedans and Jews and doubtfully Christian 'converts'. The work of reorganization undertaken by Ferdinand and Isabella in these unpromising circumstances met with an impressive degree of success. The anarchy in Castile was brought to an end mainly through the formation under royal control of *Hermandades*, 'brotherhoods' entrusted with the task of installing local law and order. These peace-gilds could have achieved little but for the accompanying process of judicial and administrative repression of the greater feudatories, who lost ground to the Crown through a great Act of Resumption of royal domain (1480), the destruction of unauthorized castles and heavy punishment in the royal courts. The Crown also assumed the masterships of the Military Orders, which possessed enormous estates; in revenue alone these were worth about half a million *reals* a year, but the indirect gains in jurisdiction were immense.

Like other monarchs—and Italian *signori*—Ferdinand and Isabella naturally looked for ministers among the 'low-born' who had no territorial stake in the country and would be dependent on royal favour alone. The main instrument of rule in Castile was the Council, a continuous body with full powers, at whose meetings one at least of the monarchs was at first always present, though later a President was appointed. The reorganized Council had twelve or thirteen members, of whom eight or nine were legists—and hence trained administrators—while of the others three were nobles and one a prelate. In 1494 the Council of Aragon was reorganized on similar lines. The Council gained in power at the expense of the *Cortes*, though not before the latter had been employed to pass anti-baronial measures in 1476 and 1480. Thereafter the parliament—as in Yorkist England—was found of little use, and it was not called at all between 1483 and 1497. Later it was summoned occasionally to grant money, but in the main other sources of revenue were preferred to extraordinary taxation. Moreover, after 1480 only the representatives of towns were called, and these were now of exemplary subservience, thanks mainly to the institution of *corregidores* appointed by the royal Council to inspect urban administration. These officials were supplemented by *veedores* (financial inspectors) and *pesquidores* (judicial commissioners). Toledo, where the city's *alcade mayor* was appointed by the Crown (though the municipality chose his two assistants), was pacified and brought thoroughly under royal control during Gómez Manrique's long tenure of office as *corregidor* (1477–90).

Financial recovery was due less to invention of new sources of revenue than to successes in checking the exemptions and corruption which had depleted the old ones. The *alcabala* tax on incomes which had rendered a mere 10 million *maravedis* a year under Henry IV realized nearly 25 million in 1478 and over 150 in 1482. The corresponding figures for total revenues have been estimated at under 1 million *reals* in 1479, 12 million in 1482 and over 26 million in 1504. In part this recovery was due to currency reform and to the increased yield of commerce and industry. Legislation played its part in stimulating the textile industry in

Castile; after 1462 the importation of cloth was forbidden, and at least one-third of the Castilian wool-crop had to be retained for home manufacture. Trading links, mainly through Bilbao, with Bruges and the Hanse ports had become important by the end of the fourteenth century and to the commerce in raw wool was now added that in Castilian cloth.

The greatest industry of Castile was pastoral farming and this implied transhumance, many of the flocks spending the winter in the southern plains and migrating during the summer to the central plateau. The organization of this vast biannual emigration of flocks (the *Mesta*) was the object of a royal privilege as early as 1273, but the financial possibilities of the *Mesta* were only fully exploited by the Crown from the time of Ferdinand and Isabella. Their manipulation of the *Mesta* provides an admirable instance of the new monarchy at work, and shows how initial intervention from above could be used to strengthen the sinews of the autocratic machine. The *Mesta* was now centralized in its judicial aspects and local taxation of migrant flocks was both systematized and restricted. Special judicial enquiries were held to investigate privileges bearing on the activities of the *Mesta*, which was encouraged to have recourse to the royal Council itself—as well as to the appellate court at Valladolid—as a court of first instance. The *Cortes* which met at Toledo in 1480 promulgated far-reaching reforms whereby royal towns had to furnish annual reports on local taxation affecting the *Mesta* and royal *veedores* were placed in charge of such taxation. Formerly royal tolls which had passed into private hands were now abolished, and in assuming the Grand Masterships of the Military Orders Ferdinand secured for the Crown their considerable revenue from sheep tolls. In 1500 royal control was formalized and again extended by the appointment of the senior member of the royal Council as *ex officio* President of the *Mesta*. All this meant great acquisitions for the Castilian treasury—and the *Mesta* itself was often used as a sort of bankinghouse for the Crown—but it also implied support, administrative and above all judicial, for pasturage in opposition to grain-farming, and such a policy had grave economic dangers.

The peculiar problem presented by Spanish religious heterogeneity has already been mentioned—and of course the differences were profound social ones, not mere dissimilarities of faith. The situation was particularly inflammable in the towns, some of which housed large communities of dubious converts of Jewish descent, whose prosperity was regarded by the 'old Christians' with an envy inextricably mingled with religious disapprobation. Hatred of Jews and *conversos* played a very considerable part in the repeated riots and revolts of Toledo, where—in the face of papal disapproval—the old Christians obtained a royal privilege denying *conversos* the right to hold municipal office.

In any case no monarch could be strong unless he controlled the fabric of religious institutions within his state. We have already noted how this was achieved by the Sforza in Milan and by the kings of France (above, pp. 219 and 244), while other examples could be given from later medieval England. Sigismund had launched a Crusade against his own Bohemian subjects rather than resign himself to rule a kingdom divorced from its Church, and it was not conceivable that Ferdinand and Isabella's crusading state should act differently, however radical the policies involved. Characteristic agreements with the papacy—facilitated by the strong Spanish influence in the Curia—gave the Crown, from 1482, *de facto* control over appointments to sees and the main abbacies. At the end of the century this satisfactory situation was further formalized by a new agreement with the Spanish pope Alexander VI. Meanwhile the authority of the monarchy in matters of belief had been secured by the quite abnormal institution of a national Inquisition, set up with the consent of Sixtus IV in 1478. Though the Supreme Council of the Inquisition represented both Crown and Church, all appointments as inquisitors were made by the kings, who also paid the inquisitors, supervised their instructions and received the property that they confiscated. In 1484 the work of the Supreme Council was extended to Aragon, where, however, it was less appreciated than in Castile.

Religious unification under the Crown implied not only the conquest of Granada but also the complete extirpation from Ferdinand and Isabella's kingdoms of both Mohammedanism and Judaism. The expulsion in 1492 of the Jews, who probably numbered some 150,000–200,000, was a religious and political act, not an economic one, but it may be noted that the Jews could now be more easily dispensed with owing to the existence of Christian bankers, and that they were forbidden to take their valuables with them. There followed the attempt to convert the Moors *en masse* (in contravention of the terms agreed when Granada capitulated in 1492) and finally, in 1502, the process of conversion by force was achieved by expelling Muslims who refused to accept Christianity.

By the last decade of the century the monarchy had won great victories, though more notably in Castile than in Aragon. It had come to dominate the baronage and the Church, its Council's administration was ubiquitous, its finances were vastly strengthened. These gains would only make Spain formidable if they were accompanied by military strength. As it was, the Spanish ranked with the Swiss as the great soldiers of western Europe. This was not due to changes in obligation and recruitment—though Ferdinand's assumption of the Grand Masterships virtually brought the Military Orders into the royal army—but to the reforms of a military genius, Gonzalo Fernández de Cordoba, the 'Great Captain'. Gonzalo organized the auxiliary arms, artillerymen and engineers, and 'brigaded' his troops so that he had at his disposition compact and self-sufficient formations accustomed to co-operate in action. His brigade included three hundred heavy cavalry and the same number of light horsemen, but most feared of all was the square of heavily-armoured Spanish pikemen, moving forward and protecting a core of more lightly armed infantry. Gonzalo was also a highly successful military tactician, and as captain-general over both land and sea forces was well-placed to ensure the efficient co-operation of the navy in the Granada campaign and the Italian ones that followed.

The final decisive war against the Moors to which Ferdinand and Isabella were committed was made easier by the internal disputes of the Granada sultanate. They were able to use Boabdil, son of a previous sultan, against his uncle Zagal; to the Moslems, indeed, it must have appeared a civil war rather than a Christian conquest. But the campaigns naturally assumed a strongly religious tinge, and volunteers came from all parts of the peninsula and beyond. Malaga was captured in 1487 and the siege of Granada itself at last undertaken in 1491, Ferdinand and Isabella being present to give solemnity to the last scene of the drama. The sultanate capitulated in November and the Catholic kings made their entry into the city on the day of Epiphany (6 January) 1492.

This triumph was soon followed by an important acquisition

for which no war had to be fought. In 1492 Charles VIII of France began to plan his Italian campaign. Certainty of Spanish non-intervention was essential for his plans, and this would not be easy to achieve, but the way to an *entente* might lie through the cession of Cerdagne and Roussillon, the provinces whence Ferdinand had not dared to dislodge Louis XI. Agreement was reached at Barcelona in January 1493 and, despite the disappointment of Charles's sister Anne over inadequate Spanish guarantees, Ferdinand and Isabella entered Perpignan in state that September. After Isabella's death (1504) Italian developments made possible yet another Pyrenean accession: the kingdom of Navarre, relinquished by Ferdinand's father, had come under the domination of the French, but in 1512 Ferdinand was able to dispossess Louis XII and secure confirmation of his hereditary title from his ally, pope Julius II.

These territorial successes on the Pyrenean frontier were but one aspect of a process, seen more clearly in Italy itself, whereby the French took the initiative but the Spaniards reaped the gains. In accordance with the agreement of Barcelona, Ferdinand stood aside while the French destroyed the Aragonese monarchy in Naples; yet the following year he was within his rights in responding to the appeals of Alexander VI when Charles VIII occupied papal territory and in helping to form the anti-French Holy League. After Charles's evacuation of Naples (1495), Ferdinand dropped hints to the French that a joint enterprise might carve up southern Italy to the mutual benefit of the two powers and in 1500 formal agreement on partition was reached at Granada. When the Aragonese house had been overthrown once more, Ferdinand was able to trump up a frontier dispute as *casus belli* and a series of brilliant campaigns under Gonzalo drove out the French by 1504. This was the beginning of the Spanish domination in Italy which was founded firmly in 1525 when Charles V, Ferdinand and Isabella's grandson and ruler of the Empire as well as Spain, shattered the French at Pavia.

The achievements of the Spaniards beyond the Atlantic lie for the most part in a period not considered in this volume. During the fifteenth century the Portuguese, barred by Castile from expansion to the east, turned south by way of the sea and played a far more important role than the Spaniards in the process of maritime exploration. The story begins with voyages to Morocco and settlement in Madeira quite early in the century, followed by continuous probing farther down the Atlantic coast of Africa in search of slaves and other trading commodities. The 'Gold Coast' was reached in 1436, Senegal in 1445, 'Guinea' in 1469. Diaz was the first to round the Cape of Good Hope in his voyage of 1486–7, and ten years later (1497–9) Vasco da Gama followed the African coast to Mombassa, then crossed the Indian Ocean to Calicut before returning to Lisbon. By that time Spain had conquered the Canary Islands and the Catholic kings had begun to finance the expeditions of Columbus (1492–1502). Columbus himself became a viceroy and governor in the New World, but the continuous history of Spanish colonial administration starts later with the setting-up of a court in Haiti in 1511. The conquests of Mexico and Peru were only initiated in 1519 and 1532 respectively.

The homeland of the Great Captain and the *Conquistadores* is for the most part harsh and barren country, yielding a stern and meagre diet and an upbringing well calculated to prepare the Castilian infantrymen for the 'flinty and steel couch of war'. Francesco Guicciardini travelled a good deal in Aragon and Castile in 1512 as the ambassador of Florence, and his diary remarks repeatedly on the sterility of the land and the lack of inhabitants. In Catalonia 'the country is mountainous, wild and very barren; one finds a village with one big house, and some of the land around is cultivated, but after that for league after league there is no cultivation. . . .' On his return home his official *Relazione* emphasized the poverty of the Spanish countryside and made the generalization concerning the Spaniards, so often to be repeated by later observers: 'they do not engage in commerce, which they consider shameful'. Industry, he says, was a no less humiliating source of income.[1] Despite the predominance of agriculture and pastoral farming, the peninsula was not self-supporting in grain, which was imported from southern and western France, from Sardinia and Sicily, and parts of the eastern Mediterranean and Black Sea regions. Seville grew to a great city of some 75,000 inhabitants by the late fifteenth century, even before it became the centre of trade and communication with the Indies, but the previously flourishing economy of Catalonia (and in particular Bar-

[1] F. Guicciardini, *Scritti autobiografici e rari*, pp. 120, 123, 128–30.

celona) was in full decline by the same period. Catalan textiles had lost their place in the western Mediterranean to English cloth, and the merchants of Barcelona had been ousted, to some extent by Valencians and Castilians but much more by the Italians and English.

The policies of the Spanish rulers did nothing to resolve the paradox of strength combined with poverty. Attempts were made to foster a textile industry by limiting exports of raw wool, but in the long run protection of trade and industry would have been incompatible with the far more deeply rooted alliance with the *Mesta* and the latifundists; grain farming could only have been encouraged at the expense of the *Mesta*, an institution which became absorbed into the nation's financial structure. Connected with all this was the profound religious difficulty. A crusading state had been reluctant to back industry and trade wholeheartedly when so many of those concerned with these occupations were non-Christians. The religious element also aggravated the economic situation through the mass expulsions: in the words of the cynic's favourite cliché, they were worse than a crime, they were an error. The opening-up of the New World, so often wrongly blamed for the decline of Spain because the importation of precious metals played a part in raising prices, perhaps came just in time to save Spain from economic disaster, but there was no escape from the country's fundamental poverty. Consideration of Spain's later decadence must also take into account the Inquisition and the discouragement of the spirit of enquiry, but there is a great danger of making use of hindsight to over-emphasize these elements of weakness. On the death of Ferdinand in 1516 his Habsburg grandson Charles I succeeded to a well-administered state. Its 'Golden Age' lay still in the future, and after 1519, when under Charles its rule was joined with that of the Empire, it became the dominant power in Europe west of the Ottoman lands.

Further Reading

R. B. MERRIMAN, *The Rise of the Spanish Empire*, Vols. I, II (New York, 1918)

J. KLEIN, *The Mesta* (Cambridge, Mass., 1920)

J. H. ELLIOTT, *Imperial Spain, 1469–1716* (London, 1963). Chapters I–IV

J. R. L. HIGHFIELD (ed.), *Spain in the 15th century* (London, 1972)

XIV

GERMAN DISUNITY AND THE ORIGINS OF
THE REFORMATION

A N earlier chapter has described the enfeeblement of central
power in Germany during and after the thirteenth century
and the gaining of *de facto* independence by the Swiss confederation. In the fifteenth century imperial territory was also lost
to Denmark, Poland and the Turks, while the emperor played an
ever-diminishing role in Italy. For the future development of
Germany, however, these losses were less important than the internal consequences of regionalism, which influenced and assisted
the Lutheran Reformation, while the Reformation in turn was to
do much to intensify political disunity.

The long reign of the Habsburg Frederick III (1440–93) was
an uphill struggle. Until 1463 Frederick had to contest the control
of his own Austrian and Tyrolean inheritance—his only territorial
base—with his brother Albert. For twenty-seven years (between
1444 and 1471) he never visited Germany west of these lands. He
was threatened with supersession first by Philip the Good of
Burgundy (1454), then by Poděbrandy, king of Bohemia (1459–
1461), and finally by his own son Maximilian, and as late as 1485
he was driven from Vienna by Matthias Corvinus of Hungary.
The constantly harassed circumstances of the reign made schemes
for constitutional reform impracticable, although these were discussed and in 1455 a detailed plan was drawn up for an imperial
council, an imperial court presided over by paid judges, and a
general tax. Frederick's solitary triumph, which was of profound
importance for the future of both the Habsburgs and the Empire,
was the marriage of his son Maximilian to the Burgundian heiress
Mary, daughter of Charles the Rash (1477) (above, p. 240). This
marriage conveyed to the Habsburgs the wealth of the Low

Countries on which had been founded the greatness of the Burgundian dukes, thereby strengthening enormously their territorial
basis and perhaps virtually ensuring the continuation of their
election as emperors. It also extended their interests so that the
north-west of Germany now joined the south-east as the two
potential strongholds of imperial power.

Frederick III's Concordat of Vienna with pope Nicholas V
(1448) contrasts with Charles VII's Pragmatic Sanction of Bourges
(1438) in a way which illustrates clearly enough the difference between the authority of these two monarchs. The Pragmatic Sanction defined and checked papal authority over the Church in France
to the advantage of the Crown. The Concordat, on the other
hand, had to be acceptable to the imperial nobility as well as to
the papacy; the German princes gained a very high price for their
adherence to it and thereafter enjoyed an increased amount of
ecclesiastical control. They won enlarged rights of presentation
and a considerable share in the proceeds of ecclesiastical taxation.
Church courts lost part of their jurisdiction to the princes, particularly in eastern Germany, and even to the municipalities. Moreover, the lay nobility even came to play a larger role in the organization of religion, by issuing legislation concerned with matters
of morality (such as gambling and false weights and measures), by
intervening to reform or suppress ecclesiastical institutions, and
through its share in higher education. Of the twenty universities
existing in Germany at the end of the Middle Ages, all but two
(Würzburg and Mainz) had lay founders. One consequence
of these developments was that religious reform came to be
thought of as in many ways essentially the responsibility of the
princes.

Ecclesiastical matters provide merely one instance of the general
movement of the greater German feudatories into a position of
complete dominance. Laymen or prelates, these men had a way
of life in common, with their vast households (the margrave of
Brandenburg had an entourage of four hundred at the end of the
fifteenth century) and their own traditions of expenditure on festi-
vities and artistic and educational patronage. The princes had
virtually carved up the kingdom. Naturally each sought to round
off his territories and in the process quarrelled with his neighbour,
particularly over disputed jurisdictional rights. Limits were set to

s

their power, however, by lack of financial centralization, by the existence of enclaves—particularly imperial cities and ecclesiastical lordships—within their dominions and most of all by the tendency to fission of lay property through division on succession. Thus there were two Saxonies (ducal and electoral) and several branches of the ruling house of Anhalt, Brunswick was divided from the early fifteenth century between three branches of the same family, and the Brandenburg lands were partitioned after the death of the Elector Albert Achilles (1486). The financial needs of the princes also subjected them to occasional pressure from meetings of estates, but in general the elements which might have kept them in check, the knights and the towns, were those which most conspicuously lost ground. As in France, the knightly class encountered great economic difficulties and began to play a much less significant part in the political scene. When ousted by professional soldiers of non-knightly origin, some of them sought an outlet from their poverty in the career of 'robber-knight'.

Though the knights complained bitterly of the social pretensions of the burghers and the enlarged jursidictions of the municipalities, the towns, too, were losing authority. The decline of the Hanseatic ports has been mentioned above (p. 108), but the failure of the towns to 'balance' the nobility is as evident in other areas where there was no general recession, the only anomaly being the continued strength of the towns on the lower Rhine. The 'average' German town was of course primarily a centre for the marketing of grain, wine and other local agrarian produce. The major exceptions to this were Cologne and the other Rhineland towns, dealing in wine, coal, iron, cloth and silk, and closely connected with Antwerp and the towns of Flanders; Leipzig and Breslau and other towns lying on the routes of the eastern and northern commerce in grain, fish, wax, honey and furs; and finally some rapidly developing cities in southern Germany. The chief among the latter were Nuremberg and Augsburg, both linked with Antwerp as well as with the commercial world of Italy, and benefiting from a spectacular advance of mining for silver and copper in the Tyrol and for gold and copper in Hungary. During the period 1460–1530 the annual output of silver and of copper in central Europe increased approximately fivefold, and in 1525 the emperor believed that 100,000 of his subjects were engaged in mining. Greatest of the Augsburg families were the Fuggers, the firm which financed Charles V's election to the Empire: bankers to emperors and popes, they were also near-monopolists in their control of Tyrolean and Hungarian metals.

Whatever the achievements of the Fuggers, of other financiers such as the Höchstetters and Welsers, of lesser-known mining engineers, and of the Swabian League of towns (which between 1488 and 1519 effectively opposed the Swiss and the dukes of Bavaria), the primary features of Germany's political landscape were the strength of the greater nobles and the impotence of the king. When Maximilian (1493–1519) succeeded his father Frederick III, there followed a still richer harvest of schemes for fundamental reform, all of them proposing a constitutional solution to the insoluble problem of governing an Empire whose sovereign lacked the means to rule. The model for these was set at the prolonged *Reichstag* (parliament) at Worms in 1495, in which the estates put forward a detailed plan whereby the emperor was to have a permanent Council (*Reichsrat*) of seventeen, the consent of which was to be required for all important royal acts: each of the six electors was to nominate one member of the council, the other spiritual and temporal princes were both to name four, the towns two, and the remaining member, the president, was to be chosen by the king. This idea was naturally rejected by Maximilian, and the scheme for a quasi-federal tax (the 'Common Penny') was no more successful. Nevertheless the *Reichstag* of 1495 bore some fruit in the form of a supreme central court of justice, the *Reichskammergericht*. In 1500 the emperor himself advanced a scheme whereby many of his powers would pass to a central council (the *Reichsregiment*), but this proposal also was unsuccessful and provoked an open quarrel between Maximilian and the electors. The latter, led by the arch-chancellor, Berthold, archbishop of Mainz, would have been satisfied with nothing short of a quasi-federation within which the emperor would have lost control of both taxation and army. After these disputes Maximilian deprived Berthold of the arch-chancellorship, but compromise between imperial and electoral interests still proved impossible. New constitutional schemes were discussed ineffectively at Cologne in 1505, at Augsburg in 1510, and at Trier and Cologne in 1512; the last of these, perhaps the most radical, proposed the setting-up of a permanent executive council of the *Reichstag* and an army organized by zones (*Kreise*).

These negotiations over constitutional change were brought about by the pressure of political events—by Maximilian's need for troops and money—but the same events made it impossible for the Emperor to concentrate on the constitutional question. He had to work at the more practicable task of unification within his own Austrian lands (in which he achieved much success), to fight the Palatinate over the succession to Bavaria (1504), and to oppose the Swiss and the Turks, as well as dealing with Germany's endemic anarchy. But the most onerous of all his preoccupations was the menace of French power in Italy. It would have been intolerable for any emperor, but it was particularly bitter for a man of Maximilian's chivalrous temperament, that his shortage of soldiers should cause the Empire to cut such a wretched figure in Italy. Again and again imperial rights fell to the French by default, and meanwhile the recreant Swiss constantly counted for much more on the Italian scene. Enmity with Venice had originally caused Maximilian to welcome Charles VIII's invasion of 1494, but he soon recognized its dangers and joined the anti-French league of 1495, only to find that he could play no active part because the *Reichstag* wanted to talk about the constitution rather than provide him with an army. By 1496 he was ready to intervene in Italy, but did so feebly and achieved nothing. Maximilian wished for war against France on Charles's death in 1498, probably to add to his Burgundian acquisitions, but again the nobles would give him no support. When Charles's successor, Louis XII, captured the imperial duchy of Milan (1500) Maximilian could not even get an army into the field. Later he joined the League of Cambrai (1508) against his old enemy Venice, but once more his military contribution was negligible and so, therefore, were his territorial gains. Even in 1512 he played a diplomatic rather than a military role in defeating the French, and in any case Milan was in the hands of the French again by 1515. Revenge in Italy was only to come with the election to the Empire in 1519 of Maximilian's grandson, the king of Spain.

One consequence of imperial weakness and German disunity was to expose the Church within the Empire to the authority, and in particular the fiscality, of the papacy. The constitutional discussions at Worms in 1495 included proposals for a 'German' Church, and Maximilian himself suggested the appointment of a permanent papal legate who should always be a German by birth, but these schemes were not put into effect and the Empire failed to acquire the national ecclesiastical 'defences' of France, Spain and England. The feeling that Germany was paying more than its share to Rome in taxation, in expenses incurred over disputed episcopal elections, and so on, was a reasonable one. Indulgences to pay for German churches were one thing but, as Ulrich von Hutten put it, why should the Germans pay for Roman churches when Italy was wealthier than Germany? Konrad Celtes the humanist had made a similar point: 'The Emperor rules in the German lands, but the Roman shepherd alone enjoys the pasture. When will Germany regain her old strength and shake off the foreign yoke?' The logical conclusion of this attitude was to come with Luther's indignant opposition to papal fiscality and his invitation to the emperor and princes to forbid the payment of taxes to Rome.

This anti-papal sentiment was interwoven with the heightened national self-consciousness which was so evident also in the France of Joan of Arc and which had become more pronounced within the Church itself during the disputes of the conciliar era, while it was natural that religion should take on a more national tone in an age when the Scriptures were increasingly diffused in the vernacular.[1] During the fifteenth century there had developed a stronger interest in Germany's past, culminating in the appearance of the first history of Germany, Wimpfeling's *Epitome Rerum Germanicarum* (1505). The material for a nation's saga, both historical and mythical, existed in abundance. In the medieval past the imperial achievement of Barbarossa stood out, beyond that lay the epic deeds of Theoderic the Ostrogoth, and further back still there had shone the primitive virtues of the folk described and praised by Tacitus in his *Germania*. This work, first printed in Germany in 1473, appealed both to the classical interests and to the national pride of the German humanists—a pride often inflamed by much contact with patronizing Italians. Konrad Celtes (1459–1508), a fierce German patriot, produced a new edition of the *Germania* and lectured on Tacitus, as well as planning a topographical

---

[1] At least sixteen German versions of the Bible were printed before Luther's.

Germania Illustrata and an epic poem on Theoderic (see below, pp. 275-6). Ulrich von Hutten (1488–1523), like Celtes, lived for some time in Italy, and shared his enthusiasm for the *Germania*, though he deplored the falling-away of the Germans from their pristine nobility. He it was who founded the 'myth' of Arminius, erecting into a national hero the chieftain who had defeated Varus's legions in A.D. 9. The strength of the patriotic currents which flowed beneath this classical surface may be gauged from the fantastic *Book of a Hundred Chapters* written in 1510 by an anonymous writer usually known picturesquely as 'the Revolutionary of the Upper Rhine'. This man believed that the Germans had once 'lived together like brothers', ruling all Europe in a Utopian communistic régime which had been destroyed by the Romans and the Church of Rome. The Latin peoples were the source of all wickedness and the eternal opponents of everything German. Yet 'the Germans once held the whole world in their hands and they will do so again, and with more power than ever'.[1]

National feeling and ecclesiastical grievances in Germany itself do not fully account for the widespread detestation of the papacy. While the humanists were confirmed in their indigation by Lorenzo Valla's exposure of the 'Donation of Constantine' as a forgery, of much greater general consequence were the effects of the prolonged, though gradual, descent of the papacy into an institution apparently concerned principally with the family policies characteristic of an Italian state. Nicholas V (1447–55) and Pius II (1458–1464) had been well-meaning men who lacked the urgent reforming drive to halt these traditions. Their pontificates were separated by that of the first Borgia pope, Calixtus III (1455–8), who promoted to the cardinalate his nephew, the future Alexander VI. Paul II (1464–71), a Venetian and a nephew of Eugenius IV, was another pontiff who passively acquiesced in the traditions that he inherited, but his successor Sixtus IV (1471–84) was a scandalously secular character who promoted his criminal nephews and was an accomplice before the fact in the conspiracy to murder Lorenzo and Giuliano de' Medici. After the harmless but rather ineffective Genoese Innocent VIII (1484–92), there followed Alexander VI (Borgia) (1492–1503), who has often been made to

---

[1] For 'the Revolutionary of the Upper Rhine' see N. Cohn, *The Pursuit of the Millennium* (1962), pp. 114-23.

bear the brunt of the moral blame levelled against the 'Renaissance' papacy. Like Sixtus, Alexander gave new impetus to the Curia's worldly outlook, and to the passionate advancement of his descendants he added more conspicuous defiance of the spiritual nature of his office. He it was who publicly kept a succession of mistresses and who threw that very gay party in the Vatican at which some most unusual games were played with the co-operation of fifty prostitutes.[1]

The prolonged political crisis in the peninsula ushered in by the French invasion of 1494 would in any case have made it difficult for the papacy to escape from the descending spiral of Italian politics and territorial rule, and in these circumstances expedience combined with bribery to ensure the election of men versed in the well-established ways of Sixtus and Alexander. Julius II della Rovere (1503–13) was a nephew of Sixtus IV and had been a very active and prominent member of the Curia during his uncle's pontificate: he no doubt found it natural that he should devote his energies primarily to the diplomatic situation in Italy and the reconquest of the Papal State. Leo X (1513–21) was no better equipped to break with the prevailing tendencies of the Curia; he was a son of Lorenzo the Magnificent, who had bought a cardinalate for him when he was thirteen, in 1489, and his preoccupation with French and Spanish power in the peninsula was complicated by the family connection which made him *de facto* ruler of Florence as well as of the Papal State.

Typical of many Germans who visited Rome at this time and reported unfavourably on it was the humanist Konrad Peutinger of Augsburg (1465–1547), who wrote of the city during Innocent VIII's pontificate:

> Here I see everything for sale, from the highest to the lowest. Intrigues, hypocrisy and servility are praised, religion is falsified, base actions without number are perpetrated, and Justice sleeps. When I look at the ruined monuments of Antiquity I bewail the fact that this most honoured City is ruled by an alien [*peregrina*] people, who commit every sort of wickedness under the fair disguise of religion, and expect to receive praise instead of blame. When I criticize this, they tell me that it is ordained by Fate, and that if God wished

[1] J. Burckard, *Liber Notarum* (Rerum Italicarum Scriptores, new series, XXXII, 1), II, 303.

otherwise people would act otherwise. The Patrimony of St Peter has to be governed thus, they say, because Fate wills it. I could write a long story, but do not wish to offend your ears further.[1]

In view of the reputation of Rome with the Germans, it is likely that the young Augustinian friar Martin Luther was prepared to find the worst when his house at Erfurt sent him to Rome in 1510, and anti-Italian feeling may surely be detected in his own comment that 'he went to Rome with onions and returned with garlic'. Whatever his expectations, he was shocked at the irreverent ways of the Roman clergy. Yet another German who came away with indignant impressions was 'Crotus Rubeanus' (part-author of the satirical *Letters of Obscure Men*), who reported of his visit to Rome in 1519: 'I saw the monuments of antiquity. I saw the chair of pestilence: what I saw both helps and disgusts me.'[2] One cause of this antagonism was presumably the contrast between northern and southern religious *mores* which persists to this day, for Catholics from northern Europe are still scandalized to find Italians walking about and talking during Mass. The same difference was noted by a visitor to Milan in the early sixteenth century who compared the 'irreligion' of that duchy with the crowded churches of Germany 'where they do not talk of merchandize nor amuse themselves as in Italy, but occupy themselves solely with hearing Mass and the divine offices and saying their prayers, all kneeling'.[3]

It would be quite misleading, however, to distinguish the pious North from the indifferent South. In both there were movements for reform: in Italy, for instance, those associated with the Franciscan St Bernardino of Siena (1380–1444) and the Puritan revivalism of Savonarola in late fifteenth-century Florence; in Germany and the Netherlands the less spectacular but more lasting and widely-diffused movements associated with the Beguines and the Brethren of the Common Life. Moreover, the upper clergy in Germany produced examples of scandalous worldliness which ranked with the worst in Italy. Rupert von Simmern, bishop of Strasbourg

---

[1] Letter from Rome to Valentin Eber, 5 August 1491 (*Konrad Peutingers Briefwechsel*, ed. E. König, p. 9).

[2] 'Fui nuper Rhomae cum Hesso nostro, vidi veterum monumenta, vidi cathedram pestilenciae: vidisse iuvat, vidisse piget' (in Ulrich von Hutten, *Opera*, ed. E. Böcking, I, 311).

[3] *Die Reise des Kardinals Luigi d'Aragona . . . v. A. de Beatis*, ed. L. Pastor, p. 107.

from 1440 to 1478, was said never to have celebrated Mass, and Diether von Isenburg, archbishop of Mainz from 1460 to 1481, to have done so once only, on the occasion of his consecration. Such men became archbishops and bishops because these offices, involving immense political and territorial power, continued to be associated with the great feudal families who struggled to secure them for their members. The Church in Germany had remained largely the 'proprietary Church' of the early Middle Ages. It was as impossible for the archbishop of Cologne or Mainz to neglect his state and devote himself primarily to spirituality as it was for the pope to withdraw from the affairs of his State and of Italy. One consequence of this was a great rift between the prelates and the lower clergy, many of whom were to give their support to Lutheranism.

The principal currents in the reforming tendencies in the North, often described generically as the *Devotio Moderna*, were those associated with the Augustinian canons of Windesheim and the 'Brethren of the Common Life' whose movement centred on Deventer in the Netherlands. The second of these had originated in the fourteenth century with the work of Gerard Groote, the founder of a hostel where pious women lived as a community. In the fifteenth century many other 'colonies' were set up in the Low Countries and Rhineland, frugal households whose members took a vow of chastity, surrendered all their possessions to a common chest, and devoted much of their time to prayer. Hostels were also opened for the children of the poor, who thus received a religious education, but men like Groote were far from being 'humanists'. Groote himself advised against the vanity of 'books beautifully adorned' and the dangers of the useless learning of 'geometry, arithmetic, rhetoric, dialectic, grammar, songs, poetry, legal matters or astrology'.

> I resolve [he wrote] never to take a degree in medicine, because I do not purpose to get any gain or preferment by such a degree; and the same resolve holds for Civil and Canon Law; for the purpose of a degree is either gain or preferment, or vain glorification and worldly honour, which latter things if they lead not to the former are simply useless, empty and most foolish, being contrary to godliness and all freedom and purity. I resolve not to study any art nor to write any book, not to undertake any journey nor any labour, nor

to pursue any learning with the purpose of extending my own fame or repute for knowledge.[1]

The characteristic and most famous book of this *milieu* is the *Imitation of Christ*, probably written by Thomas à Kempis (1380–1471). The *Imitation*, too, dwells on the dangers of intellectual pride. Knowledge has little to do with piety, 'I would rather feel compunction than know how to define it', and 'What will it avail thee to dispute profoundly of the Trinity if by your lack of humility you are displeasing to the Trinity? Truly at the day of judgment we shall not be examined on what we have read, but on what we have done.'[2]

One who received some education in the schools of the Brethren of the Common Life at Deventer and s'Hertogenbosch in the 1470s and 1480s, but was unhappy there, was Erasmus of Rotterdam (? 1469–1536). This illegitimate son of a priest of Gouda spent a period as an Augustinian canon, but left his monastery and became the most famous figure in the learned world of his day. We know much about Erasmus, thanks in particular to his letters, and there is insufficient room here to do justice to his many-sided importance or to discuss adequately the differences between his opinions and Luther's. First of all, Erasmus was a much-travelled cosmopolitan literary figure, moving between the Netherlands, France, England, Italy and Germany, and linking humanists in many lands. As a voluminous and much-read author (in Latin) he also exerted an enormous influence on the literature of sixteenth-century Europe, particularly through his collection of pithy *Adages* and the rather unoriginal but wise and well-phrased social commentary of the *Colloquies*. Erasmus's favourite targets were empty and superstitious observances and the other religious abuses of the age. Among the Spaniards the fervent commonsense of his moral criticism founded a school of thought the outlook of which is still evident in *Don Quixote*. Besides all this there was a great positive achievement in learning, of which the principal monument was Erasmus's New Testament. This was the first edition to be published in Greek (though it was made from extremely defective texts), and incorporated a new Latin translation, differing greatly in style from the Vulgate.

[1] Translation slightly adapted from *The Founders of a New Devotion* (1905), p. 57.
[2] *Imitation of Christ*, Ch. I.

Among those who made use of Erasmus's New Testament was Martin Luther, who learned from it that the Vulgate's version of the Greek of St Matthew 4:17 rendered as 'Do penance' words which meant merely 'Be penitent'. From this Luther argued that the sacrament of penance lacked scriptural authority, a conclusion which strengthened him in his stand against the sale of indulgences. The indulgence was not in itself an innovation in Luther's day: for centuries crusaders, contributors to religious buildings and foundations, and others had been promised certain defined benefits in the form of remission of sins. The idea had proved capable of considerable expansion, and indignation against its development is to be found already in the fourteenth century, when Chaucer depicted his crafty pardoner with a wallet 'brimful of pardon come from Rome all hot'. In the following century the benefit of indulgences was extended to souls in purgatory. Erasmus and other critics expressed doubts about these extensions and criticized the salesman's techniques of the pardoners, but this was essentially a grievance of the serious and educated; indulgences were not an important source of popular anti-clerical or anti-papal feeling.

The papal indulgence which aroused Luther's indignation was that preached in 1517 by the Dominican Tetzel. It was a dual affair in that half the money contributed to gain remission of sins for the donors and their dead friends and relations was to go to pope Leo X to assist in the rebuilding of St Peter's, the other half to the young Hohenzollern, Albert archbishop of Magdeburg and Halberstadt, to enable him to repay the loan of 10,000 ducats from the Fuggers which was to purchase the archbishopric of Mainz. Neither of these causes was a popular one in Germany, for the Hohenzollern had many enemies, and the long-planned rebuilding of St Peter's was felt to be a matter for the Romans. In any case it was a slow affair, the completed results of which were unlikely to be visible for a long time. The construction of a Renaissance St Peter's, which had been proposed in the middle of the fifteenth century by Nicholas V, was only begun in earnest by Julius II in 1506, and though it was strenuously forwarded by Leo X, most of the work was carried out later still, with Michelangelo as the principal architect, and it was not completed until the seventeenth century.

Luther's protest against the indulgence of 1517 (the 'Ninety-five Theses') was important not in itself but because it became the first step towards a position of outright revolt. In the summer of 1518 Luther replied to a critic in a tract which appealed to the Scriptures and by implication elevated them as an authority above both pope and Councils. When his case came before a papal legate at Augsburg that autumn he rejected the doctrine concerning the 'treasury of merit' which offered the orthodox justification and explanation of indulgences. In the argument that followed, Luther stated a new and revolutionary position when he claimed that the pope abused the Bible: 'I deny that he is above Scripture.' Luther then fled back to Wittenberg, confirmed his stand ('I damn and detest this decretal'), and appealed from the pope to a general Council. Luther went on to reject papal primacy, which he regarded as the product of the papal legislation of the last four centuries or so—the decretals—and as lacking the essential authority of the Scriptures. A bull of November 1518 ('Cum postquam') redefined doctrine on indulgences and made it clear that they did not in themselves remit guilt nor automatically diminish the penalties of purgatory, but by this time Luther had gone too far for reconciliation. Leo X's bull of June 1520 ('Exsurge Domine') condemned forty-one Lutheran errors and ordered his works to be burnt. On 10 December Luther retorted by burning the bull.

If Luther's position was already far from that of Erasmus, who could not at any price condone a schism, that of his protector Frederick the Wise, elector of Saxony, was no less far from them both. At Wittenberg Frederick had not only his cherished university, in which Luther was lecturer on the Bible, but also a magnificent accumulation of holy relics, partly inherited but mainly acquired through his own energies. The catalogue of 1509 recorded 5,005 separate relics and by 1520 the holy bones alone numbered 19,013. Yet this pious collector of relics was greatly impressed by Luther, and Luther in turn accepted Frederick's protection, without which he could have achieved little. Practical reformers in Germany had long understood that religious institutions were so rooted in society that durable religious change could only be achieved with the support of lay power. Some years earlier Konrad Celtes and the satirical poet Sebastian Brant (the author of *The Ship of Fools*) had hoped that reform might come from Maximilian, but in Germany effective lay power could only mean the princes. It was primarily to these that Luther addressed himself in his *An den christlichen Adel deutscher Nation von des Christlichen Standes Besserung* (*To the Christian Nobility of the German Nation, concerning the Reform of the Christian Estate*) of 1520, an appeal to emperor, princes and nobles, ecclesiastical and secular, to assist in the reform of the Church. Recourse to the lay powers was accepted by Luther without reluctance, and he cannot have failed to realize that emancipation from the papacy implied for the nobility an immensely attractive prospect of increased wealth and authority from enlarged jurisdiction and the spoils of ecclesiastical property. He made clear his attitude in the statement that 'earthly government is a divine order and estate' and by his criticism of the proto-Anabaptist Müntzer and other sectaries who would not come to terms with the secular state. He was willing to consult with the elector, through the latter's chaplain Spalatin, and accepted the situation whereby the elector's court came to deal with suits involving ecclesiastical matters such as marriage, tithes and even church discipline. In 1527 Luther's *Instruction of Visitors to the Pastors* asserted that lay courts and officials should punish moral offences, false religious doctrines and non-attendance at church, and later the Lutherans established Consistorial Councils, whose members were named by lay lords, to deal with such matters. By then, with the formation of the League of Torgau (1526), there was an open Lutheran party among the princes, led by the Saxon elector and the landgrave of Hesse.

Lutheranism drew strength from both German national feeling and German political disunity, but neither worked solely in its favour. Luther's defence of certain condemned articles of Huss (among them the statement that 'it is not necessary for salvation to believe the Roman Church superior to all others') earned him much unpopularity. He was hailed by his enemies as 'the Saxon Huss' in lands that had been fought over by the Bohemian Hussites, and must have lost some support through such accusations, though this label did not stick. Moreover, rivalry between electoral and ducal Saxony ensured antagonists for the Wittenberg professor in the ducal university of Leipzig, just as rivalry between religious institutions gained the Dominicans' support for

Tetzel against the Augustinian. Nevertheless the strength of the elector of Saxony *vis-à-vis* his imperial overlord was the essential element which enabled Lutheranism to become firmly rooted in the critical decade after 1517.

The diffusion of Lutheranism would also have been a much slower and more difficult process but for the printing-press. In the years before Luther's prominence Frankfurt had been the main centre for the printing of pamphlets concerning the Reuchlin controversy, a dispute over the right of a scholar to pursue biblical investigations by studying Jewish literature which had put the humanists at odds with papal authority. It was therefore natural that this city should become a sort of headquarters of Protestant printing. Erasmus was already a best-seller—seventy-two editions of the *Adages* appeared between 1500 and 1525, and about sixty of the *Colloquies* in eight years after 1518—but the publication of Luther's writings was an even more profitable, as well as a pious, undertaking. Four thousand copies of the address *To the Christian Nobility* were sold within three weeks. The pamphlet war warmed up to such intensity that in the years 1518–25 no fewer than one-third of the German books sold were copies of works by Luther, whilst many of the rest were those of his supporters and antagonists.

Much of the remaining pamphlet literature was concerned with the question of peasant discontent. Since the early fifteenth century the German peasantry had suffered serious depression of its status at the hands both of hard-pressed knights and (particularly in the east) virtually independent lords. Sporadic risings culminated in *Bundschuh*[1] peasant revolts in Alsace in 1493, around Speyer in 1502, in the Breisgau and many other parts of the west in 1513–14, in Austria in 1515, and in the Black Forest area again in 1517. In 1525 there followed the great and disastrous Peasants' War. Ultimately the principal effect of these revolts was to strengthen the already dominant position of the lords who played the leading role in their suppression, but they had religious consequences as well, in that nobles who might otherwise have devoted their energies to combating Lutheranism were distracted by the successive crises of agrarian discontent.

The principal responsibility for the extermination of heresy in

---

[1] This was a type of shoe worn by peasants.

Germany lay of course with the emperor Charles V, who had at the same time to conduct the struggle against Francis I in Italy and the critical defence of the Empire against the Turks, as well as the multifarious internal negotiations of his vast domains. Charles's burdens were so manifold that his failure to bring sufficient force to bear in time against the rapidly rising Lutheran movement is readily understandable. In 1532 he was compelled to recognize the Protestant religion by the 'Common Peace' of Nuremberg, and in 1555 the Peace of Augsburg sealed the victory of territorialism in Germany by permitting the head of each state to decide the religion of his own lands.

Further Reading

G. STRAUSS (ed.), *Pre-Reformation Germany* (London, 1972)

A. G. DICKENS, *Reformation and Society in 16th-century Europe* (Thames & Hudson Library of European Civilization, 1966)

R. H. BAINTON, *Here I Stand. A Life of Martin Luther* (Mentor Books)

J. HUIZINGA, *Erasmus of Rotterdam* (with a selection from the letters) (London, 1952)

Memoirs of a Renaissance Pope (an abridged translation of the *Commentarii* of Pius II, ed. L. C. Gabel), (London, 1960)

Appendix

German National Sentiment in Celtes' Ingolstadt Address, 1492. (Translation by L. W. Forster in C. Celtes, *Selections*, pp. 45–7.)

Let us be ashamed, I pray, that although we have waged and won many memorable wars in Hungary, France and Italy and against that cruel tyrant of Asia who wallows in Christian blood, not one of you should be found today to hand down to posterity the deeds performed by German courage. Yet many foreigners will be found who in their historical works, contrary to all historical truth, will hiss like vipers against our courage with all the pretentious cajolery of their style and seek with falsifications and lying inventions (with which that sort of men is most prodigal for the purpose of singing their own praises) to belittle our glorious achievements. And I am quite at a loss to say whether it is due to our wisdom or our carelessness that lately of our own accord we have surrendered the insignia of authors and their companion, the imperial laurel, to Rome—an unhappy omen, as it were, for our empire, this abdication to others of the right to confer the laurel, foreshadowing that in the end not a single privilege of empire will remain in our possession.

Assume, O men of Germany, that ancient spirit of yours, with which you so often confounded and terrified the Romans, and turn your eyes to the frontiers of Germany; collect together her torn and broken territories. Let us be ashamed, ashamed, I say, to have placed upon our nation the yoke of slavery and to be paying tributes and taxes to foreign and barbarian kings. O free and powerful people, O noble and valiant race, plainly worthy of the Roman empire, our famous harbour is held by the Pole and the gateway of our ocean by the Dane! In the east also powerful peoples live in slavery, the Bohemians, the Moravians, the Slovaks and the Silesians, who all live as it were separated from the body of our Germany. And I may add the Transylvanian Saxons who also use our racial culture and speak our native language. In the west is France, which is so friendly and bountiful towards us by reason of the immortal virtue and incredible wisdom of Philip, Palatine of the Rhine, who rules both banks of the famous river and will ever rule them with fair-omened sway,

While the pole wheels the stars, while winds smite the shores.

But from the south we are oppressed by a sort of distinguished slavery, and under the impulse of greed, that old and accursed aid to the acquirement of comfort and luxury, new commercial ventures are continually established, by which our country is drained of its wonderful natural wealth while we pay to others what we need for ourselves. So persistent is fortune or destiny in persecuting and wiping out the Germans, the last survivors of the Roman Empire.

XV

POLITICAL WRITERS AND THE STRONGER STATE

ORGANIZERS of curricula and authors of text-books have usually fixed and accepted a date at the end of the fifteenth century as the arbitrary dividing-line between 'medieval' and 'modern' European history, the most conventional of such dates being that of the invasion of Italy by Charles VIII of France in 1494. The very idea of such a disjunction has itself a long history, and ultimately goes back, as does the concept of 'the Renaissance', to the opinions of contemporary writers. One of the most influential works in formulating this view of 1494 as a dividing-line is Francesco Guicciardini's *Storia d'Italia*, written in about 1536–9 and published in 1561. Guicciardini begins his history of Italy with the year 1494 and his principal theme is the 'calamities' inflicted on a previously tranquil and wealthy peninsula by this and subsequent invasions.

Yet the opinion that 1494 marked a radical change in the texture of Italian political life was held long before Guicciardini wrote his *Storia d'Italia*, as may be seen from his own much earlier history of Florence, most of which was probably written during the year 1508. In this work he narrates the appearance of Charles VIII's army in Italy, and then breaks off to exclaim:

> And there had entered Italy a flame and a plague which not only changed states,[1] but also methods of ruling them and of conducting warfare. Previously, Italy being composed of five main states (the pope's, Naples, Venice, Milan and Florence), each one of these attempted to preserve its own possessions, and watched out lest any took another's territory and gained so much that all the rest should fear it. Thus they observed every small alteration, and there was excitement when even the most insignificant of fortresses changed

[1] I.e. changed their régimes.

hands. When it came to warfare the strength was so evenly balanced and the movements of the militia and the artillery were so slow that almost a whole summer might be spent over the capture of a single castle. Wars were long-drawn-out, and when battles were fought very few men were killed in them. Now, with the coming of the French, it was as though a sudden storm had turned everything upside-down. The union of Italy was broken and torn apart, and so was the thought and care that had previously been given to the commonweal ['cose communi']. When cities, duchies, and kingdoms were attacked or fell prey to tumults, each state stood aside and attended to its own interests, instead of taking action lest a nearby fire or the downfall of a neighbouring town might burn or bring down its own régime. Sudden and violent wars began, and now a kingdom was destroyed and gained in less time than had previously been taken for a village to change hands. Cities were captured rapidly and fell not in months but in days or hours, and battles became ferocious and bloody. In brief, henceforward states were preserved or ruined, given away or taken, not by schemes drawn up in the study as in the past, but in the field and by armed men.[1]

Francesco Guicciardini (b. 1483) was a member of one of Florence's great patrician families. In childhood he saw the city's Medicean régime overturned as a result of Piero de Medici's hesitant attitude and feeble opposition to the French invasion, and for the next eighteen years he lived under a republic that was too democratic (one should perhaps say insufficiently oligarchic) to suit the ideas and interests of the Florentine magnates. Thereafter he entered the service of the Medicean popes (Leo X and Clement VII) as an administrator, and in 1526–7 played a particularly important role in the attempts to withstand Charles V's domination of Italy. His practical experience as an administrator and soldier, and his concern over democratic trends in Florence after 1494, are the biggest influences in Guicciardini's political writings. These are thus—as are his historical works— essentially the products of a particular situation: even when generalizing they consider and criticize *contemporary* institutions, and hence they stand in complete contrast to the writings of Aquinas and other medieval authors (see above, pp. 10–12), which approach politics deductively by the application of general and universally valid principles.

[1] F. Guicciardini, *Storie Fiorentine* (ed. R. Palmarocchi), pp. 92–3.

V. The Italian States in 1494

His circumstances, his temperament and the wish to give practical opinions, all made Guicciardini a realist. He saw Florence's limited capacities, and thought of the city as being 'in its old age'. He prided himself, too, on not being overawed by the writers of classical antiquity—in a way he was consciously emerging from the 'Renaissance' with its uncritical enthusiasm for antiquity—and he boasted that he was no Plato, thinking up some 'imaginary government, more likely to appear in books than in reality'.[1] With characteristically cautious phraseology, he often urged a certain course of action as 'the least bad'. In a dialogue concerning the Florentine situation in 1494, written some thirty years later, he was careful to explain that 'when judging between one government and another I should not consider so much the form of these governments, but should rather take into account which has better consequences and where men are better governed, where justice is best administered and where there is most respect for the general good, each man being in his proper rank'.[2] The practical application of Guicciardini's pragmatic approach emerges in the same Dialogue. He regretted the fall of the Medicean régime, but concluded (with the advantage of hindsight) that its restoration would be harmful, since this could only come about through external attack or internal faction, or a combination of the two, and it would lead not only to the destruction of the Medici's opponents but also to the installation of a very different type of Medicean rule. This regard for particular circumstances and caution in generalization were to make Guicciardini the ideal critic of his dogmatic friend Machiavelli.

Niccolò Machiavelli (1469–1527) lived through the same critical decades of Italian history and his writings, too, are essentially the product of the humiliation of Florence and the other Italian states by the great powers, France, Spain and the Empire of Charles V. His experiences, however, differed from Guicciardini's in a way that did much to affect his ideas, for as secretary to the Florentine committee for foreign affairs he saw events from the centre without having to bear the heavy burden of responsibility and decision-making which fell to Guicciardini. Machia-

---

[1] From 'Dialogo del Reggimento di Firenze' in *Dialogo e Discorsi del Reggimento di Firenze* (ed. R. Palmarocchi), p. 99.

[2] *Ibid.*, pp. 17–18.

velli was a brilliant writer and a generalizer by temperament, but his advice comes from the study. He delighted in writing the word 'to liquidate' (*spegnere*), yet his ruthlessness somehow fails to convince. In contrast Guicciardini, who wrote in the intervals of a career as governor and military commander, had really had men put to death.

This does not mean that Machiavelli has no claim to be considered as a 'realist'. His realism is limited and generic; but in that he was obsessed by the idea of power he, too, was dealing with realities with which his medieval predecessors had had no concern. 'Power easily wins a name, but a name wins no power',[1] he wrote, and in this determination to see beneath the surface he has much in common with Guicciardini and with many contemporary writers, among them a nephew of the latter who wrote contemptuously of 'the many men in our city who consider the names of things rather than their effects and causes'.[2] Machiavelli had learnt the hard lesson of Florence's insignificance in the eyes of the great powers in a fashion that was personally humiliating. He visited France as a Florentine emissary three times between 1500 and 1510, and his treatment by the French made him realize that a state can only count with its titular allies in so far as it has power to do them good or harm. The French consistently neglected their obligations towards their Florentine ally and, to make things worst of all, they themselves met defeat in Italy in 1512, and this defeat in turn brought about that of the republican régime in Florence, as a result of which Machiavelli lost his post and was for a time imprisoned. Savonarola had failed, in Machiavelli's opinion, because he lacked military support, and 'unarmed prophets' were bound to meet with defeat. Florence could only count for something in the world of power politics if it had a formidable army, and, since each state can rely solely on its own power, this would have to be an army of Florentine citizens. Mercenaries lacked any compelling bond with the states that employed them, hence the only solution was the restoration of a civic militia, based on Roman and communal models. It was in

---

[1] *Discorsi sopra la prima deca di Tito Livio*, Bk. I, ch. 34.

[2] Niccolò Guicciardini, 'Discorso', printed in R. von Albertini, *Das Florentinische Staatsbewusstsein im Übergang von der Republik zum Prinzipat*, pp. 352–62 (this passage occurs on p. 357).

this field alone that Machiavelli held a post of real importance and had an opportunity to put his ideas into practice: he played a leading part in the organization of a Florentine militia in 1506-7, but must have been sadly disappointed by its subsequent ineffectiveness.

Machiavelli saw not only states but also men as powers whose limits were those of their own unaided strength. Thus a dictator who had gained his position by a *coup d'état* was warned against reliance on the supporters who had brought him to power; by definition they were the malcontents of the previous régime and were likely to remain malcontents under his. On the other hand he could hope for the backing of the populace if he attended to the 'common good', and their support was preferable to that of the aristocracy not only in the dictator's own interest but also because theirs was a more widely shared 'good' and hence 'a more honest aim'.

Since the potential strength of the state was the sum of that of its own citizens, it was essential to maximize this by ensuring their full support. Patriotism, or public spirit, was the assurance of such support, and the good citizen—of whom Machiavelli found examples among classical Romans and contemporary Germans—was the man who paid his taxes honestly or delivered up to the state the loot captured in war. Feudalized states, whose nominal citizens owed allegiance to a local potentate rather than to the ruler, were enfeebled or 'corrupt'. Machiavelli relied on religion to impart public spirit, but Christianity was not well calculated to perform this role, and he criticized it for that reason. His ideal citizen, gladly paying taxes and serving in the army, was surely then, as now, 'more likely to appear in books than in reality'.

Machiavelli is best known for *The Prince*, the brilliantly-written handbook for a tyrant which set up an idealized Cesare Borgia as a model to the Medici from whom the author was seeking employment. His most important political work, however, is the *Discourses on Livy*, an attempt to elucidate and propound the lessons of early Roman history. In his Introduction to the *Discourses* Machiavelli declared his inability to understand why 'in matters of constituting republics, maintaining states, governing kingdoms, forming an army or conducting a war, judging subjects, or extending rule, one finds neither prince nor republic who goes to antiquity for examples'.[1] There is expressed here a fundamental belief that the ancients can teach in politics as they have taught in architecture and literature, that the men of the 'Renaissance' may, by copying them, hope to rival their achievements in statecraft as in the other fields of human activity. In this, as in other ways, Machiavelli was more old-fashioned than Guicciardini and many of his contemporaries; at the time when he was writing his main political works, in the second decade of the sixteenth century, blind admiration for antiquity was rather out of date.

A number of letters bear witness to a most interesting friendship between the lively, rather showy Machiavelli and Guicciardini, an aloof man who was perhaps a shade patronizing to Machiavelli but was attracted and stimulated by his vivacity and brilliance. Fascinated but unconvinced by Machiavelli's generalizations, Guicciardini once reminded his friend in a typically pessimistic phrase that 'we walk in darkness, with our hands tied behind our backs so that we cannot ward off blows'.[2] 'It is a great error', he thought, 'to speak of things absolutely and without distinguishing—by rule, as it were—for there is nearly always some difference in the circumstances which prevents their being brought under the same heading, and such distinctions have to be learnt from experience, not from books.' This was really his reply to the doctrine of Machiavelli's *Discourses*: 'It is quite fallacious to judge by examples. They are useless unless they are identical, because the smallest difference between them may be the cause of a great difference between their consequences, and a very perceptive eye indeed is required to discern such small differences.' Again, such generalizations presuppose absolutely correct knowledge about the past, yet this is an impossibility 'if one comes to reflect that we have no sure knowledge of the present, even of events occurring from day to day in one's own city'. A last quotation from Guicciardini's aphorisms (the *Ricordi*) completes the case against Machiavelli: 'How mistaken are those people who constantly cite the example of the Romans! One would have to have a city [state] the conditions of which were the same as

---

[1] *Discorsi*, Bk. I, Proemio.
[2] Letter of 7 August 1525 (in *Lettere*, ed. F. Gaeta, 1961, p. 426).

theirs and then follow their example fully, but our qualities are so disproportionate to theirs that this would be like trying to make a donkey gallop like a horse.' When he came to write a specific criticism of the *Discourses*, Guicciardini returned once more to his friend's exaggerated classicism: 'One should not praise antiquity so much that one disapproves every modern institution that was unknown to the Romans.'[1]

Whatever their disagreements, Machiavelli, Guicciardini and their Florentine contemporaries inaugurated a new approach to political writing. This is not the same as saying that they were the first men since classical times to think inductively about politics, or even that they were the first to write in a 'practical' way about politics, and this is perhaps as well, for this book has surely had enough to say about Florence already. To find the same practical pragmatic discussion of the state and politics, however, it is necessary only to travel to Venice, where it may be encountered in the utilitarian reports (*Relazioni*) by Venetian ambassadors which are such an important source for sixteenth-century history. These accounts were used as the basis for the republic's decisions concerning political and economic policy, hence they were practical by their very nature. The institution of diplomatic reports of this nature was not solely a Venetian one, and it originated before the sixteenth century; but the Venetian *relazioni* were particularly copious and, by retaining its independence, Venice kept the need for such information longer than the other Italian states.

Realistic discussion of politics is of course to be sought in historical works as well as in writings on 'current affairs', and may also be found in abundance in the *Mémoires* of Commynes (*c.* 1447–1511): (see above, pp. 236–8 for some quotations from this work). Commynes' *Memoirs* is a fascinating and much-read book, which ran to no fewer than twenty-five editions in French between its appearance in 1524 and the end of the century, and was translated into many languages. Not the least of its consequences was the stimulus it gave to the great German historian Ranke, who as a boy had noted the discrepancies between Scott's *Quentin Durward*

---

[1] *Ricordi*, nn. VI, CXVII, CXLI, CX (ed. R. Spongano, pp. 11, 128, 153, 121): *Considerazioni su i Discorsi di Machiavelli*, on *Disc.*, II, 24 (in F. Guicciardini, *Opere Inedite*, Florence, 1857, p. 67).

and the 'much superior' account given by Commynes of the character of Charles the Rash.[1] Philippe Commynes came of a Flemish family (feudal in standing though *bourgeois* by descent) settled near Lille. He early entered the service of Charles the Rash, then heir to the duchy of Burgundy, and later duke, but in 1471 accepted a pension from Louis XI and the following year turned traitor to Charles. He then took employment under Louis XI, and for some forty years acted as an adviser and emissary for the French crown. He was endowed with large estates by Louis, who particularly valued his first-hand knowledge of his former master. Louis also despatched him on a mission to Florence (1478), and later Commynes accompanied Charles VIII to Italy and acted as his emissary to Venice (1494–5); he also visited Milan with Louis XII (1507). Commynes' service to the French crown was not without vicissitudes: he had great difficulty in asserting his title to the lands granted him by Louis XI, and after Louis' death he fell from favour for some years, took part in the insurrection of 1485 ('la Guerre Folle'), and was subsequently imprisoned. After a long exile from the Court he was restored in 1491 only to fall into temporary disgrace once more seven years later.

There are some curiously close parallels between Commynes' career and Machiavelli's, as well as similarities in the bearing of their experiences on the framework of their ideas. Both men conceived an admiration for the statecraft of one exemplary individual: Commynes was often the confidant of Louis XI, as Machiavelli occasionally was of Cesare Borgia, and he thought Louis wise, subtle, possessing 'perfect common sense' and, above all, skilful at extricating himself from difficulties. Each of them, too, was present at a momentous occasion in his hero's career, which profoundly affected his own ideas. In the case of Commynes the 'traumatic' episode was Louis XI's meeting with Charles of Burgundy at Péronne in 1468 (see above, p. 238) when the king was in his enemy's power and yet was allowed to go free, Commynes' own soothing advice perhaps helping to persuade his then master to spare the man who was destined to become his master. The equivalent occasion in Machiavelli's experience was the trap set by Cesare Borgia at Senigallia to capture the mercenary leaders who had been plotting against him. Machiavelli was at

[1] Ranke, *Sämmtliche Werke*, 53/54, p. 61.

Cesare's court as Florentine emissary when these men were apprehended and put to death (31 December 1502), and he described the entire event three times, with increasing care and admiration, first in his report to the republic, then in the brief *Descrizione del modo tenuto dal duca Valentino nello ammazzare Vitellozzo Vitelli, Oliverotto da Fermo, il signor Pagolo e il duca di Gravina Orsini*, and finally in *The Prince*. Both of these men travelled a good deal—as we have seen, Commynes knew Italy and Machiavelli France—and both endured spells of imprisonment, the former in 1487-9, the latter in 1513 when suspected of complicity in an anti-Medicean plot. Machiavelli suffered French insults, and even for this there is a parallel, *mutatis mutandis*, since Commynes had to return to Venice as France's emissary in 1495, after Charles VIII's humiliating withdrawal from Italy, and the Venetians then greeted him sarcastically as a 'much thinner' man than the triumphant Commynes of the previous year.

Machiavelli thought that *The Prince* would prove his 'fifteen years' study of the art of statecraft were not wasted in sleep or play' and that it would persuade the Medici that his services were too valuable to miss. Commynes felt the same conviction that his *Memoirs*, the fruit of 'eighteen years or more spent in the vicinity of princes, and certain knowledge of the most important and secret affairs of this kingdom of France and the neighbouring lordships' would not provide amusing reading-matter for silly, simple folk, 'but I think that rulers or men at court will find good advice in them'.[1] By a natural extension of the same principle, Commynes shared the Florentine's belief in the 'lessons of history', and his pessimism concerning his own times:

> One of the best ways for a man to acquire wisdom is to read histories. From these and the example of his predecessors he can learn how to act, to be cautious, and to undertake things wisely. For one man's life is so short that it does not provide sufficient experience. Moreover, we are enfeebled by age, and men live less long than they used to and their bodies are less strong. We are also weaker in observing good faith and loyalty among ourselves. I do not know where men can trust each other now, particularly among great rulers, for these are most inclined to follow their own will

[1] Machiavelli, Letter to F. Vettori, 10 December 1513 (*Lettere*, ed. F. Gaeta, 1961, p. 305); Commynes, Bk. II, 6 and Bk. III, 8.

without considering anything else and, what is worse, they are usually surrounded by men who are intent only on pleasing their masters, and praise all their actions, both good and evil.[1]

When Commynes writes of Venice he comes closer still to Machiavelli, so close indeed that some scholars have tried to maintain that he had heard of Machiavelli's ideas, though the *Discourses* were written after his death and it is virtually certain that he never met their author. Commynes envied the Venetians because 'they know, through Livy, the mistakes that the Romans made, for they have his *History*, as they have also his bones in their palace at Padua'.[2] He himself knew no Latin and regretted this deficiency. His belief that the lessons of history were best learnt from Livy is evidence, of course, not of any dependence on Machiavelli, but of the general acceptance of the superiority of the Romans over their debased successors and the consequent opinion that their achievements and shortcomings constituted the lessons of the past *par excellence*. This way of thinking was no less characteristic of the twelfth century than of the sixteenth, and was to be found in France as much as in Italy: we have already encountered it in the history book specially composed for Philip VI (above, p. 142).

Commynes certainly appears more 'medieval' than Machiavelli in some ways. Whereas the latter thought Fortune 'arbiter of half our actions', Commynes would have no truck with this essentially irreligious concept. 'Fortune is nothing but a poetic fiction', he wrote, and the downfall of Burgundy was no turn of Fortune's wheel but the work of 'the hand of God', but for whose special favours France 'would have been in great danger'.[3] Yet fundamentally they have much in common, and both Commynes and his master would have understood and sympathized with Machiavelli's political writings, a point that is perhaps best established by giving some sayings of Louis XI that are quoted appreciatively in the *Mémoires*:

He once said to me . . . that men are sometimes ruined by having served too well, and great services are most often repaid by great ingratitude. He said that this may come about not only through the

[1] *Mémoires*, Bk. III, 8 (for the last sentence, cf. *Prince*, chs. 18 and 23).
[2] *Ibid.*, Bk. VII, 15.
[3] *Prince*, ch. XXV: *Mémoires*, Bk. IV, chs. 1, 5, 7, 12.

ingratitude of rulers but also through the defects of those who have performed these services, if they speak too arrogantly and rely too much on their good fortune in their dealings with their lord as well as with their colleagues. He also said to me that, in his opinion, it was better for a man at court to have received undeserved benefits from his ruler, and thus to be much obliged to him, than to have rendered great services, so that it was the ruler who stood under a great obligation; because it is natural for a ruler to love those who are obliged to him rather than those to whom he is obliged.[1]

To Louis XI (though not by Commynes) was also attributed that quintessentially 'Machiavellian' saying: *Qui nescit dissimulare, nescit regnare*[2] ('He who cannot dissimulate cannot rule'). That such an amoral aphorism should have been on the tongue of a ruler half a century before *The Prince* was written will surprise only the most naïve, but the fact may help to disprove the ridiculous and stubborn myth that rulers and statesmen needed to read Machiavelli to learn wickedness.

More striking than Machiavelli's not very successful attempt to eliminate morality as irrelevant to political discussion is the way in which he saw statecraft as the interplay of power. Commynes had emphasized strongly the element of personal decision; the downfall of the Burgundian duchy, for instance, was for him essentially the result of a series of misjudgments by Charles the Rash. Machiavelli's view of the lessons of the last decade of the fifteenth century and the first of the sixteenth was a more penetrating one, and in this he was assisted by being an Italian and hence reflecting more on the changes wrought in the peninsula by the invasions. Like Guicciardini, Machiavelli saw the Italian states as potential victims of the 'new' powerful monarchies, particularly of the French, the Spaniards and the Ottomans. These were monarchies whose rulers could 'make the rich poor and the poor rich . . . build new cities, destroy those that already exist, and move the population about from one place to another'.[3]

Machiavelli's was indeed in many ways an utterly different world from the thirteenth-century Europe sketched in Chapter I.

[1] Bk. III, 12 (cf. some similar remarks in Machiavelli's *Discorsi*, Bk. I, 30)
[2] Giovanni Botero, *La Ragion di Stato*, Bk. V, ch. 5.
[3] *Discorsi*, Bk. I, 26.

Men still went back to the ancients—Machiavelli to Livy and Polybius, as Aquinas to Aristotle—but ways of writing about politics and the society that was written about had both changed profoundly. The Aragonese kings whose subjects would obey them if they kept their word 'and if not, not', the barons whose feudal rights made them 'sovereigns in their own baronies', the Italian 'patricians' enjoying complete political independence through the weakness of central authority, all these would have found the political atmosphere altered beyond recognition had they revisited Europe in the sixteenth century. Communications were still primitive and regional jurisdictions and loyalties, states within the state, immensely powerful; Machiavelli and men for centuries after him knew the successors of Beaumanoir's 'sovereigns in their own baronies'. Yet the main direction of change in these three centuries had been decisively in favour of the monarchies. Spain was now one powerful kingdom, France so strong that it could take Italian states 'with chalk', England, Sweden and Denmark had kings who could break the bonds of Rome and change their countries' religion. The cardinal achievement was the gradual ousting of the mighty subject by a centralizing bureaucracy, and this process was taking place in the later Middle Ages wherever circumstances were favourable. In Spain the circumstances were provided by a dynastic marriage, in France by the more complicated combination of the English challenge, the stimulus given by this to patriotic sentiment, and the collapse of the Burgundian duchy.

Granted the proviso that many ordinary folk would still be aware of the strength of local potentates more than of that of monarchs, some apology is perhaps needed also for the choice of a political criterion in assessing the greatest changes during this period of three centuries. Among writers who have seen things differently, some would point to the geographical discoveries in America and Africa as marking a fundamental change in expanding men's intellectual horizons, revolutionizing their commercial and financial existence and bringing into being new empires. The impact of these developments, though, was extremely gradual, a matter of slow dilution. The Mediterranean continued to be the most important sphere of European maritime commerce throughout most of the sixteenth century, and awareness of exotic peoples and new worlds was slow—except perhaps in the Iberian peninsula—to work significant changes in the outlook of even the most thoughtful of Europeans. Even less convincing is the claim that a 'modern' way of thought among the educated, a sloughing-off of the 'medieval mind', dates from the cosmological discoveries of the sixteenth century. Copernicus's heliocentric system was indeed published in 1543—a second edition was not required till 1566—but its effects on men's views of life were bound to be small; indeed, they remain small today. This sort of scientific truth seems compelled, in a way, to remain incomprehensible, so evident is it to each individual that there is another sense in which the earth is the centre of the universe and he the centre of earthly affairs.

To depict the growing power of the monarchic state as the great tendency of the times is not to suggest that all forces were conspiring in this direction or that this was a sort of magnetism predestined to prevail and to undergo no lasting reverse. The internal cohesion of imperial Germany, not comparable at the outset of the sixteenth century with that of France, England or Spain, was further impaired by Charles V's struggle to rule a vast Habsburg Empire and was destroyed in the following century by the Thirty Years War. The French monarchy too was to undergo an immensely harassing crisis throughout the second half of the sixteenth century, partly due to the newly disunificatory force of religion. Nevertheless the power of Charles V's state and Francis I's prepared that struggle between Habsburg and Valois which was to provide the main theme in European foreign relations right up to 1648 or even 1713.

Further Reading

MACHIAVELLI, *The Prince and Discourses* (ed. M. Lerner, Modern Library College Editions: and many other translations)

F. GUICCIARDINI, *Maxims and Reflections of a Renaissance Statesman* (Harper Torchbooks)

P. DE COMMINES, *Memoirs* (see above, p. 196)

INDEX

Dates given are those of birth and death, except in the case of popes where they are those of their pontificate

Aachen, siege of, 187
Achaia, 42, 44; William of, 44
Acre, fall of, 117, 198
Adolf of Nassau (d. 1298), 79
Africa, North, 258; Barcelona and, 46, 47
Agincourt, battle of, 147, 154, 155, 156, 183
Agriculture, in Southern Europe, 21; effect of famine on the price of grain, 105; a means of judging Europe's wealth, 111
Aicelin, archbishop of Narbonne, 60
Aigues-Mortes, 241
Al-Mahdiya, siege of, 152, 206-7
Al-Mustasir, Sultan, 46
Albania, 44, 203, 204, 205, 212
Albergati, Cardinal, 194
Albert, archbishop of Magdeburg, 271
Albert I (c. 1250-1308), king of the Romans, 79
Albert II (1397-1439), king of the Romans, 83
Albert III, Achilles, Elector of Branden-burg (1414 86), 262
Alberti, Leon Battista (1404-72), 228, 229; Della Famiglia, 164, 174-5; On Painting, 166
Albigeois, 61
Albizzi, the, 107
Albizzi, Maso degli, 220
Albizzi, Rinaldo degli, 220-1
Albornoz, Cardinal Gil Alvarez Carillo (1300-67), 120; pacifies the papal lands, 121-2
Alcaçovas, treaty of, 251
Alençon, 237
Alexander IV, Pope (1254-61), 36, 37
Alexander V, Pope (1409-10), 127
Alexander VI, Pope (1492-1503), 228, 255, 266; his immorality, 266-7
Alexandria, 45, 249; siege of, 206
Alfonso V, king of Aragon (c. 1390-1458), and Naples, 249, 250
Alfonso IX, king of Castile, and the Order of St James, 5-6
Alfonso X, king of Castile (1221-84), 5, 9, 16, 18; and the German Crown, 76, 77, 78, 247

Alfonso, king of León, 14, 15
Alfonso V, king of Portugal (1432-81), 251
Algarve, 5
Alphonse of Poitiers (d. 1271), 61
Alsace, Burgundy and, 186 7; revolt of Bundschuh peasants in, 274
Amadeus VI, Count, of Savoy, (1334-83), his 'Crusade', 206
Amboise, Concordat of, 244
Amiens, Mise of, 56
Anagni, 125; 'outrage' of, 54, 60, 65, 117
Anatolia, 199, 202, 203, 210
Ancona, March of, 36, 215, 216, 249
Andalò, Brancaleone degli, 35
Andalusia, 246
Andernach, treaty of, 188
Andronicus II, Byzantine Emperor (1260-1332), hires Catalan mercenaries, 199
Angelico, Fra (1387-1455), 228
Angevins, the, 241, 244; and Sicily, 39, 50; the papacy and, 40, 41, 50-1, 117, 118; their increased power, 55; draw France into foreign intervention, 58; and Florence, 216
Angora (Ankara), 202, 208
Angoulême, 61
Anjou, 236; a state in itself, 3-4; Dukes of, 146, 236, 241
Anne of Brittany, queen of Charles VIII (1476-1514), 243-4
Anne, duchess of Bedford, 234
Annibaldi, the, 51, 54; dispossess the Orsini, 40-1
Annibaldi, Cardinal Richard, 37
Antwerp, 108, 242, 262; growth at the expense of Bruges, 193
Aquinas, St Thomas (c. 1226-74), his political theories, 10-11, 278; and legislation, 11; his ideal constitution 11-12; uses the deductive method, 12
Aquitaine, a fief of England, 3-4, 58, 140; Philip III and, 61; French overlordship in, 63, 140; the French monarchy and, 140; enlarged by Treaty of Brétigny, 145
Aragon, 190; government of its component parts, 5; its coronation oath, 8, 250; and town representation, 13, 14;

financial arrangements, 19, 253; local administration, 20; part of the Mediterranean zone, 33, 248; emerges as a great sea power, 45, 47, 55; and the conquest of Sicily, 47, 50, 249; French claim to its throne, 54, 141; French invasion of, 57; and the Great Schism, 130; Castile and, 246, 247, 248, 250; its Reconquest, 248-9; its Mediterranean trade, 249; political institutions, 249-50; unification with Castile, 250-2; its reorganized Council, 253

Ariosto, Ludovico (1474-1533), *Orlando Furioso*, 177

Aristotle (384-322 B.C.), his influence on medieval thought, 10, 11, 71, 146, 164, 168, 169, 289

Armagnac, 237, 241; at war with Burgundy, 183

Army, the, in the Italian republics, 25; and the *popolo*, 27-8; and town Leagues, 85; and damage to land and crops, 100-2; Charles VII's reforms, 234-5; *see also* Warfare

Arnolfini, Giovanni and Giovanna, 194

Arnolfo di Cambio (1232-1301), 164

Arras, Louis XI and, 242

Arras, treaty of, 185, 234, 240, 242

Arsouf, 198

Arthur, King, exemplar of chivalry, 151, 158-9

Artois, 180, 181, 185, 191, 195, 240, 242; a state in itself, 3-4

Asia, 6; Ottoman campaigns in, 210

Asti, 244

Athens, duchy of, 44, 200, 202, 210, 249

Athès-sur-Orge, peace of, 58-9

Audenarde, 191

Augsburg, 108, 262, 272; peace of, 275

Augustine, St (353-430), 10; Petrarch and, 168, 169

Augustinians, 269, 270

Austria, 181, 240; Germany and, 78, 79, 83, 260, 264

Auvergne, 68, 236; acquired by the Crown, 61

Auxerre, 185

Avignon, 22; Petrarch and, 167-8

Avignon Papacy, 65, 116, 117-19, 167; its preoccupations, 119-20; Italian policy, 120-2; its achievements, 122-3; and the Great Schism, 124, 126

Baillis, 4, 19-20

Baldwin, count of Flanders (1171-1206), emperor of Constantinople, 42

Balearics, the, 5, 14; their conquest by Aragon, 45, 249

Balkans, Ottoman expansion into, 202-3, 205, 210

Banking, the Italians and, 106, 112; the Medici and, 109, 220, 221, 223, 225; in Germany, 263

Bar, County of, 4, 233, 241

Barbarigo, Andrea (1399-1449), his business ventures, 110

Barcelona, 108; mercantile strength of 45-6; appoints consular representatives, 46; its privileged status, 47; its recession, 249, 258-9; Agreement of, 257

Basle, Council of, 129, 131, 138

Baudricourt, Robert de, 4

Bavaria, 77, 78, 181, 264

Bayard, Chevalier de (*c.* 1473-1524), 159

Bayezid I, Sultan (1347-1403), 203, 207, 208

Beaucaire, 22

Beaufort, Cardinal Henry (*c.* 1375-1447), 138

Beaujeu, Anne and Pierre de, 243

Beaumanoir, Philippe de Remi, Sire de (*c.* 1250-96), 3, 15, 289; on oligarchy, 22-3; on lay jurisdiction, 63

Béguines, the, 268

Belgrade, 210, 212

Belleperche, Pierre de, bishop of Auxerre, 60

Benedict XII, Pope (1334-42), 122; builds a palace at Avignon, 118, 119

Benedict XIII, Pope (1394-1423), 124, 126, 127, 130; condemned as a heretic, 127

Benedictines, 10

Beneš of Weitmil, 132

Benevento, battle of, 38, 39

Bentivoglio, the, 226

Bentivoglio, Giovanni, 226

Bentivoglio, Sante, 226

Bernardino of Siena, St (1380-1444), 268

Bertrand, Cardinal Pierre (d. 1361), 123

Bertrand de Born (*c.* 1140-*c.* 1215), 150

Bessarion, Cardinal Johannes (*c.* 1400-72), 228

Bible (medieval), its influences on legal theories, 10, 11; translations of, 265 and n, 270, 271

Bithynia, 202

Black Death, 99, 103-4, 107, 111; Boccaccio and, 113-14

Black Sea, trade and, 42, 43; Ottomans and, 210

Bladelin of Bruges, 192

Blanche of Lancaster (d. 1369), 189

Boabdil (d. *c.* 1493), king of Granada, 256

Boccaccio, Giovanni, (1313-75), 162, 250; and the Renaissance, 165, 169, 170; Significance of the *Decameron*, 171

Bohemia, 3, 78, 255; Germany and, 79, 82; Hussites of, 129, 133 ff.; and the Great Schism, 130, 132,133; growth of national consciousness, 131-3; antagonism to Germany, 131, 133, 137; and the Taborites, 137

Boiardo, Matteo (1434-94), 177

Bologna, 109, 118, 121, 218; under the Bentivoglio, 226

Bonet, Honoré, *Arbre des Batailles*, 157

Boniface VIII, Pope (Benedict Caetani) (1294-1303), 70, 79; his expenditure, 50; character, 52; criticisms of, 52; his policy, 52–3; territorial acquisitions, 53–4; quarrel with Philip IV, 54, 64–5, 117; and the taxation of church revenues in France, 64; issues *Unam Sanctam*, 64–5; his posthumous trial, 66, 117, 119

Boniface IX, Pope (1389–1404), 126

Book of a Hundred Chapters, 266

Bordeaux, and trade with England, 97 and n; the Hundred Years War and, 101

Borgia, Cesare (1476–1507), Machiavelli and, 282, 285

Borgia, the, 266

Bosnia, 202, 204, 205, 210, 212

Botticelli, Sandro (1444–1510), 228

Boucicaut, Marshal, (1365–1421) 151–2, 159; his Order of the White Lady, 158

Boulogne, 180, 185, 237

Bourbon, duke of, 236, 237

Bourgneuf, Bay of, 113

Brabant, 106, 108, 142, 184, 185, 189, 191

Bracciolini, Poggio, 228

Brandenburg, 77, 81, 82, 86, 138, 261, 262

Brant, Sebastian (1458–1521), 272–3

Brenner Pass, 97

Brethren of the Common Life, 268, 269, 270

Brétigny, treaty of, 143, 145, 156

Brie, 61, 238

Brittany, 143, 241; its Celtic tongue, 3; loses its independence, 243–4

Brittany, duke of, 236, 237

Bruges, 21, 176, 187, 242, 254; 'Matins of', 58; and maritime trade, 97, 106; its decline, 108, 192, 193; and banking, 192–3

Brunelleschi, Filippo (1377–1446), 166, 172

Bruni, Leonardo (1370–1444), 166, 172

Brunswick, duchy of, its creation, 75; divisions in, 262

Brussels, 106, 191

Buch, Captal de, 145

Bueil, Jean de (d. *c.* 1478), *Le Jouvencel*, 157

Bulgaria, 3, 198, 199, 202, 204; extends its hold in Thrace, 42; the Ottomans and, 203, 205

Burghers, the, representatives in towns, 11–12 and n

Burgundy, a state in itself, 3–4, 178; acquired by the Crown, 61, 178, 180; and the Swiss Confederation, 90; allied with the English, 147; emergence as a duchy, 178; its increasing power and wealth, 178–80, 181; acquisitions, 180, 181, 185, 186–7, 195; at civil war, 183; relations with England, 183–5, 186, 232, 234; its role under Charles the Rash, 186–8, 190; sumptuousness of its court, 188–9, 194, 196–7; fails to achieve kingship, 189–90; and European affairs, 190; fails to achieve unity, 190; its

administration 190–1; its revenues, 191; and Flanders, 192–3; and the arts, 194–5; and the Crusade of Nicopolis, 207; captures Joan of Arc, 234; comes to terms with France, 234; Louis XI and, 236, 237, 239; and Germany, 260; *see also* Charles the Rash and Philip the Good

Byzantine Empire, 3, 16; part of the Mediterranean zone, 33, 97; The Fourth Crusade and, 42; Michael Palaeologus and, 44, 45, 50; its weakness, 55, 199; the Catalan company and, 199–200; its fragmentation, 202; the Ottoman Turks and, 202; Serbia and, 204; extinguished by Mahomet II, 208–10

Caetani, the, 51, 52, 53, 54, 117

Calais, 144, 145, 147, 152

Calixtus III, Pope (1455–8), 266, 267

Caltabellotta, peace of, 50

Cambrai, 20, 142, 155; League of, 264

Camino, Rizzardo de, 215

Campagna, Roman, its feudal dynasties, 40, 51; Boniface VIII and, 53, 117

Canary Islands, 258

Capetians, the, 30 and n, 74, 141

Capistrano, Friar Giovanni da (1386–1456), 210

Cardinals, college of, and papal residence, 116, 118, 119; becomes increasingly independent, 122–4; and the Great Schism, 125 7

Carinthia, 212

Carraresi, the, 218

Cassel, battle of, 142

Castagno, Andrea del (1409–80), 228

Castiglione, Baldassare, Count (1478–1529), *The Courtier*, 177

Castile, 4, 13, 130; Alfonso X and, 5, 16, 247; its *Siete Partidas*, 9 10, 12, 14n², 15; and the chancellorship, 18; its exchequer, 19; local administration, 20; its debilitation by disputed successions, 30, 247; French intervention in, 57; its history that of Reconquest, 246; weakness of the monarchy, 247, 248; the *Hermandades*, 247, 248; its decentralized administration, 247–8; unification with Aragon, 250–2; its Council, 253, 254; the textile industry, 253–4; its pastoral farming (*Mesta*), 254, 259

Castracane, Castruccio, 216

Catalan Company, in Byzantium, 199–202

Catalonia, 5, 14; its committees to watch 'non-feudal' subsidies, 15; and the *Cortes*, 16; James I of Aragon negotiates with, 30–2; the position of Barcelona, 46; its Consuls in Sicily, 47; expansion in the Mediterranean, 249; revolts of 1461–72, 249, 251, 252; its decline, 258–9

Cateau-Cambrésis, peace of, 245

Catherine, Princess, marriage to Henry V, 147, 155

U

Catherine of Sweden, St (1335–81), 124
Caxton, W. *Book of the Ordre of Chyvalry*, 159n
Celestine V, Pope (Peter of Morrone) (1294), 51–2
Celtes, Konrad (1459–1508), 265, 272
Cerdagne, 251, 257
Cervantes Saavedra, Miguel de (1547–1616), *Don Quixote*, 159–60, 270
Cesarini, Cardinal Julian (1398–1444), 138
Ceuta, 45, 47
Champagne, 30, 180, 237, 238; a state in itself, 3–4; acquired by the Crown, 61; its fairs, 97, 99; Burgundy and, 186
Champmol, Charterhouse at, 194
Chancery, the, its personnel and organization, 17–18
Charlemagne (742–814), 1, 151
Charles IV, Emperor (Charles of Bohemia) (1316–78), 206; promulgates the 'Golden Bull', 81; and Bohemia, 132–3; Petrarch and, 170
Charles V, Emperor (1500–58), 75, 195, 245, 290; and Italy, 226, 257; succeeds in Spain, 259; and Lutheranism, 274–5
Charles IV, king of France (1294–1328), and Aquitaine, 140–1
Charles V, king of France (1337–80), 157, 189; and Urban VI, 125; accession, 146
Charles VI, king of France (1368–1422), 126, 147; his insanity, 178, 181; Philip the Bold and, 180, 181
Charles VII, king of France (1403–61), 4; as the Dauphin, 145, 147, 183, 185, 189, 232–3; as king, 185–6; coronation, 233; and Joan of Arc, 233–4; his military reforms, 234–5; recovers Normandy, 235; his achievements, 235
Charles VIII, king of France (1470–98), 199; and Naples, 219, 245; his accession, 243; marriage, 244; Italian intervention, 244–5, 257, 264, 277
Charles, king of Navarre (d. 1387), 145, 180
Charles, count of Valois, and the throne of Aragon, 54, 141; and his son, 141–2
Charles the rash, duke of Burgundy (1433–1477), 83, 178; invades Switzerland, 90; and chivalry, 151; and Louis XI, 186, 187, 188, 195, 235, 237, 238, 239, 240; territorial acquisitions, 186–7; downfall and death, 188, 190, 195, 240; of English descent, 189–90; his administration, 191; revenues, 191; and aid to Flanders, 193; Commynes and, 285
Charles, duke of Calabria, 216
Charles, duke of Orléans (1391–1465), 233
Charles of Anjou (1225–85), 7–8, 16, 116, 152, 200; Innocent IV and, 35; overthrows Manfred and succeeds to the Sicilian throne, 37–8; defeats Conradin, 38–9; extends his power in Rome and Tuscany, 39; Martin IV and, 41; his fall, 41–2, 47–50; aims at the eastern

imperial crown, 44–5, 47; and the Aragonese monarchy, 45, 47; arouses discontent in Sicily, 47–9; leaves Sicily, 50; and intervention in Spain, etc., 57
Charles of France (brother of Louis XI), 237, 238
Chartres, 61
Chastellain, Georges (*c.* 1405/15–*c.* 1475), 151, 190
Chaucer, Geoffrey (*c.* 1345–1400), 271
Chios, island of, 43, 48
Chivalry, its meaning and ideals, 148–52; initiation into, 150–1; virtues of, 151, 152; exemplars of, 151–2, 159; and the conduct of war, 152–3, 154; French the language of, 153, 171; the English and, 154–5, 156; France and, 155–6; changing attitude to, 157; Orders of, 157–8, 206; social and literary aspects, 158–60, 163; its influence on Italian culture, 170–1
Christians, in Ottoman Turkey, 203; inferiority in the Crusades, 208; their frontier in Spain, 246, 248, 252; and converts, 255
Chrysoloras, Manuel (*c.* 1355–1415), 170
Church, the, as large landowner, 6; and appellate jurisdiction, 6–7; the king and, in England, 8; and the civil service, 17, 18, 29; the goal of clever younger sons, 52; its involvement with the French party in Rome, 55; the French Crown and its revenues, 63–5; achievements of the Avignon popes, 122–4; and the Great Schism, 126–7; and heresy, 131; and chivalry, 150; a necessity for monarchical control, 255; differences between North and South, 268; movements for its reformation, 268–74
Church, French, and the Great Schism, 125–7; the Pragmatic Sanction and, 244, 261
Church, Greek, 129; titular submission to papacy, 45
Church, Roman, dispute concerning papal residence, 116–20; the Great Schism, 125–7; the Council of Constance and, 127–9; Bohemian antagonism to, 132–3; Huss and, 134 ff.; Luther and, 268–9
Civil Service, its central organization, 17; a route to ecclesiastical preferment, 17; position of the chancery, 17–18; emergence of the exchequer, 19; and local administration, 19–20; lack of in Italy, 213
Classical literature, Italian culture and, 162, 167, 168, 169–70, 287, 289
Clement IV, Pope (1265–8), and kingship, 7–8; and the Sicilian succession, 38, 39
Clement V, Pope (Bertrand de Got) (1305–14), 65; supports Henry VII, 79; and residence in Rome, 116–17; **settles at Avignon**, 117

Clement VI, Pope (1342–52), 81, 118, 119, 206; his extravagance, 123; Charles IV and, 132

Clement VII, Pope (1378–94), his election, 125–6, 127; death, 126

Clergy, the, and taxation, 64–5; and nationalism, 71–2; source of educated men, 173; celibacy among, 173 and nn[2,3]

Clermont, Marshal, 144

Cleves, 142

Cologne, 10, 77, 262

Colonna, the, 51, 117, 168; Boniface VIII and, 53–4

Colonna, Cardinal Peter, 53

Columbus, Christopher (1451–1506), 258

Communes, French, seek royal intervention, 62; and taxation, 68

Communes, Italian; origins of, 27–8; their weakness, 213–14; tyrants and, 217

Commynes, Philippe de (c. 1446–c. 1511), 239; and Louis XI, 236, 237, 238, 285, 287; his *Mémoires*, 284–5, 286; his career, 285; compared with Machiavelli, 285–8

Compiègne, 234

Conrad IV, king of the Romans (1228–54), 76, and the Sicilian succession, 35–6

Conradin (1252–68), and the Sicilian succession, 37, 38–9

Constance, council of, Sigismund and, 82, 83, 134; brings the Great Schism to an end, 127, 131; elects Martin V, 127; and conciliar authority, 127–9; Huss and, 134

Constance of Sicily, 36; assumes title of Queen, 45; offered the throne, 50

Constantine XI, Emperor (1403–53), 210

Constantinople, 207, 208, 249; Genoa and, 43; Greek rule restored to, 44; Charles of Anjou's plan to conquer, 48; 49–50; deportation to, 203; Dušan and, 204; captured by Mahomet II, 208–9

Copernicus, Nicolas (1473–1543), 290

Cordova, 5

Coria, siege of, 151

Corleone, 49

Correspondence, the chancery and, 17–18

Corsica, 98

Counter-Reformation, 212, 229

Courtrai, battle of, 58, 60

Courts, centres of culture and patronage, 176

Crécy, battle of, 143–4, 154

Cremona, 35, 216

Crete, 212

Crimea, the, 249

Crotus Rubeanus, 268

Crusades, the, 152, 186; and Byzantium, 42; Louis IX and, 46, 56; the Templars and, 65, 66; need for their renewal, 117, 205; Avignon popes and, 122, 198; Burgundy and, 189, 190, 198, 207; the

daydream of the West, 198; the Crusade of Nicopolis, 205; attempts to regain lost territory, 205–7; inferiority of Christian discipline, 208

Crusades, of Nicopolis, 205, 207; of king Peter of Cyprus, 206; of Count Amadeus of Savoy, 206; Franco-Genoese, 206–7

Culture, Italian, its feeling of the countryside, 162; and deeds of chivalry, 163; its civic feeling, 163–5; the 'Renaissance' and, 165–7; and classical literature, 167, 168, 169–70; its continuity exemplified in Petrarch, 168–9; influenced by France, 170–1, 176; influenced by wealthy patronage, 171–2, 176–7, 226–9; its secular tone, 173; and family tradition, 173–5

Cyprus, 249

Czechs, the, attitude to Germans, 131–2, 133; and Bohemia, 132, 133; their national struggle, 137–9

Dante Alighieri (1265–1321), 176; and Florence, 24, 28–9; condemns Boniface VIII, 52, 54; and imperialism in Italy, 54, 80; his conception of 'Italians', 70; salutes Henry VII, 79–80; denounces Avignon, 118; and chivalry, 163, 171; and the Renaissance, 165

De la Marche, Olivier, 187, 196

Della Faggiuola, Uguccione, 216

Della Scala, the, 215, 216, 218

Della Scala, Alberto, 216

Della Scala, Cangrande, 215

Della Torre, the, 35, 120, 216, 217

Denmark, 84, 260

des Ursins, Jean Juvénal, *Remonstrances*, 157

Deventer, its Brethren of the Common Life, 269

Diaz, Bartolomew (c. 1450–1500), 258

Dijon, 190, 194

Dominicans, the, 122

Douai, 58, 106

Du Guesclin, Bertrand (c. 1320–80), 146, 151, 155

Dupplin Moor, battle of, 144

Durham, its palatinate, 6

Edmund de Langley (1341–1402), 180

Education, in medieval Italy, 161 ff; 173; family tradition and, 173–4, 175

Edward I, king of England (1239–1307), 62, 117; calls the clergy to parliament, 13; France's war with, 58; and the English language, 70; Statute of Winchester, 154

Edward II, king of England (1284–1327), and Aquitaine, 140, 141

Edward III, king of England (1312–77), 4, 57, 154, 171, 206; and the French Crown, 141, 142; and the Hundred Years War, 143–5; death, 146; and chivalry, 156; founds Order of the Garter, 156, 158

Edward IV, king of England (1442–83), and Charles the Rash, 186, 187, 188, 189, 239; lands in France, 239

Edward, the Black Prince (1330–76), 4; and the Hundred Years War, 144–5; his chivalry, 152–3; sacks Limoges, 153

Elizabeth, princess of York (1465–1503), 188

Elizabeth of Görlitz, 186

Emilia, 21; Frederick II and, 34

Empire, Holy Roman, and European kings, 1; relations with the papacy, 6; and meetings of town representatives, 13; lack of bureaucratic machinery, 17, 74; succession remains elective, 73–4; Pope John XXII and, 80; loses its strength to the princes, 81; in decline, 120; and the Great Schism, 130; and the vicariate, 215; opposes French intervention in Italy, 245; loses territory, 260; its Church and the papacy, 264–5

England, the monarchy in, 1, 5, 8, 13; strength of its powerful subjects, 4; the king's right to impose taxation, 15; its bureaucratic machinery, 17, 18, 19, 20; Venice compared with, 43; and Louis IX, 56, 57; the king's need for money to wage war, 59; parliamentary development compared with France's, 69; agreement on kingly primogeniture, 73; and military support from the Empire, 78; its growing nationalism, 79; the famines of 1315–17, 99; expenditure on Hundred Years War, 103; after the famines of 1314–16, 105 and n[1]; and Flemish cloth industry, 105–6; the Peasants' Revolt, 107; fall in land values, 112; dispute with France over Gascony, 117; and the Great Schism, 130; military successes in Hundred Years War, 143, ff.; use of the longbow, 154; less class conscious than France, 156; and the Armagnac-Burgundy civil war, 183; relations with Burgundy, 183–5, 186 ff.; 195, 232; and Flanders, 188, 192; and the later crusades, 207; accepted as heir to French throne, 232; and Joan of Arc, 233–4; France and the civil war, 238–9; end of its claim to French crown, 239

Epirus, despots of, 42, 44, 198

Erasmus (? 1469–1536), 272; his learning and influence, 270; and indulgences, 271; printing of his works, 274

Ernest of Pardubice, archbishop of Prague, 132

Estates, the French, and the disasters of the Hundred Years War, 145–6, 147; *États Généraux*, 243

Este, the, 35, 177, 215, 217, 227

Euboea, 210

Eudes IV, duke of Burgundy (1315–49), 180

Eugenius IV, Pope (1431–47), 266; and Council of Basle, 129

Europe, economic expansion in the Middle Ages, 96–9; reasons for decline, 99–103; effect of the Black Death on, 103–104; popular unrest in, 107; technological progress in, 112; fragmentation of its S.E. regions, 202; conquest of the S.E. by Ottoman Turks, 202–4, 205, 210–12; division between medieval and modern history, 277; changes between thirteenth and sixteenth centuries, 288–90; *see also*, under individual countries

Exchequer, the, emergence of, 19

Eyck, Jan van (*c*. 1389–1441), 194

Falkirk, battle of, 144

Famines, of 1315–17, 99–100; of 1314–16, 105

Felix V, Pope (1439–49), 129

Ferdinand III, king of Castile (1217–52), 246

Ferdinand IV, king of Castile (d. 1312), 16

Ferdinand V of Castile, II of Aragon and Sicily and III of Naples (1452–1516), 246, 250–1; ruler of Spain, 251 ff.; organizes the *Mesta*, 254; relations with the papacy, 255; war against the Moors, 256; Pyrenean acquisitions, 257

Ferrara, dominated by Estensi, 35, 177, 215, 217

Ficino, Marsilio (1433–99), 227, 228

Flanders, 6n[3], 30; a state in itself, 3–4; its autonomous units, 20, 21, 29; relationship between trade and agriculture, 21; opposition to oligarchy, 27; relationship with France, 27, 58, 61, 106, 117, 130, 142, 181; its *échevins*, 29; Louis IX and, 56; Philip IV's campaign in, 58–9; and the German Crown, 76; cultivation of new land in, 96; the famines of 1315–17, 99, 100; decline of the cloth industry, 105–6, 107, 192; popular unrest in, 107, 108; Edward III becomes vicar-general, 142; its bankers and Charles the Rash, 187; England's bid for her aid, 188; administration of, 191; its improvement under Philip the Bold, 192; affected by industrial decline, 192; Louis XI and, 242

Flanders, count of, 20, 142

Fleta (*c*. 1290), 14

Florence, its increasing prosperity, 23–4, 35, 172; Dante and, 24, 28–9; Villani and, 24, 106, 107, 161; moves against magnates, 26; efforts to prevent a tyranny, 28; the Bardi, 98, 106, 109, 171; and banking, 106, 109, 171–2; and the cloth trade, 106–7; popular unrest in (the *Ciompi*), 107–8; and the Medici, 109, 220–6, 278; 'War of the Eight Saints', 120; and the papacy, 122; education in, 161–2; position of its artists 164–5, 166; its certainty of rebirth, 166–7, 172–3; patronage of the arts in, 171–2, 176; under tyrants, 214; the Angevins and, 216; in opposition to the Visconti, 218; the Sforza and

219; Lorenzo Medici and, 222–5; Council of the Hundred, 223; becomes an annexe of the papacy, 225; its patrons, 227–8; Guicciardini and, 277, 278–80; Machiavelli and, 281
Flotte, Pierre, 60, 64
Foix, 237
Folgore of San Gimignano (thirteenth century), 163
France, position of its monarchy, 1, 3, 4, 8–9, 13, 55, 56–7, 73, 145, 290; its linguistic divisions, 3, 70; territorial lordships, 3–4; bureaucratic machinery, 17, 18, 19, 57, 59; its local government, 19–20; autonomous units in the South, 21–2; relationship with Flanders, 27; hereditary descent of the Capetians, 30 and n, 74, 141; predominate influence in south and central Italy, 37, 55, 56; Sicily's hatred of, 48, 49; war with Edward I, 58; the king's need for money to wage war, 59, 63; the monarchy's territorial acquisitions, 61–2, 74; its increased control in the municipalities, 62–3; its appellate jurisdiction, 63; levies a tax on Church revenues, 63, 67, 145; methods of taxing the laity, 67–8; informality of its parliamentary gatherings, 69; minor reform in Crown policy, 69–70; growing sense of nationality, 70–2, 79; moves towards strong central government, 72; and hereditary succession to the Crown, 73, 74; relations with Empire, 78; the famines of 1314–17, 99, 100, 105; disasters wrought by Hundred Years War, 100–3, 107, 143, 145; popular unrest in, 107; and the papacy, 116, 117, 118–20, 125 ff.; dispute with England over Gascony, 117, 141; struggle to resist domination by England, 130; and the possession of Aquitaine, 140–1; change of dynasty in, 141–2; in the Hundred Years War, 143–5, 147–8; at its nadir, 148, 232; fails to learn from defeat, 155–6; begins to consider causes of defeat, 157; influence on Italian culture, 170–1; Burgundian ambitions and, 178, 181, 185, 186–8; and the later crusades, 207; ambitions in Italy, 224, 225; comes to terms with Burgundy, 234; its recuperation, 234 ff.; acquires Brittany, 243–4; intervention in Italy, 244–5, 257; loses power in Italy, 245, 281; and the affairs of Castile, 247; effect of her invasion of Italy, 277 ff.
Franche-Comté, 61, 79, 180, 181, 190, 195
Francis II, duke of Brittany (d. 1488), 243
Franciscans, the, 71, 122
Frankfurt, 81; and printing, 274
Frederick II, Emperor (1194–1250), 10, 12, 13, 25; his attempt to dominate Italy, 33–4, 39, 76, 216; effect of his death, 34–5, 54; dislike of Germany, 75; deposed by Innocent IV, 76
Frederick III, Emperor (1415–93), 83,

159; the house of Burgundy and, 188, 189, 240; his harassed reign, 260; his Concordat of Vienna, 261
Frederick II, king of Sicily, 50, 199
Frederick, prince of Meissen, 82
Frederick, prince of Nuremberg, 82
Frederick of Habsburg (d. 1330), and the German Crown, 80, 87
Frederick III, elector of Saxony (1463–1525), and Luther, 272–4
Friesland, 81
Frisia, 185, 191
Froissart, Jean (c. 1333–c. 1405), 97n, 102, 114–15; and chivalry, 155, 156
Fuggers, the, 263, 271

Galicia, 5
Gallipoli, 199, 202
Gama, Vasco da (c. 1469–1525), 258
Gascony, 96, 97; disastrous effect of the Hundred Years War, 101–2; Anglo-French dispute over, 117, 130, 140–1, 142
Geneva, 241
Genoa, 36, 37, 107, 190, 218; its trading rights in Byzantium, 43, 97; defeats Pisa at Meloria, 46; and the arts, 176; its mercenaries, 199, 202; its Crusade, 206–7
Germany, without a ruler, 1–3, 77; church lands in, 6; its episcopate, 6n[2]; its laws, 6n[3]; its *Reichstage*, 12, 13; its *Landstage*, 13; fails to instal hereditary succession, 30, 73; elective nature of kingly succession in, 73–4; enfeebled by its lack of unity, 74–5, 79; effect of Frederick II's policy on, 75–6; under double rule, 76–7; its electoral college of princes, 77–8, 79, 81; under the Habsburgs, 78–9, 80, 260, 290; relations with the papacy, 80, 81, 119, 261, 264–5; importance of the 'Golden Bull', 81, 83; its history in its principalities, 81, 83; Pius II on its political troubles, 83; the Hanseatic and other Leagues, 83–5; warfare between towns and barons, 85; colonization of its frontier territories, 96; the famines of 1313–15, 99, 100; farming conditions, 111–12; and the Great Schism, 130; and Bohemia, 131, 138; the Lutheran Reformation and, 260; and the Low Countries, 260–1; the Concordat of Vienna and, 261; increasing power of its feudatories, 261–2, 263; poverty of princes, 262; its towns lose authority, 262; impotence of its monarchy, 263; efforts at constitutional reform, 263–4; position of the Church, 264–5, 268; interest in its past, 265–6, 275–6; detestation of the papacy, 266, 267; Luther's efforts at reform, 272–4
Ghent, 21, 58, 181; oligarchical government, 23, 27; its *échevins*, 29; Burgundy and, 191, 192, 193
Ghibellines, the, 36, 120, 214, 216; and Alfonso X, 77; and Henry VII, 79–80

Ghirlandaio, Domenico (1449–94), 228
Gibraltar, Strait of, and trade, 99
Gilds, the, 62; the *popolo* and, 27; the *Ciompi* and, 107–8
Giotto di Bondone (1267–1337), 165, 166, 171
Gonzalo Fernández de Cordoba (1453–1515), 256, 257, 258
Government, local, in the Middle Ages, 19 ff.
Granada, 252; remains in Muslim hands, 246; reconquest of, 255, 256–7
Grange, Jean de la, bishop of Amiens, and Urban VI, 125
Granson, battle of, 90, 188
Great League of Upper Germany, 91
Greece, 204; its empire in Trebizond, 42; Venetian conquests in, 42, 43; and the Genoese, 43; Michael Palaeologus and, 44, 55; return of its Empire, 55; Italian culture and, 170; Ottoman Turks and, 202, 203
Gregory IX, Pope (1227–41), 55
Gregory X, Pope (1271–6), 78; resides at Lyons, 116
Gregory XI, Pope (1370–8), 119, 122; restores the papacy to Rome, 118, 124
Gregory XII, Pope (1406–15), 127, 133
Groot, Gerard (1340–84), 269–70
Guelders, 187
Guelfs, the, 214, 216; assist Charles of Anjou, 38
Guicciardini, Francesco (1483–1540), 22, 258; and the invasion of Charles VIII, 277–8; his career, 278; political writings, 278–80; compared with Machiavelli, 280, 281, 283
Guicciardini, Niccolò, 281 and n²
Guines, 61, 237
Guy of Dampierre, count of Flanders, (*fl.* 1300), 27
Guyenne, 235, 238

Habsburgs, the, 195; election of Rudolf I, 78; and the Swiss Confederation, 87–8, 89–90; and Spain, 259; and Germany, 260, 290
Hainault, 81, 142, 181, 185, 191; separated from Flanders, 61
Halidon Hill, battle of, 144
Hanse, the, 97, 108, 112, 239, 254; and Antwerp, 193
Hanseatic League, 86, 192, 262; its formation, 83–4
Harfleur, 61; siege of, 147
Henry VI, Emperor (1165–97), 34, 36, 42, 77; strives for hereditary succession, 74
Henry VII (Henry of Luxembourg) *c.* 1269–1313), Emperor, his Italian ambitions, 79–80, 120, 217; and the vicariate, 215
Henry II, king of Castile (d. 1379), 247
Henry III, king of Castile (d. 1406), 247
Henry IV (the Impotent), king of Castile (d. 1474), 247, 250, 251, 253

Henry III, king of England (1207–72), 35 and n, 37, 56, 76
Henry IV, king of England (1367–1413), 183, 198
Henry V, king of England (1387–1422), 198; and the Hundred Years War, 147, 155; and Burgundy, 183, 184; feted in Paris, 232
Henry VI, king of England (1421–71), 184, 236; his birth, 232; deposition and restoration, 239
Henry VII, king of England, (1457–1509), 188
Henry II, king of France (1519–59), 159
Henry, son of Frederick II, 76
Henry of Ghent (d. 1293), 71
Henry of Langenstein, and Conciliar authority, 128
Henry 'the generous', count of Champagne, 149
Herder, J. G. (1744–1803), 160
Hohenstaufen, 77; the papacy and, 35, 36, 37, 77, 129
Hohenzollern, 271; foundation of their power, 82, 86
Holland, 81, 181, 185, 191
Honorius IV, Pope (1285–7), 50–1
Hospitallers, the, 67
Humanists, Italian, 167; German, 265, 266
Humphrey, duke of Gloucester (1391–1447), 184–5
Hundred Years War, destruction wrought by, 100–3, 107; Avignon popes and, 119–20; events leading up to, 141–2; military successes of England, 143–5, 147; Burgundy and, 178; its liquidation, 239
Hungary, 3, 82, 83, 204, 207; and the Great Schism, 130; and Turks, 208, 212; mining in, 262–3
Hunyady, John (*c.* 1387–1456), 208, 209, 210
Huss, John (*c.* 1369–1415), early career, 133; excommunicated, 133–4; death, 134; his preaching, 134–5
Hussitism, 82, its wars, 101, 135, 137; in Bohemia, 129, 133; its tenets, 134–5; the Taborites and, 135–7; becomes a national war, 137–9; and the 'Compactata' of 1436, 139; consequences of, 139; Luther and, 273
Hutten, Ulrich von (1488–1523), 265, 266

Industry, the growth of towns and, 21; and long distance commerce, 97
Innocent III, Pope (1198–1216), 13, 71; *Contempt of Worldly Things,* 163
Innocent IV, Pope (1243–54); deposes Frederick II, 34, 39, 55, 76; and the Sicilian succession, 35–6; resides at Lyons, 116
Innocent VI, Pope (1352–62), 119, 121, 123
Innocent VII, Pope (1404–6), 127
Innocent VIII, Pope (1484–92), 228, 266, 267

Inquisition, its institution in Spain, 255
Isabel, Queen, wife of Charles VI, 183
Isabella, Queen (1292–1358), wife of Edward II, 140, 141, 142
Isabella, Queen, wife of Ferdinand II (d. 1504), 246, 250–1; her character, 252; as a ruler, 252 ff.; *see also* Ferdinand
Isabella of Portugal, 189; queen of John II of Castile, 247
Italy, relationship between trade and agriculture, 21; origin of the communes, 27–8; strife within its city-states, 28; Frederick II and, 33–4; effect of Frederick's death on, 34–5, 54; Henry VII and, 79–80, 215; Lewis IV and, 80–1; cultivation of new land in, 96; and the cloth trade, 105, 106–7; commercial setbacks, 106–7; economic recovery in, 112; and papal residence, 116–19; its cultural and intellectual history, 161 ff.; civic patriotism in (*Campanilismo*), 164–6; did it really experience renaissance, 167 ff.; invaded by Ottomans, 212; weakness of the communes, 213–14, tyrants and the republics, 214–15; defeat of republican institutions in, 216–17; French claims in, 224, 225, 244; shattering of French supremacy in, 245; Spanish domination in, 249,257; Maximilian I and, 264; effect of Charles VIII's invasion on, 277–8
Italy, Central, autonomous units, 20, 21; claimed by the papacy, 33; French predominance in, 37; the Black Death and, 103 and n¹; popular unrest in, 107; loss of papal authority in, 120; and the vicariate, 120–1, 215; under tyrannies, 215, 226
Italy, Northern, without a ruler, 1–3; its republics, 5, 213 14; its autonomous units, 20, 33, 34; and the *contado*, 28 and n²; internal strife in its towns, 28–9, 214; Frederick II and, 34; dominated by single lords, 35; Charles of Anjou and, 37, 39; gains from the imperial withdrawal, 54; the famines of 1315–17, 99; under tyrannies, 215–26; loss of French power in, 245
Italy, Southern, the monarchy in, 5, 13; destruction of its archives, 18; its bureaucratic machinery, 18, 19; part of the Mediterranean zone, 33; Frederick II and, 33; in theory a papal fief, 35; French predominance in, 37, 56; loss of French power in, 245

Jacoubek of Stříbo, 135
Jacqueline, countess of Hainault, 184–5
Jacques de Lalaing (1421–53), 151–2, 159
James I (1213–76), king of Aragon, 14, 36; negotiates with the Catalan Estates, 30–2; and Barcelona, 45–6; and Morocco, 46–7
James II, king of Aragon (*c.* 1260–1327), 50

Jerusalem, 58; duties of ruler and ruled in its monarchy, 9; its Court of Burgesses, 9
Jews, the, 59; in Spain, 252, 255; their expulsion, 255–6
Joan of Arc, St (*c.* 1412–31), 4, 185, 233–4
Joan of Navarre, marries Philip IV, 61
Joanna II, queen of Naples (d. 1435), 244
Joanna *la Beltraneja* (b. 1462), 250, 251, 252
John XXII, Pope (1316–34), 119, 122; and Lewis IV, 80; his nepotism, 123
John XXIII, Pope (1410–15), his election, 127; and Ladislas of Naples, 134
John, king of Bohemia, 80, 81, 120, 142
John I, king of Castile (d. 1390), 247
John II, king of Castile (d. 1454), 247, 250, 251
John, king of England (1167–1216), 18
John II, king of France (1319–64), 144, 206; imprisonment, 145, 155, 180; death, 146; his Order of the Star, 158; acquisitions in Burgundy, 180
John V Palaeologus, Emperor, 202, 205
John VI Cantacuzenus, Emperor, 202
John VIII Palaeologus, Emperor, 210
John I, king of Portugal (1357–1433), 151
John IV Lascaris, 44
John of Lancaster, duke of Bedford (1389–1435), 184, 234
John, duke of Berry, 180, 181
John, duke of Bourbon, 181
John the Fearless, duke of Burgundy (1371–1419), 147, 181–3, 184, 189; and the Crusade of Nicopolis, 207
John IV, duke of Burgundy, marriage to Jacqueline of Hainault, 184
John, duke of Calabria, 237, 239
John of Gaunt, duke of Lancaster (1340–99), 4, 130, 189
John of Procida, 48
Joinville, Jean, Sire de (1224–1317), 4, 7 and n¹; and chivalry (*Life of St Louis*), 148–9
Juliers, 142
Julius II, Pope (1503–13), 226, 257, 267, 271
Justinian I, Emperor (*c.* 482–565), influence of his legal code, 9, 13, 16

Kingship, medieval theories of, 7–12; hereditary and elective, 73–4; *see also* Monarchy
Knighthood, Orders of, 156, 158
Kossovo, battle of, 205; (second), 209
Küstendil, battle of, 204

La Marche, 61
Ladislas, king of Naples, John XXIII's crusade against, 134
Ladislas, kings of Poland, 208
Lancaster, Edmund, earl of (1245–96), and the Sicilian succession, 35 and n, 76
Lancia, Conrad, 45
Landucci, Luca, 224

Languedoc, 118, 119, 145, 237; its lawyers and notaries, 21
Latini, Brunetto (*c.* 1210–*c.* 1295), 171
Law, the, the monarchy and, 5–6, 8, 15; appellate jurisdiction, 6 and nn[1,3], 63; lawyers and notaries, 21
Lawyers, 21; their employment as ministers in France, 59–60; in medieval Italy, 167
Leo X, Pope (1513–21), 223, 225, 229, 267, 271; his bull 'Exsurge Domine', 272
León, 5, 14, 16, 18
Leonardo da Vinci (1452–1519), 227, 228; offers his services, 229–31
Leopold, duke of Austria, 87; Leopold, nephew of above, 88
Lepanto, battle of, 212
Levant, the, 9, 55; Venice and, 43; Genoa and, 43
Lewis IV, Emperor (Lewis of Bavaria) (*c.* 1287–1347), 142; intervention in Italy, 80–1, 120; fails to achieve an imperial revival, 81; supported by Swiss cantons, 87
Liége, 20, 29, 142, 186, 238
Liguria, 176
Lille, 58, 191
Limburg, 184, 191
Limoges, sack of, 153
Lodi, peace of, 221
Lombardy, 20, 37, 59, 107; Frederick II and, 34; subject to tyranny, 35, 216; Charles of Anjou and, 39; its textile industry, 112
London, governed by the wealthy, 23; and maritime trade, 97
London, treaty of, 187, 239
Lorraine, 79, 186, 188, 240
Louis IX, St, king of France (1215–70), 1, 3, 4, 35, 63, 246; and kingship, 7, 9; and the Sicilian succession, 37; Crusade against Tunis, 46; his reputation for justice, 56–7; canonized by Boniface VIII, 64
Louis X, king of France (1289–1316), 67, 69, 140
Louis XI, king of France (1423–83), 90; Charles the Rash and, 186, 187, 195, 235, 238, 239, 240, 285; his gains for France, 195, 236–7, 241; as Dauphin, 235; his character, 235–6; coalition against, 237; prisoner at Péronne, 238, 285; and the English civil war, 238–9; buys off Edward IV, 239; his preference for financial methods, 239–40, 241; and Burgundy, 240; his achievements, 241–3; and Flanders, 242; his fiscal machine, 242–3; and Aragon, 251; Commynes and, 285
Louis XII, king of France (1462–1515), 245, 264
Louis, duke of Anjou, 180
Louis, duke of Orléans, 181, 232, 241; in rebellion, 243; marriage, 244
Louis II de Bourbon, and the Franco-Genoese Crusade, 206–7

Louis de Male, count of Flanders, 180, 181
Louis of Bruges, lord of Gruuthuse, 193
Low Countries, 142, 191–2, 195, 260–1, 269
Lübeck, 82, 84, 234
Lucca, 107, 109, 216, 218
Lucerne, 88
Lull, Ramon (1232–1315/16), and reconquest of Syria from Moslems, 205–6
Luna, Alvaro de (d. 1453), 247
Luther, Martin (1483–1546), 6, 260, 269; opposition to papal taxation, 265; and Rome, 268; and Erasmus, 270, 271; protests against indulgences, 271–2; address to the German princes, 273; strength of his teaching, 273–4
Luxembourg, 142, 186, 190
Lyonnais, 79
Lyons, acquired by the Crown, 62; papal residence at, 116, 117; Louis XI and, 241

Macedonia, 204, 205
Machiavelli, Niccolò (1469–1527), 214; and the Swiss, 90; his writings, 280–1, 282, 285; career, 281–2, 285, 286; friendship with Guicciardini, 283–4; compared with Commynes, 285–8; and Cesare Borgia, 285–6; and statecraft, 288
Mâcon, 185
Madeira, 258
Maghreb, the, Barcelona's trade with, 46
Magna Carta, 8
Magnates, relationship with the monarchy, 1, 3, 5, 12–13; movements against in Italy, 26–7; their privileges in Germany, 75
Mahomet II, Sultan (1430–81), captures Constantinople, 208–9, 210; character, 209; further campaigns, 210
Maine, 236, 241
Mainz, 77, 132, 271; and leagues of cities, 84; archbishops of, 83, 85, 263, 269
Malaga, capture of, 256
Malatesta, the, and Rimini, 15, 121, 215
Malory, Sir Thomas (d. 1471), and chivalry, 158–9
Manetti, Giannozzo (1396–1459), 163, 228
Manfred, king of Sicily (1232–66), 8n[1], 39, 44; his accession and conquests, 36; overthrow and supersession, 36–8; Jean de Meung and, 41; discontent of his exiles, 47, 48
Manrique, Gómez, 253
Mantegna, Andrea (1431–1506), 228
Mantua, 170, 177
Marcel, Étienne (*c.* 1317–58), 146
Marcell, Aymergot, 102; and pillaging, 114–15
Marck, 142
Margaret, countess of Flanders, 180
Margaret, wife of Philip the Bold, 180–1

Margaret of Anjou, queen of Henry VI (1429-82), 239
Marignola, Giovanni da, 132
Marigny, Enguerrand de, 68
Marseilles, 108, 241, 244
Martin IV, Pope (1281-5), 54; and Charles of Anjou, 41, 45, 49, 50, 57; and the Germans, 41 and n[1]; excommunicates Sicilian rebel towns, 49; succeeded by a Roman pope, 50; and France's Aragonese campaign, 63
Martin V, Pope (1417-31), unifies the papacy, 127; and conciliar authority, 128-9
Martin I, king of Aragon (d. 1410), 250
Mary of Burgundy, daughter of Charles the Rash, 195, 240, 260-1
Matthias Corvinus (c. 1443-90), king of Hungary, 260
Maximilian I, Emperor (1459-1519), 90; and chivalry, 159; his marriage, 195, 240, 244, 260-1; and constitutional reforms, 263-4; his need for troops and money, 264
Medici family, 176, 187; and Florence, 109, 220-6; their forty-year crisis, 225; as patrons, 227-8; and the papacy, 267
Medici, Alessandro dei, 226
Medici, Cosimo dei (1389-1464), 109, 172, 220, 226; his rule, 221; character, 221-2, 225; as a patron, 227
Medici, Foligno dei, 109
Medici, Giovanni dei (d. 1429), 109; (II) 227
Medici, Giuliano dei (d. 1478), 223-4, 266
Medici, Giulio (later Clement VII) (1478-1534), 225-6, 229
Medici, Lorenzo dei (1449-92), 244, 267; his duality in government, 222; his autocratic rule, 222-3; the Pazzi conspiracy against, 223-4, 266; his reputation, 224-5; as a patron, 228
Medici, Piero dei, (1414-69), 222, 227-8, 278; (1471-1503), 225
Mediterranean Zone, its traditional town life, 21; its unity, 33; Venetian ambitions in, 42-3; the Genoese and, 43; Aragonese sea power, 45, 55; expanding maritime trade, 97; Louis XI and, 241; its enduring importance, 289
Meloria, battle of, 46
Mercenaries, 199, 202, 216; Catalan, 199; French, 234, 235
Merchants, make use of representatives and agents, 98-9
Messina, 48; revolts against Charles of Anjou, 49, 50
Meung, Jean de (c. 1250-1305), and Manfred, 41
Mexico, 258
Meyr, Martin, 83
Mézières, Philippe de, 206, 208
Michael VIII, Palaeologus, Emperor (1234-82), 3, 43; comes to power through usurpation, 44; his shrunken heritage, 44, 198; submits the Greek

Church to the papacy, 45; and Charles of Anjou's ambitions, 48, 50
Michelangelo (1475-1564), 271
Middlebourg, 192
Milan, 21, 37, 109, 110, 264; dominated by Della Torre, 35, 216, 217; dominated by Visconti, 35, 120, 215, 216, 217-18; acquires the title of Duchy, 215, 217; the Sforza and, 215-16, 217, 218-20; its administration, 218; relations with Venice, 218, 219, 221; relations with Florence, 221, 224; fear of France, 224; Orléans and, 244
Milič, John (d. 1374), 132
Mohacz, battle of, 212
Mohammedans, the, in Spain, 246, 249, 252; their expulsion, 255-7
Molay, Jacques de (d. 1314), 66
Molinet, Jean (1435-1507), 150
Monarchy, the, its position in France, 1, 3, 4, 8-9, 13, 55-7; in Spain, 5, 246, 248, 249-50, 252; and self governing areas, 5; and the law, 5-6, 15; relations with its vassals, 7; medieval theories of kingship, 7-12; coronation oaths, 8; and the development of parliament, 13-15; and taxation, 15; its bureaucratic machinery, 16-20; and local administration, 19-20; weakness of its central control, 29-30; and hereditary succession, 30; its need for money to wage war, 59; and concessions in return for taxation, 69; agreement on primogeniture, 73; Charles VII and, 235; its impotence in Germany, 262; strengthened by the sixteenth century, 289-90
Mons-en-Pévèle, battle of, 58
Montaperti, battle of, 36, 38
Monte Cassino, monastery of, 10, 169
Montefeltro, the, 215, 227
Montereau, 183, 185, 234
Montferrat, Boniface of, king of Thessalonica, 42
Montferrat, marquis of, 37
Montfort, Jean de, 143
Montlhéry, battle of, 237
Montpellier, 62
Morat, battle of, 90, 188
Moravia, 79, 83; the Hussites and its Church, 139
Morgarten, battle of, 87, 90; description of, 91-4
Morocco, 258
Mortimer, Roger, earl of March (1287-1330), 141, 142
Mühldorf, battle of, 80
Municipalities, see Towns
Muntaner, Ramon, his *Chronicle*, 199-200
Müntzer, Thomas (c. 1490-1525), 273
Murad I, Sultan (d. 1389), 205
Murad II, Sultan, 208, 209
Mussato, Alberto (1261-1329), 165, 167
Mytilene, Mahomet II and, 209, 210

Nancy, battle of, 188

Naples, 10, 18, 66, 98, 120, 130, 167, 190, 236; the Sforzas and, 219; the Medici and, 224; fear of France, 224; the Angevins and, 244; passes to Charles V, 245; Aragon and, 249, 250, 257

Nationalism, in France, 70–2, 79, 233; and conciliar authority, 129, 130–1, 265; in Germany, 265, 275–6

Navarre, 145, 243; French intervention in, 57; acquired by the Crown, 61; claimed by Aragon, 251; acquired by Spain, 257

Nemours, 241

Nepotism, 266; Nicholas IV and, 40, 51; Clement V and, 121

Neri Acciauoli, lord of Corinth (fl. 1390), 202

Netherlands, England and, 78, 79; German acquisitions in, 81; and the Hundred Years War, 142

Nicaea, 42

Niccoli, Niccolo, 227

Nicholas III, Pope (1277–80), 67; rules through family connections, 39–40, 51

Nicholas IV, Pope (1288–92), 51

Nicholas V, Pope (1447–55), 129, 266; as a patron, 228, 271; Frederick III and, 261

Nicholas of Dresden, 135

Nicopolis, 155, 186, 189; crusade of, 205–6, 207, 208

Ninfa, 53–4

Nogaret, Guillaume de (d. 1313), 60; and Boniface VIII, 54, 65; and the Templars, 66

Normandy, 237, 242; acquisition of, 7, 30; increased maritime trade, 112–13; and the Hundred Years War, 143, 144; recovered by Charles VII, 235

Northampton, John of (fl. 1376–90), 23

Novellino, Il, 98, 162

Nuremberg, 108, 262; 'Common Peace' of, 275

Nymphaeum, treaty of, 43, 44

Oldřich of Rožmberk, 139

Oligarchy, in the towns, 22; defeats itself, 23; must assimilate new members, 25–6; opposition to, 26–7; in the college of cardinals, 123–4

Ordelaffi, the, 121

Order of St. James, Alfonso IX and, 5–6

Orders, military, in Spain, 248, 253, 254, 256

Orders, religious, 10, 71, 122; and the papal schism, 1378–9, 126; in the Northern Church, 269

Orléans, 242; relief of, 233; house of, 237

Orsini, the, 51, 53, 54; and the papacy, 40–1

Orvieto, 28n[1], 37

Otranto, 212

Ottokar II of Bohemia, 77

Ottoman Turks, 155; origin and expansion, 202–3, 205; government of subject people, 203–4; and Nicopolis, 207; extinguish Byzantium, 208–10; further

campaigns, 210–12; growth of seapower, 212; effect of their conquests on Europe, 212; Italian fear of, 224

Padua, 21n, 35, 107, 167, 171–2, 216, 218

Palermo, 36, 50; and the 'Sicilian Vespers', 49

Palestine, its diminishing Christian strip, 198

Pallavicino, Hubert, 35, 36, 216

Palmieri, Matteo (fl. 1439), 163–4, 176; and Giotto, 166; and education (*Della Vita Civile*), 175

Papacy, 33; seeks to control whole Church, 6, 64–5; and appellate jurisdiction, 6–7; and refusals to grant taxes, 15; and correspondence, 18; relationship with the emperor, 34, 55, 264–5; and the Sicilian succession, 35–9, 49, 50; vacant after Clement IV's death, 39; split into French and Italian factions, 40 and n[1], 50, 70, 116, 129; burdened by the Sicilian war, 50; appointment of a Roman pope, 50–1; its involvement in the fate of south and central Italy, 55; and taxation of church revenues, 63–4, 265; Boniface VIII states its supremacy in *Unam Sanctam*, 64–5; Lewis IV and, 80–1; the Medici and, 109, 221, 223, 225; and residence in Rome, 116–19, 126; institutes the vicariate, 121, 215; relations with the college of cardinals, 123–5; rivalry between Urban VI and Clement VII (the Great Schism), 125–7, 129–31; unified under Martin V, 127; conciliar authority and, 128–9, 130; political background to Great Schism, 130; and Philip VI, 142; as art patron, 228–9; Spain and, 255; German detestation of, 266, 267; its descent into nepotism and worldliness, 266–7; Luther and, 271–2

Papal States, 6, 12, 13, 36, 66; weakening of imperial power, 35; during the vacancy in the papal see, 39; Martin IV and, 41, 63; Nicholas IV and, 51; Avignon popes and, 120; and the vicariate, 121; pacified by Albornoz, 121–2; tyrants of, 226

Paris, 10, 185, 241; fetes the English, 232; remonstrances of, 232; reoccupied by French, 234

Paris, University of, and papal election, 125, 127–8; founding of, 148

Parliament, development from municipal representation, 13–16; its activities, 16; early difficulties of representation, 16; a means of demonstrating national solidarity, 67; its informal nature in France, 68–9

Parma, 216

Passerini, Cardinal, 225

Paul II, Pope (1464–71), 266

Paul III, Pope (1534–49), 229

Pavia, 35, 216; battle of, 226, 245, 257

Pazzi conspiracy, 223–4

Peasant, the, 96–7, 111; and the Hundred Years War, 101–2; revolts by, 107, 274
Peasants' War, 274
Pepoli, the, 226
Percy, Bishop Thomas (1729–1811), 160
Péronne, 186, 238, 285
Perpignan, 257
Peru, 258
Perugia, 107, 218; laws against magnates, 26; the Five and, 28n[1]; papal conclave at, 116
Perugino (*c.* 1450–1523), 228
Peter III, the Great, king of Aragon (1236–86), 36, 152, 250; and the conquest of Sicily, 47, 48, 49–50
Peter the Cruel, king of Castile (1334–69), 247
Peter I, king of Cyprus, 206
Peter of Alençon, 58
Petrarch, Francesco (1304–74), 250; and papal residence, 118–19; love of the countryside, 162; his significance for the Renaissance, 165, 168–9; his career, 167–8; and intellectual authority, 169; meeting with Charles IV, 170
Peutinger, Konrad (1465–1547), on Rome, 267 ff
Philip II (Philip-Augustus) king of France (1165–1223), 56, 61, 69
Philip III, king of France (1245–85), 7, 8; his conservative nature, 57; his need for money, 57–8, 67; territorial acquisitions, 61
Philip IV, the Fair, king of France (1268–1314), 16, 27, 44; and Boniface VIII, 54, 64–5; his Flemish campaign, 58–9, 71; employs lawyers as officials, 59–60; territorial acquisitions, 61; relationship with the papacy, 63–5, 67, 69, 117; and the Templars, 65–7; taxation of the laity, 67–8, 71
Philip V, king of France (*c.* 1293–1322), 67, 140; taxation of the laity, 68; his assemblies, 70
Philip VI, king of France (1293–1350), 119, 287; his accession, 141; character, 142; declares Gascony confiscate, 142; death, 144
Philip II, king of Spain (1527–98), 245
Philip the Bold, duke of Burgundy (1342–1404), and Charles VI, 180, 181; his marriage, 180–1; extends his power, 181; his revenues, 191; and Flanders, 192, 194
Philip de Rouvres, duke of Burgundy (d. 1361), 180
Philip the Good, duke of Burgundy (1396–1467), 190, 192; founds Order of the Golden Fleece, 158, 189, 194; and the English, 183–5; and Joan of Arc, 185; and Charles VII, 185–6, 234; European acquisitions, 186; and van Eyck, 194; his personal tastes, 194–5; his Banquet, 196–7; and the Crusade of Nicopolis, 207; and Frederick III, 260

Philip, duke of Touraine, allotted the duchy of Burgundy, 180
Phocaea, 43, 48, 200
Picardy, 195, 237, 240
Picquigny, treaty of, 188, 189, 239
Piedmont, 37; Charles of Anjou and, 39
Piero della Francesca (*c.* 1420–92), 228
Pierrefonds, 61
Pinturicchio (1454–1513), 228
Pisa, 43, 46, 55, 98, 108, 109, 218; and Alfonso X, 77; and trade with Byzantium, 97; acquired by Florence, 112; Council at, 1409, 127, 130, 133
Pius II, Pope (Cardinal Aeneas Silvius Piccolomini) (1458–64), 219, 228, 266; and the woes of the Church in Germany, 83
Plague, 100, 103
Plegamans, Raymond, 46
Podèbrandy, king of Bohemia (1420–71), 260
Poitiers, 61, battle of, 143, 144–5, 152, 154, 180
Poitou, 30, 61
Poland, 3, 83, 130, 260
Polenta of Ravenna, 15
Poliziano, 228
Polo, Marco (1254–1324), 171
Ponthieu, 141, 145
Popolo, the, 26; origin of, 27–8, its organization, 28
Population, European increase in, 96; outstrips food production, 99
Portovenere, 98
Portugal, 190, 193; and the Great Schism, 130; Spanish ambitions and, 247; invades Spain, 251; maritime adventures, 257–8
Poujet, Cardinal Bertrand du, 121
Pragmatic Sanction of Bourges, 244, 261
Prague, under Charles IV, 132, 133; held by Žižka, 138
Presles, Raoul de, 60
Printing, and Lutheranism, 274
Prokop the Bald, General, 138, 139
Provence, 3, 37, 45, 236, 241; and trade, 98; its troubadours, 171
Prussia, 83, 112
Pulkava, Přibik, 132

Quercy, 61
Querini, Guglielmo (*c.* 1400–68), his business ventures, 110–11

Ragusa, 249
Raspe, Henry, anti-king (d. 1247), 76
Reformation, the, 1; splits Christian Europe, 212; intensifies German disunity, 260
Reggio, 216
Renaissance, the, 54; meaning of, 161; concept of the term, 165–7; was the term really justified, 167, 171, 177; effect of clerical celibacy on, 173 and n[3]; its bourgeois nature, 173–6; and patronage, 176–7, 226–9; *see also* Culture, Italian

Rentiers, increase in, 111
Representation, Parliamentary, its early difficulties, 16
Resumption, Act of, 252
Reuchlin controversy, 274
Rheims, 187
Rhenish League, 84–5
Rhens, 81
Rhineland, its towns, 262
Rhodes, 212, 249
Riccobaldo of Ferrara, admiration of the austere past 25
Richard I, king of England (1157–99), 73, 198
Richard II, king of England, (1367–1400), 146, 157, 181, 207, 232
Richard, earl of Cornwall (1209–72), 35; and the German Crown, 76–7, 78
Richemont, Constable, 233
Rimini, the Malatesta and, 15, 121, 215
Robert II, the Pious, king of France (d. 1031), 178
Robert of Naples, 216
Roger of Flor, his Catalan mercenaries, 199–200
Rolin, Nicholas, 194
Romagna, 15; the papacy and, 40, 41, 58, 118, 120, 121, 215; under tyranny, 216
Roman de la Rose, 41, 171
Romano, Ezzelin da, 35, 216
Rome, 35; its legal system, 9, 11, 18, 167; Charles of Anjou and, 38, 39; the papacy and its senatorship, 40, 41, 51; Boniface VIII and, 53; the Medici and, 109; papal residence at, 116–19; sacked by imperial troops, 225–6; rebuilding of St. Peter's 228, 229, 271; a 'Renaissance' city, 229; Germany and, 267–8
Rouen, 232, 241, 242
Rourergue, 61
Roussillon, 251, 257
Rucellai, Giovanni (1475–1525), and Florence's greatness, 166–7, 172–3, 176
Rudolf I, King of Romans (1218–91), 1, 40; summons a 'general court', 13; his chancery, 18n; his election, 78, 87; relations with France and England, 78–9
Rupert III, king of Romans (1352–1410), 82
Russia, under Tartar domination, 3; trade with, 111
Rustichello of Pisa, 171

Sacchetti, Franco (c. 1330–1400), 162
St Maur, treaty of, 237
St Pol, 241
St Sardou, village of, 141
Saisset, Bernard, bishop of Pamiers (d. c. 1314), 64
Saladin (1137–93), 198
Salinguerra, the, 217
Salutati, Coluccio, 163, 165
Sancho IV, king of Castile (d. 1295), 16
Sardinia, 45, 98, 249
Savelli, the, 51

Savonarola, Girolamo (1452–98), 244, 268, 281
Savoy, 181
Saxony, 7, 73, 77, 82; its double rule, 262
Scander Beg (c. 1405–68), 208, 212
Scandinavia, 3, 84, 99, 105, 108
Scotland, 117, 143, 144, 154; and the Great Schism, 126, 130; its universities, 130
Scrovegni, Enrico, 171–2
Scutage, 15
Selim I, Sultan (1467–1520), 212
Sempach, battle of, 88
Seneschal, the, 19–20
Senigallia, 285–6
Serbia, 202, 203; its brief empire under Dušan, 204–5; and battle of Kossovo, 205; regained by Mahomet II, 210
Seville, 5; recovered from the Moors, 246
Sforza, the, and Milan, 215–16, 217, 218–20, 255; and patronage, 227
Sforza, Francesco, duke of Milan, 218–9, 220, 221, 226, 227; and the papacy, 219; and Louis XI, 236, 237
Sforza, Francesco II, 219
Sforza, Gian-Galeazzo, 219
Sforza, Ludovico ('Il Moro'), 219, 227, 244
Sforza, Massimiliano, 219
Sheriffs, the, not recruited locally, 19
Sicily, its famous parliament, 13, 16; Frederick II and, 33; the struggle for its succession, 35–41, 58; and Byzantium, 42; conquered by Aragon, 47, 120; the Sicilian Vespers, 48–9, 199, 249; revolts against Charles of Anjou, 49; trade with, 98; passes to Charles V, 245
Siena, 28n[1], 36, 218; popular unrest in, 107; the Chigi of, 112; Council of, 1423, 129, 131
Sigismund, Emperor (1368–1437), 90, 188, 255; his character and achievements, 82–3; and Huss, 134; and Hussitism, 137–8; grants Alsace to Charles the Rash, 187; at Nicopolis, 207
Signorelli, Luca (c. 1441–1523), 228
Silesia, 83
Simmern, Rupert von, bishop of Strasbourg, 268–9
Simonetta, Cecco, 219
Sixtus IV, Pope (1471–84), 223; as a patron, 228; and the Inquisition, 255; his nepotism, 266, 267
Slav lands, 99; their bishops and monasteries, 6; rivalry with Germany, 131–2
Sluter, Claus (c. 1350–1405/6), 194
Smyrna, 43, 206
'Somme towns', 185, 186, 191, 234, 237, 240
Songe du Verger, Le, 157
Sorbon, Robert de (1201–74), 148–9
Spain, position of its monarchy, 1, 5, 246, 248, 249–50, 252–6; ubiquity of ecclesiastical lords, 6; its *cortes*, 14, 16,

248, 249, 253, 254; the king's right to impose taxation, 15, 253; its inadequate bureaucratic machinery, 17, 19; Frnech interventions in, 57; cultivation of new land, 96; and the Great Schism, 126; Flanders and, 193; opposes French intervention in Italy, 245; composed of different elements, 246; domination in Italy, 249, 257; joining of Castile and Aragon, 251 ff.; its religious disunity, 252, 254–6, 259; the *Hermandades*, 252; institution of *corregidors*, 253; financial recovery, 253–4; and the Inquisition, 255; military prowess, 256; maritime conquests, 258; sterility of the land, 258–9; its fundamental poverty, 259; *see also* Castile and Aragon

Spenser, Edmund (1552?–99), 160
Stans, Compact of, 90
Stephen Dušan (*c.* 1308–55), 'Emperor' of Serbia, 202, 204–5
Stephen Uroš III, Emperor of Serbia, 204
Stralsund, Peace of, 84
Strozzi, Palla (1372–1462), 172
Styria, 78, 79, 212
Swabian League, 90, 263
Swiss Confederation, 82, 187, 188, 240, 264; its development from existing corporations, 86–90, 260; united geographically, 86–7; and the Habsburgs, 87–8, 89–90; its new unions, 87–8, 88–9; acquires adherence of neighbouring zones, 88, 89, 90; the *Sempacherbrief*, 89; its dependence on armed strength, 89, 90; prestige of its pikemen, 90, 256; strength of its flexible constitution, 91
Syria, 45, 46, 49, 97

Taberner, 48
Taborites, 135–7, 138, 139
Tacitus (*c.* 55–120), *Germania*, 265–6
Tagliacozzo, battle of, 39
Talliapanis, Lazario, exports hats to Sicily, 98
Tartars, 3
Tavernini, 121
Taxation, rights of the king and, 15; in the Middle Ages, 23; and the monarchy's need to finance wars, 59; of Church revenues in France, 63–5, 67; the papacy and, 63–5, 67, 265; of the laity in France, 67–9; its relationship to concessions by the Crown, 69–70; justification of, 71–2; a result of war, 103, 145; the Hundred Years War and, 145
Templars, the, 59, 60, 119; founding of the Order, 65; accusations against, 66; suppressed by Philip IV, 66–7
Tetzel, Johann (*c.* 1455–1519), 271, 274
Thessalonica, 42, 44
Thessaly, 200, 202, 204
Thomas à Kempis (*c.* 1380–1471), 270
Thomas, Pierre de, 206

Thrace, 42, 111, 199, 203, 205
Thuringia, 79
Timur (Tamerlane) (1336–1405), 203, 208
Tlemcen, 46
Todi, Jacopone da (*c.* 1230–1306), and Boniface VIII, 52
Toledo, 5, 248, 253; recovered from the Moors, 246; and the *Mesta*, 254; in revolt, 255
Torgau, League of, 273
Toro, battle of, 251
Tortosa, 47
Toulouse, 30; a self-governing unit, 22; acquired by the crown, 61
Tours, 241, 242, 243; truce of, 234
Towns, powers of self-government, 5; their representatives attend great councils, 13; and the development of parliament, 13–16; and the powers of representatives, 16; position of autonomous units, 20; derive their strength from a powerful population, 21; oligarchy and, 22–4; must assimilate 'new men', 25–6; and royal taxation, 68; Sigismund's policy towards, 82–3; the Hanseatic and other Leagues, 83–5; their expansion in the Middle Ages, 96; the Black Death and, 103; declines offset by expansions, 108–9; the *Hermandades* in Castile, 248 and n[1]; *see also* under individual towns
Trade, the growth of towns and, 21; possibility of profit from, 23–4; expansion in the Middle Ages, 97; local fairs and markets, 97–8; use of representatives in markets, 98–9
Trades, 21, 42, 97, 101, 103, 105, 106–7, 109, 113, 192, 194
Trade, Maritime, 21; Venice and, 42–3, 97, 98; Barcelona and, 45–6, 47, 55; expansion in the Middle Ages, 97; linked by land routes, 97; minor routes, 98; Normandy and, 112–13
Transylvania, 208
Trapani, 50
Trebizond, 210; Greek empire in, 42
Treviso, 215, 216
Trier, 77
Troyes, treaty of, 147, 184, 232
Tunis, 58; Barcelona and, 46
Tunisia, 249; Peter III and, 49–50
Turks, the, 3, 260; the universal enemy of the West, 198–9; Catalan Company and, 199–210; *see also* Ottoman Turks
Tuscany, 20, 21, 40, 79, 107, 120, 166; Frederick II and, 34; dissolution of imperial power, 35; subject to the Ghibellines, 36; Charles of Anjou and, 39; under tyranny, 216
Tyrants, Italian, methods of achieving power, 214–15; and the vicariate, 215; defeat republican institutions, 216, 217; dominate northern and central Italy, 216 ff.; overawe the Commune, 217; as patrons of art, 226–8

Tyrol, the, 81, 260; mining in, 262–3
Tyrrhenian coast, 53, 98, 244

Ulpianus (*c.* A.D. 170–228), 11
Umbria, 41, 117, 215, 216
Urban IV, Pope (1261–4), 41, 57, 116; and the Sicilian succession, 37–8
Urban V, Pope (1362–70), 121, 122, 180; and papal residence, 118, 119
Urban VI, Pope (1378–89), 130, 206; his election, 124; his character and achievements, 124–5; deposition, 125–6; death, 126
Urbino, Montefeltro of, 215
Utrecht, 20, 186
Uzzano, Niccolo da, 220

Valencia, 5, 14, 103n², 108, 249; its fleet, 47
Valla, Lorenzo (*c.* 1405–57), 228; and the 'Donation of Constantine', 266
Valladolid, 251, 254
Varna, battle of, 208
Vasari, Giorgio (1511–74), 167
Vendôme, Mathieu de, abbot of St Denis, 57
Venetia, 20, 107; Frederick II and, 34; under tyranny, 35, 216
Venice, 21, 109, 112, 176, 204, 207; closes its great Council, 23 and n²; its Mediterranean trade, 42–3, 97, 98, 110, 111; its leading position, 43, 110, 111; and Charles of Anjou 48; the Medici and, 109; and Antwerp, 193; and the Turks, 208, 210; maintains its independence, 213, 218; relations with Milan, 218, 219; Maximilian I and, 264; its *Relazioni* by ambassadors, 284; Commynes and, 287
Verona, 35, 167, 215, 216, 218
Vicenza, 216, 218
Vienna, 212; concordat of, 261
Vienne, 117; Council of, 66
Villani, Filippo, 165
Villani, Giovanni (*c.* 1275–1348), and Florence, 24, 106 and n, 161; and Giotto, 165
Villehardouin, the, 42
Visconti, the, 226; and Milan, 35, 120, 215, 216, 217–18; the papacy and, 121, 122; acquire the title of Duke, 215, 217; territorial acquisitions, 217–18; their powers of administration, 218 replaced by Sforza, 218

Visconti:
—, Azzo, 217
—, Filippo Maria (1392–1447), 218
—, Gian-Galeazzo (1351–1402), 215, 218, 244
—, Giovanni (d. 1354), 217–18
—, Luchino, 217
—, Matteo (1255–1322), 215, 217
—, Ottone (d. 1295), 217
—, Valentina, 244
Viterbo, 39, 40
Vlachs, the, 209

Waldensians, 139
Waldhauser, Conrad, 132
Wales, 143, 154
Walter of Brienne, duke of Athens, 200; and Florence, 107, 216
War of the Common Weal, 186, 237–8
Warfare, attitude to looting, 89; its ruinous economic consequences, 100–2, 120; causes heavy taxation, 103; influence of Žižka on, 137; use of the longbow, 144, 154; chivalry and, 148, 150, 152–3, 154; the English and, 154–5; France and, 155–6, 157
Warwick, Richard Neville, earl of (1428–71), 239
Wenceslas, king of the Romans and Bohemia (1361–1419), 82, 85, 133, 215
William of Hainault, 152
William of Holland, Count (d. 1256), 13, 76
Wimpfeling, *Epitome Rerum Germanicarum*, 265
Windesheim, Augustinian canons of, 269
Wittenberg, 272
Worms, *Reichstag* of, 90, 263, 265
Wyclif, John (*c.* 1320–84), Huss and, 133, 134–5

Ypres, 58, 100, 192, 193

Zaccaria, Benedetto (*c.* 1240–1307), 43–4, 48
Zeeland, 81, 181, 185, 191
Žižka, General John (*c.* 1376–1424), Hussite leader, 137
Zlata Koruna, monastery of, 139
Zürich, 88, 91
Zwin, 193